Issues in Curriculum Development

A BOOK OF READINGS

Professional Books in Education

VAN MILLER

Consulting Editor

Issues in
Curriculum Development

A BOOK OF READINGS

EDITED BY

MARVIN D. ALCORN

AND

JAMES M. LINLEY

San Diego State College, San Diego, California

WORLD BOOK COMPANY
Yonkers-on-Hudson, New York

Foreword

An analysis of the citations in the *Encyclopedia of Educational Research* indicates that the body of literature of education is about 60 per cent serial in content with emphasis on periodicals, and fairly recent in date with a median age of about twelve years. A general charge made by those outside the field, admitted by many on the inside, is that much of this publication is trivial and of little use.* Nevertheless, within this same body of literature have been buried some of the most timely, pertinent, and valuable contributions to the field. Nowhere is this more true than in the area of curriculum where the periodical and fugitive pamphlet publications are prolific. To keep abreast of the tide of such publication, the reader, student, teacher, or researcher must wade through the mass, ignoring much of it, to cull out those articles of lasting worth.

This book has been designed to make easier the task of those who wish to become acquainted with or to keep up with recent developments in curriculum. It represents the result of a comprehensive survey of recent articles in the field and the selection of those of representative merit. The criteria for selection were usefulness, significance, quality, timeliness, insight, and readability.

The organization and classification have followed the pattern suggested by the number and quality of the selections themselves. No attempt has been made to emphasize or deemphasize any aspect of curriculum, but rather to report the degree and kind of emphasis the literature presents. Hence the compilation reflects both the recurring

* Robert N. Broadus, "The Literature of Educational Research," *School and Society,* 77:1985, January 3, 1953, pp. 8–10.

problems in the curriculum and the special stresses of the last five years. For example, there may be some question about the balance of space given to the slow learner and the gifted. Whereas twenty years ago the gifted was scarcely mentioned and the slow learner was in the spotlight, today the reverse is true.

In some areas, naturally, very little material was available. In other phases materials existed in quantity but were highly specific, reportorial, applicable to local situations only, fragmentary, repetitive, or exhortative. It was then necessary either to dismiss them or to make a brief analytical summary of the gist and content.

In general, however, it has been the intent to let the original authors speak for themselves through reprint of the articles or through direct quotation of pertinent parts. By means of introductions, transitions, notations, and summary, the attempt was made to weave the parts into an organized whole.

The resultant work then is useful either as a text or as a supplement to a text, and to keep professional workers up-to-date in the area of curriculum. The stress always is upon the original sources which might otherwise be lost or difficult and time-consuming to obtain.

No undertaking of this kind could succeed without the cooperation of the authors and publishers concerned. Aside from brief recognition given under titles of quoted articles, gratitude is expressed to them not only for their making the materials available, but for their genuine interest in the project in the form of suggestion and encouragement. Acknowledgment for helpful and proficient service is due to the librarians of Northwestern University, Evanston, Illinois, and of Western Michigan University, Kalamazoo, and especially to Frances Schalles, Curriculum Librarian, San Diego State College.

M. D. A.
J. M. L.

Table of Contents

PART ONE

The Curriculum: Its Setting

1

THE CURRICULUM MOVEMENT

Everyone knows what schools are and has some idea about what they should accomplish. Not everyone is familiar with the term *curriculum,* especially as it is used by educators today. The task of the schools is old; the curriculum movement as such is comparatively new.

It was only about two or three decades ago that the word *curriculum* was rather abruptly added to the teacher's vocabulary, and for a long time it seemed to have little if any practical meaning for the average teacher. Even the definition in the standard dictionary was confusing—and still is. [16:5]

Reference to standard dictionaries as an authoritative source of generally accepted meaning and usage is revealing. Barclay's Universal Dictionary does not list *curriculum* in the 1812 edition, nor does Webster in his early editions. By 1856 the word had made its dictionary debut with two definitions: "1. a race course; a place for running; a chariot. 2. a course, in general; applied particularly to the course of study in a university" (Noah Webster, *An American Dictionary of the English Language,* Springfield, Mass., G. & C. Merriam, 1856). Seventy-two years later, in the 1928 edition, slight changes had occurred: the omission of "a chariot" from the first definition, and the addition to the second of "a specified, fixed course of study as in a university." In 1955 these two meanings are given: "a. A course; esp., a specified fixed course of study, as in a school or college, as one leading to a degree. b. The whole body of courses offered in an educational institution, or by a department thereof;—the usual sense."

It appears then that *curriculum* has been a technical word in generally recognized use for only about a century. Its meaning has under-

3

gone slight, slow change and this but recently. The latest definition given by Webster reflects but one facet of a broad concept, or cluster of concepts, held generally by educators today.

Although the roots of the concept go deep, the outward manifestations of change appeared about three decades ago. In 1928, Walter D. Cocking wrote:

A few years ago the term *curriculum* was generally used as meaning a group of subjects leading toward a particular end. . . . During the past few years, however, there has come a new conception of the term *curriculum* as it is ordinarily used in modern educational parlance. It seems to be a much more inclusive term, as well as a much more general term. [7:41]

Since then, educators have been attempting to define, clarify, or express the concept. In 1934, Harold Rugg did it thus:

The "curriculum"—an ugly, awkward, academic word, but fastened upon us by technical custom—is really the entire program of the school's work. It is the essential *means* of education. It is *everything* the students and their teachers do. Thus it is twofold in nature, being made up of activities, the things done, and of the materials with which they are done. [13:18]

Saylor and Alexander say "The curriculum is the sum total of the school's efforts to influence learning, whether in the classroom, on the playground, or out of school." [14:5]

Carter Good, in order to break down and define the broad concept, gives three basic definitions of *curriculum*. In addition he requires two pages to list and define some forty sub-entries, including activity, articulated, broad fields, child-centered, correlated, integrated, social, traditional, and vocational. [11:113–115]

A recent summary finds that although a discussion of curriculum terminology does not belong in a treatment of historical perspective, it cannot be ignored because it has been culturally generated. Three basically different definitions were identified in the literature: the first in terms of the experiences of children under the jurisdiction of the school, the second in terms of social need and design for institutionalized education, the third in terms of the psychological changes in children brought about by their school activities. [1:245]

Attempts to define the term will do little more than indicate the breadth and complexity of the curricular concept held by educators today. To understand the reasons for this complexity and the nature of it, the influences which fostered it must be examined.

An excellent brief analysis of the past century, not yet available for reprint, finds that the clearest evidence of the changing life of the school is found in the changes in its curriculum. They reflect the pressures, insights, aspirations, and needs of society. The major changes were not born in the past hundred years but evolved from the thinking of teachers long before. Many ideas, however, are unique to this last century and derive from the development of the new sciences of psychology, psychiatry, cultural anthropology, and sociology.

The first significant change is from emphasis on memorization and mental discipline to emphasis on purpose, meaning, and goal seeking in the learning process.

The second change is from reliance on tradition and subjective judgment to use of scientific methods and findings as the basis for educational procedures.

A third change involves the idea that how we learn is as important as what we learn. The change is from stress on subject matter alone to a realization of the importance of motivation and of teaching method.

The fourth change is in the pattern of curriculum building from selection of materials by experts who organized them according to the logic of a field, to the participation of teachers, pupils, and the community in identifying goals to be achieved and ways to reach them. [3]

While the curriculum has changed both in meaning and in operation, it has been subject to continuous criticism. Dissatisfaction with the school's program is perennial. Here, too, historical perspective is necessary. For example, about the year 1200 Peter of Blois said:

For what does it profit them to spend their days in these things which neither at home, nor in the army, nor in business, nor in the cloister, nor in political affairs, nor in the church, nor anywhere else are any good to anyone— except only in the schools? [5:392]

If some have found the curriculum too far detached from life, others have decried its being changed too much by it. In 1797 a New England schoolmaster voiced this complaint:

I am heartily sick of this modern mode of education. Nothing but trash will suit the taste of people at this day. I am perplexed beyond all endurance with these frequent solicitations of parents, to give their children graceful airs, polite accomplishments, and a smattering of what they call the fine arts; while nothing is said about teaching them the substantial branches of literature. If they can but dance a little, fiddle a little, flute a little, and make a handsome bow and courtesy, that is sufficient to make them famous, in this *enlightened* age. Three-fourths of the teachers of those arts, which once were esteemed most valuable, will soon be out of employment, at this rate. For my part, I am convinced, that, if I had been a dancing master, music master, stage player, or mountebank, I should have been much more respected, and much better supported, than I am at present. [4:189]

These remarks come from a period in our own background when, from our present point of view, the old disciplines supposedly were cherished. As Will Rogers is reputed to have said: "Things ain't what they used to be and probably never was."

Anyone responsible for curriculum-making will be obliged to heed the demands made by persons and groups of different philosophical orientations, without being unduly influenced by any particular one. In this connection, John Dewey has made this significant comment:

It is the business of an intelligent theory of education to ascertain the causes for the conflicts that exist and then, instead of taking one side or the other, to indicate a plan of operations proceeding from a level deeper and more inclusive than is represented by the practices and ideas of the contending parties. [8:v]

Today it is necessary to face the challenge of the present by seeing it in perspective, by recognizing that whatever uniqueness it has is not without antecedents. It is none the less a time of unprecedented cultural change and stress. Lawrence Cremin has given historical perspective to the persistent problems of the curriculum maker.

The Curriculum Maker and His Critics: A Persistent American Problem   by LAWRENCE A. CREMIN

From the *Teachers College Record,* February, 1953, pages 234–245. Reprinted by special permission of the author and the publisher, Bureau of Publications, Teachers College, Columbia University. Lawrence A. Cremin is Professor of Education, Teachers College, Columbia University.

Lawrence K. Frank, in a challenging essay first published in 1944, has given us a curious but suggestive conception of the role of the historian in modern society. The essay is entitled "The Historian as Therapist," and in it, Frank pleads for a continuing rewriting of history from generation to generation.[1] The historian as therapist, Frank argues, "is needed to

[1] Lawrence K. Frank, *Society as the Patient* (New Brunswick: Rutgers University Press, 1948), Chapter 25.

release man from the coercions and distorted versions of his traditions, of his 'past.'. . . . Man is at the mercy of these versions of his past, these selectively organized presentations of traditions and events from which he derives his cultural heritage, his image of himself, and ideas of his future." Only, he concludes, as man frees himself from the fetters of outmoded interpretations of his past can he use history as a resource for enlightened solutions of his present problems.

Frank's argument becomes less curious as we apply it to our contemporary situation in American education. One might say without overstatement that a generation of our educators has grown up on the writings of Ellwood P. Cubberley and Paul Monroe. These men were writing during a period of phenomenal educational expansion. As they looked about them, they saw a school structure which was the envy of other nations—an elementary system which embraced the vast majority of America's children and a secondary system which enrolled more youngsters than other secondary schools the world over. It is little wonder that they looked to the future with optimism, and that they painted a picture of educational struggles which had been waged and won, and enemies which had been routed and destroyed. The great battles—to use Cubberley's phrase—were over; and Americans might presumably look forward for many years to the happy business of peacefully perfecting their school systems.

One soon realizes why the present generation of educators, nurtured as it has been on this version of history, finds itself so perplexed and disgruntled over the recent attacks on American public education. To those who received their charge to duty from the writings of Cubberley and his contemporaries, the Allen Zolls, Lucille Crains, Milo McDonalds, and Merwin K. Harts and their insidious work in Pasadena, Englewood, Port Washington, Scarsdale, and a dozen other American communities are an anachronism—phenomena out of another age. To phrase the problem in Frank's terms, what is needed is another look at the history—a reassessment of the past which will more effectively equip us to deal with the problem at hand. It is as a brief introduction to this task that I should like to develop my discussion.

Certainly, one fact soon becomes clear even on the briefest perusal of the growth of American education: attacks on public schools and public-school people are as old as the public school itself. They were present in the early days, when the fathers of the public school were beginning their work, and they have only become intensified in the years since. Rather than constituting a given enemy which was fought and destroyed, the attackers have been the constant companions of the American schoolman—hounding him during some periods in guerrilla actions, waging full-scale warfare in others. While this discussion might well deal with any number of these periods, I should like to concentrate on two: first, the years during which Horace Mann was redesigning the conception and program of moral education in the common school; and second, the years when Francis W. Parker was building the foundations of a new educational method. From a reassessment of those years, I think we can draw some useful conclusions about our present predicament.

Mann and His Critics

Horace Mann fought many battles during his lifetime, but none was so fundamental as the one he fought to remove sectarian religion from America's public schools. Mann had been one of the earliest leaders to help in the building of a new educational ideal for America. The years after 1789 had witnessed the extension of the suffrage, the widening of candidacy for public office, the growth of industrialism, the rise of the labor movement, and the emergence of a vehement (almost querulous) nationalism. More and more it was felt that the school would have to take on certain tasks which could no longer be left to chance education by family and church, and therefore that schooling would have to be made available to all future citizens. The answer of Mann and his colleagues was the common school, a school not common in the traditional European sense of "for the common people," but common in a new sense of common to all the people.[2] Only in a school where children of all economic classes, religious creeds, and political persuasions could meet on a free and equal basis did these leaders see the amelioration of divisive influences which threatened the social cohesion so necessary to the new Republic. All their faith was expressed, perhaps, in the optimistic statement of a Massachusetts clergyman before a citizens' association for the improvement of common schools in 1839:

I want to see the children of the rich and poor sit down side by side on equal terms, as members of one family — a great brotherhood — deeming no one distinguished above the rest but the best scholar and the best boy — giving free and natural play to their affections, at a time of life when lasting friendships are often formed, and worldliness and pride have not yet alienated heart from heart.[3]

Not only was this common school to serve the public, it was also to be supported and controlled by the public. In this way, no child could ever be banned for poverty, and no partisan political, economic, or religious group could ever control the school for its own private purposes.

[2] See Lawrence A. Cremin, *The American Common School: An Historic Conception*, Part II (New York: Bureau of Publications, Teachers College, Columbia University, 1951).

[3] *The Common School Journal*, Vol. I (1839), p. 60.

Given such a school—supported by, controlled by, and serving the public—what would it teach? What ideally would be its curriculum? Generally, the reformers came fairly close to what we would today call a common-learnings-type curriculum. They, thinking in the terms of their nineteenth-century outlook, called it a common branch curriculum—meaning those branches of knowledge which should be the common equipment of every citizen. Specifically, these fundamentals embraced three areas of instruction: training in reading, writing, and arithmetic for everyday use; moral education so that knowledge could be put to proper use; and education for patriotism and citizenship. While there was some argument over which studies would best nurture patriotism and loyalty, it was generally agreed that history and geography would accomplish this purpose. When the problem of a proper moral education was raised, however, bitter controversy ensued.

In the nineteenth century, the moral good was so intimately bound up with religious faith that the two were practically inseparable in the minds of the people. Thus, morality would have to be inculcated by and through a religious faith. Yet how could this be done in view of the multiplicity of churches, each holding its own doctrinal interpretation of the Christian religion? Educational leaders wanted youngsters of all religious convictions in the same

school. Yet the teaching of any given religious faith in the schools would be tantamount to proselytism and the eventual exclusion, by reason of conscience, of members of other faiths.

It was to this seemingly insurmountable problem that Horace Mann turned in his role as curriculum maker. Mann was a deeply religious person—one who always took his religion seriously. His quest was for a program which would enable him to serve this new common-school ideal without giving up his loyalty to Christianity and the need for it in an educational program.

The solution he proposed profoundly influenced the future of American schooling. Why not, Mann queried, cull from the various creeds the common elements on which all agreed and teach these in the school? More extensive doctrinal instruction could be left to the home and the church. "The diversity of religious doctrines," he wrote in 1839, ". . . would render it difficult to inculcate any religious truths . . . were it not for two reasons: first, that the points on which the different portions of a Christian community differ among themselves are far less numerous than those on which they agree; and, secondly, were it not also true, that a belief in those points in which they all agree, constitutes the best possible preparation for each to proceed in adding those distinctive particulars, deemed necessary to a complete and perfect faith." [4] To accomplish this, Mann proposed two devices: the Bible would be read without comment (for, as he urged, the Bible is God-made while sectarianism is man-made); and the teacher by his every word and action would counsel the great moral truths of Christianity in a non-sectarian context.

It is one thing to have a good idea about a curriculum change, but quite another to get it accepted. How did Mann's idea fare in Massachusetts? Any picture of the struggle which ensued must be framed in a knowledge of the continued hammering at the common-school idea which went on throughout the period. Attacks on political, economic, and social grounds were particularly vehement. Newspapers in every part of the country complained that educational taxation was "worse than highway robbery," that universal schooling would disturb the time-honored social-class structure, that the poor would abuse their privileges and irresponsibly multiply like rabbits, and that the whole idea was "socialistic" to begin with. "Schools are sufficiently plenty . . . ," wrote a correspondent to the Raleigh (North Carolina) *Register* in 1829, and children "should pass their days in the cotton patch, or at the plow, or in the corn-field, instead of being mewed up in a school house, where they are learning nothing. . . . I hope you do not conceive it at all necessary, that everybody should be able to read, write, and cipher." [5] Others undoubtedly agreed with the alarm expressed by the New Jersey Presbyterian Synod in 1845 that "The race of religious and infidel youth, such as may be expected to issue from public schools . . . will not be fit to sustain our free institutions." [6]

Within this context, Mann went to work. The story has been told often, but it is worthy of reiteration. When Mann became secretary of the Massachusetts State Board of Education, in 1837, there had already been in effect for ten years a state law giving local school committees the authority to purchase schoolbooks provided that none be included "which are calculated to favour any particular religious sect or tenet." [7] Moreover, shortly before the board had been created, the state had also passed a law authorizing school districts to raise by taxation funds for local school libraries. Few districts went ahead and did so, and in 1838, Mann took steps to arrange with a commercial publisher for two reasonably priced sets of books which might be made available to district officers.

[4] *Ibid.*, p. 14.

[5] Charles L. Coon, *The Beginnings of Public Education in North Carolina* (Raleigh: Edwards & Broughton, 1908), p. 432.

[6] J. J. Janeway, *Report to the Synod of New Jersey on the Subject of Parochial Schools* (Philadelphia: n.d.), p. 5.

[7] Laws of 1827, Ch. CXLIII, Sec. 7.

When the plan was announced, the American Sunday School Union, through its secretary, Frederick A. Packard, inquired as to whether Abbot's *The Child in the Home*—published by the Union—might be used. Mann read the book and found it imbued with Calvinist preachments which would undoubtedly have offended the Universalists in Massachusetts. Therefore he replied that he would rather abandon the whole scheme of libraries completely than include a single book of that sort on his list.[8]

Packard's response, carrying with it the implied weight of the American Sunday School Union, was sharp and acrimonious. Packard vehemently attacked Mann and the Board, first at a meeting of orthodox Congregational clergymen in New Bedford, and later in a pair of anonymous letters to a New York newspaper. On both occasions he questioned the worth and practicability of Mann's program of religious education.[9] Neither Mann nor the Board replied directly to his charges.

The embers of the Packard controversy smouldered for six years, and again burst into flame in 1844. In that year a group of Philadelphia citizens had engaged Daniel Webster to argue before the United States Supreme Court against the will of Stephen Girard of Pennsylvania—a will which had established a school where no sectarian religion was ever to be taught and no ecclesiastic ever to enter. The heightened interest in the case led the Reverend Edward A. Newton, a former member of the Board of Education who had resigned during the library controversy, to attack the non-sectarian policy of the Massachusetts schools.[10] Such a policy, he argued, could only lead to an unhealthy and godless skepticism in the school children of the state. Mann replied courteously, using his note to clarify and support the program he espoused. In response, the editor of the *Christian Witness and Church Advocate,* an Episcopalian organ, accused him of so diluting religious instruction in the attempt to be non-sectarian that the program was worthless. The weight of editorial opinion in other journals seems to have been with Mann.

The third and probably the most vitriolic exchange came in 1846. The Reverend Matthew Hale Smith, in a sermon entitled "The Ark of God on a New Covenant," accused Mann of sponsoring godless schools from which the Bible and religion had been removed. Interest flared, and in a subsequent exchange of tracts and letters, Mann once again simply and

---

[8] Mann to Packard, March 18, 1838 [Correspondence bound as *Mann Papers* in Massachusetts Historical Society Library].

[9] *New-York Observer,* Vol. XVI, No. 42, October 20, 1838, p. 16, and No. 43, October 27, 1838, p. 172.

[10] See *The Common School Controversy* (Boston: 1844).

clearly stated what was actually going on in the schools and the philosophy behind the program.[11] Here, too, editorial support seemed strongly to favor the new approach, and the program continued and flourished.

What were some of the things Mann had done to gain him this support from his constituency? A principal clue, perhaps, lies in the many ways in which he continually explained and publicized his new approach. Every two weeks from 1839 through 1848, Mann edited and published an issue of his *Common School Journal*—a periodical which did much to set forth and explain his views to the public as well as to his confreres in education. A similar purpose was served by his much publicized twelve annual reports to the Board—every one of which was a simple and forthright statement of his beliefs. Mann also lectured as often as possible to groups of every kind and persuasion, and used these lectures to bring his views to the people. Many of these lectures were to groups of teachers, and he diligently used these occasions to talk with them about the program they were carrying on. Finally, Mann—particularly in the controversies with Newton and Smith—answered his attackers quickly, directly, and forcefully. Moreover, he had worked closely enough with the forces in the community who supported him—in

this case, church groups and ministers—that they entered the fray in his behalf. Mann had found his friends in time of calm, and they were ready to serve him in time of stress. In 1847, a year after the Smith controversy, Mann's success was epitomized by a glowing commendation in the inaugural address of Governor George Briggs, an ardent Baptist, who noted that Mann's work would "earn for him the lasting gratitude of the generation to which he belongs." [12]

Much more might be said about Mann and his work, but let us turn to our second focus of attention—the years roughly a third of a century later, when Colonel Francis W. Parker was attempting his fundamental innovations in the realm of method.

Parker and His Critics

In October, 1837, less than four months after Horace Mann had become secretary of the Massachusetts Board, Francis W. Parker was born in what is presently the city of Manchester, New Hampshire. The thirty-eight years between that time and the time of Parker's appointment as Superintendent at Quincy, Massachusetts, were eventful years for American education. The public-school idea had firmly taken root on the American scene, and enrollments had risen to approximately eight mil-

---

[11] See *The Bible, the Rod, and Religion in Common Schools* (Boston: Redding and Company, 1847).

[12] Acts and Resolves of 1847, pp. 576–578.

lion, with an annual expenditure in the neighborhood of seventy million dollars. While these figures seem modest when compared with contemporary enrollments and expenditures, they represented phenomenal advances for those years.

As I have asserted, these advances were made in the face of continued attacks throughout the years. In spite of Horace Mann's "victory," one notes any number of public men and ministers dubbing the public school a godless institution. All of the arguments of the 1840's were advanced and reargued. For many a newspaper editor, the public school was still "socialism"—in fact, they had coined a new word, "agrarianism." School taxation was still denounced, and the leveling tendencies of the common school were still decried. Compulsory attendance, thought by many to be a logical culmination of the common-school ideal, was for others a final subjection of humankind to arbitrary state authority. There were these attacks and more. The public school had been operating for fifty years now, and was a fitting scapegoat for every ill of industrial civilization. For example, one man urged in a scholarly treatise that there were no crimes to speak of in colonial Virginia—and no schools. In 1880 Virginia's crime rate was rising and so were public school enrollments. The "logical" conclusion was clear: public schools caused crime.[13] And so it was with suicide, divorce, insanity, and tuberculosis. A growing body of tracts, pamphlets, editorials, and lengthy books proclaimed these exposés to the American people during the next twenty years. This, then, was the workshop of Francis W. Parker.

And what of the schools themselves? There is every indication that while in many places their physical appearance had improved and their offering expanded, the character of their program was much the same as it had been a century before. In many cases one "kept" school instead of "teaching" it, and that often involved activities ranging from chopping wood for the stove to beating up the larger students—or keeping order, as it was called. In those places where one could devote more attention to the actual teaching of school, there was much to be desired. The teacher had a body of content—usually contained in prescribed textbooks—for the youngster to learn. Learning usually involved being able to read and recite from memory this required content. While there is no doubt that much of this content was useful and applicable in given situations, the situations usually eluded the youngster. Learning and schooling were thereby so often a continuing, intolerable drudgery. Semester after semester, book after book, and recitation after recitation the process went on until at a given point the youngster was adjudged to have completed

[13] Zach. Montgomery, *The School Question from a Parental and Non-Sectarian Standpoint* (Washington: Gibson Brothers, 1886).

his elementary studies and to be fit for the world or perhaps the high school.

There is no doubt that some teachers worked admirably within this pattern, dealing with the materials in an interesting, often engrossing, manner. Also, there is no doubt that some youngsters thrived under it, and many of its products are numbered among the great of America. But the waste of human resources must have been appalling.

There were those in Europe during the nineteenth century who were beginning to realize this. Pestalozzi and his colleagues were working out radically new educational methods at Yverdon in Switzerland, and attracting world-wide attention. The educational revolution they were creating involved a complete shift of emphasis from the subject matter to the child himself. How, they asked, can we best develop the mental, moral, and manual capabilities of each individual youngster with whom we work? Their answers worked havoc with the traditional approach; for, realizing that meaningful learning could come only from the senses, they put the books away for much of the early program and took the child outside the classroom to learn about the world around him. Others, in and out of universities, were looking at the manifold problems of method. No

less a man than Johann Friedrich Herbart, who had taken Kant's chair of philosophy at Konigsberg, initiated a whole school of thought (particularly with respect to teaching method), while Froebel in the 1830's and 1840's was developing his conception of the kindergarten.

These stirrings inevitably had their repercussions in America. Pestalozzian ideas are clearly discernible in journals, textbooks, and even given school programs during the years after 1805.[14] They received their first great advance, however, in the work of Edward A. Sheldon at the Oswego State Normal School in New York during the late 1850's and early 1860's. Oswego soon became one of the important creative centers of educational thought in America; its teachers were eagerly sought after, its classes were visited by hundreds from every part of the nation. Kindergartens made their appearance in the 1850's, while Herbart's ideas began to enjoy currency during the 1870's.

Parker, too, on his return from service in the Civil War, became disturbed with the traditional approach. During a period of teaching in Dayton, Ohio, between 1860 and 1871 he began avidly to read the works of Sheldon, Horace Mann, and a number of European educators. When an aunt died and left him a small legacy he determined to follow Mann's ex-

[14] Will S. Monroe, *History of the Pestalozzian Movement in the United States* (Syracuse: Bardeen, 1907).

ample and spend a period of study in Europe. In his two and a half years there he not only studied at the University of King William in Berlin, but traveled widely through Holland, Switzerland, Italy, France, and Germany, eagerly observing the innovations in the schools he visited. On his return to the United States, Parker was determined to sponsor similar changes in American schools.

His opportunity came soon. In 1873 the school committee of Quincy, Massachusetts, sensing that all was not well with Quincy's schools, decided to conduct the annual school examination themselves. When the committee appeared for the examination, no less a man than John Quincy Adams, president of the Board and descendant of the House of Quincy Adams, took the place of the teacher. The expected occurred. While the youngsters knew their rules of grammar thoroughly, they could not write an ordinary English letter. While they could read with facility from their textbooks, similarly graded material that they had not seen confused them. They could spell the authorized lists with alacrity, but could not spell in the letters they wrote. The committee had made its discovery and was determined to change the curriculum. After some brief exchanges, it was decided that Colonel Parker was the man for the

job, and he was elected superintendent in 1875.

Things soon began to happen in Quincy. They are described well in a short biography of Parker published in 1900:

The set program was first dropped, then the speller, the reader, the grammar, and the copy-book. The alphabet, too, was treated with slight deference; it was not introduced to the children by name, but they were set at once to work making words and sentences. The teachers woke up, and had to depend upon lively wits for success. No longer could they comfortably hear recitations from convenient text-books — there were no text-books. Other books there were in plenty, and magazines and newspapers. Teachers and pupils had to learn first of all to think and observe. Then bye-and-bye they put these powers to work on the required subjects.[15]

The program itself was an immediate success and attracted national attention as "the Quincy System." Interestingly enough, Parker himself decried this labeling, protesting that there was nothing particularly revolutionary in the new approach. "I repeat," he wrote in his report of 1878–79, "that I am simply trying to apply well-established principles of teaching, principles derived directly from the laws of the mind. The methods springing from them are found in the development of every child. They are used everywhere except in school. I have introduced no

---

[15] Marion Foster Washburne, "Col. Francis W. Parker; The Man and Educational Reformer," *Francis Wayland Parker: His Life and Educational Reform Work* (New York and Chicago: E. L. Kellogg, 1900), p. 19.

new principle, method, or detail. No experiments have been tried, and there is no peculiar 'Quincy System.' " [16]

What, then, were some of these well-founded principles that Parker was advancing? Many are at the heart of what we today conceive of as a program of good education. Parker wrote constantly of self-activity as the key to all education. "We learn to do by doing," he said in 1883, "to hear by hearing, and to think by thinking. The greatest delight of all teaching is to place the difficulty squarely before the pupils . . . and then, let them work it out for themselves." [17] Parker was constantly concerned with the interests and problems of growing youngsters, and sought to tailor his program to these interests. Much of this tailoring came in the form of opportunities freely to model, paint, draw, and sing. Nevertheless, he was always conscious of social motives and needs, and never lost sight of them in gearing the curriculum to individuals. Above all, Parker inveighed against rigidity in the educational program, and sought in its place a supple flexibility which would release both the teacher and the child to a stimulating and productive freedom. Parker himself in

1900 remarked, "There never was a Quincy method or a Quincy system, unless we agree to call the Quincy method a spirit of study and the Quincy system one of everlasting change." [18]

What of Parker's critics? They were untiring in their resistance. As early as the years he spent in Dayton he had been roundly attacked by the textbook publishers, who saw in Parker's innovations a threat to their sales. With the notoriety of the work at Quincy the attacks mounted. Some elements in Quincy felt strongly that Parker and his program were far too expensive to warrant continuation; and each year between 1875 and 1880 the Board and Parker had to fight to maintain the new curriculum. From other quarters came the criticism that the children might very well be happy, "but did they learn? Could they spell?" And these persons were not at all quieted when in 1880 a survey of the whole county by an inspector of the Massachusetts State Board revealed that Quincy's youngsters did better at every one of the fundamentals except arithmetic—where they stood third or fourth—than those of any other town in the county. [19] No, the report was attacked as unfair. From still other quarters—

[16] *Report of the School Committee of the Town of Quincy for the School Year 1878–79* (Boston: Cochrane and Sampson, n.d.), p. 15.

[17] Francis W. Parker, *Talks on Teaching* (New York: Barnes, 1883), p. 115.

[18] Francis W. Parker, "The Quincy Method," *Report of the Commissioner on Education for the Year 1902* (Washington: Government Printing Office, 1903), pp. 239–240.

[19] See Charles Francis Adams, "Scientific Common-School Education," *Harper's New Monthly Magazine,* Vol. LXI (1880), p. 934.

in fact from the ranks of educators themselves—came criticisms that the system was falsely grounded, that it made false claims, and that it embodied nothing new anyway.

When, after a brief interlude in Boston, Parker assumed the principalship of the Cook County Normal School in the suburbs of Chicago and there attempted to continue and perfect his methods, his critics grew even more vehement and more bitter. Of the many which might be cited, none was more representative than Charles S. Thornton, a member of the Cook County Board of Education. Parker had early come into conflict with Thornton by dismissing a teacher friendly to the latter. Thornton's continual sniping after this incident came to a head in the report of an examination of the normal school which he submitted to the Board in November, 1891. Needless to say, it was decidedly reminiscent of the Quincy criticisms. "It is with great regret," Thornton wrote, "that I must report that the results indicate desultory work and careless, inattentive, and idle habits." He had found the students he tested unable to write even the simplest expositions about everyday objects, and did not blame them for it in view of the great deal of class time wasted on "celebrations, excursions, and show work to please visitors." [20] When the fact was later brought to light that Thornton had concentrated on a half dozen slow learners which Parker had brought into the practice school to keep the group heterogeneous, Thornton himself seemed little disturbed.

Parker's retort at the same Board meeting was sharp but considered. "I should like to know," he queried, "how we could measure physical culture, musical growth, or moral development. . . . This man who has never taught school a day in his life comes up and states that I am a failure after thirty-seven years of practice. When he comes to the school and acts like a gentleman, I will give him any information he wants." [21] The exchange set off a seesaw of examinations, reports, and counter-reports. A month later the county superintendent of schools carried on some tests and denied *in toto* Thornton's accusation. It was then argued, however, that the superintendent—a close friend of Parker's—had done a whitewash. Therefore, a third examination was given by another member of the Board, with disastrous results for the students. Nevertheless, when the county superintendent gave the same questions to students in fourteen schools of Chicago, the results were equally poor. Needless to say, the whole affair caught the eyes of local newspaper editors, and throughout the remainder of the 1890's the Chicago *Tribune,* *Times-Herald,* and *Evening Post* carried charges that fads such as

[20] *Chicago Tribune,* November 22, 1891, p. 3.
[21] *Ibid.*

music, drawing, and physical culture were ruining youngsters, and counter-charges about the failure of the traditional school. Throughout the stormy period, the Normal School and its principal stood.

What were some of the ways in which Parker fought back during these years? The resemblance to Mann's methods is interesting. Early in the controversy, the editor of the *School Journal* opened its columns to Parker, and Parker used them often and well over the years to explain his position to his colleagues in the profession. Moreover, Parker was always direct and prompt in his responses to criticism—speaking out forthrightly yet courteously when he was attacked. Parker, like Mann, was careful to make his ideas clear to the teachers who worked with him. In fact, lectures to teachers form a major part of his published works. Probably the most potent characteristic of Parker in this respect was his ability to keep the community groups which were backing him not only informed but working in his behalf. This was clear in the Quincy situation, where his Board not only remained with him throughout the fray but helped to defend him with articles in important journals of opinion, with public statements, and with personal approbation. So it was also during the Cook County and Chicago experience. Finally, Parker had a remarkable ability to inspire personal loyalty among his staff

members, even when the latter were divided with regard to policy.

Some Prescriptions for Action

If the historian can really act as a therapist perhaps this is the place for a prescription. Seriously, it appears that this conception given us by Cubberley and his contemporary historians that the battles have been fought and won has clearly acted to becloud the present situation. Mann won his battle; but it is quite evident that we are still fighting vigorously to maintain the non-sectarian character of the public school. Parker won his battle; but aren't many of us still fighting to secure his kind of program, and aren't others of us fighting to hold advances that have been made? No, I'm afraid that although Mann and Parker won their battles, they did not win them once and for all. Perhaps, like the struggle for liberty, these battles have to be won anew by each and every generation of educators. What, then, do we learn from this changed view of the history of American public education? It seems to me we learn a number of things.

First, I believe we must study these attacks of the past, and study them carefully. George Santayana has counseled that those who forget the past are condemned to repeat it; and this is good counsel for the situation at hand. What men have made these attacks, and why? What have been their arguments? What were the so-

cial, political, economic, religious—
or for that matter, personal—factors
involved? To what extent were the
attacks expressions of deeper currents and controversies in American
life—as are so many of the present
ones? How have great educators of
the past coped with these attacks,
and what can we learn from their
successes and failures? These and
other questions should be our constant concern. And this introduces
another vastly important task for the
historian: that is, to tell us what
kind of man is able to stand his
ground in the face of such attacks.
In our recent concern with "social
forces" in history—and it is a very
valid concern—we historians have
perhaps de-emphasized biographical
elements to too great an extent. It
seems to me that we have the responsibility of telling today's would-be
curriculum maker that he enters
what can be a perilous occupation,
and of telling him "what it takes" to
withstand the pressures.

Second, I believe that curriculum
makers must root themselves in the
historical values of our public-school
ideal more than they ever have before. For, as in other times, it is not
just this or that curriculum which is
being attacked, it is the whole conception and institution of public education. When the public-school idea
is attacked as godless, materialistic,
irreligious, or atheistic I think we

have a responsibility to inform the
American people about the deeply
religious men who conceived it and
have since dedicated their lives to its
realization. Similarly, when the idea
of a secular public-school curriculum
is pronounced "totalitarian"—as it
was not long ago in a lengthy statement by a group of prominent
clergymen in one of our leading de-
nominations [22]—I think we must
forcefully point out the sincere devotion to American democracy of
those who in the past have espoused
this idea and who do so today. Democratic and equalitarian principles
have been the lifeblood of the public
school; and if, as Dean Hollis Caswell urged in his Steinmetz Lecture
last spring, there is now going on a
"great reappraisal of public education," then it seems to me that we
owe it to the people to use every
agency at our disposal to bring these
values before them—on radio, in
newspapers, in current periodicals,
and on television.

My third point stems from my second: it is that we must always maintain a self-critical attitude about our
own work. One of the things about
the recent attacks which has been
moderately discouraging has been
the tendency toward self-righteous-
ness on the part of many educators
who are criticized. There is a vital
difference—not always easily discernible, I grant, especially under

[22] See *The New York Times,* November 16, 1952, p. 80.

stress—between those who exercise their legitimate right to criticize public educational policy and those who would undermine the structure of public education itself. For the latter we must have our own ringing justifications of public education. We must be ready, however, to grant the loyalty of the former critics while answering them, as did Mann and Parker, with our evidence and our contentions. We must also ever be able—to borrow a phrase from a speech during the recent Presidential campaign—"to recharge our own batteries." By this I mean that we have to fight the apathetic and the lunatic fringe within our own ranks as well as the attackers from without. Parker spent many an article disclaiming those who were heaping every educational excess under the rubric of "the Quincy method"; and it seems to me that we are faced with much the same task today with respect to "progressive education."

My fourth point calls to mind the great facility of both Mann and Parker in finding and organizing their supporters in the community. If there is one lesson to be learned from Willard Goslin's recent experience at Pasadena, and from a hundred similar setbacks, it is that the friends of the program under attack were unorganized, and remained so until it was too late to matter. The story of organized assistance to Mann and Parker—and most assuredly they would have gone down to defeat without such help—should

counsel every curriculum maker about the value of organizing favorable public sentiment long before an attack comes. This always involves long and patient deliberation, and tireless effort in writing, meeting, lecturing, and just plain talking with people about schools. More than this, it implies the necessity of being able to talk about our schools in words and phrases that people understand and appreciate. This matter of communication and interpretation has occupied the best minds in our profession for many years now, but despite their efforts, there are literally thousands of parents for whom "activity program," "heterogeneous grouping," and "enriched curriculum" remain utterly incomprehensible phrases.

And this brings to mind the fifth and strongest point I have to urge. Actually, we have the greater part of our future citizenry in the schools under our charge for twelve years, and we are so busy interpreting other important areas to them that we virtually ignore our own vital work. It seems to me that we should see to it, in our civics courses, in our core programs, in our social studies and history classes, that every child has ample opportunity to gain a basic citizen's understanding of universal, free public education—its value, its meaning, and the great struggles which have been and are being fought to secure and preserve it. This, it seems to me, would be our best guarantee of an interested and informed citizenry, mature and sophisticated in its ability to judge and weigh the great educational issues of our time.

One final remark: neither Mann nor Parker nor any other great curriculum maker ever achieved his goals by becoming preoccupied with his critics. The great curriculum maker in a democracy knows that in the last analysis his most persuasive arguments lie in the favorable results he can produce in children themselves. No therapist ever made his reputation by looking exclusively to the past; and I suspect that I can close most fruitfully by urging that while you read my prescription and wield the sword against your attackers, you save the greater part of your effort to build the best educational programs possible for the youngsters who are your charges. Only you who have made curricula know how much of yourselves you will have to give.

2

THE VOICES OF OUR TIMES

THE CULTURE: ITS INFLUENCE ON THE CURRICULUM

Man makes his culture. In our instance, at least, we have created a culture which is beyond our power fully to comprehend, to control, or to transmit. Each generation, to some extent, has faced the same problem. Each considers its challenge unique. In a sense, this assumption is true. What basis is there, then, for the belief that our own people in our own times today face a very special challenge?

In concluding a portrait sketch of the American people, Henry Commager says:

No analysis of American character could omit optimism, amiability, energy, self-confidence, enterprise, materialism, idealism, practicality, sentimentality, progressiveness, conservatism, inventiveness, carelessness, intolerance, equalitarianism, individualism. The characteristics are not, in themselves, profoundly different from the characteristics of some other peoples. . . . It is not so much the particular elements as the juxtaposition of all the elements that gives them peculiar interest. Nor is it realistic to lose sight of the obvious fact that it is the combination of these qualities with immense power that gives them significance.*

Such a complex of attributes might well be expected to produce complicated results at any time. We may question whether the situation today has in reality any unusual significance. Concerning this point, Goldman has said:

* From Henry Steele Commager *et al., Years of the Modern: An American Appraisal,* John W. Chase, editor (New York: Longmans, Green & Company, 1949), p. 31. Quoted by special permission. Henry Steele Commager is a noted historian, author, and Adjunct Professor of American History, Columbia University.

Each era, with the egotism of the present, has seen its age as a turning point, and often history, with a mocking toss of her head, has decided not to turn. Yet the Fifties know, with unchangeable certitude, that mankind is hurtling through a process that recurs not in centuries but in millenniums. [10:460–461]

Our culture is complex and contradictory. It is "neither static nor homogeneous. It is, in many respects, a culture of paradoxes." [2:3] It is, moreover, moving at an enormously accelerated pace.

Since the school is a controlled environment designed by a social group to perpetuate its existence, the nature of a society will determine the curriculum of its schools. The demands have been many and conflicting. They have changed the curriculum. "More laws affecting the curriculum were passed in the Thirties than had existed in 1928." [18:524] Wish further notes that the period 1945–1954 showed influences of a different nature, more complicating and problematic than helpful. Among these influences are the tremendous influx of pupils, slow teacher pay rise, the advent of FM and TV, the G.I. Bill and increased college enrollments, the "Red" scare, loyalty oaths and questions of academic freedom, and the cheering potentials of the Fulbright and Smith-Mundt exchange programs. [18:674–675]

The situation is inescapable: more people to be served in more ways for more purposes. The needs are there; the answers are not. "Out of conflicting issues and forces has arisen a new sense of national insecurity." [2:40] Since the schools reflect the society they serve, they reflect, too, the insecurities.

What do our people think of our schools? The Roper Survey makes two main points: "Today's parent is inclined to feel that the school, good or bad, is just as responsible as he for most of the upbringing of his child . . . and, when Americans think about education, they are complacent as a whole and dissatisfied in particular; they feel that the overall situation is sunny but not so good at the school down the street." [17:11]

The implications of this picture have been summed up by Commager:

Many of the failures we ascribe to contemporary education are in fact failures of our society as a whole. A society that is indifferent to its own heritage cannot expect schools to make good the difference. A society that slurs over fundamental principles and takes refuge in the superficial and the ephemeral cannot demand that its schools instruct in abiding moral values. A society proudly preoccupied with its own material accomplishments and well-being cannot fairly expect its schools to teach that the snug warmth of security is less meaningful than the bracing venture of freedom. In all this, to reform our schools is first to reform ourselves.

For a century and a half the American schools have served and strengthened the commonwealth. They provided a citizenry as enlightened as any on earth. They justified and vindicated democracy's promise. If society clearly defines the new duties it wishes our schools to fulfill and if it steadfastly supports them not only with money but also with faith, they will surely justify that faith in the future as they have in the past.*

Our society is in the process of making that definition. It is doing so through voices clamoring out a cross fire of conflicting demands. These demands are expressions of the result of examination of public school programs from given points of view.

CRITICS AND DEFENDERS OF THE CURRICULUM

Never before have so many had so much to say about education. Albert Lynd has repeatedly attacked the philosophy of John Dewey and his followers and the progressive education movement in general. Mortimer Smith has lamented the lack of intellectualism in the public schools and the resultant "diminished mind." Rudolf Flesch has specifically condemned the current methods of teaching reading. To each of these critics replies have been made. The National Education Association in its December, 1957, *Research Bulletin* summarizes the arguments pro and con under the title "Ten Criticisms of Public Education." To the unbiased listener who lends an ear to the conflicting voices lifted for and against the curriculum of America's public schools, all is confusion. What is the truth about public education? The average man has difficulty in distinguishing fact from fiction in the welter of voices. Just what are the points of controversy? A number of them are highlighted in *U.S. News & World Report* in an interview with Professor Arthur Bestor, one of the best known of those spokesmen who have been sharply critical of present-day public education.

* From an editorial by Henry Steele Commager, "Our Schools Have Kept Us Free," in *Life* Magazine, October 16, 1950, pp. 46–47. Copyright 1950, Time, Inc. Reprinted by special permission of the publisher.

We Are Less Educated Than Fifty Years Ago

An interview with ARTHUR BESTOR

Reprinted from *U.S. News & World Report,* an independent weekly news magazine published at Washington. Copyright, 1956, United States News Publishing Corporation. This interview appeared in the November 30, 1956, issue (the portion reprinted is taken from pages 68–72, 74). Arthur Bestor is former President of the Council for Basic Education and Professor of History, University of Illinois.

Q. There is a lot of talk these days that our schools are not doing their jobs properly. What do you think is wrong with education in America today, Dr. Bestor?

A. When you come right down to it, what's wrong is that the schools have lost their sense of purpose. Schools today are undertaking a large number of activities that aren't essential to education at all. The result is that these unessential activities are squeezing out the basic subjects for a very large number of our students.

Q. We hear it said that reading, writing, and arithmetic are not taught any more, or that they are not taught as widely as they should be. Are those statements true?

A. The subjects are being taught, of course, but they are not being taught as effectively as they should be. It's not a question of omitting them entirely. It is a matter of treating them too casually all the way through school. It takes long and steady effort to teach a boy or girl to write, for example.

Q. What do you mean by that?

A. Well, by writing I mean a great deal more than being able to form letters on paper. When a youngster has finished twelve years of grade school and high school, he ought to be able to write clearly and grammatically about the subjects he is studying. In college we find that an appalling percentage of them can't, and we have to have large staffs to teach elementary grammar and punctuation to college students.

Q. Are the schools paying less attention to the teaching of science, mathematics, history, and foreign languages than they used to?

A. Yes, they are. In fact, lots of American high schools don't even offer courses in the basic sciences and advanced mathematics, that is geometry and algebra. And an increasing percentage of American students aren't taking the courses when they are offered.

Q. How bad is that situation?

A. Well, more than half of the high schools in the United States offer no physics; roughly a quarter offer neither physics nor chemistry. And even geometry is missing in 23 per cent of our high schools.

Q. Is the situation getting better or worse?

A. Worse. A responsible estimate is that last year some 1,500 high schools reduced the number of their courses in science and mathematics, or dropped them entirely.

Q. Is there a relationship, do you think, between the shortage of scientists you hear so much about today and what we have been doing with education in the last thirty to fifty years?

A. A very obvious relationship. The figures of the U.S. Office of Education show that in 1900 nearly 84 per cent of all American high-school students were taking some science courses. That has dropped to only 54 per cent today. In mathematics the drop has been from 86 to 55 per cent.

Q. Where does that put us in comparison with other nations?

A. Behind the eight ball, I should say. What we know about education in the Soviet Union is causing real alarm in scientific and military circles. The Russians are giving intensive training in these fields. In the upper grades of their secondary schools, 40 per cent of the time is spent on the sciences and mathematics. And they aren't playing at it. The school day has more hours, and the school weeks and terms are longer. The competition among students for academic honors is intense.

Q. When did this deterioration in American schools begin?

A. It became noticeable about twenty-five or thirty years ago. But the roots go back further than that.

Q. How does a thing like that come about?

A. Those who defend the present state of affairs blame it on the greatly increased enrollment in high schools. This was a factor, but it isn't the whole story.

Q. Why not?

A. Well, for one thing, the money that was available for schools has increased even more rapidly than the number of students.

Q. Doesn't the declining value of the dollar have something to do with it?

A. Even after taking that into account, the money spent per pupil has steadily increased. There was no financial reason why the quality of education should have declined with the increase in the number of students.

Q. But was there some relationship between the decline in quality and the coming of mass education?

A. Yes, but only because a number of fallacious ideas about education took hold at the same time.

Q. What do you mean, fallacious ideas?

A. Well, for one thing, the professional educators began to get very confused about the fundamental purposes of education. And here I mean the professors of education—those who teach teachers—and the school administrators, that is, the superintendents and principals, not the actual classroom teachers. The teachers themselves were just obeying orders.

In my judgment, the real purpose of a school is to teach youngsters how to use their minds effectively. You have reading, writing, and arithmetic as the first steps in this process. Then, in high school you get science, history, English, and foreign languages.

Of course, you have other school activities, too. But these ought to be additions to the school program. And what the professional educators are really doing is pushing the fundamentals aside in favor of the other things. What they are saying is that the fundamental subjects, the ones I just named, are not really fundamental, except for a small number of students. The other pupils, they say, should be getting something different in school.

Q. What are they giving them in place of the fundamentals?

A. Well, they say a student should be trained for his job. Or, that he should be taught what these people call "life adjustment." They say, for example, that instead of teaching a child history or geography, you should teach him how to act when he goes out on a date. This they call "social studies." Or, instead of requiring him to study literature, they give him pointers on how to select a good radio program.

Q. How do they defend this?

A. They call it "democratic."

Q. But you don't consider it so?

A. Emphatically not. The worst enemy of democracy could not invent a more grotesque parody of democracy.

The object of education in a democracy is to raise the intellectual level of the population, not to level it down. You don't raise it by teaching the fundamentals to a small group of students only, and letting the others go.

Q. Are you saying that what you call the fundamentals—English, foreign languages, science, mathematics, and history—are the things that every student needs?

A. Precisely. All of them have to live in the modern world where these things are fundamental. All of them are citizens and will have to use their intelligence in making decisions. Otherwise the nation is headed for disaster.

Q. Are you against what might be called "selective education"—that is, taking the gifted students and enabling them to go forward as rapidly as possible without being held back by the others?

A. I approve heartily. There is no reason why a capable student should not get as thorough an education in an American public school as in the best school in another country.

A democracy needs trained minds. It actually needs them more than a country where power is in the hands of a few. We can't uphold our way of life by committing intellectual suicide. We have got to give our best students the toughest mental training they can take.

Q. We hear a lot about provisions for "exceptional children." Isn't this a hopeful sign?

A. It ought to be. But, in educational jargon, "exceptional children" doesn't mean what you expect. Let me quote a definition given by an official of the U.S. Office of Education: "Among them are the blind and the partially seeing, the deaf and the hard of hearing, the speech-defective, the crippled, the delicate, the epileptic, the mentally deficient, the socially maladjusted, and the *extraordinarily gifted.*" (The emphasis is mine.)

To me this definition—it is a common and accepted one—is utterly shocking. How can we ever offer able students the education they desire if we classify them with mental defectives because they deviate from the normal? There is far too much emphasis, nowadays, on fitting the school program to the average or below-average child, and then adapting it to suit the more able ones.

The job should be done the other way round. The able child should set the pace for the school, and the program should be adapted, if necessary, for the others. You have to give the average children equal opportunities, but not by sacrificing the best minds.

Finding Ability Early——

Q. Isn't there some stage at which the student who might have the ability to become a scientist or engineer could be attracted into that type of education and yet is not?

A. Yes, intellectual ability can be detected early. Some countries rely on detecting it by the age of eleven or twelve. I think we should keep the door open for a longer time. But, as soon as we know that a given child does have ability, we should not allow him to waste his time. If he hasn't learned the fundamentals by the time he graduates from high school, it may be too late for him ever to learn them well enough to make the most of himself in an advanced career.

Q. Isn't there a problem in educating children of merely average ability? Can they get anything out of the subjects that the ablest pupils are studying?

A. They certainly can, and a great deal more than many educators apparently believe. One great weakness of our system is that it is not getting anything like enough out of the average student. Our schools permit him to get by by electing courses that haven't any real content.

Because we never really challenge a student of this kind, we don't really discover what he can do. Of course, the slow learner creates problems. But our schools are taking the easy way out. They don't solve the problem, they just dodge it. If he doesn't learn to read well, we try to teach him with pictures. And if a girl can't—or won't—get mathematics, we let her take cooking instead. And we try to cover up by saying that all subjects are equally valuable in training the mind. The fact is, they aren't.

Q. Would you draw a distinction between fast learners and slow learners, bright students and dull students, and recommend a division in the classes or schools as between those?

A. I would.

Q. Are we doing that today, though?

A. In my judgment, we're not doing nearly enough of it.

Q. Can you draw a distinction between students who have and those who don't have aptitudes for certain studies, or would the division be solely on the basis of what we call fast and slow learners?

A. The term "fast learners" or "slow learners" merely means aptitude or lack of aptitude. One must admit, of course, that individuals have greater aptitudes for certain things than for others. The best studies show, however, that students with high ability are good in almost all subjects. The popular notion that these things compensate—that a student who is very bright in mathematics is apt to be stupid in other subjects—is simply not true.

Q. Is there anything to the idea that students from low-income families are not as bright as those from families with a greater amount of cultural background?

A. No, there is no real evidence to show that innate intellectual ability has anything to do with economic level.

Students who come from families of low economic background are handicapped to some extent, of course, but the handicap arises from their background, not their ability. They haven't had the advantage of being surrounded from birth with books and with opportunities for intellectual and cultural activity.

It's my judgment that it is the function of the public school to make up these deficiencies in background, not to accept and perpetuate them.

Q. Is this something that can be made up in school?

A. Certainly. Schools exist for that very purpose. History is filled with examples of boys and girls born in poverty who became leaders in intellectual activities which were unknown in the homes where they were raised.

Q. Isn't it true, however, that children learn at different speeds?

A. Of course. This is a central problem, when you have a system of mass education like ours.

Difference in "Mental Age" — —

Q. How great is the difference?

A. To take one example, the average child reaches what is called a "mental age" of twelve at the same time he reaches the chronological age of twelve. This is simply the definition of mental age. But intelligence tests show that a substantial number of children reach the mental age of twelve at the age of ten. Then you have another group, slow learners— not the slowest, merely those toward the end of the scale—who don't achieve mental age of twelve until they actually are fifteen years old.

Q. And yet we put all these children together in the same grades and classes, don't we?

A. We do.

Q. Isn't that one of the troubles?

A. I think it is a basic trouble. The facts are inescapable, but far too little thought has been given to working out a systematic plan for education based on these facts.

Q. Apparently we haven't been progressive enough then?

A. Quite right.

Q. One would think that educators would have discovered the difference between the mental age and the chronological age long before this——

A. They discovered it long ago. But it seems to me that they have been running away from the facts, instead of facing them by reorganizing the system.

Q. Well, then, would you eliminate the system of "grades" in the schools —first grade, second grade, and so on?

A. Certainly not. Any school system that handles masses of students must be based on a regular progression of grades, from first grade right on up through high school and college. You can't have a tutor for each child to carry him along at his own pace. You have to have school grades, but my point is that they should be based on mental rather than chronological age.

Q. How could you go about setting up such a grade structure?

A. First of all, there must be a series of grades through which a slow learner can proceed regularly and systematically. Perhaps more grades than we now have would be necessary. But the students of higher ability must be allowed—or rather encouraged—to skip certain of the grades, in a regular and systematic way, not haphazardly.

In the second place, we must separate the grade-level concept completely from the chronological age of the student.

This last point is very important. One of the serious objections to setting up a system based on mental age is that it puts very young students together with much older ones in social situations where such relationships are quite undesirable. My feeling about this is that you could organize things so that extracurricular activities are carried on by groups of children of the same chronological age. Then academic activity could be carried on in groups where the basis is the mental age.

Q. Do you feel that the schools will be in good shape when they are able to offer, say, the work of the top elementary grades to the slower learner at the chronological age of fifteen and to the rapid learner at the chronological age of ten?

A. That is exactly what the figures on mental age show. If you are going to have a system that takes full advantage of the abilities of all students, you've got to have something approaching that.

Q. Wouldn't it be true that some of those who were slow due to their slowness in maturing would ultimately catch up and be as bright as any of the others?

A. There would certainly be a far greater chance if they were carried along at a pace they could follow without getting hopelessly discouraged. They must learn steadily, even if slowly.

Q. Would you say that education in America has kept pace with the requirements of modern life?

A. No. American education has changed rapidly, but the changes seem to me to have been in the wrong direction. The schools have retreated from modern life.

Q. By de-emphasizing science and mathematics?

A. Yes. But not only there. Foreign languages have been neglected just as badly.

Q. Has there been an actual decline in teaching languages, too?

A. Yes. The figures I gave a while ago for science and mathematics can be matched for foreign languages. In 1900, nearly three quarters of all high school students were taking some foreign language. Today less than 22 per cent are doing so.

Q. Is this because Latin is being given up?

A. No, all foreign languages are suffering. Over these same years, French has dropped from 7.8 per cent of all students to 4.8 per cent,

and German from 14.3 to less than 1 per cent.

Q. Those figures on languages would seem to indicate that somebody has an idea that languages are not worthwhile in the modern world. What do you think?

A. I consider this view part of the retreat from the facts of modern life.

Value of Languages — —

Q. Is the study of languages a form of mental discipline, or is it a background to education — or what?

A. I would say that the first argument for foreign languages is essentially practical. The United States is deeply involved in world affairs and needs men and women who can understand the language and get the ideas of both our allies and our potential enemies.

Moreover, studying a foreign language is an essential part of learning to use one's own language. It was Goethe, I believe, who said that no man knows his own language until he knows another. One of the reasons for the decline in effective use of the English language is that so few students today have any knowledge of any other language, and, therefore, any knowledge of the principles of language in general.

Q. What do you think is to be said for the idea that, when you study other languages, you study the literature and culture of other peoples and therefore you begin to understand how their minds work, so that in this world of misunderstanding we can bring about some form of understanding? Is there anything to that theory?

A. I think there is a great deal to it. I subscribe to it wholeheartedly.

Q. We notice in the newspapers page after page of advertisements asking for engineers and scientists. Companies in the defense program are unable to find them. Is that shortage going to be serious?

A. It's already very serious, and it will grow much worse if we don't reverse present trends promptly. The bottleneck is the high school. I don't care how bright a student may be, he can't learn science or mathematics or foreign languages if he goes through a high school that does not offer the whole range of courses in these fields.

Q. Are the universities and their faculties aware of this—the boards of trustees? Or are they indifferent to it?

A. I think the faculties of colleges and universities are intensely aware of it. They are very much alarmed, virtually unanimously.

Q. Are you speaking now for teachers?

A. I am, yes.

Q. Teachers who would like to see more of their own subjects taught?

A. Not exactly. Most university professors are just as concerned about subjects other than their own. It's not a question of historians lamenting the fact that students are inadequately trained in history. I'm a historian. One of my worries is that students come to college unable to write good English, lacking in any foreign language, and too ill-informed about science ever to grasp its historical significance.

Q. Then, are university faculties pretty well agreed on what a good high-school education ought to include?

A. Yes, with one exception: Professors in departments of education—most of them, not all—are at odds with all the rest. They have been the principal sponsors of the watering-down process I have tried to describe.

Q. Are they part of what we call the "progressive education" movement?

A. I suppose one could say so. On the other hand, "progressive education" has meant a good many things, and some of the ideas, particularly at the beginning of this century, were perfectly sound. I don't like to condemn progressive education indiscriminately. One should make a distinction.

So long as the effort was mainly to improve methods of teaching, particularly by making subjects more alive to the pupils, progressive education was on the right track. When progressives began to think that interesting the pupil was the main thing, rather than how substantial might be the knowledge he acquired, then I think the movement began to be regressive education.

Q. Where did this progressive education idea originate? Was it at Columbia University?

A. A great many of the ideas stem from John Dewey, who was, of course, a professor of philosophy at Columbia and deeply interested in education. Frankly, I consider that many of the ideas which are given in his name are distortions of what he was, in fact, saying. But he did emphasize the importance of connecting education closely with the personal interests of students.

As I read Dewey, this was merely a step toward introducing the sciences, mathematics, and foreign languages in a systematic way. Many educators, however, took his philosophy to mean that formal and systematic training in the fundamentals was not necessary, and all that was required was for the students to spend their time according to their own interests without direction from above.

Education in 1900 — —

Q. Under your definitions, would you say that boys and girls are better educated today than they were in 1900, or less so?

A. On the whole, less well educated. You have to break this down a bit. The student who completed high school in 1900 was pretty sure to have gone through courses in the fundamental subjects and to have met well-recognized standards. He wasn't allowed to waste his time on trivialities, and he was under pressure to work at his studies.

Today the able student in a good city or suburban high school can doubtless obtain an equally good education if he wants to. But he is much less likely to be kept to the fundamentals if he decides he wants to fool around with easy courses. And, of course, he may live in a town where the high school has gone all-out for "life adjustment" education and doesn't offer enough of the basic work to give him what he needs.

The story is a little different for students of merely average ability. Lots of them would have dropped out of school in 1900. Now they are likely to continue, and so, on paper, they are better educated. But the courses for them have usually been so watered down that the real gain isn't very great.

I can't help thinking, moreover, that many of them have developed sloppy habits of thinking that are almost worse than ignorance itself. They have been allowed to get by without serious effort for so long that they've lost the ability to buckle down to hard work with their minds.

Q. In other words, we have retreated and slipped in our educational process?

A. I believe we have. Actually, I would rather compare the present achievement of American public schools not so much with the past as with the results we ought to be getting out of the much greater invest-

ment we are now making in education. We're spending enough to give
every American child the kind of
sound education that only a fraction
of them could have had half a century ago.

The average child today ought
to be as thoroughly educated as the
exceptional child of 1900, because he
is spending much more time in
school and receiving far more costly
instruction. And the exceptional
child ought to be receiving a much
better education than he could have
got in 1900. Neither result has, in fact,
occurred. This seems to be downright
failure on the part of our educational
system. . . .

Specific response among schoolmen to these pronouncements was instant. An editorial in a professional magazine made two charges:

1. Dr. Bestor is guilty both of drawing damaging conclusions unwarranted
by the facts and of presenting facts in a misleading manner—*and he knows it.*
2. Bestor tries to drive the wedge deeper between so-called scholars and
professional educators. [9:121]

The first of these charges was taken up later and substantiated by a
careful documentation and analysis of U.S. Office of Education statistics.
The result scarcely makes for easy reading but is proof again of the integrity and caution required both of the person who presents figures
and of the reader who is asked to accept them.

New Flaws in Arthur Bestor Diatribe   by HAROLD C. HAND

> This letter was first sent to the *St. Louis Post-Dispatch* and then it ap-
> peared in the March, 1957, *Phi Delta Kappan,* pages 254, 256. Reprinted
> by special permission. Harold C. Hand is Professor of Education, Univer-
> sity of Illinois.

In your "The Mirror of Public
Opinion" space on December 31,
1956, you reproduced Professor Arthur Bestor's answers to several of
the questions put to him by the editors of *U.S. News & World Report*
in an interview reported in its November 30, 1956, issue.

Professor Bestor said that the U.S.
Office of Education figures show that
only 55, 54, and 22 per cent of all
American high school students are
taking one or more courses in mathematics, science, and foreign languages, respectively, at the present
time. He also said that more than
half of the high schools offer no physics, that roughly a quarter offer nei-

ther physics nor chemistry, and that geometry is missing in 23 per cent. Further, he said that, on the whole, our boys and girls are less well educated today than they were in 1900.

The enrollment figures given by Professor Bestor are grossly in error and give the present-day high schools a completely undeserved black eye. His statistics regarding the number of schools not offering physics, chemistry, and geometry are correct but utterly misleading. And his statement that our boys and girls are less well educated today than in 1900 is ludicrously false, for, on the basis of the very criteria which he employed, it can be shown that the very opposite is the case.

Now to prove these charges in the order given.

Here are the enrollment figures reported by the U.S. Office of Education for 1950:

Mathematics—Algebra, 27 per cent; general math, 13 per cent; geometry, 13 per cent; trigonometry, 2 per cent. *Science*—General science, 21 per cent; biology, 18 per cent; chemistry, 8 per cent; physics, 5 per cent; physiology, 1 per cent; botany, 1⁻per cent; zoology, 1⁻per cent; earth science, 1⁻per cent. *Languages*—Spanish, 8 per cent; Latin, 8 per cent; French, 5 per cent; German, 1⁻per cent; Italian, 1⁻per cent; Portuguese, 1⁻per cent; Russian, 1⁻per cent.

When these percentages are added up, the resultant sums are 55, 54, and 22 for the three divisions, respectively.

What Professor Bestor did was to add up the U.S. Office of Education figures in this way and to call his sums the percentages of "all American high school students" who are taking any work in mathematics, science, and foreign languages these days.

But this is not at all what the above figures tell us. The table in the U.S. Office of Education bulletin which reports these figures says that each is the percentage of the *total student body* taking the subject indicated in that *one* grade of the pupils' *four* grades in high school in which they happened to be located in the *one school year of 1950*. What Professor Bestor did was to treat the data for but the *one school year of 1950* as though they were the percentages for the entire four years which our recent graduates spent in high school. A reasonably bright fifth-grade school boy should know better.

Let us take the figures for mathematics to demonstrate how grossly Professor Bestor misled everyone who took him seriously. The U.S. Office of Education reports that its 27 per cent algebra figure includes the data for both elementary algebra (20 per cent), a ninth-grade subject, and intermediate algebra (7 per cent), an eleventh-grade subject. It also reports this breakdown for its 13 per cent geometry figure: plane geometry (10 per cent), a tenth-grade subject, and solid geometry (3 per cent), a twelfth-grade subject. General mathematics is a ninth-grade subject, but about one-fifth of the pupils who take it are tenth-graders. Trigonometry is a twelfth-grade offering.

The U.S. Office of Education also reports that of all the high school pupils in the U.S., 31 per cent, 27 per cent, 23 per cent, and 19 per cent were enrolled in the ninth, tenth, eleventh, and twelfth grades, respectively, in 1950.

Let us take a high school whose enrollment fits these percentages exactly: ninth grade, 155 pupils; tenth, 135; eleventh, 115; twelfth, 95. Total, 500. In 1950, the enrollment in algebra was 135 pupils (27 per cent of the total student body). Of these 135 pupils, 100 (20 per cent of the student body) were enrolled in elementary algebra. Since algebra is a ninth-grade subject, these 100 pupils were ninth-graders. The 1950 enrollment in general mathematics was 13 per cent of the total student body, or 65 pupils. Four-fifths, or 52, of these pupils were ninth-graders. In 1950, then, 152 of the 155 pupils in the ninth grade studied mathematics. *This was 98 per cent of the class.* Let's allow for repeaters and call the figure 95 per cent. Professor Bestor told his readers that the U.S. Office of Education figures show that 45 per cent of all American high school pupils take no mathematics in high school. As we have just seen, these figures actually show that the proportion is about 5 per cent.

By the process just noted, it can be demonstrated that 49 per cent, 30 per cent, and between 16 and 26 per cent of the tenth, eleventh, and twelfth-grade pupils, respectively, took mathematics in 1950.

Professor Bestor's figures for science and foreign language enrollments were just as far wrong as his percentage for mathematics was, and for exactly the same reason.

Now for his statistics regarding the percentages of high schools not offering chemistry, physics, and geometry, which we said were correct but utterly misleading. The U.S. Office of Education which gives the figures says very clearly—in bold-face type, in fact—that it is only in the smaller schools that these subjects are missing from the curriculum, that taken all together the little schools in which neither chemistry nor physics is offered enroll fewer than 2 per cent of all the high school pupils in America, and that fewer than 6 per cent of all pupils are found in schools not offering geometry. It also pointed out that it is a common practice to teach chemistry and physics in alternate years in the smaller high schools, and that the data reported were for but one given year. The presumption, therefore, is that only half of that 16 per cent of all pupils who are found in the approximate half of the schools in which physics was not being offered the year of the survey had the opportunity to take this subject either the year preceding or following. To say, as Professor Bestor did not, that from 2 to 8 per cent of the *pupils* in this country have no opportunity to study chemistry, geometry, or physics creates quite a different (and a far more accurate) impression of the situation than to say, as he did, that from a quarter to a half of the *schools* do not teach these subjects.

Finally, Professor Bestor failed to tell his readers that only 8 per cent of all youths of high school age were attending the public high school in 1900 but that his figure was 64 per cent in 1950. In 1900, then, no more than 8 per cent of our boys and girls could possibly have been taking public high school courses in English, mathematics, science, and foreign languages. In 1950, on the other hand, 64 per cent of *all* the 14–17 year old boys and girls in this country were taking English, 63 per cent were taking mathematics, at least 58 per cent were taking science, and the proportion taking Latin I alone was greater than the percentage included in the entire student body in 1900. It is sheer nonsense to say, as Professor Bestor did, that on the whole our boys and girls are less well educated now than they were some fifty years ago.

See also "High Schools: Are They Doing Their Job?" from *Changing Times,* pages 373–379 of this book.

NOTE: The reader who is interested in making a further study of current educational criticisms should read a penetrating analysis of "The Good Guys and the Bad Guys" by James D. Finn in the *Phi Delta Kappan* for October, 1958, pages 2–5, 29–32. It includes an excellent, up-to-date bibliography.

Even more subtle and involved is the philosophic-psychological question of what constitutes intellectual development. The article which follows deals with this question.

Intellectual Development in Modern Schools

by LAWRENCE E. METCALF

From the *Phi Delta Kappan,* April, 1957, pages 277–280. Reprinted by special permission. Lawrence E. Metcalf is Associate Professor of Education, University of Illinois.

In *U.S. News & World Report* Professor Arthur Bestor says that the "real purpose of a school is to teach youngsters how to use their minds effectively." He goes on to say that this purpose is today less well achieved than in the past. He believes that fundamental intellectual disciplines are being squeezed from the curriculum by less essential content. He argues that mastery of history, English, foreign languages, mathematics, and the sciences is necessary to everyone's intellectual development, and that such mastery would include an understanding of the methodology basic to each discipline. The student of history, for example, should learn the historical method as well as the content acquired through this method. Unlike Dewey, and pragmatists in general, he does not speak of a methodology, reflective thinking, as a basis for all our knowledge. Some replies to Bestor have taken the direction of quarreling with his figures, and asserting, for instance, that there is more mathematics in the curriculum than he is willing to admit. A less common approach is to argue with his theory of intellectual development. The latter is the approach I choose to make. In other words, I believe that it is time that we examine what is meant by those who accept intellectual development as the major purpose of education in a democracy.

Before giving consideration to a pragmatic conception of a program in intellectual development, it clears the air to recognize how formidable is the task facing us if we buy Bestor's approach. It is indeed a formidable task, since the kind of mastery he wants is seldom achieved even by Ph.D.'s in a discipline. And the case he makes for studying a foreign language would apply to all languages, just as the case he makes for American literature or English literature would hold for all the literatures of

all the lands in the world, and for every historical period of all the lands in the world. In fact, Bestor's argument, if applied logically, would mean that an intellectual is a person who understands everything in his environment, and this, of course, is no longer an achievable educational purpose for even our most gifted youngsters.

Many critics of Bestor have successfully refuted his statistics, and Bestor has somewhat contemptuously referred to this kind of criticism as a numbers game. It is indeed a numbers game started by Bestor. The game has some point only if it establishes the fact that Bestor's figures are distorted and misleading. This point has been well established, but even so we are left with the task of determining whether his recommended curriculum would foster the intellectual growth that is intended. Intellectual development in every educable youngster is a decent and necessary educational objective for a democratic society. There is the theoretical problem of determining what means would lead to this noble end. A consideration of this means-ends problem will include a study of theories of mind and learning. There is nothing more practical than a good theory, and a good curriculum theory will be based upon research data on how people learn. Most of the data now available have been garnered not by educationists so much as by liberal arts professors in departments of psychology. I believe that it is now fairly well established that the pragmatic theory of mind and learning is most consistent with the data made available from psychological research.

Bestor has never really made clear to his followers the exact nature of his theory of learning. But it is increasingly clear that he does not like pragmatism, and much of this dislike is based upon a superficial acquaintance with the philosophy of pragmatism. His view on pragmatism was best expressed almost two years ago in a book review which he wrote for the *New Republic*. At the risk of inaccuracy, I would paraphrase his argument somewhat as follows:

He attributes to pragmatists the notion that genuine liberalism is possible only if liberals abjure the absolutes of non-pragmatic philosophies. He then says that any identification of liberalism with pragmatism is a handicap to American liberalism at this time. There was an alliance between liberalism and pragmatism in the early half of the twentieth century, but this alliance was a fortuitous one called forth by a particular historical situation. Historically, so says Bestor, liberals have appealed to ideal and unchanging principles of ethics and justice (see the Declaration of Independence) while conservatives have deprecated the changeless and absolute in favor of realistic and pragmatic adjustments of men and institutions. But these opposing doctrines changed partners in the latter part of the nineteenth century, and Dewey's pragmatism helped liberalism to challenge the absolutes and preconceptions of conservatism. From 1890 to 1930 pragmatism served liberalism well. But it became evident in the thirties that pragmatism could not offer liberalism either content or direction. It offered a mere methodology rather than a full-fledged philosophy. It offered no system of values other than an unexamined acceptance of the preferences that men of good will had been expressing for two or three generations past. Then, according to Bestor, even Dewey saw the light, and in one of his later books, *Freedom and Culture*, revised his view to the extent of saying that democracy is a thing of ultimate worth unaffected by the vicissitudes of time. Bestor concludes his argument with the comment that this revised view is good liberalism but poor pragmatism.[1]

Bestor's History Is Distorted

In addition to the fact that democracy is called a thing, there is much that is wrong with this argument. Bestor's history of liberalism is a distorted one, and it is the kind of distortion that frequently occurs when historians use a so-called historical method as a basis for freely interpreting the past so that it rationalizes whatever pre-determined view they

[1] "John Dewey and American Liberalism," a review by Arthur Bestor of Irwin Edman's *John Dewey, His Contribution to the American Tradition*, *New Republic*, 133:18–19, August 29, 1955.

have of the present. But more appropriate to our discussion is the shallow understanding of pragmatism exhibited in this review. It is a typically undergraduate view of pragmatism. Pragmatism is pictured as a philosophy empty of ideals, and offering man nothing more than a method by which to examine the truth of factual propositions. Value preferences within this philosophy are reflexes, either emotive, or conditioned, or both. As philosophy it has no theory of reality, no theory of knowledge, no theory of value, and little more than a theory of logic. It is also interesting to note that the review reflects two meanings of pragmatic, and these two meanings are used interchangeably with no indication to the reader that the reviewer is engaged in a shell game. Pragmatic is sometimes used as an adjective for a technical philosophy, and at other times it is used as a synonym for practical, and in this case practical means expedient rather than moral. The latter use of the term is quite common among historians who have never had time to master philosophy as well as history. This use of the term is somewhat forgivable in a political historian, but it is inexcusable for the specialist in intellectual history. It is the kind of error that is seldom made by a historian of Merle Curti's stature, for example.

Be Pragmatic, or You'll Be Dogmatic

The review also leaves out of account the fact that liberals can be as prejudiced as conservatives, and that no matter how shattered conservative preconceptions may be at this time, liberalism can always profit from a re-examination of its own premises. If pragmatism tends toward continuous re-examination and reconstruction of democracy and its premises, then a reunion of pragmatism and liberalism is needed whenever liberalism tends toward dogmatism. As long as there is an alliance between liberalism and pragmatism, the appearance of authoritarianism within liberal movements is kept to a minimum. Even more striking is the fact that Bestor fails to recognize that no matter how ultimate is the worth of democracy, the actual meaning of democracy to people who believe in it will change with the times. It is the fixed meaning given to individualism by both conservatives and liberals which hampers our efforts to deliberately plan for a more democratic society.

Bestor's view of pragmatism, however distorted and superficial it may be, is at least consistent with his perception of progressive education. Progressive education, in his opinion, was at its best in the 1920's when its emphasis was upon developing better methods of teaching. But its decline began, and it wreaked positive harm, when it invaded the field of content. It is characteristic of Bestor's thinking that he separates content from method. Content is that which professors of the liberal arts teach. Methods of teaching are taught by professors of education. And by methods of teaching he means slick tricks by which to put across the content that everyone needs in order to be an intellectual. There is very little content in a methods course, and theoretical knowledge (which I take to be the only knowledge we have) is entirely missing from courses in education. This schism in his thinking, when taken seriously by teachers' associations, unions, and accrediting agencies, has an unfortunate effect upon our thinking about patterns of teacher education. We slip into the habit of trying to figure out how much content (subject matter) and how much methods (slick tricks) to include in teacher education without raising a more fundamental question of how much educational theory to include. The old battle between theory and know-how seems to have reached a truce as we return to an even older battle between content and method.

Content Courses Must Include Method

As a matter of fact, a methods course that lacks content has no business in a teacher education curriculum, and a content course is equally misplaced if it fails to develop an understanding of sound intellectual method. One of the reasons that teachers may not teach an intellectual method is that they have not acquired one from their content or methods courses. What we need most of all in teacher education are courses which include intellectual method as a significant part of their content.

It is true that in the foregoing I have used the term method in at least two different senses. An intellectual method is a method by which we know truth. A pedagogical method is a method by which a teacher teaches truth. The scientific method is what most people today mean by a sound intellectual method, and discussion is one example of what people mean by a pedagogical method. This distinction between intellectual method and pedagogical method breaks down whenever one's approach to teaching knowledge is basically a pragmatic approach. A good pragmatist would say that the intellectual purposes of education can be achieved only when teachers use pedagogical methods which stimulate and direct scientific thinking in learners.

Much of the instruction in methods as well as much of the instruction in subject matter fails to teach prospective teachers any meaning of science and scientific method, with the result that they do not know how to use their precious content for intellectual ends. We do not remove this deficiency by including in liberal education a formal study of logic and scientific method. I do not oppose their inclusion, but I do feel that our knowledge in theories of transfer suggests strongly that prospective teachers are not likely to use principles of logic in their teaching except as those principles are illustrated over and over again in their subject matter and education courses. If this is what Bestor means by teaching the historical method as well as history, I am all for his view. But it has been my experience that historical method is seldom taught in history courses other than those labelled as methodological. A course called "The Renaissance," or "The Winning of the West," seldom comes close to any concern with historical method, even when the courses are graduate level in their numbering. Also, I believe that Bestor overemphasizes the uniqueness of the method basic to each discipline. Basically, the method is scientific, and Dewey's more general concept, reflective thinking, is the concept that needs to be progressively clarified throughout undergraduate and graduate instruction.

I agree with Bestor that not all content is equally stimulating of the intellect, but I disagree with the idea that certain content must be mastered by everyone if intellects are to develop. And it is begging the question to say that those who fail to master this pre-determined content lack intellectual capacities. In order for intellects to develop, two things are needed. First, students must think, and second, a conceptualization of the thinking process must take place. If there is a content that everyone must master, it is not history but rather the content of scientific method. We begin to acquire this content when we begin to think about our thinking. And this practice of examining our thinking must permeate all our in-

struction, and not just our instruction in a logic course.

When Education Doesn't Affect Conviction

Students possess many convictions. It is characteristic of so much of our education that it leaves our convictions uncontaminated by change. Students who study racial differences continue their dislike of Negroes. Their beliefs about Negroes lack an intellectual basis, even though they have learned from the intellectual discipline of sociology that socially significant differences among races are cultural rather than biological in origin. Much of this failure resides in the fact that we have paid too little attention to the content of student minds.

A pedagogical solution of this problem would involve students in a logical and scientific study of what they believe. The content of our various disciplines would supply students with the evidence they need in order to determine whether their beliefs are any longer worth believing and acting upon. This approach points straight toward a problem-centered curriculum rather than the subject-centered curriculum that Bestor seems to prefer. Historical data would be taught only if it clarifies some conflict of concern to the learner. This approach would not mean that we teach students only what they "want" to learn. This is a distorted view of the doctrine of interest, and is the view which Bestor attributes to educationists. A more accurate view says that we build interest in a socially significant conflict —whenever that interest is lacking in students—and proceed to help students resolve the conflict at a level of understanding appropriate to their maturity. Much history will not be taught under this approach, but whatever history we teach will have intellectual meaning and worth to the students who learn it.

Bestor will reject this solution as a watered-down one. But I see nothing diluted in a curriculum which requires students to test in a rigorously scientific way any convictions they may hold in areas of belief such as religion, race, economics, social class, and sex. The experience of most teachers is that students find this approach so demanding that they usually exhibit at times a preference for the good old days of recitations and regurgitations. I want to make it perfectly clear what the newer approach really means. It means that we address our instruction to the felt and latent conflicts of our students, and we demand that our students use intellectual content and intellectual method as a basis for resolving their conflicts. And even though students will at times resist this challenge, many of them will begin to sense a worth to intellectual living which is seldom sensed by students in conventional high schools.

If a student believes that marriages are indissoluble contracts drawn up and signed in heaven, and if he also believes that there is positive harm to be derived from keeping promises that no one wants to keep, he is likely to have a conflict over whether to be heavenly or practical. I humbly submit that anyone who has this conflict will be interested in its resolution. I further submit that the attempt to resolve such a conflict is tough enough to avoid the charge of watered-down education. And I further submit that logic, scientific method, and social science content are essential ingredients to a wise resolution of this kind of conflict.

If Bestor rejects this proposal for a curriculum in intellectual development, it is because he has assumed throughout his discussions of educational theory and practice that intelligent study of everyday problems has little to do with the fostering of human intellect.

David H. Russell's article, "The Fundamentals in Schools Today," pages 226–232, is used in a different context in this book, but it also contains a defense against Bestor's contention that present-day schools are doing a less efficient job than schools of fifty years ago.

It is easier to criticize than to defend, especially if one wishes to avoid arm-waving and glittering generalization. Sloan Wilson has made some pertinent remarks on this subject in the following quotation from *Harper's Magazine.*

Ever since the war, I've put up with about as much debate concerning the public schools as I can stand quietly, and I'm going to get into the act. Of course, I'm no great expert on the technical aspects of the thing, but I need only to inspect the torrent of recent books and articles attacking or defending the schools to realize that this is a subject which offers marvelous opportunities to a writer tired of research. Here is a field in which uninformed opinions are at a premium. A truly ignorant man can easily work himself up into a feverish fury about the public schools, and in a brief article or book can unburden himself of enough righteous indignation to heat a summer hotel in January.

On the other hand, a person who has really learned something about the schools is almost hopelessly crippled when it comes to writing genuinely dramatic books and articles. He finds he has to qualify his generalities, and all kinds of awkward facts keep getting in the way of rich, rolling prose and sweeping accusations.*

Occasionally one finds a citizen, not a public educator, who is deeply concerned with the task of the school and who is capable of both objective analysis and skillful writing. The following article is an example.

The Great Debate in American Education

by NORMAN COUSINS

Reprinted by special permission from Norman Cousins and *The Saturday Review*, from the September 11, 1954, issue, pages 11–13, 47. Norman Cousins is editor of *The Saturday Review* and recipient of the 1956 Education Award of Wayne State University.

Recently, in Tokyo, an opinion poll established that the Japanese people regarded public education as the nation's greatest single asset and source of potential strength.

Recently, in New Delhi, contesting political parties differed on almost everything except the need to push forward with one of the most far-reaching educational programs in the world's history.

Recently, in Istanbul, officials of Turkey assessed with pride the nation's progress in attempting to compress in a single generation progress of a type that might ordinarily re-

* From Sloan Wilson, "Public Schools Are Better Than You Think," *Harper's Magazine*, September, 1955, p. 29. Quoted by special permission of the author. Sloan Wilson is a "best-selling" novelist. Formerly education editor of the *New York Herald Tribune*, he was assistant director of the White House Conference on Education, 1956.

quire a century or more. And in that inventory education was at the top of the list.

This year throughout the world, in fact, education has become a historic concern on a par with the other great issues—food, health, housing, freedom. This year was not markedly different from the year before in this respect; what it did was to lend additional dramatic evidence to the fact that in the middle of the twentieth century there were few bigger issues before the world's peoples than the development of the human mind.

And in the United States this year education in all its aspects—public and private, elementary and secondary, college and university—was being debated as it had never been debated before. Exactly how the controversy would be resolved no one could tell, but at least one thing was certain: whatever happened in the United States would have an effect throughout a large part of the world. For America and Americans today are occupying the center of at least half of the world stage. Like Athens or Rome or Byzantium or Great Britain at the pinnacles of their power, America is exercising a profound gravitational pull on the values, institutions, and cultures of other peoples. It has engaged their hopes and fears. America might inspire or appall, but it could not leave people indifferent. It could neither ignore nor be ignored.

The main problem or challenge facing American education today is how to get it all in. How to maintain certain values and approaches that have proved themselves through 160 years of public education and yet enable the individual to feel at home in the middle of a century which has already seen more change than has been accumulated in the previous thousand years. The central problem is not to find new principles but to make the old ones work, not to create new values but to get rid of old assumptions.

So far as education is concerned the old definitions of what constituted an educated man are perfectly in order for the new age. The only thing that is lacking so far is a workable way of applying them. For the old definitions had to do with the making of a rounded man; they spoke of values that had to be awakened and protected. They spoke of service to the community-at-large. They spoke of the awakening of a proper ambition, of its pursuit and fulfilment. And they spoke about things of the spirit. In short, the old definitions believed in equipping the individual for a career, for citizenship, for balanced living. These definitions are as good and essential today as they were during the age of Jefferson—or of Aristotle, for that matter.

Less than one hundred years ago these definitions began to run into trouble. The new age had produced new complications, but the new concepts that were devised to meet them were inadequate. Society began to make new demands on the individual. More and more the individual was called upon to do fewer things that required greater knowledge and to do them with increasing skill. This involved more than the need for individual assent and cooperation; it required vast changes in the structure of education itself. By the end of the Second World War specialization had come into its own. Each of the parts of the new educational design was beautifully assembled, oiled, and operated. But a science of the whole was lacking; indeed the relationship of one part to the next was only imperfectly understood. What, then, about the old definitions of an educated man as someone who knew what the world was up to; who enlarged his concepts to embrace new conditions; and who had a knack for tying things together? The old definitions had stressed integration. How much integration was possible in a world geared to compartmentalization and complexity?

WHAT should the school do to meet this new challenge? How does it address itself to the job of teaching a human being three or four times as much as it did only a generation or two ago in order to qualify him as an educated man?

Already formal schooling accounts for almost one-third of the average life span. In the upper reaches of specialized training the fraction comes closer to two-fifths. Until there is a colossal expansion far beyond anything that is now anticipated in the average life expectancy—say, to a hundred years or more—the schools cannot expect merely to tack on new content by tacking on additional years of schooling. It must look to new techniques; it must study more closely the means by which the human mind masters facts, ideas, skills. It must, in short, find out more about the mechanism of human thought, for education fails in direct proportion to its failure to teach the individual how to think.

It is with respect to these objectives, and the possible means of teaching them, that the Great Debate on American Education can most profitably be conducted. Educators welcome the widest possible public participation in this debate. They ask only that the parties to the debate subscribe to the principle of public education.

The American people must be alerted to the danger that some of the groups which come before the public as critics of the schools do not seek the correction of certain flaws, minor or major, so much as the reduction or even the repudiation of public education itself.

A number of misconceptions cloud the Great Debate. There is the charge that educators regard their profession as a closed corporation; that they communicate with each other in a language replete with academic gobbledygook and magic signs inexplicable to all except members of the favored fraternity for the express purpose of excluding the public; that they have turned their backs on such fundamentals as the three R's; that they have become exponents of a strange, unidentified alien system known as Pragmatism; that they are anti-religious as a group; and, finally, that many of them are in the forefront of the conspiracy against the traditional American institutions on which our freedoms rest.

To take these misconceptions up in order:

First: Do educators seek to keep the schools to themselves and for themselves—apart from parents, community, or society?

No; teachers are part of the community. They value their place in that community. They neither expect nor desire unfettered control over the minds of the nation's children. They believe that the great enterprise of American education requires vital and creative participation by the community as a whole.

The books placed in the hands of young people, the lessons put on their desks, the writings on the blackboards, the teacher's own words— these are not privileged. These are public matters. The school cannot— and should not even if it could—arrogate to itself sole jurisdiction over the facts, the ideas, and the interpretations that are introduced into the minds of children. This is a composite responsibility of which teachers are but the custodians.

There is no doubt in the minds of responsible educators that this open-house attitude was too long in coming. It is true that the old tradition stressed a certain spirit of separateness and that public education was not the partnership between citizen and school it ought to have been. The dominant direction has been reversed in the past decade. At almost every teacher or school administrator's convention since the end of the war— state and national both—the question that has been more often discussed is "How can the schools promote increased public interest?" Countless proposals and plans towards this end have been studied and adopted. The various districts and regions have exchanged progress reports; representatives have been appointed to approach community leaders by way of convincing them that their participation is not only welcome but essential. The educational organizations have urged governors or state legislatures to appoint citizens' committees for the purpose of undertaking fact-finding surveys about the schools. Where fact-finding commissions have been appointed educators have pledged and given full cooperation.

Second: Do our teachers and educators use a professional jargon that tends to mystify and separate them from the public?

This charge, unfortunately, contains enough elements of truth to warrant the severest self-scrutiny by members of the profession. As in most other callings, there has been a tendency to develop the occupational disease of specialized references and apparent obscurantism. Whether this tendency is worse in pedagogy than it is, say, in law or medicine or architecture or the physical sciences, or for that matter, among aviation cadets or bobby soxers, it is difficult to say. In any event, the tendency has gone much too far and should be arrested. Apart from this, it is important to correct the misconception that the only reason teachers communicate with each other in this apparent mumbo-jumbo is to set up a barrier between themselves and the public. There is no need to ascribe ulterior motives; the tendency is bad enough. The need to humanize and simplify this language is a necessary challenge to the profession as a whole.

Third: Are our teachers and educators intent on shelving or replacing the three R's?

There has never been any argument among educators concerning the importance of the three R's as fundamental building blocks in early schooling. There has, however, been some difference of opinion concerning the methods by which the three R's should be taught. Many educators are not convinced that the possibilities for improvement in techniques of instruction were long ago exhausted. Nor are they convinced that the most rigid form of teaching the three R's is necessarily the best. Are they completely satisfied with the present methods in teaching the three R's? Hardly. They believe that much thought and work remain to be done. They believe in the need for additional improvement and ask the

patience and help of parents in this respect—as in all others.

Apart from this, there is a growing concern among educators that some people would have the schools regard the three R's as ends in themselves. Having defined the three R's as the essentials, these critics define almost everything else as non-essential or even as "frills." While they describe the three R's as the entrance-way to education, there is at least an implication in what they say that it is also the exit.

Educators call for general recognition of the fact that there are subjects beyond the three R's that equally deserve to be regarded as basic. To be sure, these subjects all rely heavily on the three R's as fundamental tools; but in themselves they represent the tools to an education that is more than mere literacy. In this case, too, no educator will say that better techniques cannot be worked out for these subjects than the techniques now obtaining.

In any event, educators generally regret the fact that "Back to the Three R's" has become a slogan and battlecry rather than a responsible approach to responsible debate.

Fourth: Have educators been infected by a strange new philosophy called "Pragmatism," and doesn't it come into conflict with what is known as "the American Way"?

As in the case of the debate over the three R's, the charge of "Pragmatism" has been used as a battering ram to knock down aspects of public education that the attackers appear to dislike. Generally the term has not been defined when it is used to criticize or condemn. Rather than get into a debate over Pragmatism educators would prefer to describe what the methods are that they do use, to the extent that they may be said to favor any single "set" of methods or techniques.

Wherever possible today's teachers try to stress the practical aspects of learning. A child has a firmer grasp of a subject if it can be related to his own experience. He learns how to make a model plane by making it, not by reading about it. A textbook is a valuable aid, but it is not the be-all and end-all of education. A student learns about citizenship in the community not only by reading about it but by participating in it while at school. It is proved to him in terms of his own experience that certain patterns of work are better than others, and that the subjects he studies are not empty things but part of a real world that he can feel with his own hands. His relationship with his neighbors or his fellow human beings, wherever they may be, are not academic matters but the stuff of life, and have to be worked at to be understood.

All this is what is meant basically by "learning by doing." As a "system" it is not the sole possession of one or two contemporary philosophers. Its exponents and exemplars would include, to mention a few, Benjamin Franklin, Abraham Lin-

coln, Ralph Waldo Emerson—and not solely William James and John Dewey, the latter of whom has been blamed indiscriminately for almost everything that is wrong with contemporary education. In terms of a democratic approach to democratic living "learning by doing" is truly at the core of what historians regard as "the American Way."

Fifth: Are educators "anti-religious" as a group? Why are they opposed to spiritual teaching in the schools?

Of all the misunderstandings concerning the true positions of most educators this is perhaps the most serious and widespread. This misunderstanding fails to take into account an important distinction that educators make. It is the distinction between *providing a place* in the schools for spiritual values, and avoiding any *indoctrination* in spiritual values in the schools. A man cannot claim to be truly educated who is oblivious of the great religions and their part in the shaping of history and human aspirations. Nor can he ignore the fundamental spiritual urge that is deep within man and that helps to establish his uniqueness. But the teacher must respect the right of each Church to take care of the spiritual needs of its followers. The schools cannot prescribe for the spiritual health of the nation. They cannot indoctrinate, they cannot presume to give weight to one belief over another. They are aware, however, that the clause in the United

States Constitution prohibiting "an establishment of religion" means that they must abstain from doing anything that would seem to favor one denomination over another. At the same time, they can help make our young people aware of the universality of spiritual values.

Sixth: Aren't many teachers disloyal, or subversive in one way or another? Why is there so much news in the newspapers linking them to controversies over loyalty tests and the like? Are they trying to conspire against a democratic society, of which the schools are a vital center?

Our educators do not believe that our schools should disregard, discard, or devitalize the moral, spiritual, and political values of a free society. Nor do they believe that the main purpose of the schools is to serve as a sanctuary for those who profess freedom the better to weaken it. They believe that the main purpose of the schools is to prepare free men for purposeful life in a dynamic world. That purpose, too, is to help the individual to discover his own potential and help him to develop it. There is no place in the schools for the idea that the object of education is to cultivate human robots for the convenience of totalitarian systems, public or private.

Our educators believe in the democratic responsibility of democratic education for the democratic good.

This, in turn, is directly tied to democratic equality and respect. Our teachers and educators do not ask or expect special privileges because of their calling. Neither do they believe that their position on the public payroll should mark them out as special targets for abuse or deprive them of status in the community. They take a proper pride in their profession. They do not believe this profession should be regarded as fair game by headhunters or headline hunters.

What our teachers say or do in the schools should not be exempt from scrutiny or review. But it is vital that such scrutiny or review be conducted in an atmosphere of trust rather than distrust, of friendliness rather than hostility. Loyalty in the public service must be an abiding principle, but this should not be taken to justify a presumption of guilt against any teacher whose work is under review. A real difference exists between random accusation and documented proof. Slogans are not quite the same as evidence or due process of law.

There is a difference between conspiracy and honest controversy. Unless this difference is clearly recognized by the Government and people we sever one of the vital arteries in the circulatory system of a free people. Conspiracy seeks to subvert representative government. Controversy can sustain it and strengthen it. The bloodstream of democracy circulates best when it can draw upon the full and free flow of ideas. Honest dissent should be more than merely tolerated; it should be encouraged. A vital point of difference between the totalitarian state and the free state is that totalitarianism does not permit, and could not survive, the right of protest.

The free state remains free not only because its citizens are given the right of protest but because they use it. The citizen must be above the state; this is the essence of a free society.

THESE, then, are some of the principal misconceptions about educators and the public schools which if cleared up could contribute substantially to the usefulness of a Great Debate on American Education.

Apart from the clarification of misconceptions, what are some of the positive ideas that parents and educators alike should bring to the Great Debate?

These ideas should concern freedom.

First of all, it is the freedom to do one's best in an atmosphere that makes possible one's best. It is the freedom to believe in and act upon the need for enduring improvement and progress as a basic law of life.

Next, freedom from stagnation. We want the kind of freedom that provides elbow room for inspiration and the imagination; that sees education not in terms of tight and fixed compartments but in terms of the limitless possibilities of a free mind.

This freedom has something to do with the great American diversity and the power that is inherent in it. Education must deal with this diversity and indeed reflect it.

This freedom if it is to work must also keep the schools clear of pile-driving pressures and political stampedes. The schools must be operated soberly and responsibly with the needs and interests of the young people and the entire community in mind. The schools must have freedom to protect themselves, and the means to protect themselves, against mobilized attack directed against free education itself.

Finally, freedom that has to do with the spirit of adventure. Nothing in human history is as fascinating or as wondrous as the growth of the human mind. The educated man believes in the infinite capacity of the mind for continued development. So long as the community-at-large is free to examine, explore, and experiment we have every confidence that the basic problems confronting education—as indeed, all basic problems confronting the country—can be met and solved.

Educators today do not profess to have all the answers about their own craft. They have yet to determine how formal education can get everything in that should get in within the limited time available to the school. But they are working on the problem and will do a better job if they realize that we are working alongside them to the same ends. And they know that a constructive and affirmative atmosphere can provide a powerful stimulant and incentive in arriving at wise and effective decisions.

For if the job of educators is to increase the stretching capacity of young people in the attainment of great ideals, it is no less their own responsibility to transcend their own past and present limitations. In fact, the crisis of our time is a crisis in growth. It concerns man's ability to use his vast power for his own good. That cannot be done without growth.

The part of free education in making such growth possible is necessarily a big one. In calling attention to the spaciousness and grandeur of the challenge, educators are appealing to the best in America. Freedom thus defined is freedom to serve the cause of freedom.

Only an intelligent citizenry can hope to hear and heed the voice of leadership amid the hue and cry. Again, Sloan Wilson has shrewdly assessed the situation.

The job of figuring out how righteous indignation about weaknesses of the schools can be converted into constructive action will not be done by people who wave their arms while criticizing the schools as though they were fighting bees. It will be done by serious-minded people calmly appraising the schools in their own community. It will be done by people who have learned to be patient of differing points of view, and who know how to enlarge areas of agreement, rather than capitalize on controversy. Somehow an ancient fallacy will have to be righted. *The schools are no good,* many people are saying nowadays, and they imply, *therefore, do not support them.* I certainly agree that many schools are pretty poor now, as they have been always, and I believe that they therefore should be supported doubly. The job of creating schools capable of developing all the abilities of all American children will never be easy, but without any doubt the American people are in their own curious way plodding toward it. There is certainly hope in the fact that for the past fifty years, they have plodded with the speed of hares.*

AREAS OF CONFLICT

When active forces meet, either of two things may happen: cleavage on clear-cut issues or joint action on areas of agreement. The two results need not be mutually exclusive. The latter course will pave the way to desirable changes in school practice; the former will continue to make the public schools a battleground. In the article that follows, Terrien, a sociologist, identifies the areas of conflict and their sociological roots, points out the dire consequences of inaction, and challenges the teaching profession to cope with the situation in a positive manner.

* From Sloan Wilson, "Public Schools Are Better Than You Think," *Harper's Magazine,* September, 1955, p. 33. Quoted by special permission of the author.

The Sociology of the Attacks on the Schools

by FREDERIC W. TERRIEN

Reprinted by special permission from the *California Journal of Secondary Education,* March, 1953, pages 134–141. Frederic Terrien is Assistant Professor of Sociology, San Francisco State College.

There are more than one and one quarter million teachers in the United States. In their generous numbers, they could have a considerable share of temporal power, and in the acknowledged virtue of their calling, they could have the glory of worldly reward. There are enough of them to exert as much political pressure as the National Association of Manufacturers, to fight for their own interests more effectively than any labor union, and to control professional standards as stringently as does the American Medical Association. Yet none of these things is happening. A proportionately increasing number of jobs in the field go begging each year, and a great many of those that are filled are rewarded so poorly, in a material sense, that their holders are hard pressed to maintain themselves. Now more trouble besets the profession, for in addition to the critical attacks on performance to which teachers are subject, there has been added an attack upon their loyalty to the democratic ideology.

All of this is not new. Any professional group may expect to have its detractors; it is only their current vigor which would seem, paraphrasing Charles Lamb, to press incivility out of season. Attacks on the performance of educators are as old as the profession of teaching. Brickman notes that "public criticism was a concomitant of education even in the early days," [1] and Burton points out that earlier writers from Confucius and Socrates to William Penn grumbled that a "return to fundamentals" would be a most salutary thing for the educational systems of their times. "Parents are always saying," he comments, "that schools were better in their day, or in their parents' day. . . . *The schools of any earlier day, revered by today's critics, were under the identical criticisms made today.*" [2]

If there is little novelty in these attacks, only a brief recapitulation of their main charges is necessary; it will be the purpose of this paper to examine, from a sociological point of view, the possible reasons for the attacks. The literature anent the cur-

[1] William W. Brickman, "Attack and Counterattack in American Education," *School and Society,* Vol. 74, No. 1923, October 27, 1951.

[2] William H. Burton, "Get the Facts: Both Ours and the Other Fellow's," *Progressive Education,* Vol. 29, No. 3, January, 1952.

rent wave of criticism is already sufficient to have warranted a published bibliography.[3] Summarizing from the thoughtful pieces by Benjamin Fine,[4] Ernest O. Melby,[5] Archibald W. Anderson,[6] Paul Woodring,[7] and Harold Alberty,[8] and from *Newsweek's* "Platform," [9] the principal charges against education today seem to be eight in number. The critics hold that:

1. *The fundamentals are not being taught.* Various fads and frills, rather than the three R's, are the subject matter of the day, which means that

2. *A lack of discipline prevails.* Just as drill and hard work in learning have been abandoned, so has disappeared a respect for authority, and so, inevitably,

3. *Moral and religious values are neglected.* The test of expediency has been substituted for the test of ultimate values. If the latter may be questioned, it is no wonder that

4. *The schools are seedbeds of un-Americanism.* If all these things are true, then the contention that

5. *The schools are too expensive* finds ready support, along with the concomitant charge that

6. *Education offers poor preparation for making a living in the world of today.* This is held to be true chiefly because

7. *The schools are pre-empting the functions of the home,* endeavoring to provide institutional substitutes for much that should be accomplished within the family framework. This would never have come about if it were not that

8. *Control of education has passed out of the hands of the people* and into those of a group of self-appointed experts who make no effort to consult with or inform the community which pays their salaries.

The replies which have been prepared by educators to these charges would seem to be more than adequate defense. Point for point, the critics have been answered—perhaps nowhere more ably than by the various contributors to the January, 1952, issue of *Progressive Education,* and by

---

[3] *A List of Articles and Books Concerned with the Wave of Attacks on Public Education* (Washington, D. C.: Defense Commission of the National Education Association).

[4] Benjamin Fine, "Why Our Public Schools Are in Serious Trouble," reprinted from *The New York Times* (no dates).

[5] Ernest O. Melby, "American Education Under Fire," *Freedom Pamphlets,* 1951.

[6] Archibald W. Anderson, "The Charges Against American Education: What Is the Evidence?" *Progressive Education,* Vol. 29, No. 3, January, 1952.

[7] Paul Woodring, "An Open Letter to Teachers," *Harper's Magazine,* Vol. 205, No. 1226, July, 1952.

[8] Harold Alberty *et al.,* "Let's Look at the Attacks on the Schools" (Mimeo.) (Columbus, Ohio: College of Education, The Ohio State University, 1951).

[9] "New Crises for Education," *Platform* (New York: Newsweek Club and Educational Bureaus, Weekly Publications, Inc.), January, 1952.

the group which prepared the symposium entitled "Let's Look at the Attacks on the Schools" (both previously cited). The catalogue of reasons for such attacks is as long as that for the attacks themselves, and can be related directly to them. If human beings may be said to talk most about what they do not have, so may they also be said to attack most readily that which is related to their own shortcomings. Reviewing the charges, then, let us consider the reasons behind them.

First is the charge that the fundamentals are not being taught. While innumerable surveys have shown, as Melby says, that "the test scores of present-day children are superior to those made by children of thirty or forty years ago and by youngsters of the early days of our country," [10] many people are hard pressed to accept this supported truth. In the long view, the educators should not take umbrage at this feeling. There are good reasons for it, and it has nothing to do with the earnestness with which educators are performing their duties.

The simple truth is that the fundamentals are being taught, but that along with them, other things are also being dealt with—things so much more complex than the essential three R's that they defy easy explanation. Perhaps the chief difference between the schools of our day and those of Horace Mann's time is the venturesome step which the educators have made into the realm of interacting variables. Instead of relying upon simple didactic repetition of letter and number combinations, the teachers have dared to venture into the fields of psychology and sociology—to bring such processes as controlled motivation and sociometrics to their work. These things are not easily understood and are much less easily explained. Since the changes embodying these more recondite principles have been continuous and relatively rapid, each succeeding generation of parents has had to accommodate itself to new concepts of educational practice—in sum, to learn all over again what education was doing.

This apparent departure from the fundamentals invariably incurs the suspicion of learning which appears to be generic to all cultures. The widespread ambivalence toward knowledge is solidly rooted in primitive experience. Knowledge is everywhere revered because it tends to explain the otherwise inexplicable, thereby giving man increased control over an essentially hostile environment, and contrarily, knowledge is everywhere feared because it deals with the unknown, and is in part an unknown itself. The unknown, in Nature, is coincident with danger. Since some knowledge, by definition,

---

[10] Ernest O. Melby, "Challenge to the Critics of the Schools," *The New York Times Magazine*, September 23, 1951, quoted in *Platform, op. cit.*

is beyond the capacity of all but the ablest members of any group, the "higher learning" of that group, and the people who deal with it, must always remain in the shadow of suspicion. Present-day educators, and progressive educators in particular, by venturing into the never-never land of the interacting variables of social science, force themselves to accept the condition that all such advances beyond those completely within the grasp of the least able members of their societies will invite criticism and hostility.

The second point of the attack — that a lack of discipline prevails in the public schools, is partly valid. The most casual observation would indicate that discipline is in short supply in most of our public schools. Casual observation, however, might well be supplemented by two important considerations. The first is that complete discipline of the kind which produces "pin-drop" silence and instant obedience is not desirable either from the point of view of its implications in regard to personality or politics. The "authoritarian personality" exists in American life, as has been demonstrated,[11] but thanks in part to the intelligent permissiveness of the schools, this type of personality is by no means in the majority. Further, critics of the schools err when they

fail to take account of the fact that a relative absence of discipline is a characteristic of the American culture pattern. America was, as Commager notes, "born of revolt, flourished on dissent." [12] Therefore it is not surprising that something less than a complete regard for authority has found its way into the schools. Authority resting on its own weight is not consonant with that part of the democratic ideology which requires a free appraisal of values; we cannot expect the public schools to define, in the short time in which they work with the average American, that point where freedom ends and license begins — particularly when this definition is not made in many homes, nor indeed, in the lives of some adults. When the parents have, for the last generation, so freely misinterpreted the psychologists' moderate strictures against frustration of the child that they abandon even nominal training restraints, they are asking the impossible in their demand that the schools re-structure overnight their children's behavior to fit the requirements of adult life. Discipline, like charity, begins at home. Undoubtedly, we are going through a period in our development which will have the effect of assaying the utility, and indeed the meaning of discipline. Many Americans feel that discipline, like

[11] T. W. Adorno, E. Frenkel-Brunswik, D. J. Levinson, and R. N. Sanford, *The Authoritarian Personality* (New York: Harper & Brothers, 1950).

[12] Henry Steele Commager, "Who is Loyal to America?" *Harper's Magazine,* Vol. 195 (July, 1947). Quoted in Robert C. Sorensen, "Assassins at Large," *The Christian Register,* August, 1951.

truth, is a fixed ideal which should be maintained. More accurately, it is a mechanism for controlling behavior, and its best use is legitimately judged on a pragmatic basis. Suffice it to say that if the children of today are learning more and attending school longer, as is demonstrably the case, the problem of discipline is perhaps not paramount.

The third charge, that moral and religious values are neglected, would be difficult to refute even if the schools taught nothing *but* moral and religious values. The reason for this is that these values are ideologies, and ideologies resist change with implacable tenacity. All people tend to look backward for their definitions of the good, the true, and the beautiful, and anything taught today which is not the same as it was yesterday is bound to conflict with our relatively static values.

The slowness of change in the value structure is quite possibly a long-run "good" for a society which generates technological alteration as fast as does our own. Too-rapid change on all fronts would challenge the stability of the society—a statement for which microcosmic evidence is available in the resistance of

the individual to a shift in values, or to the teaching of anything which seems to neglect the world of right and wrong as he understands it. The individual's resistance is rooted in his memory of primary-group values and necessary youthful idealism; his judgments of the world are made essentially in terms of the ideals laid down for him in his youth. Hence, any group which not only perceives change but interprets its meaning, as does the teaching group, is bound to encounter resistance. Since teachers are "paid agents of cultural diffusion . . . hired to carry light into dark places," they are also, as Waller has so aptly stated, "martyrs to cultural diffusion." [13]

If the people accept the fact that education is "a value-conditioned activity . . . never morally neutral," [14] they will have to make up their minds as to whether they will go along with Buckley in his belief that the teacher has been hired to teach according to certain specified policies, [15] or whether they will support the aims of education stated by the Harvard Committee: "To think effectively, to communicate thought, to make relevant judgments, *to discriminate among values.*" [16]

[13] Willard Waller, *The Sociology of Teaching* (New York: John Wiley and Sons, Inc., 1932), p. 40.

[14] John L. Childs, *Education and Morals* (New York: Appleton-Century-Crofts, Inc., 1950), p. 16.

[15] William F. Buckley, Jr., *God and Man at Yale* (Chicago: Henry Regnery Company, 1951), as prepared and paraphrased in *Platform, op. cit.*

[16] The Harvard Committee, *General Education in a Free Society* (Cambridge, Mass.: Harvard University Press, 1946), p. 65 (italics added).

The fourth criticism, which holds that the schools are seedbeds of un-Americanism, is perhaps the one which is currently most threatening to the average teacher. With committees from both houses of Congress planning investigations of the colleges, and with organizations such as the National Council for American Education and the Friends of the Public Schools of America castigating the schools, the educator is reminded of the hysterical days of the Alien and Sedition Acts, when "there was hardly a word to allay the alarm, a warning against too hasty action, or a plea that civil liberties be preserved, from the Federalist spokesmen in Congress. Instead, the party elders seem to have acted upon the assumption that their duty was to whip up the frenzy by screaming 'Jacobins, Hell, and all the Devils' at every street corner." [17] When Representative Velde (R., Ill.) makes statements to the effect that teachers in perhaps twenty-five major colleges and universities have been "identified as subversives," [18] and when Senator McCarthy (R., Wis.) says he expects "all hell" to break loose upon the occasion of his "going into the educational system," [19] it should not be surprising that educators "were wary and felt varying degrees of inhibition about speaking out on controversial issues, discussing unpopular concepts, and participating in student political activity." [20]

The degree to which communism is an active force in the public schools should be considered, if only for the record. Some Communists have been discovered among teachers as among people of other callings. But in terms of the relative number of teachers who follow the communist line, the general charge of treasonable adherence would be laughable, if it were not potentially so tragic in its effect upon individuals. The simple truth is that no group has yet been found which is less likely than the teachers to espouse communism, or more successful than the teachers in imparting democratic values. Melby has stated that "sociological studies have shown American schoolteachers more conservative than the total population." [21] Significantly enough, after one of the most vigorous attacks leveled at a school system in recent history, a committee of Pasadena citizens found that "no textbook used in the schools contained so much as a line that could be considered subversive." [22]

The reasons behind the attacks on

---

[17] John C. Miller, *Crisis in Freedom* (Boston: Little, Brown and Company, 1951), p. 22.

[18] U. P. wire story, Washington, D. C., December 29, 1952.

[19] A. P. wire story, Washington, D. C., January 5, 1953.

[20] Kalman Seigel, "How Free?" *The New York Times,* May 10–11, 1951, quoted in *The Key Reporter,* Vol. XVI, No. 4, Autumn, 1951.

[21] Ernest O. Melby, "Challenge to the Critics of Schools," *op. cit.*

[22] Joseph A. Brandt, "This, Too, Happened in Pasadena," *Harper's Magazine,* Vol. 205, No. 1230, November, 1952.

schools partake chiefly of the schools' normal function of transmitting the cultural heritage. The educators' chances of doing the "right thing" in the judgment both of those who wish the cultural heritage, particularly its values, preserved intact, and of those who want the schools to prepare the student for a changing world, are clearly nonexistent; the aims of these groups are mutually exclusive. If there is any charge which may be successfully brought against the educators, as persons, which might help to explain their current susceptibility to attack, it is that even as a group they seem to generate something of a power vacuum. For reasons which will be discussed, the educators are singularly unable, or unwilling except on the university level, to resist the attacks of the irresponsibles who cry "Havoc!" and let slip the dogs of calumny. Justices Douglas and Black have wisely noted of freedom of thought and expression that "none needs it more than the teacher"; [23] they might have added that few are less able to protect themselves against the loss of it.

More immediately, the present wave of charges that the schools are questionably orthodox is directly related to the current hysteria over the threat of communism. This exacerbated fear is difficult to combat because it is based in reality; communism is a genuine threat, and the Communists themselves linger on the brink of a global fire fight with the free world which civilization cannot afford. However, the *social* dangers inherent in this situation stem as much from ourselves as from our enemies. Traditionally, civil liberties suffer in a time of reaction, and Americans are reacting not only against communism, but from the effects of twenty years of change as profound as has occurred in any period in our history. It is clear that social change is cyclical in at least some of its aspects, and that the trend of the present is toward extreme conservatism.

The fifth charge against the schools—that they are too expensive—requires no insight, sociological or otherwise, to understand. The schools are expensive. In the typical American community, they constitute the largest single item in the municipal budget. The question revolves entirely around the word "too" in the criticism. What is "too" expensive? The question is one which must be decided in the light of the conflicting values which are discussed in reference to all the other criticisms.

The sixth point, that education offers poor preparation for making a living in the world of today, could, like most of the criticisms, be leveled at education no matter what was taught over and above the three R's and the trades. The paramount dilemma for the critics is their difficulty in deciding what is related to making

[23] Adler v. Board of Education, Justices Douglas and Black dissenting. Quoted in *New Republic,* Vol. 126, No. 11, March 17, 1952.

a living, and the paramount truth which educators have to explain to them is the fact that making a living is both the easiest and the last thing which needs to be taught any student. The high degree of technological specialization in our society renders superfluous a long period of specialized training in advance of the job; what employers seek are those very qualities for which only a generalized training is effective—awareness, adaptability, and maturity. Yet the schools are forced, in response to the demand for "useful" training, to play down the generalized social studies in favor of what the public deems practical courses. As Barzun says, "one of the great obstacles to a decent organization of the intellectual life is that it is at the mercy of the majority's snap judgment." [24]

Whatever the wish of the taxpayers, the schools are never going to be entirely "practical" in the popular sense because they are undertaking the task of preparing a collection of divergent personalities for divergent life roles by means of a standardized set of techniques. The knowledge that they purvey is doomed to generalities, and the activity that results from learning is thus harder to connect to the initial learning, subjecting the latter to a certain amount of devaluation—

hence Znaniecki's observation that "the knowledge that is needed as a condition of success in practical activity is always less highly esteemed socially than the success to which it is subservient." [25]

More important, however, is the widening gap between the increasing amount of complex knowledge totally available in the modern world, and the potentiality of the average individual for absorbing it, or of the schools for teaching a major portion of it. The only recourse for the school, in the face of the vast body of information accessible to it, is abstraction and again abstraction, until what is taught has little apparent relation to reality, however certainly it may stem from reality. Grambs has commented on this process, to the effect that "the complexities of today's world have tended to make in-school learning ever more remote from reality, since reality itself is too huge, too confusing, too unmanageable." As a consequence, she says, "the learner develops a general tolerance of the school, but a mistrust of education since it is so remote from his daily problems and immediate interests." [26]

Little or no argument can be offered to the seventh criticism—that the schools are pre-empting the func-

---

[24] Jacques Barzun, *Teacher in America* (Boston: Little, Brown and Company, 1946), p. 300.

[25] Florian Znaniecki, *The Social Role of the Man of Knowledge* (New York: Columbia University Press, 1940), p. 91.

[26] Jean D. Grambs, "The Sociology of the 'Born Teacher,'" *The Journal of Educational Sociology,* Vol. 25, No. 9. May, 1952.

tions of the home. Most sociologists agree that the schools, along with other institutionalized agencies of society, are removing from the family not only the educational, but also the economic, religious, recreational, protective, and status functions. Whether or not the parent sees this process objectively, or verbalizes it *in toto,* he is certainly aware that it is happening. The fact of which he is perhaps unaware is that the shift in the functions of the family constitutes, like minimal discipline, a pattern characteristic of American culture.

Because the teachers deal with those individuals most important to parents—their children—their dominating, judging role in the children's lives is the subject of close attention on the part of parents. If the parents feel that the increasingly important teachers are in any respect competitors for their children's affections, or that their own performance as parents is in any sense inadequate, they will, as Grambs says, feel "exposed" in their relations with the teacher, "with consequent belittling, belligerence, or retreat into inferiority." [27] Rugh believes that the work of the teachers, paralleling and sometimes exceeding the effectiveness of the home in socializing the young, may account for the current position of education as a kind of scapegoat. He holds that "well-intentioned Ameri-

cans are conscious of the fact that American democratic ideals are not being realized in our social, economic, and political life," and that this frustration results in a tension which leads to aggression against education, "one of the most docile and undefended institutions." Such aggression, he contends, projects upon the scapegoat education the blame for a situation for which the people feel an inner guilt, whereby the guilt is relieved. There is, as he says, "little if any danger of retaliation or reprisal." [28]

The causes underlying the last criticism—that control of education has passed out of the hands of the people—do not seem to lie, as might first appear, entirely in the wish of the people for control of an important social institution. The people evidently like to feel that they have ultimate authority over such professionals as lawyers and doctors, business managers and civil servants, but they do not everywhere form associations designed to tell these groups how to do their work. The crux of the matter appears to relate partly to the peculiarly public and universal nature of teaching—educational experience is something which no one escapes—and partly to the basic personality type which is associated with teaching either in actuality or in the common belief. As

[27] Grambs, *op. cit.*
[28] Douglas Rugh, "The Scapegoat Value of American Public Education," *School and Society,* Vol. 74, No. 1908, July 14, 1951.

with all occupations, teaching appears to select or to mold personalities with certain identifiable characteristics. If there is not a unity among the people who are educators, there is at least a concentration of attributes which serves to distinguish them from persons who follow other occupations.

The Cooks,[29] Warner, Havighurst, and Loeb,[30] and others have shown that the teaching group is largely feminine, of native white stock, predominantly Protestant in religion, unmarried, conservative in social attitudes, and from middle class to upper lower class families. The process of stereotyping has served to fix these and other characteristics in the public mind, reifying them to the exclusion of sharper perception in individual cases. It should be recognized that this synthesis of characteristics is not one which attracts power, wields influence, secures worldly goods, or even inspires confidence. Thus it is the unhappy truth that the group characteristics of teachers tend to mitigate against their chances for improving their lot, or even of holding their own in times of attack. When pressure mounts in a community, teachers may expect partially to lose control of their vital institution un-less they take determined and intelligent steps to avoid this. If they recognize their competitive limitations, and are aware of the ultimate potential of their numbers in a society which recognizes both the weight of the majority and the rights of minorities, they are better prepared for effective action.

Finally, then, let us consider briefly what may be done to withstand the current attacks on education. The fortunate truth, which Alberty's monograph and the cited issue of *Progressive Education* have made clear, is that the vast majority of the people are favorably oriented toward the teachers and the educational institution. In some communities, they are even willing to pay more in support of education, as Brandt has demonstrated of Pasadena.[31] The teachers can be sure, then, that they begin any action to improve their lot with the strong support of the public.

The present would seem to be the time to take that action. Instead of relapsing into the "frustration and cynicism" of which Canon Bell has accused them,[32] teachers should understand that "these are days when those who believe in tolerance and rational discussion of public matters must realize the consequences of pas-

[29] Lloyd Allen Cook and Elaine Forsyth Cook, *A Sociological Approach to Education* (New York: McGraw-Hill Book Company, Inc., 1950).

[30] Lloyd Warner, Robert J. Havighurst, and Martin B. Loeb, *Who Shall be Educated?* (New York: Harper & Brothers, 1944).

[31] Brandt, *op. cit.*

[32] Bernard Iddings Bell, "The Fault Is Not the Teacher's," *The New York Times Magazine,* November 18, 1951.

sivity and inaction on their part." [33] Educators have been content merely to defend themselves long enough; they have made a practice of turning the other cheek until they are in a veritable whirl of submission. Although the policy of *ahimsa* or passive resistance has been finally successful for the people of India in their centuries of relationships with the British, and although most Americans might be willing to accept the dictum that the meek shall inherit the earth, it may seriously be doubted that the teachers now practicing their profession are entirely willing to await the millennial deliverance of this legacy. None would advocate aggression, because aggression on a worldwide scale and its direct corollary, fear, are to a considerable degree accountable for the present state of siege in which the teachers now operate—but neither should any advocate merely standing firm and weathering the storm. Other storms will come, as they have in the past, and the net result will be that the group will be only the more weather-beaten.

Rather should the teachers undertake positive action on community, state, and national levels. Organizations are already in existence to put their efforts to good use. Citizen groups may be formed; these have, as demonstrated in Englewood [34] and Scarsdale,[35] successfully stood off the purveyors of intimidation and reaction. The vast numbers of teachers and the essential esteem in which they are held can serve, if the group is united and above all determined, to make ever more effective the high purpose to which it is dedicated.

COMPARATIVE EDUCATION

In "the Great Debate on education" many critics compare European and American schools, with the latter suffering by comparison. James B. Conant, president emeritus of Harvard University and former ambassador to the Federal Republic of West Germany, has made some pertinent observations on the relative merits of European and American education after spending four years in Europe and after recently visiting fifty high schools in seventeen states, where he interviewed principals, superintendents, thousands of teachers, and hundreds of students. A summary of his observations appears in the following reprint from *Better Schools*.

[33] James B. Conant, "The Superintendent Was the Target" (a review of David Hulburd's *This Happened in Pasadena*), *The New York Times Book Review Section*, April 29, 1951.

[34] Fine, *op. cit.*

[35] Robert Shaplen, "Scarsdale's Battle of the Books," *Commentary*, Vol. 10, No. 6, December, 1950.

American Schools Reflect Our Culture

by JAMES B. CONANT

Reprinted from *Better Schools,* May, 1958, page 8, published by the National Citizens Council for Better Schools.

In attempting to explain American education to Europeans, I often sum it up by saying that our schools must be regarded to a large degree as instruments by which we seek to come nearer to the goals of our society, equality of opportunity for all children, and equality of respect for all forms of honest labor.

Under the influence of these ideals, through the expansion of our state-supported universities and the persistence of our four-year colleges, we have in the United States in the last fifty years greatly increased the percentage of our youth who are attending college and, as a consequence, enormously increased the full-time enrollment in our high schools. With us, 75 per cent of the 16-year-olds are going to school. In no European land is the figure more than 10 or 15 per cent. And right at this point I might mention a matter of terminology which illuminates the difference between the European and American concepts more than table upon table of accurate statistics.

In a large book devoted to European schooling, the percentage of each age group who are attending school is shown graphically, but no distinction is made between those who attend school four hours a week supplementary to their apprentice work in factories, and those who go five days a week for many hours in order to prepare themselves for entrance to a university.

There is no German word for full-time education; the best that can be done is a literal translation of the English phrase. More than one European would probably say, "Essentially all our youth attend school until they are 17 or 18 years old. But for the vast majority, 90 per cent or so, who are going to be farmers or workers in various forms of industry, or even shopkeepers on a small scale, a few hours of schooling a week is ample."

* * *

This selection of one group, 10 per cent of those in the elementary schools who are separated from the others and are sent to what are essentially university preparatory schools, is a characteristic of European education.

What is often not recognized in comments on European education is the fact that only this group of 10 per cent or so receives the kind of education which is essential for those who are to be professionally competent in this modern world.

For the European youth who

starts at age 10 or 11 in his long journey towards the university, and of whom about half will become in fact university students, the instruction is far more rigorous, the work far harder than we can imagine here in the United States.

But let us look at the other side of the picture; of the other 90 per cent—few if any will have studied any foreign language, few if any will have studied mathematics beyond the simple algebra, few if any will have been exposed to the type of studies which we consider so important for the development of an understanding of our government and the rights and duties of a citizen in a democracy.

Now let me make it plain that, in making this comparison between the European scheme of education and our own, I am not for a moment suggesting that the European nations should accept our pattern. And I am certainly not advising that we should revert 75 years to the European tradition. I use the word "revert" advisedly, for I think it fair to say that, in the closing quarter of the nineteenth century, our college preparatory schools, whether they were supported by public money or private means, were very similar to the university preparatory schools in Europe.

Let me further make it plain that I am not advocating a return to the type of high school curriculum which was appropriate fifty years ago when less than a third of our youth attended a high school and when less than

5 per cent entered a college or university. I believe that we must continue to hold fast to the ideal of providing an education full-time for all American youth. Furthermore, that our education in the schools should be connected to a system of colleges and universities by which as much as a third of the youth enter these colleges and universities; that there continue to be such a variety of subjects offered that there is the room for development, through full-time education up to the age of twenty or twenty-one, of a great variety of talents and interests; and, above all, that we keep the present flexible arrangement by which a boy or girl can postpone the decision as to whether or not he or she goes on to education beyond the high school until the closing years of his or her high school course.

"But does this mean," some may ask, "that we cannot hope to educate a considerable number of our youth so that they, like their European contemporaries, have mastery of a foreign language, a greater mastery of mathematics than at present, a more detailed and greater grasp of factual material than provided by most of our public or private schools?" My answer would be, "No. I am by no means a defeatist. We can greatly improve our education in our schools along lines similar to those considered conventional by Europeans, *provided* we do this primarily on a selective basis."

The point I wish to make is that

I believe it is possible for our schools to do far more for children with special gifts and talents than at present, without jeopardizing our basic educational philosophy. To me it is unthinkable that we should give up the common American practice of having in one school boys and girls with different talents and different interests. I am convinced the comprehensive high school is an excellent American invention.

* * *

To my mind, the way out of this educational quandary lies in identifying scholastic talent young and then providing for teachers who will stimulate the selected students to do their utmost because they want to and as a matter of pride. The substitute for the European pressures from the family and from the accepted mode of a European society must be found in America by the early discovery of talent and its stimulation.

The difficulty with the study of mathematics in our schools, for example, is in no small part due to our failure to identify at a relatively young age those pupils who have more than the average talent for mathematics. If such pupils were identified and then were stimulated to proceed rapidly with their studies, a respectable fraction of the incoming freshmen of our better colleges would have sufficient mathematical aptitude to tackle the first-year physics and chemistry courses with both enthusiasm and success.

I have spoken of appealing to the pride of selected students. To some degree this can be stimulated by the spirit of competition which is not something to be deplored if kept in bounds by a spirit of fair play; it is a healthy aspect of our American emphasis on sports.

In short, identification of talent, motivation through aroused interest and competition should enable our schools to utilize much more than now the rich sources of talent in each generation.

Let me make it plain that what I have just suggested can be accomplished, I believe, by modifications in our educational practices so slight that they will not jeopardize the essence of the American tradition. We need not retreat one step from our goal of providing education for all American youth.

Equality of opportunity for all children and equality of respect among all occupational groups are two doctrines that are as significant for our future as for our past. These are the fundamental premises of American education. Every citizen needs to understand them; every citizen needs to realize how they differ from the premises in other lands.

He will then see how our American educational philosophy differs from the European and reflects the special nature of our own free society. He will be then more ready to support in every possible way the further development and improvement of our American schools. If one understands why and how these schools differ from those of other free societies, one will be more ready to support them and make the sacri-fices that are required to improve them, even at a time when they face the staggering problems presented by the drastic upswing in the size of our population.

The May, 1958, issue of *Better Schools* includes a report on Hol-linshead's conclusions, which indicate that Europeans are not entirely satisfied with their schools.

American Education System Needn't Kowtow to Europe
from BETTER SCHOOLS

Reprinted from *Better Schools,* May, 1958, page 8, published by the National Citizens Council for Better Schools.

Europeans don't think their education is better than ours, and we're mistaken if we think so, says a noted American scholar and educator who returned to the U.S. last fall after serving five years in Paris as director of the Technical Assistance Department of UNESCO.

Byron S. Hollinshead, author of an eight-page reply to critics of American education, reports that European countries feel "intense dissatisfaction" with their educational systems and look with envy on the United States. He said that while in Europe he was asked:

"You Americans, you are always several steps ahead of us. How do you do it?"

Europeans are impressed by American techniques and equipment in science, the stability of our government, the chance for the individual to get ahead, and the large number we educate. "American textbooks are the envy of the world" because publishers can afford to produce for the many a quality book that they could not afford to produce for a few.

Dr. Hollinshead said that it was a shock to him upon his return home to be confronted with such questions as:

"Is European secondary education superior to American? Is it true that European science is better than ours? How is it that Europeans do better in foreign languages than we do?"

* * *

Dr. Hollinshead has some of his own questions to ask:

Does anyone seriously contend that the almost amazing lack of development of the social sciences in European schools and universities, except the Scandinavian, is a good thing?

Do we want life in America to be as static as that in Europe?

Dr. Hollinshead points out that the scope of the European education systems is hardly comparable to that in America, since based on percentages of young people in high school at the end of the sixteenth year, 70 per cent of the American age group is in school compared with only 10 per cent of the age group in England and France. At college age, he reports, about 25 per cent of the American age group is attending, compared with 5 per cent of the European group. "In other words, in the United States some seven times as many of the age group attend high school and at least five times as many attend college as in Europe."

For the reader who is interested in further analysis of the "debate" over comparative education, the following two articles are recommended: Admiral H. G. Rickover, "A Comparison: European vs. American Secondary Schools" (pages 60–64) and William W. Brickman, "Rickover as Comparative Educator" (pages 64–67), both in the November, 1958, *Phi Delta Kappan*.

A thoughtful report on the history and present state of both U.S. and Soviet schools is contained in Fred M. Hechinger's book, *The Big Red Schoolhouse* (New York: Doubleday and Company, Inc., 1959). According to *Better Schools* (February, 1959, page 4), this book "should lay the ghost of comparing incomparable systems of education once and for all." Another recent publication, *The American High School Today*, by James B. Conant (New York: McGraw-Hill Book Company, Inc., 1959) is rapidly becoming the most widely read educational book in America. It summarizes the findings which resulted from Conant's two-year study of the American high school (briefly described on page 63 of this book). In answer to the critics of American secondary education, Conant not only reaffirms his belief in the comprehensive type of high school (an American innovation) but also points out that educational problems vary from state to state and from community to community within a state and that, aside from the need to reorganize and combine small high schools, no drastic revision of "the basic pattern of American education is necessary."

3

FORCES AFFECTING OUR
CURRICULUM

Any analysis of forces affecting the curriculum should take into account, at the outset, the traditions which have developed in the evolution of education. The 1958 *Yearbook of Education* editors stress the point that "tradition, the accumulated experience of teaching, is after all, the basis of curriculum. . . . Most unconscious answers to a request to define the forces that have shaped the curriculum boil down simply to a statement that 'that is the way it has always been done'. . . . At present, all over the world the schools are faced with the necessity of adjusting their programmes to the drastic change around them. Yet all over the world, nations not only cling to outmoded educational programmes but also rationalize eagerly the justifications for so doing." [19:25] The influence of tradition on educational institutions and their programs is further emphasized by Smith, Stanley, and Shores in these words: "The relations between school and society are important in a period of relatively little change. In a time of profound social change, the relationship is even more important because society then is not all of one piece. Old and new social elements are to be found side by side— and frequently in competition with one another for survival. In such a period the school tends to reflect the older elements of society." [15:1–2]

In the last analysis, not great movements but many forces are shaping the curriculum of our public schools. Some of these forces can be identified as groups or agencies; others are not so clearly defined. An understanding of the complexity of pressures upon modern education can be gained from the article which follows.

Forces Affecting the Curriculum
by ROY E. LARSEN and HENRY TOY, JR.

From the *NEA Journal,* December, 1955, pages 562–563. Reprinted by special permission of the National Education Association, the National Council for Social Studies, and the authors. Roy E. Larsen is president of Time, Inc.; Henry Toy, Jr. is president of the National Citizens Council for Better Schools.

The curriculum is the nerve system of the school. It is influenced, in one way or another, by almost everything that affects the school. It is also, because of its importance, the aspect of the schools that receives most attention from those forces which seek to change or modify the schools.

Forces affecting the curriculum are almost infinitely varied. We usually think of "pressure" or "pressure groups" as largely bad, if not evil. This is an oversimplification. Most pressures may be constructive or destructive, depending on how they are applied.

There are, to be sure, pressures that are almost wholly destructive. Self-seeking politicians and other groups may try to use the schools for personal profit. A few people may be solely interested in the tax rate and never realize the stake they have, as Americans, in good education for all children. And an occasional individual may seek personal publicity from the schools. But these are not the pressures that exert real and lasting influence.

The typical forces that have made our schools what they are today, and even now are shaping the schools of the future, truly seek the improvement of the schools. They do so from many points of view and in behalf of ideals that are often conflicting and contradictory. But they have a common commitment to the ideal of public education.

It is impossible to list all of the forces that help to shape our schools and the curriculum. Some of the more important ones will have to serve as representatives of the many others that range from the subtlety of a public attitude toward athletics to the obviousness of an overcrowded classroom.

State Agencies

Education is, constitutionally, a state function. Much of the responsibility for schools is delegated to local communities through the formation of school districts and provisions for their administration by locally selected school boards. A considerable measure of authority is, however, retained by the individual states, and they probably play a more important role in shaping the curriculum today than ever before.

The Federal Government

The U.S. Office of Education was established to collect facts and statistics on education and to disseminate information concerning the schools. Over the years, however, a number of administrative and leadership functions have devolved upon the Office which have made it a vital force in the area of curriculum. The Smith-Hughes and later vocational-education acts give the Office of Education considerable administrative authority over vocational programs at both the state and community level.

The publications of the Office of Education have exercised a potent influence over the thinking and action in our classrooms. And the agency's leadership in sponsoring curriculum research and experimentation (as in the case of life adjustment education) is widely known.

The Profession

Professional school men, from the time of Horace Mann and Henry Barnard to the present, have been one of the powerful influences in shaping the curriculum. The individual classroom teacher is doubtless the most important single influence on the school program. His ability, training, and attitude largely determine what is taught, and, even more important, what is learned.

Professional educational associations are a closely related and, also, powerful influence. Today there are over 500 national and regional organ-izations, more than 100 state bodies, and thousands of local units. Not all of these, of course, work directly on curriculum problems, but all are concerned with the manner in which educational goals are translated into classroom practice.

The National Education Association and the various state education associations, for instance, have a general interest in all aspects of school affairs. The Association for Supervision and Curriculum Development, NEA, promotes curriculum research and knowledge specifically. The National Council for the Social Studies, NEA, typifies professional concern for a special area of interest. All of these educational organizations exert a major influence, directly or indirectly, on the schools and their problems.

Accrediting Agencies

Accrediting associations are an important factor in secondary-school curriculum. The six regional associations set up minimum standards for curriculum, physical-plant facilities, and teaching qualifications. Local high schools find it advantageous to meet these standards, since they signify a measure of educational achievement which carries prestige both within and outside the community.

Special-Interest Groups

Many special-interest groups give considerable attention to what they think the schools should teach. Very often such groups fasten on a single objective that seems important to them and insist that it be given precedence over other goals. Some such organizations have national programs that they push through their local chapters; others are purely local in character.

In addition, individuals in any community may band together, without formal organization, to promote special interests that they agree are important. Out of this multiplicity of interests and objectives emerge many forces which influence the curriculum.

Business and Labor

Both business and labor contribute to the flood of free materials available to teachers today. These materials sometimes tell the story of an industry and its importance to the nation's economy, something of the history of labor and the crucial role it plays, or present the publisher's views on economic problems and the American way of life. Pressure is also brought to bear on textbook publishers to present the views of industry and labor accurately and fairly.

Patriotic Groups

Numerous organizations devoted to perpetuating our national ideals are eager to establish through the schools the ideas and ideals which they advocate. They work for the inclusion of citizenship courses and promote the study of American

history and national heroes. In some cases they oppose the inclusion of certain controversial issues in the curriculum and have also opposed individuals and instructional materials which they believed tended to disparage America.

Racial and Religious Groups

Racial and religious groups frequently express themselves on what they think the schools should or should not teach. Immigration has brought to America millions of non-English-speaking people who have special needs and interests which they seek to have the public schools fulfill. Other groups seek public funds for the direct or indirect support of parochial schools. And still others, because of religious convictions, insist that science teaching in the school conform to their point of view.

The Community

A study of the forces affecting the school curriculum almost inevitably becomes a study of the American community. All local schools are affected by many of these pressures, and few communities, on close inspection, would fail to muster at least a representative collection of such individuals and organizations. Any attempt to describe these forces separately, then, does violence to them because they do not function in isolation. They are each a part of the complex pattern of conflicting interests and pressures that make up the life of an American community.

At the same time, the community exerts certain characteristic influences of its own. For instance, the school board is one of the most important factors in determining the nature of a community's schools.

The community usually decides, and any community is likely to get just as good a school board as it deserves. The public's knowledge of school affairs and interest in them is the major determining factor. Communities also vary widely in their ability to support good schools.

The nature of the community and its location will also influence the curriculum for good or ill. A rural school is likely to place considerable emphasis on training for agriculture; a suburban school is likely to send a higher share of its students to college; and the school in an industrial community may place more emphasis on vocational training for the skilled trades.

But the influences operating on the schools are not that simple. The majority of parents in the various communities probably also have differing concepts of what constitutes good schools, and their ideals are directly reflected in what their classrooms teach.

Harnessing Pressures for Curriculum Improvement

Like other democratic institutions in our society, the schools assume that many conflicting pressure groups tend to offset each other. Also, necessary, however, is the stabilizing role of the informed, responsible citizen who combines respect for the past with a sure vision of the future. On him, more than any other, falls the responsibility for successful operation of the democratic process. And it is this same citizen whose influence has been felt all too rarely in the field of education during the past half century.

Finally, there must be full co-operation between schoolmen and other citizens. The citizens need the schoolmen's expert knowledge of education and their broad social understanding. The schoolmen need the layman's detailed knowledge of the community and broad perspective on community-school affairs.

In combination, citizens and schoolmen can develop a school program geared specifically to the requirements of the community and its children. In combination they have already been doing it in many communities from coast to coast.

In June, 1957, the *Review of Educational Research* found that even such a thoughtful classification as the foregoing does not allow for the more impersonal impact of social and political forces on a wider canvas. Among these are processes of racial and intercultural relations and of technological and industrial change, the impact of ideological differences, and the cleavages due to clashes within the community power structure. The conclusion reached in summary is as follows:

Altogether, studies made during the period under review seem to indicate much preoccupation with educational ideologies but small concern over the uniqueness of the community and what that means for curriculum. The forces which seem to be pressing education into new directions are the great impersonal ones. They seem to indicate pressure to conformity. There is little sense of direction given by purposive efforts. Another facet of importance which seems to be indicated is that there is still great disagreement about the function of the secondary school in America. This debate will undoubtedly be accentuated as increased enrollments are more widely felt.*

The obligation of our public schools in general—that of fulfilling society's needs—has not changed. Cultural change and social demands have expanded enormously. Perennially these demands take expression in discontent with and criticism of the curriculum. The period of the fifties has seen the wave of such criticism reach tidal proportions.

It is heartening to note that the constructive forces affecting the curriculum appear to be gaining ground. First, there is recognition of the fact that most disagreements are more the result of misunderstanding than of genuine difference of opinion. [6:477–478]

Second, the Commission for the Defense of Democracy through Education has recently reached the following conclusion: "In general, the tide of attacks on the public schools seems to have ebbed in recent months. Destructive criticism is still causing problems in many communities and a few teachers feel an increased pressure against academic freedom. An encouraging note is that more teachers mention sources of encouragement than of discouragement." [12]

In the third place, there is evidence of more clear thinking and a willingness to face the challenge to free public education today.

More recently space satellites have changed the picture (see pages 404–406 of this book). A survey covering the period through the first six months of 1958 shows a renewed wave of criticism with a different focus. The shift appears to be from the public school curriculum *per se*

* American Educational Research Association, "Curriculum Planning and Development," *Review of Educational Research,* Vol. 27 (June, 1957), p. 266. Quoted by special permission of the Association and the author, Dan W. Dodson, Professor of Education, New York University, New York.

to certification requirements and programs of teacher education. For example, see James W. Popham and Suzanne W. Greenberg, "Teacher Education: A Decade of Criticism," in the *Phi Delta Kappan* for December, 1958 (pages 118–120).

THE PROFESSION LOOKS AT ITSELF

Educators themselves have become more aggressive in their resistance to outdated, unfounded criticism. They have likewise looked to themselves and their roles as leaders.

An Editorial　　　by LOGAN M. ANDERSON

From the *Phi Delta Kappan,* November, 1955, pages 57–58. Reprinted by special permission. The author was formerly editor of the magazine.

We present in pages 59 to 92 of this issue the results of nearly two years' research and interpretation by the Phi Delta Kappa Commission on Free Public Education. It is a highly constructive report to which our personal reactions are: first, that educators are too often failing to keep in touch with their publics in "public" education, are too often failing to perform necessary salesmanship functions; and second, that no good is served by ignoring this condition. The personal, personnel, factor is present and undeniable in almost every administrative situation whether handled successfully or not.

And however well the research specialist, the curriculum expert, the tax and financial wizard, and the professor of education may live and do their work behind the barricades of purely professional interests and contacts, it is fatal for those on the firing line to attempt to do so. The classroom teacher, the school principal, and the school superintendent cannot wall themselves in from their publics even if they so wish.

One of the hazards in professionalizing an occupation is the tendency it has to promote isolation on the part of its practitioners. As these become more and more professional in their attitudes and skills they tend to "withdraw," to be concerned mainly with their specialities, to congregate only with their peers, to think and to talk "shop" mostly, and to disregard more and more the public the occupation presumably serves. Such has actually occurred in most of the professions, notably medicine, for example, and with the development of a profession of education these past fifty years it has happened in our own profession as well.

Even the virtues of educators are

often their faults. Generally of high character, devoted and dedicated to their work, they often develop an excessively proprietary attitude, an over-identification with their jobs. So common is this tendency that it affects the public relations of education itself, from local school districts basic to educational organization to national associations.

Now, there are two kinds of identification. Reasonable identification of oneself with one's work is good, say the psychologists. It adds interest to work, it betters morale, and commercial employers die a thousand deaths trying to get it. But the other kind of identification, that of personalizing one's work in oneself, is bad, and leads to the development of several unfortunate habits.

The first of these is an extreme possessiveness. The wrong kind of identification develops a strong proprietary attitude. Among educators, particularly administrators, the word "public" is too often forgotten in the well-known phrase "public school." It becomes "my school, my faculty, my school board, my curriculum," and so on. How many evils (and ulcers) would be avoided if we could bring teachers and administrators to realize that the schools simply do not belong to them, but to "the public." Not even the patrons, the parents, have an exclusive, proprietary interest in the schools. The schools do not "belong" to any branch of government—local, state, or national—nor

to the school board, and least of all to the professional staff. They belong to that rather amorphous, general group we call "the public" but which the specialists in public relations subdivide into "the publics" including, don't forget, pupils and students, themselves. (Incidentally, this possessive tendency has been well caricatured by the principal in "Our Miss Brooks"—again proof of its frequent incidence.)

There is one big-city superintendent we know who boasts that he doesn't have ulcers and doesn't intend to get any. The schools aren't "his schools" but the schools of that city. There, the curriculum is being built by representatives of the lay public and likewise the budget—by 275 community leaders in the latter case. When the professional staff told these lay budgeteers, "We need six new school buildings, we could use seven; which do *you* want?" the answer came back, "We want seven, and we will pay for them." What a relief it must be to put the burden of this sort of decision where it belongs!

How difficult it is to draw the fine line between leadership, the responsibility for recognizing and for presenting problems, and the assumption of responsibility for making all the decisions therewith. Yet we maintain that anyone committing himself to a career in public education must make that distinction if he is to remain mentally as well as physically healthy. If one wants to develop and maintain a proprietary attitude, he should go into private education with a school really his own!

A second evil of the wrong kind of over-identification is that it tends to develop a strongly defensive attitude. The least criticism is taken as a personal insult, a personal disparagement. One of the most valid comments which Bestor (and others) makes of "educationists" concerns the latter's extreme sensitivity to adverse criticism. Men in other professions and disciplines publish tentative conclusions based on partial data, fully expecting them to be reviewed thoroughly and either confirmed or disproved by further experimentation. In fact, some of the exceptional progress made in the physical and biological sciences may be traced to this willingness to throw partial facts, tentative findings, into the crucible for further independent testing. In medicine, for instance, we have known physicians to publish theories and suggest methods of treatment based upon as few as five cases. The idea is horrifying to the statistically-inclined "educationist."

A third and even more important result of this sort of over-identification is the development of an extreme resistance to change. To puncture the defensive attitude may hurt the puncturee, the defendant, but it is often the only way to get or to keep the wheels of progress turning. One is inclined to love what he has done; to look upon his handiwork and

think it good. The defensive attitude loves the *status quo*. This attitude comes more or less naturally with age, we suppose; at least our retirement systems recognize it as a fact. What we are concerned with, however, is the hardening of the mental arteries in the relatively young, say before fifty, as so often happens and, pity 'tis to have to say it, Science Research Associates reports that *teachers are the slowest of all groups* to change, and they have studied many professions and many occupational groups.

Further, we are about convinced that this extreme possessiveness, which breeds fear of change, is largely responsible for the lack of progress in the science of education. The essence of science is experimentation, but why experiment if you are fearful of, or unwilling to make changes? Why make it unpleasant for yourself by discovering something which may challenge one of the most pleasant situations in life, namely, the assumption that you are "doing all right," the assumption of the absolute? The sequence is this: Over-identification spans the proprietary attitude, possessiveness; possessiveness breeds content; content fosters absolutism, and absolutism discourages experimentation, which is the progenitor of change.

It is not by accident that we have the feeling, after a thirty-year gap in our connection with public education, that here, *now,* is just about where we came in thirty-five years ago. We were debating formal discipline and transfer of learning then; we argue it now. We were learning about individual differences then; we make but scant provision for them even now.

Well, there you are, as George Gobel would say. The wrong kind of identification results in the proprietary attitude, brings on extreme possessiveness, automatically defensive attitudes, resistance to change, failure to adopt the principles, methods, and attitudes of experimental science, poor executive ability through inability to delegate responsibility and authority to subordinates, and a lack of interest in development of good public relations, because your excessively over-identified person has an extreme insensitivity to the matter of how others feel.

And if you think Science Research Associates' judgment upon educators is too severe, let us ask, "How many of you make budgetary provisions for change, even if it is only moving a partition?" Yet industry, with which we are somewhat familiar, recognizes that unless some changes are made almost for the sake of change, *people go dead* on their feet, to say nothing of their minds. We submit

that education is not so different that school management can afford to overlook the stimulating effects of deliberate change. As Earle Rugg quotes in this issue, "Change is a social fact." School programs and practices must change with the times, it is the educator's professional responsibility to determine their *nature*. Educators must also assume the educational leadership, and sales responsibilities for explaining them and of "selling" the "backward" element found in any population distribution or group.

That word "management" reminds us that one of the best antidotes to this over-personalized feeling, this over-identification, is the development of the concept of management. "Management" has an impersonal quality, and among those who often find it most difficult to grasp the concept are the *managers* themselves!

The self-centered over-identification too often found among educators needs to be superseded by dedicated impersonalization sensitive to all the influences and the nuances of public contact. When this occurs we shall have teachers and administrators both responsive to and skilled in their relationships with their employers—the public.

Leaders in every phase of American endeavor face the same enigmatic challenge. The educator today, more than ever, must fulfill his particular responsibility to the mandate of a people who, though it has never fully achieved its goals and is often uncertain as to what constitutes real progress toward them, has never seriously considered abandoning them.

Bibliography

1. AMERICAN EDUCATIONAL RESEARCH ASSOCIATION. "Curriculum Planning and Development." *Review of Educational Research,* XXVII, June, 1957.
2. ASSOCIATION FOR SUPERVISION AND CURRICULUM DEVELOPMENT. *Forces Affecting American Education.* 1953 Yearbook. Washington, D. C.: Association for Supervision and Curriculum Development, a department of the National Education Association, 1953.
3. ———. *One Hundred Years of Curriculum Improvement, 1857–1957.* Washington, D. C.: Association for Supervision and Curriculum Development, 1957.
4. BINGHAM, CALEB. *The Columbian Orator.* Boston: Manning and Loring, 1797.
5. BURTON, W. H. *Introduction to Education.* New York: Appleton-Century, 1934.
6. CARTWRIGHT, WILLIAM H. "What's the Shooting All About?" *NEA Journal,* 44:477–478, November, 1955.
7. COCKING, WALTER D. *Administrative Procedures in Curriculum Making for Public Schools.* Contributions to Education No. 329. New York: Bureau of Publications, Teachers College, Columbia University, 1928.
8. DEWEY, JOHN. *Experience and Education.* New York: The Macmillan Company, 1938.
9. ELAM, STANLEY. Editorial. *Phi Delta Kappan,* XXXVIII, January, 1957.
10. GOLDMAN, ERIC F. *Rendezvous with Destiny.* New York: Alfred A. Knopf, Inc., 1953.
11. GOOD, CARTER V. *Dictionary of Education.* New York: McGraw-Hill Book Company, Inc., 1945.
12. NATIONAL COMMISSION FOR THE DEFENSE OF DEMOCRACY THROUGH EDUCATION. "State of the Nation in Regard to Attacks on the Schools and Problems of Concern to Teachers." Washington, D. C.: the National Education Association, December, 1955.

13. Rugg, Harold. *American Life and the School Curriculum*. Boston: Ginn and Company, 1936.
14. Saylor, J. Galen, and William M. Alexander. *Curriculum Planning*. New York: Rinehart & Company, Inc., 1954.
15. Smith, B. Othanel, William O. Stanley, and J. Harlan Shores. *Fundamentals of Curriculum Development,* Revised Edition. Yonkers-on-Hudson, New York: World Book Company, 1957.
16. Spears, Harold. *The Teacher and Curriculum Planning*. New York: Prentice-Hall, Inc., 1951.
17. "What U. S. Thinks about Its Schools: a Roper Survey." *Life,* October 16, 1950, pages 11-12, 14, 16, 18.
18. Wish, Harvey. *Contemporary America: The National Scene Since 1900*. New York: Harper & Brothers, 1955.
19. *Yearbook of Education: The Secondary School Curriculum*. Prepared under the auspices of the University of London Institute of Education and Teachers College, Columbia University. Yonkers-on-Hudson: World Book Company, 1958.

PART TWO

The Curriculum: Its Operation

Introduction

Public schools are responsive to the society which creates and supports them, but a society upset by fear of sputniks and dizzy from the "big change" of the last fifty years fails to provide a clear blueprint for educational action. Furthermore, an educational system governed by forty-eight separate school authorities, each responsive to the will of its local communities, makes the difficulty of sharply defining the direction of American education become further evident.

The problem of securing agreement on educational purposes and functions is not new. The following remark attributed to Aristotle indicates that ancient educators also had difficulty in achieving unanimity: "All people do not agree in those things they would have a child learn . . . from the present mode of education we cannot determine with certainty to which men incline, whether to instruct a child in what will be useful to him in life, or what tends to virtue, or what is excellent; for all of these things have their separate defenders." [35:6]

Why is the age-old problem of securing agreement on educational objectives a recurring one? Any satisfactory answer is dependent upon time, place, and the kind of society under consideration. Reemphasizing what has just been said above, Goslin (17:518–519) states two reasons why it is difficult to decide on what should be taught in our schools: (*a*) We live and teach in the period of most rapid change in history, and (*b*) the people of our nation differ so widely on economic, social, political, material, and religious issues.

Barlow's conclusions listing the three situations affecting the present status of secondary education are also significant: (*a*) "First, *society does not agree concerning the desirable content or major emphasis in secondary education.*" (*b*) "*The community does not understand what is going on inside the school.*" (*c*) "*Instructors are not completely successful in translating educational theory into practice.*" [5:40–42]

Roads to agreement on educational objectives, especially at the secondary level, are further blocked by hasty generalizations about the success or failure of education, by a tendency to search for simple answers to complex problems, and by a paucity of research to validate the achievement of professed objectives. Concerning the complexity of the problem, Conant has this to say: "What is a 'good' high school education? A meaningless question to my mind unless you specify the pupil, his environment, his capabilities, and his ambitions." [35:14]

The need for more research relative to the achievement of objectives is substantiated by the following conclusion from the February, 1954, issue of the *Review of Educational Research:* "There is a dearth of studies at the secondary level which have as their major purpose *the determination of the degree of attainment of objectives.*" [4:40]

How are the public schools to escape from what appears to be an impasse with regard to objectives? Participating in a round-table forum on education conducted by the editorial staff of the *Ladies' Home Journal,* Woodring describes in these words a policy decision that must be made by *all* the people:

I think the current educational crisis grows out of our failure as citizens to decide just what we want the schools to accomplish. What are the aims of education? Should the schools be responsible for the child's intellectual development only or should they be responsible also for his social, moral, religious, vocational, physical, and emotional development as well as for his recreation? If the schools are to be responsible for everything, are all these things of equal importance; and if not, what is the order of priority—what comes first? Unless we decide what is more important and what is less important the schools are faced with an impossible task for there is not adequate time to do everything well.

This is a policy decision to be made by all the people—not by educators alone. The failure of the people to make the decision, and to communicate that decision to the educators, has brought about the present crisis.* [26:56]

* Reprinted by special permission of the *Ladies' Home Journal.* Copyright 1954 by the Curtis Publishing Company.

The final responsibility for curriculum development devolves upon the professional educator. He must be responsive to and interpret the needs and desires of both his immediate community and the country as a whole. From the preceding discussion, it is obvious that his task is not an easy one.

4

PURPOSES AND FUNCTIONS
OF PUBLIC EDUCATION

The difficulty of reaching consensus in setting up the purposes and functions of public education has just been noted. However, other problems present themselves in this area. For instance, many excellent statements of the objectives of education appear in the literature. Indeed, some are classics. But, unfortunately, they have been so often repeated that they have become trite and have lost their power to affect educational practice. Furthermore, any extensive survey of school policies and practices, especially at the secondary level, is almost sure to reveal a lack of serious effort on the part of many schools to define objectives at all. In addition to that, when attempts are made to evaluate the achievement of stated objectives, results are likely to be stated in quantitative terms only. With or without clearly-defined objectives, scope and depth of program vary so much from school to school that critics have only to pick out the weakest link for an easy target to discredit the entire system of public schools.

After reminding the reader that there are several agencies of education in our society and after tracing briefly the historical aims of education, Mayer furnishes a comprehensive discussion of the "broad goals of education."

The Aims of Education   by FREDERICK MAYER

From *Education*, Vol. 76, No. 10, June, 1956, pages 630–638. Reprinted by special permission of the Palmer Company and the author. Frederick

Mayer is a Professor of Philosophy at the University of Redlands, Redlands, California.

The Meaning of Education

The dilemma of the twentieth century is that we have more institutions than ever devoted to educational purposes, yet real interest in education has not kept pace with the technological changes of our time. Often the emphasis in education has been purely quantitative, instead of qualitative. The stress has frequently been upon buildings rather than teachers, upon equipment rather than motivation, upon training rather than genuine growth, upon vocationalism rather than the liberal arts, upon specific knowledge rather than general education.

Education has been defined in various ways. Plato thought that "a good education consists in giving to the body and to the soul all the beauty and all the perfection of which they are capable." Herbert Spencer believed that "education has for its object the formation of character." Horace Mann felt that "education alone can conduct us to that enjoyment which is, at once, best in quality and infinite in quantity." Thomas Henry Huxley thought that "education is the instruction of the intellect in the laws of nature, under which I include not merely things and their forces, but men and their ways, and the fashioning of the affections and of the will into an earnest and loving desire to move in harmony with these laws."

One of the most famous contemporary views of education is that of Dewey, who regards education as a reconstruction of experience which gives meaning to our existence and which aids us in the direction of subsequent experience.

The trouble with this definition is that experience covers a multitude of meanings; the term experience is almost as broad as the term life. Experience may be directed, as the experiments of Hitler and Mussolini indicate, through indoctrination and propaganda as well as through rational training. Education, I believe, demands a *qualitative* concept of experience. Thus I regard education as a process leading to the enlightenment of mankind.

This implies not merely intellectual growth as a criterion for education, but also emotional maturity and ethical awareness. This means that education is incomplete without the formation of critical habits. This definition also implies the need for a continuous reexamination of educational methods and objectives.

The objection may be made that this definition neglects the importance of vocational training. How can vocational efficiency add to the enlightenment of mankind? The answer is that human progress depends upon techniques as much as upon intellectual stimulation. Without vocational skills and technological efficiency, education tends to be an exercise in contemplation and abstraction. The purpose of education is not merely to contribute to the continuity of culture, but also to change peacefully and rationally the material foundations of civilization.[1]

The difference between education and indoctrination is that while indoctrination depends upon the closed mind and preconceived viewpoints, education is open-minded and accepts no absolutes. Indoctrination appeals mainly to our emotional biases, while education appeals primarily to our rational capacities. Indoctrination gives us only partial knowledge, while education seeks complete knowledge. Indoctrination is intensely subjective, whereas education tends to be an objective process.

Dogmatism is the keynote of indoctrination, while tolerance is the watchword of education. The conclusions of indoctrination lead to rigidity and compulsion; the conclusions of education are subject to scientific verification and thus are *tentative.*

Education, as Dewey often pointed out, is not the preparation for life but represents the continuous changes and processes of life. To identify education with book knowledge is a rather narrow view, for education often arises in the matrix of practical activity. Education implies not merely discipline of thinking, but also a passion for creativity.

The Agencies of Education

Almost everyone will recognize the importance of the family in the diffusion of education. For our primary attitudes are shaped in the home and much of our later success depends upon the cultural atmosphere and stimulation of the home.

The community likewise aids in the diffusion of knowledge. Certain communities, like Boston, have a tradition of education, while others, especially small agricultural communities, may regard education as a rather unessential activity. The resources of the large city, particularly its libraries, universities, and museums, aid in intellectual and esthetic growth, while small communities tend to lack this type of stimulation, and thus tend to be more narrow intellectually than many large cities.

National differences condition, to a large extent, the development of education. Thus Russia emphasizes totalitarianism in education, while the United States cherishes democratic ideals. South American countries frequently have at least indirect ecclesiastical control over education, while the United States system of education

[1] Cf. Dewey, *Democracy and Education* and *Experience and Education.*

is based upon the *separation of state and church*.

Religious factors, however, cannot be excluded from education. Noticeable in our time is the rapid growth of parochial education, sponsored especially by the Catholic Church. Denominational colleges have made a significant contribution to higher education in the United States. It must be remembered that religious organizations were responsible for the founding of the early colleges. Thus the Congregationalists established Harvard, the Anglicans gave impetus to the founding of King's College (Columbia), and the Presbyterians were active in the establishment of Princeton.

The economic system, as well as the church, influences the prevalent educational structure. Capitalism encourages private support of education as can be seen by the activities of such great foundations as the Rockefeller, Ford, and Carnegie foundations. Under a fascist economic system, on the other hand, the state controls all activities of education, and private support is extremely limited.

The type of work we do influences our outlook upon education. In Greece education was mainly a preparation for leisure; thus philosophy to the Athenians was the noblest subject. In recent times, on the other hand, the gospel of labor has conditioned our educational views, and education has been more vocational and less literary and philosophical.

The newspaper, as we all know, has had a significant impact upon education—perhaps less through the editorial page than through the comic section, which has become a universal medium of entertainment. Newspapers in the nation range from the staid and objective *New York Times* to the tabloids which specialize in sex, crime, and sensationalism.

The radio, like the press, not only is an agency of entertainment, but also transmits information and education. The radio has done much to popularize music; millions listen to the New York symphony orchestra. Furthermore, discussion groups give an opportunity to various political parties to voice their views. News commentators illuminate the trends of current events. Commentators may specialize in an objective view of the news, as does Edward R. Murrow, or they may appeal to sensationalism.

The library is another agency of culture and educational diffusion. It preserves the books and manuscripts of the past and is a storehouse for the valuable documents of the present. The free public library is one of the bastions of the democratic way of life; here rich and poor, young and old meet on the basis of equality—all engaged in the search for knowledge and truth.

It would be impossible to omit the contribution of the motion picture and television to education. Great motion pictures, like *All the King's Men, A Place in the Sun,* and *The Good Earth,* give a dramatic view of man's life and they present important moral implications. The motion picture is fundamental in shaping the mores of American youth; millions of American girls will imitate their favorite actress, while boys will often speak and act like Humphrey Bogart. Television promises to be an even greater force than the cinema in shaping popular education. It is possible in the future that a television set may become part of the regular classroom equipment, and that television will greatly aid the teaching process.

We all know the educational effects of travel. Through traveling we come into direct contact with foreign nations and through it we often overcome prejudice and bias, and develop a cosmopolitan and broad-minded philosophy of life. Formal education tends to be abstract and theoretical, while traveling gives us a sense of *immediacy and directness.*

We often learn more through play than in our regular classroom. We realize today that education fails if it does not prepare us for a creative use of leisure time.

The mores which exist in our city or nation may influence our outlook upon education. In the study of Middletown by the Lynds it was established that poetry and the arts were thought to be more suitable to women than to men. This explains why poetry has not become too pop-ular in this nation, for it is thought quite often that men should not be interested in the arts. Their function is to earn a living, not to think about impractical subjects. Confucius thought that no one is truly educated who does not appreciate poetry; this, however, is not the viewpoint of our utilitarian civilization which tends to view the poet as being impractical and much less important than the businessman.

We cannot omit the influence of war upon education. Usually war intensifies the mood of chauvinism and encourages the development of applied science, while inhibiting the advancement of the humanities. War thus contributes to the cultural lag, and adds to the discrepancy between the moral and scientific development of man.

Technology, like war, exerts an important influence upon education. Technology creates new inventions which improve the teaching process and which aid in the art of communication. Often technology becomes an idol of the educator who believes in mechanical solutions, instead of stressing the importance of inspired and inspiring teaching.

The conclusion is that education involves not merely the formal school environment, but also the informal agencies of communication. We learn through multiple sources; education thus is pluralistic rather than monistic. All this implies that the school cannot exist in an atmosphere of isolation, and that it must contribute to social change and social advancement.

The Historical Aims of Education

The goals of education have differed in various historical periods. In primitive society, education enforced the status quo and became the bastion of tradition. While primitive education was conservative, modern education tends to be progressive and looks to the future rather than to the past.

Hebrew civilization stressed the religious purpose of education. Through education a correct knowledge of God was to be achieved. Education not only taught the fundamentals of ethics, but was also concerned with history, dietary laws, and the meaning of the ritual. The rabbi was not only a spiritual leader, but also a teacher who would comment upon the meaning of religious laws and the nature and destiny of man.

In Athens the purpose of education was both rational enlightenment and preparation for citizenship. No infallible book was acknowledged; religion was subordinated to philosophy. Sparta, on the other hand, regarded militarism as the goal of education and specialized in the art of warfare rather than in the arts of peace.

In Rome education was more practical than in Athens. The obligations of citizenship were stressed, rather than the pursuit of speculative philosophy. The Roman ideal in education was to produce an individual who would sacrifice for his fatherland, who would be temperate and moderate in his habits, and who would never be discouraged by reverses.

In the Middle Ages the spiritual qualities of education were foremost. It was thought that this life was only a preparation for the beyond, and thus education aided in asceticism, in curbing natural appetites and passions, and in preparing for celestial bliss. The sciences in the Middle Ages were subordinated to theology, which was regarded as the queen of the sciences.

During the Renaissance a different ideal of education emerged. Now the natural capacities of man were glorified; education emphasized individualism rather than spiritual collectivism. The educated man of the Renaissance, Castiglione indicated, could speak several languages, he was versed in the art of love, and he looked down upon the rustic manners of the medieval knights.[2]

In modern times the scientific goals of education have been stressed. Did not Bacon point out that knowledge means power over nature? Did not science revolutionize the physical world? Did not science give us the basis of the industrial revolution? Modern education, as Thorndike has indicated, is based upon psychology

[2] Cf. Waugh, *History of Europe,* Chapter 21; Taylor, *Thought and Expression in the 16th Century,* Volume I, Chapter I.

and biology, rather than upon theology.

Tentative Goals

Several attempts have been made to describe the aims of education. Thus in 1918 the Commission on the Reorganization of Secondary Education pointed to seven basic goals of education:

1. Good health
2. Command of fundamental processes
3. Worthy home membership
4. Vocational efficiency
5. Civic efficiency
6. Worthy use of leisure
7. Ethical character [3]

In 1933 a committee of the National Education Association formulated social-economic goals to be realized through education. Among the members of the commission were Leon C. Marshall, Robert C. Moore, Edward A. Ross, John Dewey, and Fred J. Kelly. According to the commission the goals to be achieved were the following:

1. Hereditary strength
2. Physical security
3. Participation in a growing civilization
   a. Development of skills and techniques
   b. Development of values, standards, and meaningful philosophies
4. A dynamic, flexible personality
   a. Personal initiative

b. Discriminating viewpoints and choice
c. Flexibility of thought and conduct
d. Individual differences
e. Need for cooperation
5. Suitable occupation
6. Economic security
7. Mental security
8. Equality of opportunity
9. Freedom
10. Fair play [4]

The Educational Policies Commission in 1938 issued a report on *The Purposes of Education in American Democracy*. The report centers upon four major areas. (*a*) Self-realization, including the inquiring mind; command of fundamental processes, including speech, reading, writing, arithmetic, sight and hearing, health knowledge and habits, interest in public health, recreation, intellectual and esthetic interests, and the formation of character. (*b*) Human relationships are also stressed in the report, especially respect for humanity, friendship, cooperation, courtesy, appreciation of the home, conservation of the home, homemaking, and democracy in the home. (*c*) Economic efficiency is emphasized, particularly the importance of good workmanship, occupational information, occupational choice, occupational efficiency, occupational adjustment, occupational appreciation, personal economics, consumer judgment,

[3] Commission on Reorganization of Secondary Education, *Cardinal Principles of Secondary Education*, 1918, 32 pp.

[4] Cf. Committee on Social-Economic Goals, *Implications of Social-Economic Goals for Education*, N.E.A., 1937, p. 126.

efficiency in buying, and consumer protection. (*d*) The importance of civic responsibility is upheld by the report. Particular attention was drawn to the need for social justice, social activity, and social understanding. Also critical judgment, tolerance, social applications of science, world citizenship, law observance, economic literacy, political citizenship, understanding of the principles of conservation as related to the national resources, and devotion to democracy are stressed by the report.[5]

The Broad Goals of Education

The main aims of education can be summarized under fifteen headings. Naturally, these objectives are tentative.

1. Reflective thinking is a primary need. Few of us are aware of the resources of our minds. Thus we spend most of the time in daydreams and we rationalize our preconceived beliefs. Reflective thinking involves an attitude of objectivity whereby we formulate tentative theories and try to verify them in a laboratory manner. Reflective thinking is a purposeful activity; it changes, as Dewey points out, an indeterminate into a determinate situation.

2. Appreciation of culture should be emphasized. Education is incomplete without the enjoyment of the arts and humanities. A knowledge of the great works of art of the past may illuminate our appreciation of the present. The alarming trend in education, as Whitman already pointed out, is the reign of vulgarity. Often a monistic viewpoint exists which equates industrial arts with Sophocles, Edgar Guest with Robinson Jeffers, Dale Carnegie with Socrates, and Michelangelo with an illustrator of the *Saturday Evening Post*. Appreciation implies more than a recognition of the great works of art; it means a transvaluation of our attitudes whereby art becomes a way of life and conditions our basic values and goals.

3. Development of creativity should be stimulated. Too often education is concerned merely with the imitation of the past; too often education stresses discipline for the sake of discipline; too often the individuality of the student is overlooked; too often the educational process is so boring and anemic that it kills our creative drives. Creativity demands not only insight, but concentration and dedication. Thus Thomas Wolfe would revise his novels many times, and when he was engaged in creative work, all other interests and concerns would be secondary. The teacher can aid creativity by stimulating students, by uncovering hidden talents, and by respecting the originality and individuality of his students. The goal of the teacher should be to lead the student from passivity to activity, and from imitation to creativity.

[5] Educational Policies Commission, *The Purposes of Education in American Democracy* (Washington: National Education Association, 1938), p. 157.

4. Understanding and application of science are significant, for science, perhaps more than any other field, has contributed to the advancement of civilization. At the same time, the new scientific weapons have created immense dangers for the survival of man. Science thus offers no magic solutions and no magic utopias for modern man.

A clear distinction should be made between the scientific method and technology. The scientific method is open-minded, tentative, tolerant, and abhors absolute conclusions. It can be used in the natural as well as in the social sciences. Technology, on the other hand, represents the application of science, and from a moral viewpoint, may have either constructive or destructive effects. For example, an airplane may be used for transportation or it may be used for purposes of destruction.

The task of education is to give us a balanced view of science, to see both its possibilities and limitations.

5. Education should bring us into contact with great ideas, for we learn by critical thinking as well as by doing. Too often philosophers have been concerned mainly with abstractions and they have looked upon ideas as things-in-themselves. Ideas, it must be remembered, are functional and they initiate social change as in the case of those presented by Darwin and Freud.

Contact with great ideas leads us away from the immediate and gives us perspective regarding our own time and our own culture. The emphasis in our educational thinking, however, should not be mainly upon description of events and ideas, rather upon the ways and means through which life can be changed and improved.

6. Moral and spiritual values cannot be excluded from the educative process. Yet too often moral and spiritual values have been regarded in a rather narrow manner. Thus teachers have been subjected to multiple tabus, especially in small towns. They have been evaluated by their conformity, rather than by their sense of originality.

A commentator recently said that he wanted to preserve the spiritual values of our civilization. I asked him how this would be accomplished. He replied by saying that he wanted to banish writers like Steinbeck and Hemingway from the high school anthologies, for these writers, according to the commentator, give a "perverted view of life."

Now genuine spirituality implies quite a different perspective than that represented by the commentator. It implies a questioning spirit and an identification with the highest symbols of culture. Like Jesus and Buddha, the truly spiritual teacher will regard all men as equal and he will disregard the barriers of race, religion, and nationality.

7. Fundamental skills are basic in education. This implies not just a mastery of reading, writing, and arithmetic, but an emphasis upon the

art of communication and the development of esthetic sensitivity. To be able to read, to write legibly, and to understand the basis of mathematics —all these capacities are not to be equated with genuine education. What counts is the critical analysis of books, the ability to distinguish between propaganda and truth, and the capacity to arrive at rational decisions.

8. Vocational efficiency has become a primary concern of modern education. For we are interested not only in the enjoyment of life, but also how we can best make a living. Unfortunately, we often choose the wrong profession; the result is that we feel frustrated and we may develop a severe neurosis.

Once we realize that we are in the wrong type of work we may react as violently as Gauguin who sacrificed respectability and economic success and devoted himself to art in the garrets of Paris and in the wilderness of various South Sea Islands.

Vocational efficiency should not be equated with economic success; otherwise we are dominated by the idol of materialism. Often the most important profession, like teaching, is certainly not the most remunerative. We should develop a respect for all, as much for the mechanic as for the banker, as much for the poet as for the scientist.

9. Effective education implies a better adjustment to family life. Through education we can improve our appreciation of the home and we can become more considerate of others. We learn the destructive ways of conflict and the importance of mutual sharing and understanding. Confucius pointed out that the educated man should be an example, not merely in his thinking, but also in his conduct.

Education can change both the spiritual and physical aspects of the home. It can create a more esthetic atmosphere, and improve our homemaking capacities. It can also change our basic attitudes, whereby we cease to regard our own needs and desires as primary and instead learn to cooperate with others.

10. Education is the most adequate preparation for citizenship. Citizenship implies more than the fulfillment of elementary political duties, it implies the need for tolerance and social justice and the development of genuine social conscience. Effective citizenship demands not only a verbal allegiance to democracy, it requires also the daily application of democratic principles in the home, classroom, business, and political affairs.

11. Without physical and mental health all the other objectives are superficial and visionary. While good health, to some extent, depends upon our heredity, modern science has made immense strides, and through correct habits, emphasizing the interdependence of the mind and body, we can achieve not only a long life, but also a happy life.

Mental health requires balanced

perspective and the avoidance of extremes. If we are sadistic or masochistic, if we hate others, if we are imperialistic in our behavior, if we act on an infantile plane, then certainly psychological conflicts are bound to occur.

Education can become the tool of maturity. It should be, as Spinoza said, a reflection upon life rather than upon death, and should indicate our possibilities—both physical and mental—rather than our limitations.

12. Genuine education ought to change our personality. Whitehead one time stated that being interesting is more important than being factually correct. If education has made us boring and uninteresting then certainly it has missed its goal. Real knowledge ought to make us more dynamic and fascinating and ought to radiate our zest and yearning for truth.

13. Education ought to give us permanent interests. Activities that are merely confined to the classroom are superficial. If we read only the books that are assigned we are inferior students; rather we should read on our own and we should become imbued with the *adventure* of knowledge.

Our leisure-time interests ought to reflect our yearning for education. Certainly sports, movies, an active social life are to be recommended; still all these activities are not ends in

themselves and are inferior to cultural activities, which raise our level of understanding and sensitivity.

14. The achievement of peace is one of the fundamental objectives of education. Any system of education which contributes to mistrust among nations and which glorifies chauvinism and military force is to be condemned. Thus we read in *All Quiet on the Western Front* about the educational system of Germany before 1914. Technically, it was proficient. The German youths had an excellent classical background, and a comprehensive knowledge of science, but their minds were poisoned by myths about the superiority and infallibility of the German fatherland.

15. Education aims at a *perpetual renaissance* of man. It indicates that man is the measure of the universe, that knowledge is an infinite process, and that enlightenment must radiate and must not be confined to the few. As educators it is our task to create not only original minds in art, literature, music, philosophy, religion, and science, but also to develop an interested audience which can appreciate creativity.

Education thus looks to the future; it indicates that man has not finished his task, rather that he has only begun. Education is not the prelude to despair and cynicism, but the eternal overture to hope and expectancy.

Confusion over the purposes and functions of secondary education has divided spokesmen into a number of camps. Some say that the public high school fails to prepare students for college, thus neglecting its primary function; others, that too much stress is placed on the college-preparatory function; and still others, that the high school has no objectives at all. A time span of better than 300 years has marked a transition in secondary education from a school with but one function—namely, to prepare *boys* for college—to one that serves many purposes and functions of *all* youth, regardless of sex, race, or creed.

Perkins, in the following article, is concerned mainly with the high schools in their function of preparing students for college. However, he makes a number of points which are vital to our general discussion of the purposes and functions of the public schools: (*a*) College-preparatory subjects should not be discarded. Failure to fulfill the needs of the able student will result in a great loss to society. (*b*) *All* students must be taught proper work and study habits. (*c*) The community must create a climate where teachers enjoy high professional status and where things of the mind are treated with the greatest respect. Only then will the *quality* of public education be assured.

What Is a High School For?   by JOHN A. PERKINS

From *The Saturday Evening Post,* March 17, 1956, pages 25, 104, 107. Reprinted by special permission of the *Post* and the author. John A. Perkins is President of the University of Delaware.

We should do well to remember that the American high school grew out of the private academy, and came into being largely to prepare young people for college. Until recent decades, there was a stronger link between the high schools and colleges than between high schools and elementary schools. The subjects taught were steppingstones to further study. High school algebra and geometry prepared for calculus; Latin syntax and grammar paved the way for study of other languages. These subjects were taught in a manner that warmed up the student for what was to come in college: laboratories, lectures, term papers, and examinations.

The emphasis was much to the liking of the universities and colleges. Some of the great state universities had begun by 1875 to admit students from specially accredited high schools upon presentation of diplomas. College-board examinations were thought unnecessary.

Soon after 1900, however, the tongue-and-groove relationship between high schools and colleges began to pull apart. This change has continued into our own day. There now exists what might be called a breach between secondary education and higher education—even between state universities and public high schools.

Why have the colleges and high schools grown apart? At bottom, the answer lies in the great expansion of high school enrollments. The growth is continuous. Fewer and fewer young people have to quit school early and go to work, because mechanization and modern technology enable more fathers to support their families unaided. This has been true even in rural communities ever since tractors and mowing machines began to replace horses and the scythe. Today, one man can till almost twice as much acreage as he could in 1910.

In time, the general rise in family incomes made social reform possible. Child-labor laws and compulsory-school-attendance laws were enacted in all states, and the legal age for leaving school was advanced well into adolescence. Consequently, the percentage of children of high-school age in actual attendance rose sharply. It was 11 per cent in 1900, 15 per cent in 1910, 32 per cent in 1920. In the same age group today, about 80 per cent are in high school.

With almost everyone going to high school, whatever his mental ability, the school can no longer be concerned primarily with the preparation of youngsters for college. Yet it is remarkable how many high schools held to this purpose long after

their enrollments included boys and girls with ambitions running from automobile repairing to biochemistry. Even now some high schools are following the old line, abetted by an occasional parent-teacher association and vehement critics like Canon Bernard Iddings Bell and Prof. Arthur E. Bestor. Here is an attempt to withstand far-sighted educational thinking that was spelled out a generation ago.

Back in the 1920's leading school authorities such as Profs. Thomas H. Briggs, Henry C. Morrison, and William C. Bagley pointed out that for certain children the high school program must be terminal. It should be a vocational program. It should be "pupil-centered." It needs to be concerned with "life adjustment" and with citizenship. The high school program must be all these things. At the same time it must prepare about one-third of the graduates for college.

The better high schools for years now have had not one purpose but many purposes. Also, research in psychology, physiology, and anthropology has revealed so much about how people learn that it has become necessary to adopt new teaching methods. High school courses have been developed to capture the interest of pupils who learn slowly as well as those who learn rapidly. Seen from the viewpoint of the high school and its job, these adaptations are understandable, even praiseworthy.

In another development, the modern high school has become a community center concerned with mental and physical health, community projects, and adult education and recreation. The doors are open from eight in the morning until ten or later at night, at least five days a week. This change followed upon the extra-curricular movement and its valid premise: learning by doing. Those who play in the band come to know music, musicians, and composers. Through dramatics the pupils learn literature, oral expression, and aesthetics. It is all fun, too, and a source of parental pride. Still, what began as education has sometimes become mere entertainment. This fusion of school and community has its virtues, but the preparation of pupils for college entrance has not benefited.

Not everyone has been made happy by these developments. The parent who wants college for his child often charges that college preparation is a neglected aspect of the high school curriculum. Some older teachers, devoted to academic subjects, are also disgruntled. Nor have the colleges fully appreciated the enlarged responsibility of the high school. Their faculties believe that the new-style "comprehensive" school often prepares students less well than the old-style academic school. When young folk go off to an accredited college and fail, their home-town people are dismayed and sometimes angered. Some lose confidence in their high school. Others think the college unreasonable in its academic standards.

Actually, there is no one especially to be blamed, unless it be our society as reflected by our home communities. The high school has seen its large job and has tried to do it. Almost any high school administrator will admit, at least to friendly critics, that the secondary school's job has not been done perfectly. On the other hand, the universities and colleges have not always moved as rapidly as they might in the circumstances. The boy or girl leaving the new-type high school to enter an institution of higher learning has trouble adjusting to a place where students are treated as men and women devoted to intellectual growth. Many freshmen benefit from college-supervised dormitories and counseling services, aided by better testing of intelligence, aptitude, and social adaptability, but these advances have come all too recently.

Colleges have been slow to emphasize the fact that some young men and women should not go to college. It should be made clear to parents that the meaning of high school graduation has changed. Not every recipient of a diploma is eligible for college admission. The situation has been further complicated by the decided financial and social value of the college degree. Our national welfare depends more and more on technological complexities, and the self-made man of the future will probably make the grade only if he enjoys a college education. To the man of tomorrow, higher education will be as vital as were the proverbial good wife, sharp ax, and strong back to the pioneer.

Well-to-do parents often want their children to go to college even if their offspring lack the essentials for success—adequate preparation, desire and determination to learn, and enough mental ability to pursue studies which require abstract reasoning. These prerequisites for success in college are basic. They cannot be waived or altered. The college that adapts itself to the applicant who lacks ability, serious ambition, or preparation soon loses its integrity. No, the intellectual requirements of a true college education cannot be made easy to accommodate all comers.

At the same time, there is a pressing need for more college graduates. The natural resource which is in shortest supply in the United States today is trained brain power. The shortage is so acute as to endanger our national health, security, and prosperity. Someday you may have to do without a doctor in an emergency; it is estimated that by 1960 the country will have 30,000 too few doctors. Shortages of dentists and nurses will be equally grave. Our colleges are now graduating annually 20,000 fewer engineers than are needed. More scientists and mathematicians are needed. These are the people whose efforts in research laboratories make jobs for us all. It is they on whom we depend for defense against atomic bombings.

There are shortages everywhere. Last year the land-grant state universities graduated 8500 men in agriculture. Over 15,000 jobs requiring such training are available each year. We are all familiar with the serious shortage of teachers. It has brought into the classrooms many teachers without the bachelor's degree. We try to encourage young people to enter the teaching profession, but the shortage of qualified teachers remains critical. The colleges and universities of America provide only 45,000 elementary-school teachers annually; almost 100,000 are needed. To meet the total demand, 200,000 additional teachers at all levels will be needed each year for the next decade.

Another problem: a great many young people in the United States have the ability to do intellectual work of high caliber, but only half of them are enrolled in college. A Minnesota study of high school graduates ranking in the upper tenth of their class revealed that for every one who went to college, one did not go. This is pretty much the picture everywhere.

One of America's most distinguished university presidents, Harold W. Dodds, of Princeton, advises parents who want to prepare their sons or daughters for college to send them to a private secondary school. But tuition at private schools costs more than most fathers can afford. The really massive job of preparing capable youngsters for college must be done by public high schools. Their graduates will be admitted to college, welcomed there, and will succeed, if school and community adopt sound policies.

In the first place, high schools should maintain the integrity of all the programs they offer, particularly the program leading to collegiate preparation. This means offering solid courses in mathematics, English, modern languages, and at least one of the sciences. To do this will be expensive for the smaller high schools, but not to do it is eternally to handicap capable small-town boys and girls. Last year, some 1500 high schools dropped courses in mathematics and science, on the ground that there were not enough students to justify these courses. But the value of courses cannot always be determined by enrollments. To discontinue courses basic to success in college is to retain the small high school at the expense of capable pupils and the need of the country for trained manpower. We are now sacrificing superior pupils in the small high school. In evidence is the fact that graduates of small-town and rural high schools go on to college in smaller proportion than graduates of city high schools.

Studies introduced largely to provide teaching matter for less interested pupils should not push out subjects which are still basic for able youngsters. The community must not let its values be distorted by the excitement of hearing the local school band playing a Sousa march. The parents whose pride expands when son Tom has a leading part in a dramatic production should be concerned lest their satisfaction be at the expense of the boy's future. If Tom really has ability, he is more apt to develop it at the state university than in Hollywood.

Another point: pupils should not be permitted to waste time or work carelessly in high school, whatever their curriculum. The habits of hard and careful work are basic to success in all human endeavors. In its own way, each high school subject should be made to call forth the best efforts of the learner. To demand less is to make young people unfit for life. High schools often must be geared to the average mind; if they are not careful, they come to expect too little of all students, superior students in particular. The high schools must be sure that they are not turning out the only product made in America that is not "quality controlled."

Further, the importance of the high school teacher should be given greater emphasis. Too often community leaders point with pride to the new school building, exclaiming, "Haven't we a wonderful high school?" This is assuming too much. What they really mean is that the building had a good architect, a reliable contractor, and up-to-date plumbing. Only great teachers can make a school wonderful. The community determined to have dedicated, capable teachers will have to pay to get them. Money alone is not enough. Esteem and security are also important to satisfaction in a career.

We might do something, too, about improving the community's regard for things of the mind. The intellectual climate of the high school is affected by the intellectual climate of the town. If young people don't want to study, they may be reflecting the social climate in which they have grown up. Plaudits in home towns throughout our land are for the boy who makes touchdowns, rather than for the boy who makes the highest grades in mathematics. The girl who twirls the baton is more complimented than the girl who writes superior essays. If the community puts more money into lights for the football field than into books for the library, this sense of values is adopted by the boys and girls. In some communities learning is even ridiculed. Does your town poke fun at those interested in ideas by calling them "eggheads," "longhairs," or "highbrows"? Are your young people ever reminded that high-brow thinking gave us television, hybrid corn, relief from the scourge of polio? Who is more admired, the man who buys the biggest car or the man who buys books?

The community that gives the right answers to these questions need not worry about the quality of its high school and the probable success of those who go on to college. Such a community will also attract the beginning teacher who is now more drawn to the cultural life of the big city.

Of course, universities and colleges need to understand the modern high school better, and be ready with help. One state university has prepared for smaller high schools correspondence courses in such subjects as algebra, solid geometry, and trigonometry. Correspondence pupils receive a kind of tutorial help from a single high-school teacher. For the most part, these schools must emphasize "practical" subjects, a need that is not well appreciated by the college professor. He doesn't recognize that a course in automotive mechanics in the high-school shop, properly taught, can be an avenue of critical thinking. It can prepare students in the logical arrangement of ideas, in reading for meaning, and even in an understanding of our civilization.

Out of that civilization has grown the problem that besets us. How heal the breach between high schools and colleges? There is no convenient whipping boy. The problem has not been deliberately created by troublemakers or the misinformed, nor is it without solution. However, like most problems, it will not be solved by emotional response. Honest thinking and courageous action are called for, lest we spoil the child.

For an analysis of the changes that have taken place in the nature of objectives, in the sources used in their formulation, and in the range of objectives appearing during the past fifty years, the reader is referred to the article by Tyler on pages 176–192 of this book.

5

AN OVERVIEW OF OUR
PUBLIC SCHOOLS

Despite divisive factors which affect the purposes and functions of public education in the United States, the schools continue to operate five days a week throughout the school year with a minimum of friction and fanfare. Although education has been charged with social lag, the schools have been peculiarly responsive to the needs of the dynamic society in which they operate. The school of today is quite a different institution from that of fifty years ago.

During the years of World War II, as is the case in any period of national crisis, educational innovations were at a standstill. However, the renewed interest in curriculum improvement and experimentation in the short interval since the cessation of hostilities has been noted by a number of observers.

In the following pages, trends in elementary education are first described, followed by a description of secondary-school trends, then subject-matter and special developments, and finally an over-all picture of developments during the past fifty years, so well outlined by Tyler (pages 176–192).

TRENDS IN ELEMENTARY EDUCATION

While the June, 1957, number of the *Review of Educational Research* includes the generalization that "specific studies of trends in the elementary-school curriculum" are lacking [2:242], Harap is able to point out some specific, discernible differences between today's elementary school and that of only twenty years ago.

Today's Elementary School by HENRY HARAP

From the *NEA Journal,* Volume 46 (February, 1957), pages 78–80. Reprinted by special permission. Henry Harap is Professor of Education and Associate Director of the Division of Surveys and Field Services, George Peabody College for Teachers, Nashville.

The new elementary classroom bears no resemblance to the gloomy room of yesterday with its dark-hued walls and heavy, fixed desks in straight rows. New buildings have more space, movable furniture, and more equipment for active and creative learning.

As a result, the classrooms are more flexible and informal. Although many existing classrooms still have a rigid and formal atmosphere, the new room is gradually becoming a center where children live and work together.

Today virtually every American elementary-school child has access to free textbooks purchased with state or local funds. The textbook, more than any other factor, still determines what the elementary-school child learns in school. The textbooks include the whole range of school subjects—reading, spelling, handwriting, English usage, geography, history, science, health, music, and others.

In addition to the basic collection of textbooks, the pupils have access to several sets of supplementary books and a small classroom collection of books and pamphlets.

Twenty years ago it was not uncommon to see a whole primary class begin a reading period with, "Mary, turn to page 30 and read aloud." The children would then take turns reading until they came to the end of the story.

Today, reading is taught to small groups of the same level of ability or need, and reading aloud is the last of several preparatory steps.

Before the child begins to read books, such activities as telling a story from pictures, sharing an easy picture book, and listening to stories that are told or read help him develop readiness to read. The amount of emphasis on phonics varies widely.

The basic texts and directed reading are continued in the upper grades, but the child also reads more independently and more widely. Using the classroom or the library collection, he reads extensively for information and pleasure. The child becomes more familiar with poetry, short stories, plays, biographies, and books of travel.

Written expression often begins with the writing of group stories dictated by the children and written on the chalkboard by the teacher.

Later, pupils write simple letters to invite their mothers to a party or for some other useful purpose. As the pupils move to the upper grades, they have many occasions for original writing with correction of individual errors. Many teachers assign formal writing tasks suggested in language texts and workbooks. Creative writing of poems and stories is encouraged by the imaginative teacher.

Generally speaking, the elementary schools are putting greater emphasis on the development of good speaking and listening habits. The long-neglected art of conversation is engaging the attention of many teachers. As the opportunities to plan, to share, and to evaluate become more plentiful, the children are learning to think quickly, talk fluently, and listen attentively.

Grammar is part of the language-arts program. The simpler definitions and rules are incorporated in the language text, which is usually a part of the pupil's collection. This language or English book is one of the important tools used in the child's study of punctuation, sentence structure, word study, and the elements of good usage.

Spelling as a separate subject is generally taught from a text or workbook in which the child encounters the new word in context and in isolation. The words learned in the spelling book are supplemented by new words used in all subjects and by words that have been misspelled in pupils' written work.

In this generation, the teaching of handwriting has undergone a phenomenal change. Today few children learn cursive writing until they reach the end of the second grade or the beginning of the third grade. The mechanical exercises in writing rows of ovals to the rhythmic timing of the teacher have disappeared.

Beginning writing involves learning the letter forms. Soon thereafter, the child writes for a purpose such as telling about a trip to a farm. The child continues to learn to write legibly, not in isolated exercises, but as the need for written communication arises in all subjects throughout the school day. Purposeful writing is supplemented by drill given to groups on their common difficulties.

The whole range of arithmetical processes from simple addition to the division of decimals runs through all the elementary grades. The skeleton upon which figuring is hung consists of the four fundamental operations — addition, subtraction, multiplication, and division — applied successively to whole numbers, fractions, and decimals, as well as to measures and graphs.

Each grade or group of grades gets its special emphasis from the particular arithmetical steps for which the children are supposedly ready. There is a tendency to introduce topics several years before they are presented for mastery and to extend them beyond the mastery to provide for maintenance of skill. The applications of numbers to real situations in home and community living are being increasingly used in the classroom and in textbooks.

Drill still has a dominant place in the teaching of arithmetic, although it is more commonly introduced after the child has encountered the number fact in a familiar setting and is more likely to understand it.

The sequence of steps is largely determined by the particular textbook in use. The addition and subtraction of whole numbers are learned in the first and second grades, and the multiplication and division of integers in the third and fourth grades, although some schools continue them into the fifth and sixth grades.

While fractions and decimals are learned simply and concretely in the earlier grades, their formal learning is confined to the fifth and sixth grades. The children study the simpler uses of money, time, length, and weight in the primary grades and the more difficult applications in the upper grades. The study of graphs is assigned to the three upper grades.

The schools are devoting more time and are giving greater emphasis to the social studies. There is a growing tendency to push the schoolhouse walls farther outward into the community. The sequence of social studies in the first six grades parallels the expanding environment, beginning with the home and school and radiating outward to include a view of the world. While the *here* and *now* are studied in all grades, the emphasis on the *far away* and *long ago* is not begun until the fourth grade.

History and geography are combined in some classes and taught separately in others. The present trend is to combine history and geography in the elementary grades. In the curriculum guides that I have studied recently, geography as a separate subject has been disappearing. Geography is fused with United States history in the fifth grade and with world history in the sixth grade.

On the basis of curriculum guides that have come to my attention, I can report that seven school systems have fused science with social studies in recent years. The more adventurous teachers are using the lengthened period as a bridge to a larger ongoing unit of work. With this approach, pupils have ample opportunity to do group planning and to have an abundance of active and creative learning.

Science, which originally made its way into the elementary school as nature study, appears to be attaining a broader and more important status. The teaching of science at the elementary level is still in its formative stage. To my observation, the content is largely dominated by the text with very little experimentation and practical work.

Many teachers have been influenced by those courses of study and series of textbooks which are based on a classified list of concepts. For example, the concept, "Plants need air, sunshine, water, and food," is introduced in the first grade and is expanded as the child moves up from grade to grade.

The categories into which study of this concept most commonly fall are: weather and climate, earth, living things, health and nutrition, and energy and machines.

Arts and crafts, stories, music, dance, and dramatics are quietly gaining greater acceptance. The once violent and widespread criticism of these so-called fads and frills is now barely audible. In fact, the public is demanding artistic and musical training for its children.

Many schools still devote a separate period to art, although the theme of the children's work is frequently related to reading, social studies, and other subjects.

Teachers do not follow a sharply defined grade sequence of mediums or skills as they do in arithmetic. The children work with clay, finger paint, crayons, water colors, charcoal, colored paper, cloth, wood, and metals. The particular art mediums used in a school, however, vary from place to place.

On the art frontiers, one finds children weaving and making puppets, block prints, and cloth designs. The appreciation of masterpieces of art is usually limited to the upper grades.

The most common types of musical experience in all the elementary grades are singing, listening, playing instruments, and creative and rhythmic activity. Rhythm bands, folk dancing, and group dances frequently supplement the customary musical activities. Note reading develops from the rote singing of new songs.

The teachers of the upper elementary grades are giving greater emphasis to appreciation of classical music. In the better classrooms, music permeates the total life of the children. For example, one group of third-grade children whom I observed had developed an extensive repertory of songs pertaining to sea life, to which they were giving special study at the time.

Since most of the elementary teachers are women, the program of physical activities is informal and consists largely of outdoor free play and seasonal games. Where the teaching of physical education is organized, it consists of group games, individual activities, dancing, and singing games as well as other rhythmic activities.

The sequence of activities follows the seasonal pattern of games and sports. (Although educational leaders disapprove of competitive athletics for elementary-school children, the fathers in some schools have succeeded in overpowering their influence and in launching baseball and football tournaments for boys.)

Some teachers are required to follow a rigorous time schedule of subjects and others have considerable freedom to plan the weekly program of studies. A teacher who adheres slavishly to a time schedule tends to allot a fixed period to each of the ten or more subjects for which he is responsible, unmindful of their relative importance.

Some schools are tardily beginning to give some attention to balance in the total life of the school.

In such schools, teachers are helped through supervision to determine how much emphasis to give to the suggested basic components such as social living, basic skills, expressive arts, individual needs, and routine activities.

TRENDS IN SECONDARY EDUCATION

In tracing the historical development of the high school, French [16:1–62] indicates that the role of the school has changed from that of an *exclusive, selective,* and *autocratic* school to one that is *inclusive, adaptable,* and *democratic*. This has resulted in the development of a new school—the comprehensive high school.

Such trends as the following in the junior and senior high school curriculum have been summarized by Beauchamp in the June, 1957, issue of the *Review of Educational Research:* a trend "away from subject-centered programs toward integrated programs" in junior high school; participation by pupils and laymen in curriculum planning; emphasis upon preparation for citizenship; multiple-type curricula offered in over 50 per cent of the large high schools; "fusion of language-arts subjects"; attempted adaptation of "subject content to life needs"; and increased course offerings for "slow learners and gifted children." [2:242]

Four trends in curriculum development at the secondary level are discussed in the following article by Romine: (*a*) concern with present-day problems of living, (*b*) development of a unified program from the kindergarten through grade 12, (*c*) use of newer types of organization, and (*d*) more attention to individual differences.

Trends in the Secondary-School Curriculum

by STEPHEN ROMINE

From the *Proceedings* of the Northwest Association of Secondary and Higher Schools, Annual Convention, 38th Year, held at Salt Lake City, Utah, November 28–December 1, 1954, pages 43–47. Reprinted by special permission of the Association. Stephen Romine is Associate Professor of

Education and Director of the Bureau of Educational Research and Service, University of Colorado.

One of the fundamental trends in curriculum building today is that of moving toward a broader concept of the job which the high school is called upon to do and a more functional concept of how this job can be done. The two-by-four curriculum, as someone has aptly called it, with its restriction to the two covers of a book and the four walls of the school, is becoming a thing of the past. It is obvious today that the school alone cannot accomplish the challenging and complicated task of educating our youth for productive citizenship. This is a job calling for the effort of the entire American community. Only to the degree that we can secure such effort will American education be able to retain its forward thrust.

This broader and more functional viewpoint is growing in general acceptance and is reflected in at least four less inclusive but related trends, each of which merits consideration.

First, there is a trend for the high school curriculum to be more concerned with important, present-day life problems than was true in the past. Courses which have been in the curriculum for years—in English, mathematics, science, social studies, and other fields—are being given a more practical slant and a more truly cultural focus in the broad sense of the term. Problem-centered courses are more prevalent today, and out-of-school experiences are given

more consideration than in years past.

The use of a wider range of resources also fits into this broader and more functional concept of the curriculum. Many books instead of one, audio-visual aids of many types, and the use of out-of-school personnel and places illustrate this trend. School libraries are becoming communications centers and laboratories of learning, instead of merely serving as repositories of books. School librarians are spending less time with the technical details of "minding the library" and more in working with teachers and students in learning situations.

Work experience and camping also reflect the broadened concept of curriculum. More and more effort is going into the development of a high school curriculum which really makes a difference in the way people live and behave. This effort is carrying the school beyond its four walls and bringing the student body in contact with the ongoing turmoil of the world in transition. Distributive occupations courses and school-work programs are enlarging and enriching educational opportunities in a realistic manner.

Also part of this larger trend is the move toward cooperative school-community curriculum planning. In numerous communities committees are working on problems of curriculum building, and they are making it possible to bring about needed changes which would otherwise be unacceptable. Both the support of the public and the counsel of enlightened citizens are essential to a curriculum designed and operated to meet the needs of boys and girls and of American communities in this modern age.

Another major trend in curriculum building is that of the development of K–12 programs. For too long our elementary and secondary school curricula have been somewhat like an odd pair of pants and an odd coat which do not always make a good suit of clothes. Elementary and secondary-school teachers frequently have not known about or understood what was being done on levels different from their own; sometimes they have not cared very much. As an unfortunate result, our total curriculum has sometimes been a patchwork, even to the extent of having patches upon patches. All of this has led to lack of unity within the teaching profession and has been a source of criticism from the lay public.

As we really come to believe in the theory that human growth and development is a continuous process, we are sensing the need for a continuous and well articulated curriculum from the kindergarten through the twelfth grade. Especially in the basic fields of English, health and physical education, mathematics, science, and social studies are these K–12 programs becoming more common. These provide a means of help-

ing all teachers to see their own spheres of activity in better perspective to the total program, and they aid in establishing better cooperation of teachers on all levels. A stronger curriculum and a more generally satisfied public also result from the K–12 idea.

In the future we shall likely see the emergence of what may be called a K–13 program involving closer cooperation between secondary schools and colleges and universities. Next week in Colorado, for example, we are holding the third in a series of conferences aimed at coordinating more closely the curriculum in English in the Denver high schools and in the University of Colorado and pointed also at helping students to bridge the gap between English instruction on these two levels. If we are successful, and the approach thus far has real promise, the plan is to expand the effort to include other subject fields. This is a cooperative project in which neither level is attempting to dominate the other. The focus has been on common problems and what we can do together for the welfare of our common student body.

As a third major trend, newer types of curriculum organization are also becoming more common than in the past. Broad-fields courses which combine elements of courses formerly taught as separate entities are helping to bring some sense and unity out of the hundreds of courses accumulated over the years through a process of addition. As you know, all roads have led into the curriculum, and once a course has become established it has tended to enjoy permanent tenure. Curriculum surveys have revealed much unnecessary overlapping among such courses, as well as important gaps in the total education program.

The core curriculum also continues to become more popular, especially on the junior high school level. More commonly this now develops slowly through the unification of language arts and social studies, and group approaches to guidance are also associated with the core program. Many schools are avoiding a mistake all too common in years past —that of identifying such courses with a special label.

Another major trend consists of increased activity in the revision of courses within the existing framework of organization. Many teachers are beginning to doubt that what they have done and are doing is necessarily the best that they can do. In the past, we sometimes have been like overconfident George— "often in error, but never in doubt!" This is not so true nowadays, and the revision of existing courses is taking several healthful directions which go beyond "fussing with the fringes."

For example, just as the K–12 idea promotes better vertical articulation, more effort is now going into establishing better correlation and articulation among courses taught on the same grade level. Teachers of English and social studies, as an illustra-

tion, are doing much to relate and reinforce their instruction. In many fields common goals, themes, or experiences are serving as bases which promote a more effective total curriculum and a more efficient learning process.

There is also a shift within courses from emphasis on subject matter *per se* to content and experiences justified on the basis of making a genuine contribution to important educational goals. Increasingly the curriculum is coming to be viewed as a means instead of an end. Pupil-teacher planning is finding a place in the scheme of things, and courses are being broadened to include a richer variety of activities pertinent to a broader range of outcomes beyond academic information and skills.

This trend toward the revision of existing courses is important, not alone for the improvements which are involved, but because success with this process lays the groundwork for more comprehensive curriculum revision. Only as teachers can bring about improvements in an atmosphere of security and with the more familiar aspects of their work can we reasonably expect them to tackle projects which require more educational pioneering.

Growing attention to individual differences marks another major trend in curriculum and instructional procedures. In furtherance of this, an increasing number of schools are considering ability grouping or some other plan of reducing the heterogeneity of instructional groups. Temporary grouping within heterogeneous classes is also employed, and various schemes of assignment are being utilized to provide greater opportunity and challenge to students of varying abilities, backgrounds, interests, and needs.

Especially is concern for the more able student growing. For too long we have neglected this group in many schools, not because we wanted to, but because of circumstances. Many such students have not developed their real potentiality to the degree necessary for their own welfare and the general welfare of society. And some potentially able students have never been recognized as such simply because the high school curriculum has not been sufficiently challenging to motivate them. This whole problem is complicated, too, by growing enrollments and promotion practices prevalent in the majority of our schools.

Along with and as part of these trends is another which is perhaps more administrative than curricular. For a long time study halls have posed a very real problem. Many students use them badly, if at all, and teachers have been unhappy with them also. Particularly because of this, and recognizing that students might more profitably be occupied in classes, activities, and study under supervision, many schools are moving toward a schedule of fewer and longer periods in the school day. Students are also carrying heavier loads, which

permit them to pursue basic courses fundamental to the education of all youth and still elect other courses and activities in accordance with their particular interests and needs. We have come to realize that the elective system, carried to unreasonable extremes, has contributed to the multiplicity of overlapping courses found in some schools and has permitted students to avoid experiences which they should have. Often it has been easier to add courses than to appraise critically and revise those which we have in order that they might serve more effectively. The new trends seem to be giving students a richer experience in high school, as well as yielding greater educational returns on the tax dollar.

Related to these changes, and pertinent to meeting individual needs and interests, there is a trend toward greater flexibility in time requirements for high school credit. The Carnegie Unit, as old and revered as it is, has serious weaknesses. Consequently more attention is being given today to the qualitative aspects of learning and to the growth and development which students attain, rather than to the time they spend in studying a given subject. On this point accrediting agencies may be a great help or a serious handicap.

In one of our high schools last year, and doubtless this sort of thing has been duplicated in other schools, a selected group of students met their advanced algebra class only three times per week, the other two days being spent on another project. A standardized achievement test administered at the end of the year clearly indicated the superiority of this group in algebra over two other classes meeting five times per week, even though the two latter classes compared favorably to national norms. With unselected groups in other schools we have found that careful planning permits wiser use of time than is customarily made, the net result of which is a richer course of instruction and more efficient learning. In the future we shall doubtless see some classes meeting only two or three times a week; of these some may be only one semester in duration and others may extend over a period of several years. Other courses may meet for longer blocks of time. As we clarify our objectives and improve our techniques of evaluation we can make a number of modifications in scheduling which will be beneficial. These changes will pose some administrative problems, but they will not be insurmountable to competent and forward-looking school principals.

The trends which I have mentioned are not developing in a vacuum or without cause. They have grown out of experience and research. As our educational theory advances and matures, there is a tendency for practice to change also. Very important to this is the quantity and quality of administrative leadership given to our schools and the focus of this leadership. Over the nation at large high school principals seem to

be giving more time and energy to curriculum improvement than in the past, either by personal attention or through coordinators, supervisors, or similar personnel. And yet, many schools are understaffed in this regard. Few, if any, industries would think of providing only one supervisor for fifty to a hundred or more workers, yet this condition exists in public education.

Nonetheless, high school principals are increasingly concerned with curriculum and instruction, and growing enrollments will not lessen the need for this attention. In forward-looking school systems the improvement of curriculum and instruction is becoming a major undertaking, and the men and women advancing into positions of leadership are increasingly chosen from those who can work effectively with people in bringing such improvement about.

In speaking of these trends I have also attempted to think of both theory and practice. We all realize, I am sure, that practice lags behind theory. Growing enrollments and the concentration of attention and resources on housing our students also pose problems to be solved in moving ahead toward a better curriculum. So also do rising costs of education. The teacher supply bears directly on all of this, and in some quarters unwarranted criticism of the schools and a call to return to the fundamentals are to be reckoned with.

Nevertheless, we must look ahead hopefully as well as realistically.

Whatever the odds and however great the difficulties, an age of skepticism can only be fruitless; it has never been otherwise in the history of mankind. What I have suggested here today represents only a trend up to now; the future lies as much, if not more, with you than with any other group. Progress—real, substantial, and lasting progress—does not come without sustained and intelligent effort, even in the face of discouragement. I am confident that our secondary-school principals can and will give the leadership necessary that our curriculum may become increasingly potent in educating our American youth. Upon this trend—greater and wiser educational leadership—rest not only the other trends which have been mentioned, but the future of American education.

With respect to two of the areas indicated by Romine—"the reorganization of general education in the secondary school" and "more extensive provisions for individual differences"—Alberty briefly traces historical backgrounds, makes a penetrating analysis of conflicting philosophies and practices, and suggests what yet remains to be done.

Some Trends and Issues in Secondary-School Curriculum Development   by HAROLD ALBERTY

From *Frontiers of Secondary Education I*, pages 31–40. Proceedings of a Conference on Secondary Education. Compiled and edited by Paul M. Halverson, Professor of Education, Syracuse University, and published by the Syracuse University Press, 1956. Reprinted by special permission. Harold Alberty is Professor of Education, Ohio State University.

In these days of mounting school enrollments, high tax rates, and confusion on the part of the general public as to what should be expected of our educational institutions, it seems appropriate to take a careful look at our educational frontiers in order to discern in what direction we are moving and to appraise the nature and extent of this movement.

At the present time the spotlight is turned on the secondary school for a number of reasons. The effect of the increased birthrate during World War II is about to be felt in the already crowded secondary schools which now enroll 75 to 80 per cent of American youth. The number and percentages of those demanding a secondary-school education are bound to increase and we are not sure that we can house and teach nine or ten million teen-age boys and girls.

As the secondary-school population becomes more and more a cross section of the general population, the secondary school will be called upon to reorganize its program to meet the needs of an increasingly heterogeneous group. Even under present conditions 50 per cent of those who enter fail to graduate, a fact which gives us pause when we consider how far we are from the American dream of a secondary-school education for all youth.

And even among those who graduate and wish to go on to college, the road is likely to be barred for many because of the avowed plans of many of the colleges to deny admission to many high school graduates on the ground that they are incapable of succeeding in college without a costly program of "spoon-feeding." The multiplication of junior or community colleges seems to be the only solution of the problem of providing equality of educational opportunity for all American adolescents.

The question of how to provide buildings, equipment, and teachers for the increasing hordes of students who rightfully demand an education creates staggering problems which must be solved. These problems cannot, except for purposes of discussion, be divorced from the curriculum; for if we are to meet the needs of all American youth, it is necessary to look at the instruments which we use to do the job. Another challenge closely related to the curriculum concerns delinquency and failure.

Why do so many youngsters drop out of high school? Why do the colleges complain about the failure of the high school to teach reading and simple mathematics? What is back of

the charge that the high school is not providing adequately for gifted or talented youth? Add to these challenges the indictment that is being made against today's youth in the fields of delinquency and the alleged disregard for human rights and responsibilities, and you have a challenge to those who are responsible for curriculum development in the high school.

There are many curricular trends on the horizon that have a bearing upon the problems that have been raised. It is the purpose of this brief paper to look critically at some of these trends and the issues which arise from them. Because of its brevity, the discussion will be limited to two trends and the resulting issues.

General Education

There is a trend toward a reorganization of general education in the secondary school in the direction of making it function more effectively in common citizenship education.

For purposes of this discussion general education is defined as that part of the total curriculum that is designed primarily to provide for the development of the common attitudes, understandings, and skills needed for effective citizenship, and hence is required of all students.[1]

The customary design of the area of general education as defined above is a series of required Carnegie units —sometimes referred to as "man-

---

[1] For a more detailed discussion of this definition and its interpretation, see Harold Alberty, *Reorganizing the High School Curriculum* (New York: The Macmillan Company, 1953), pp. 156–166.

dated" units. Thus in a four-year high school requiring sixteen units for graduation, there are likely to be required three units of English, three units of social studies, one or two units of science, and possibly two units of physical education. Or, more specifically in the ninth grade, *all* students might be required to take English composition and literature, civics, and physical education. In this grade the student might choose between general mathematics and algebra, and elect a unit in science, and another in music, fine, or applied arts. If he were interested in business education, he might take all of his elective work in that area. For purposes of our discussion *all* elective activities, be they vocational or nonvocational in character, are designated as special-interest education, *not* as general education.

The importance of developing attitudes, understandings, and skills common to all citizens of our democracy has long been recognized. While the uniqueness of the individual is cherished, yet this uniqueness must be cultivated along with education for the common life if our democratic institutions are to survive the threats coming from within and without.

While there is general dissatisfaction with our present program of general education in the high school, as indicated by the vast amount of criticism coming alike from laymen and professional educators, there is marked disagreement as to what should be done to remedy the situation. The major issue seems to be this: *Shall general education continue to be organized as a series of separate subjects or fields of knowledge, or in terms of the common problems which adolescents face in the process of achieving increasingly mature relationships in the various aspects of our culture?*

This issue is likely to engage the thinking of both laymen and educators for a long time. Actually it is not new, for the search for a basis of organizing learning activities more closely related to the needs, problems, and interests of the learner has been going on for several decades. Dewey's laboratory school at the University of Chicago, founded in 1896, demonstrated dramatically the soundness of direct experience and a problems-approach to learning.[2] Ellsworth Collings, building upon the theories advanced by Dewey and Kilpatrick, reported in 1923 the success of an elaborate experiment in learning which abandoned completely the separate-subjects approach to curriculum development.[3] Good elementary schools began to reconstruct their programs

---

[2] For a clear presentation of the philosophy and psychology underlying this school see John Dewey, *The School and Society* (Chicago: The University of Chicago Press, 1899), and *The Child and the Curriculum* (Chicago: University of Chicago Press, 1902).

[3] Ellsworth Collings, *An Experiment with a Project Curriculum* (New York: The Macmillan Company, 1923).

in terms of the "comprehensive unit of work" approach, discovering that children learned the so-called fundamentals more effectively when motivated to work on problems which were related to their needs and which they had helped to plan.

The Eight-Year Study which got under way in 1932 stimulated high schools to experiment with new types of programs, particularly in the field of general education. Out of the more than thirty schools that participated in the study a half dozen organized "core" programs which were based upon studies of the needs and problems of adolescents and which knew no subject boundaries. It was found that the graduates of these schools did college work as well as or better than did paired graduates from conventional schools, or graduates of an equal number of Eight-Year Study schools that had retained conventionally organized programs in general education.[4]

Since 1942 further impetus has been given to the reorganization of general education in the high school by the Life Adjustment Movement and the program of the American Council on Education and the National Association of Secondary-School Principals which published *Education for All American Youth* in 1944, followed in

1951 by a revised edition entitled: *Education for All American Youth, A Further Look*.

Strangely enough, the new psychology of direct experience and purposeful learning has had little effect upon the design of general education in the secondary schools. Wright reported in 1950 that only 3.5 per cent of the public high schools reported courses which "meet for at least six periods a week and combine subjects which cut across major areas of the curriculum."[5] And of the schools reporting it has been estimated that less than one hundred public high schools out of a total of 24,000 have a program of general education which could fairly be designated as an adolescent-problems core. Probably most programs are best described as fusions or unified studies embracing the language arts, the social studies, and in some cases science, making use of the fine and applied arts in a more or less incidental manner.

No comprehensive study has been made since Wright's follow-up study in 1952 but there is reason to believe that great headway has been made since then in the reorganization of the junior high school program. Under such designations as multiple-period classes, common learning, self-contained classrooms, core programs,

[4] Dean Chamberlin *et al., Did They Succeed in Colleges?* (New York: Harper & Brothers, 1942), Chapter VII.

[5] Grace S. Wright, *Core Curriculum in Public High Schools. An Inquiry into Practices, 1949.* Bulletin, 1950, No. 6. (Washington: U. S. Office of Education, 1950.) See also Mrs. Wright's excellent follow-up study: "Core Program Why and What?" *School Life*, XXXIV (February, 1952), p. 71 ff.

seventh and eighth grade subjects are being reorganized as fusion or unified studies programs taught by one teacher who has charge of the group for three or four periods per day. In some cases, teachers actually organize the work around major problems of adolescent living, teaching the so-called fundamentals as they are needed in the solution of problems. In other cases the teachers utilize the allotted periods to teach the separate subjects, much as they were taught before the reorganization.

Considerable impetus to the trend toward curriculum reorganization at the junior high school level has been given by the recent studies of the effectiveness of the core in New York City junior high schools which were carried out by J. Wayne Wrightstone, Director of Research.[6] He found that improved mastery of the "fundamentals" and marked improvement in personal-social adjustment took place in classrooms characterized by fusion or the adolescent problems core. As a result of these studies the core is being extended in the New York City schools.

It must be clear, even taking into account the New York City situation, that the trend toward a significant reorganization of the program of gen-eral education in our secondary schools is amazingly slow when one considers the vast amount of experimentation and successful practice during the past half-century. Yet, it must also be clear that there are promising signs as well. There is rather widespread dissatisfaction with the conventional departmentalized program of the junior high school and this fact alone is having a marked effect upon the curriculum reorganization in this area. The fact that a teacher is given a group of youngsters for three or four periods per day, together with the responsibility for guidance and homeroom activities, is at least an invitation to curricular reform. If such a teacher has resourcefulness and is given some freedom to depart from traditional methods and materials, something significant is bound to happen.

Schools that have been most successful in reorganizing the general-education program as the basis of adolescent problems have built their programs upon preplanned problem areas. Roughly, a problem area is defined as an aspect or area of living in which all or most adolescents are likely to have problems. While much is to be desired in improved ways of deriving and validating problem areas, it still remains true that the

[6] J. Wayne Wrightstone, *A Second Report on the Evaluation of Pupil Growth in the Core Program in Two Academic High Schools, 1952–53* (New York: Board of Education of the City of New York, March, 1954). (Mimeographed.) J. Wayne Wrightstone, *A Second Report of the Study of the Introduction of the Core Program in Selected Vocational High Schools, 1952–53* (New York: Board of Education of the City of New York, March, 1954). (Mimeographed.)

concept is a useful one in defining the scope of general education in the high school. The following are illustrative areas taken at random from many lists: Problems of School Living, Problems of Communication, Problems of Values and Beliefs, Problems of Self-Understanding, Problems of Living in the Community, Problems of Conflicting Social, Economic, Political and Religious Ideologies, Problems Involving Selecting and Preparing for One's Life Work, Problems of the Application of Scientific Method and Technology to Living, Problems of Personal and Community Health, Problems Involving Face-to-Face Relationships, Problems of Reconciling American Ideals with Practices, Problems of Understanding and Changing Human Behavior, Problems of Intercultural Relationships, Problems of Developing and Maintaining International Understanding.[7]

Many schools have found it helpful to develop resource units or guides around each of the problem areas selected by the faculty as making up all or part of general education. These materials then serve as helps for the teacher in the cooperative planning of units of work in the classroom.

What can be done to facilitate even greater progress in the reorganization of general education in the high school? The newly formed Commission on Core Teaching of the Association for Supervision and Curriculum Development is giving some attention to this problem on two fronts: moving from a purely fusion or unified-studies approach to the Adolescent Problems Core, and attempting to extend the core to the senior high school.

There are many blocks that will need to be removed before present gains can be substantially extended. Among them are these:

1. The time-honored conception that graduation from high school shall be defined in terms of the mastery of sixteen Carnegie units—each one of which is a separate entity.

2. The action of state legislatures in prescribing what shall be taught.

3. The rigid certification requirements of state departments of education.

4. The traditional programs of teacher education which for the most part are based upon the teaching of separate subjects.

5. The persistent charges of lay groups that the "fundamentals" are being neglected.[8]

Providing for Individual Differences

A second major trend may be defined as follows:

There is a trend toward more extensive provisions for individual differences among students—particularly at the upper levels of ability and talent.

---

[7] See Alberty, *op. cit.,* Chapter VI.

[8] For example see C. Winfield Scott and Clyde M. Hill, *Public Education Under Criticism* (New York: Prentice-Hall, Inc., 1954), especially Chapters III, IV, VI.

Providing for individual differences among students has always been the concern of our American schools. To recognize and cultivate the uniqueness of the individual is an important part of our democratic tradition. Beginning about 1920 when the testing movement was at its height, educators began to be conscious of the wide range of differences that existed among students. These differences manifested themselves in intelligence quotients, reading ability, mathematical ability, as well as along lines of special aptitudes in music, art, science, and the like. The search was on for some scheme that would make it possible for youth to realize its fullest potentialities. It was natural in such a climate for much experimentation to take place. Perhaps the most widespread plan for providing for the wide range of differences was homogeneous or ability grouping. By the use of complex batteries of tests, educators divided children into larger numbers of groups. The issue became: "Shall the brighter students be allowed to move more rapidly through the curriculum or shall their program be enriched?"

The issue was fought bitterly. The results were inconclusive, partly because it was impossible to measure the intangible values which were present in the learning situation. The opponents of grouping charged that while the bright students might well master the so-called fundamentals more rapidly, yet to segregate them meant that they were losing an important aspect of democratic living —namely, rubbing elbows with their fellows who had less ability. It was also charged that ability grouping made snobs of those students who were fortunate enough to be placed in high groups, and on the other hand that such grouping tended to frustrate students who were assigned to low-ability groups.

The experimental evidence is difficult to evaluate because of the many variables involved, but apparently there was a rather marked decline in the use of ability grouping after World War II. Perhaps this was due to the fact that schemes for individualizing instruction, such as the Dalton, Winnetka, and Morrison Plans, had become somewhat popular and provided a means of providing for individual differences within the class group. While these plans never succeeded in supplanting the daily recitation system with its reliance upon assignments from textbooks, they did serve to point up the possibility of recognizing and making provision for individual differences within the normal heterogeneous class group.[9]

At the present time, there seems to be resurgence of interest in this problem of providing for individual dif-

[9] For a critical discussion of the various plans for providing for individual differences, see Vivian T. Thayer, *The Passing of the Recitation* (Boston: D. C. Heath and Co., 1928), Chapters XIII-XIV.

ferences. The reasons are not hard to find. Increased enrollments have tended to increase class size and teachers have complained that they can no longer give the necessary attention to individual students. Along with increased enrollments has come greater heterogeneity, particularly in reading ability. This again has complicated the problems of meeting common standards on the one hand, and recognizing differing abilities on the other.

Probably more important than these factors is the present trained manpower situation. The shortage of trained engineers and scientists has led many of our industrial and governmental leaders to demand that the high schools do a better job of identifying and training talented youth— especially in the field of science and technology. President Eisenhower's recent appointment of a committee to study the problem of training scientists is evidence of this trend. An important factor in this demand is the oft-quoted statistic that the Soviet Union is giving more attention to this aspect of education than are the Western democracies.

The important issue which grows out of this trend may be stated in this manner: *Shall talented youth be dealt with within the regular class groups or shall they be segregated into special classes and/or special schools?*

At the outset of the discussion of this issue, it should be pointed out that in the conventional high school there is a segregation of students on the basis of interest and ability in the elective or special-interest areas of the curriculum, even though the students may be heterogeneously grouped in the general education phase of the program. For example, the students who expect to go to college elect algebra rather than general mathematics, physics and chemistry rather than applied science, the foreign languages rather than art or shop. On the other hand, the students who are not college-bound tend to elect the vocational or practical subjects. Consequently, even though the school makes no attempt to segregate students on the basis of ability, the students with the higher intelligence quotients tend to be found in the subjects usually thought of as college preparatory. It will also be found that this student group usually represents the higher economic level of society.

But this situation does not satisfy the proponents of segregation of the talented. The reasons are not difficult to discover. First of all, even though the college bound students tend to elect certain courses, this group is becoming more and more heterogeneous as even larger numbers of students hold college aspirations. A few years ago less than 10 per cent of the graduates of high schools applied for admission to colleges while now we enroll at least 30 per cent, and this percentage is bound to increase markedly within the next decade.[10]

[10] For a discussion of this problem see James B. Conant, *The Citadel of Learning* (New Haven: Yale University Press, 1956).

In the second place, these classes are usually taught by means of daily assignments from an adopted textbook with little or no attempt to recognize and deal with individual differences except from the standpoint of differentiation in marks. That little beyond this is being done in regular classes is indicated in a recent survey of the literature by a group from the Horace Mann—Lincoln Institute of School Experimentation.[11]

Those in favor of making special provisions for the gifted point to the need of better programs for locating talented students. Such a program would make use of intelligence tests, academic and non-academic aptitude tests, and would of course also take into account such more or less intangible factors as personality, interests, and motivation. Having identified the gifted or talented, the next step would be to make administrative and curricular adaptations. If the school were large enough, sections of all classes in the fields of both general and special interest education could be set up; and a special curriculum might be developed to permit this group not only to "cover more ground" but also to deal with challenging materials especially adapted to the interests and talents of the students.

If conditions permitted, the proponents of this plan of segregating the gifted or talented would undoubtedly favor the "career" high school as it is being developed in certain of our large cities. J. Wayne Wrightstone describes the New York City program in a recent article.[12] These high schools provide for the academically gifted who expect to enter college in such schools as Bronx High School of Science, Brooklyn Technical High School, the High School of Music and Art, the High School of Performing Arts, and Stuyvesant High School.[13] For those students who desire terminal courses, the following schools among others are provided: Brooklyn High School of Automotive Trades, Brooklyn High School for Home-Making, Central Commercial High School, Central High School of Needle Trades, Food Trades High School, Machine and Metal Trades High School, Manhattan High School of Aviation Trades, and the Metropolitan Vocational High School which has special schools within its organization such as the Maritime High School which "trains young boys to enter into such maritime occupations as those of able-bodied seaman, quartermaster, and deck storekeeper."[14]

The opponents of special plans for

---

[11] A. Harry Passow, Miriam Goldberg, Abraham J. Tannenbaum, and Will French, *Planning for Talented Youth* (New York: Bureau of Publications, Teachers College, Columbia University, 1955). This pamphlet contains probably the best analysis of the problem, and certainly the most complete bibliography.

[12] J. Wayne Wrightstone, "The Career High School," *Educational Leadership*, XIII (January, 1956), pp. 236–240.

[13] *Ibid.*, p. 238.

[14] *Ibid.*, pp. 239–240.

segregating the talented or gifted, either within the school or by means of special schools, are haunted by the same arguments that were advanced against homogeneous grouping and segregation a quarter of a century ago. These arguments were sketched earlier. To them may be added at least two others that have been emphasized recently.

There really is no such thing as a homogeneous group of students. The extent of heterogeneity may be reduced by the careful use of multiple criteria, but there still would remain a wide diversity of interests and abilities that is not taken into account by the screening device that is used. It is also well established that good teaching will tend to make a group more heterogeneous rather than less.

Regardless of the care taken in grouping, the resulting distributions usually roughly follow the class system in society. The students from higher-economic-level homes tend to be grouped together, not necessarily because they have more scholastic ability or talent *per se,* but because they have had better home opportunities for learning and development. At the other end of the scale are to be found the students who live on the "other side of the tracks"—again not because they are less intelligent but because of unsatisfactory home conditions.

These arguments are not new or conclusive, but they are persistent and need to be checked carefully by any school that is considering any form of ability grouping or segregation. There is an abundance of literature in this area.[15] Some of it is frankly philosophical in character, making the case for or against ability grouping or segregation on the ground that it supports or is inconsistent with democracy. Many of the so-called experiments are inconclusive because of the number of untested variables and hidden assumptions.

And so the problem is still with us. A striking and fairly typical example of its expression is to be found in a recent article appearing in the May, 1956, issue of the *Atlantic Monthly* by Caspar D. Green.[16] He is greatly concerned because the required courses in the small high school where he teaches contain a normal distribution of students. In a tenth-grade English class of twenty-six students, he finds three of them outstanding, thirteen medium to poor, four or five *very* poor, and the remaining five or six incapable of learning anything that remotely resembles tenth-grade English. At the upper end of the scale he thinks the three outstanding (talented) students can be taken care of by special assignments, but the "dullards" at the

---

[15] Passow *et al., op. cit.,* list 162 titles dealing with all known ways of providing for individual differences.

[16] Caspar D. Green, "What Shall We Do with the Dullards?" *The Atlantic Monthly,* CXCIV (May, 1956), pp. 72–74.

lower end should be dropped from school. The possibility of a different organization for learning is not discussed by the author.

A great deal of the current difficulty in providing for individual differences can be traced to the tremendous lag between theory and classroom practice. To put the matter bluntly, enough is now known about ways of organizing curricular activities to abandon the daily recitation system with its textbook assignments and substitute for it a unit plan which is applicable to any learning situation and which would provide for the wide variety of individual differences usually found within a normal high school group.

As was pointed out at the outset, during the early twenties while the devotees of scientific method were experimenting with homogeneous grouping as a means of providing for the individual differences which they had discovered through a wide variety of tests covering hundreds of talents and aptitudes, other groups were experimenting with a new classroom methodology.

Henry C. Morrison contributed his now-famous modification of the Herbartian Formal Steps which identified the true learning products (understandings, appreciations, special abilities, and skills). William Heard Kilpatrick, building upon the experiences in agricultural education, popularized the project method and identified the successive steps in the carrying-out of the "whole-hearted purposeful activity." The field theory psychologists, rejecting the passive-learning theory of Thorndike, gave educators confidence that Dewey's concept of the complete act of thought provided a vehicle for dynamic learning. The various experimenters with individualized instruction showed how the lock step of the daily ground-to-be-covered recitation system could be broken.

V. T. Thayer brought these concepts together into a three-step unit plan which laid the groundwork for a more realistic approach to cooperative classroom planning, providing for individual differences in speed of learning and in abilities and talents through a work period which, while holding the class together for common cooperative enterprises, encouraged those who could do so to move faster, develop deeper understandings, and explore their own interests.

In recent years these unit plans have been refined by the use of the vast research into the field of group dynamics and group processes,[17] by the consolidation of what we know about adolescent growth and development, and by groups of teachers in the field representing different areas of interest working together to build resource or instructional guides which tend to break down the nar-

[17] See for example Herbert Thelen, *The Dynamics of Groups at Work* (Chicago: The University of Chicago Press, 1954).

row specialism which has characterized secondary education, and cut through to the actual problems of boys and girls.

Thus, if the tenth-grade English class discussed by Green,[18] instead of trying to make students "more aware of the practicality of the scholastic," had actually worked on real problems of living in a multiple-period core situation, there is a chance that even the "dullards" might have found themselves. For example, in a unit dealing with modern living in Columbus, Ohio, there would be much to do besides performing what Green refers to as the school's central function—academic training. Some groups would surely want to make maps of the city's growth, of its plans for developing a modern transportation system, of its blighted areas and housing projects, and these changes would involve first-hand investigations, interviews with city officials, mastery of facts and skills involved in drawing to scale, etc. Other groups would want to look at the city's park and recreation system, others at the way people make a living in Columbus, and the problem of encroachment of industry upon the residential sections of the city. Those students primarily interested in the arts would find plenty of outlets for their endeavors as they explore the achievements of the city's writers, architects, creative artists, and builders.

Once we could be freed from the

[18] Green, *op. cit.*

academic tradition of the daily recitation system, our youths might, under the direction of the school, identify themselves with the life of the community, participating for periods of time in industrial and commercial organizations, governmental agencies, museums, studies, and charitable and welfare organizations. The ideal would be for the school to serve as the coordinating agency for mobilizing the educational possibilities of the community.

The type of curriculum and procedure described above does not neglect the "fundamentals." Experiments have shown this over and over again to the point where one wonders why anyone ever needs to raise the question whether such a program provides the matrix in which the "fundamentals" can be taught meaningfully. Neither does such a curriculum neglect the talented, for the wide variety of activities called for in the normal process of solving the problems that the teacher and students set for themselves will bring into play, will even tax to the utmost, the abilities of the talented, and will open up avenues for the cultivation of new interests and concerns. And it will all be done within the framework of democracy and its deep concern for the recognition of the uniqueness of the individual and its steadfast devotion to the concept of living and working together to achieve common ends and purposes. The boy who helps with the cleaning of the paint brushes and the filing of materials will work along with the creative artist—and each will be cognizant and appreciative of the contributions of the other. That is the essence of democracy—and we must not, in our zeal to train more engineers than the Soviets, abrogate the principles of living that have made us great.

It is hoped that in this brief exposition, the writer has made two major points:

1. General education in the high school is in dire need of drastic reform and the direction of that reform lies along the lines of a direct approach to dealing with the problems of youth in our confused culture.

2. We now are in possession of the facts and techniques to introduce a teaching procedure which will protect our democratic ideals and at the same time provide adequately for developing the uniqueness of every individual, be he identified with the vast group of youth roughly designated as the common man, or with the infinitely small group that we are fond of calling the intellectually elite or gifted.

What are the chances that these changes will come about in our time? In current practice we can find schools that have already moved far in these directions. Given a generation of peace with attendant freedom from fear and frustration—and there is a good chance that the next decade or two will become noteworthy in the history of educational progress.

TRENDS IN SUBJECT-MATTER AREAS

Although there have been innovations in the organization of classroom experiences—in terms of broad fields, problems of living or activities, for example—which offer considerable promise, organization in terms of separate subjects is still the usual pattern. In the pages that follow, discernible developments in subject-matter areas will be discussed as they have appeared in the fields of language arts; mathematics and science; fine and practical arts; health, physical education, and recreation; and social studies.

LANGUAGE ARTS

The importance of the language arts (reading, writing, speaking, and listening) in the school program has been well expressed by Krug: "There is no other single field on which the development of the entire school curriculum so heavily depends." [23:133] If that be the case, then developments in the language arts are of utmost significance to every curriculum worker, regardless of his or her special area of interest.

(In the reprints below, it should be noted that the term "English" is virtually synonymous with that of "language arts.")

Developments of a general nature which have occurred in English or the language arts during the past fifty years have been summarized by Hatfield in terms of the achievement of more democracy in the classroom, broader aims and activities, better provision for individual differences, and closer integration of the several language arts.

Advances in the Teaching of English   by w. w. HATFIELD

From the *NEA Journal*, February, 1956, pages 90–92. Reprinted by special permission. W. W. Hatfield was editor of *The English Journal* from 1922 until his retirement in 1955.

The English curriculum, alias language-arts curriculum, from the first through the twelfth grade is now regarded as a single ramp—rather than as a series of steps—up which each class or individual moves at the best speed personal abilities and teachers' skill make possible. The general order of the items in the curriculum is determined by our improved knowledge of child growth.

Progress in the teaching of English in this huge and democratic country has been, like the advance of a glacier, slow but never reversed. Since I began to teach, in 1906, we have had no revolution in English curriculum or method, but we have had a significant evolution. Anyone who doubts our progress has only to compare the qualifications of teachers then and now, or to note the superior selection and presentation of material in today's textbooks. Not only is the best teaching of English today better than any of the past; the proportion of excellent to poor teaching has increased.

The Leaven

For a good many years, the two ideas which have, to a considerable extent, transformed the teaching of English were accepted by a quite limited number of theorists and by a very small proportion of classroom teachers:

1. The fastest, surest, most thorough learning comes through experience which includes the learner's deciding or helping to decide what he will do and taking or sharing the consequences of his action. John Dewey was formulating this principle about fifty years ago.

2. Education should be a preparation both for rich living and for making a living. (The transmission of the cultural heritage is not an end in itself but a means to these two

ends.) This idea was emphasized at the founding of the National Council of Teachers of English in 1911.

Classroom Democracy

American democracy supplied a most favorable climate for the spread of the experience doctrine. As James F. Hosic early impressed upon me, the sure way to train children for democracy is to practice it with them —without abdicating the adult's right and duty to give needed information and advice and even, when there is danger of serious harm in action children seem about to take, to issue and enforce orders. Nor does this mean a soft pedagogy of following pupils' evanescent *whims.*

So today teacher-pupil planning is generally accepted in principle and quite commonly practiced. An occasional failure is reported, apparently because pupils unaccustomed to planning were asked to plan a big unit at first instead of just the details of today's or tomorrow's work.

Students who have helped to plan an undertaking understand what is to be done, and why. They work earnestly and successfully because their proprietary interest provides strong motivation. That they are also learning to make decisions thoughtfully and methodically is an important incidental.

Broader Aims and Activities

A corollary to our basic idea is that powers, attitudes, and habits are even more important than mere knowledge. Of course, we wish students to know English usage, we are aware of the value of acquainting them with good literature, and we see the usefulness, for able students, in knowledge of the pertinent features of the settings in which the literature they read was produced. But we care even more that they think good speech worthwhile, that they habitually employ generally approved locutions, that they be considerate of others in discussion, that they be clear and conscientious in what they say.

The more and the better the literature they experience—not just learn or learn about—the better; but we are concerned yet more that they become able to read worthy literature perceptively when no teacher is at hand and that they develop discrimination in their choice of reading matter. We believe that the social attitudes and the understanding of themselves and others which they acquire from their reading are very important, and that we should think of these as we suggest literature for class study or individual reading.

With these dynamic aims have come more dynamic activities in the classroom. Drills in usage or in analyzing textbook sentences are used only when both teacher and students can see the need for them. Discussions, reports to classmates on topics under group study, letters to be mailed to real persons for real purposes, replace oral themes and pointless essays.

Literature chosen for class study is within the linguistic comprehension of the pupils and suited to their social and emotional maturity. Students are led to approach literature at different times in the different ways cultured adults do—sometimes for illumination of a topic or problem, sometimes for entertainment through adventure, humor, or esthetic delight.

Ability to understand and enjoy the best radio and TV programs and to perceive the tawdriness of the worst is an important equipment for living. For years, outstanding school curriculums have included consideration of radio programs, and now, discussion of television programs is increasing as teachers see that these programs vary, as do books and magazines, from the vapid or pernicious to the truly excellent.

A few teachers encourage comparison of comic-book versions of classics with the masterpiece originals; students soon discover the thinness of even "good" comics.

Individual Differences

One of the earliest kinds of provision for individual needs was the inauguration of remedial instruction in reading, because objective tests drew the attention of administrators to this area. (But even some high schools still do not have it.) Many schools now offer remedial work in speech. Occasionally one hears of remedial instruction in written language, most often in a minor but conspicuous element—spelling.

Recently, several leaders in language-arts education have been eloquently urging us to make more adequate provision for the brilliant students whose talents are stunted for lack of exercise.

Ability grouping is the most obvious means of providing for individual differences and is the one most often tried. But serious objections to it are voiced by many. Grouping based upon tests of intelligence or of subject-matter achievement may not serve important differences in temperament and tastes. The dull need the leadership of the bright, and the quick need to learn to work with the slow. Perhaps stratification by ability is no more democratic than stratification according to wealth or length of time ancestors have been in this country.

Moreover, a recent study of freshmen at the State University of Iowa showed that despite the most careful screening, "A" students will get into "C" sections, and vice versa. Still further, the same students may rate "A" in one of the four language arts but "C" in another. At the most, sectioning is an incomplete provision for individual differences in the language arts.

A few high schools are trying— and liking—parallel courses of different difficulty and somewhat different intention, with each student taking his choice. This draws together students of like aims and tastes and roughly similar abilities, but its users agree that teachers still need to individualize within each class.

Integration of the Language Arts

Educational psychology shows clearly the relatedness of the four language arts. Initially they develop, in succession, listening, speaking, reading, and writing, each one depending upon all the preceding ones. Later each art constantly influences the others. More important, in the normal activities of out-of-school life they are often used simultaneously and still more often in rapid alternation on the same piece of work.

Even fifty years ago alert teachers in the primary grades enlisted all these arts in the service of single activities and made them support each other. Today the many college courses in "communication" instead of freshman "composition" are an acknowledgement that the four language arts are a very closely knit family.

Language-arts curriculums in the upper grades and the high schools are beginning to fall into line with the primary grades and the colleges. They are introducing "topical units" in which all four language arts are practiced and literature is employed. Instruction in the skills is given during the planning and evaluation periods, which occur at the beginning, at the end, and—in long units —at several junctures of the study. If the teacher is well versed in literature suited to the age and skill of the students and uses excellent available reading lists and bibliographies, a great deal of literature may be used.

The difficult tasks in reading, interviewing, or other investigation are undertaken by the able students, who fail to find any real challenge in assignments planned for mediocre capacities. The weak students choose or are assigned parts of the study which are suited to their abilities. Since the most common use of literature outside school is for leisure reading and recreation, leading advocates of topical units urge that every semester's work include at least one unit centered in literature, and that at all times real effort be made to stimulate and guide students' individual reading.

Et Cetera

This brief survey omits more than it reports. For example, a whole article would be required for even a cursory account of the developments in reading alone: extension of the aim to include assimilation and reaction to content, the shift of stress from oral to silent reading, the change from beginning with sentences or at least words, insistence upon the reader's use of all that he knows in interpretation and evaluation, the application of semantics, the emphasis upon speed—in short, realization of the complexity of the reading art, and of the need that instruction continue through the high school into college.

Here are just a few of the many significant developments in the teaching of the English language arts.

Forty years ago no one but primary teachers preparing to teach phonics thought of giving instruction in listening, whereas we now realize that listening is an art as complex as reading and as improvable through instruction and guided practices.

"Creative" writing, almost a fad in the 1930's, is now less talked of, but today teachers who have sufficiently sympathetic personalities and any confidence in their own literary judgment find some way to encourage such writing, often called "personal" or "expressional."

The usage "rules" set up by eighteenth-century theorists ignorant of the development and actual current usages of the language they spoke have been replaced with objective study of the language used by literate persons in America today. Divided usages and acceptable regional variations are recognized. The teaching of grammar has been streamlined by the paring away of such useless or unsound items as the elaborate conjugation of verbs with six forms for each of six tenses in each of two voices, the subclasses of adjectives and adverbs, and the cases of nouns.

Further broad changes in the method of grammar teaching are foreshadowed by the work of the linguistic scholars, who analyze sentences by examining the inflections and arrangement of the words in them, instead of beginning with the meaning of the sentences. They insist that these inflections and arrangements are the means by which we indicate the relations of the words in our sentences. These are the grammatical tools which we actually use in constructing or understanding sentences.

The few secondary-school experimenters with this approach report greater satisfaction than with the old. Teacher correction of student writing tends to be less complete than formerly. Many teachers mark only one or two types of errors each time, and emphasize worth of content, clarity of organization, and effective bits of expression. They inspire more and nag less.

Hard but Rewarding Work

Teaching English, alias language arts, under today's conditions and according to our present ideals, is a challenging task. But it is one that pays rich dividends in satisfaction.

A specific language-arts problem, indicated by Hatfield, has often been this: What is the place of grammar in the language-arts curriculum? As a "declaration of independence" of the elementary school from high school and college pressures, Pooley contends that the elementary school should determine the program of grammar instruction that is most suitable for its pupils—one which "combines a maximum of practice in the use of English for communication with a minimum of formalized rules and rote learning. . . . A sound knowledge of less is a surer foundation than confusion over much." Pooley further points out the need for both elementary and high school teachers to meet together to discuss the problems of grammar and to reach agreement on the responsibility of each school with respect to it. [39:195–197]

Specific changes which have taken place in English or the language arts, especially in "methods and teaching aids," have been summarized by Boeshore for the Metropolitan School Study Council in the following article. (The reader is also referred to Shane's review of research in teaching the language arts on pages 204–207 of this book.)

Trends by ELIZABETH A. BOESHORE

From Elizabeth A. Boeshore, *English and the Secondary School Program* (New York: Metropolitan School Study Council, January, 1954). Reprinted by special permission. Elizabeth Boeshore is a member of the staff of Weehawken Public Schools, Weehawken, N. J.

Most of the ideas expressed in this pamphlet are summarized in this list of trends. Some of these trends were specifically identified by the English teachers themselves and some were inferred from their descriptions of what they are doing.

1. Greater emphasis on *learning by self-discovery*—self-discovery both of the need to learn specific things and of the content itself.

2. More teaching of *language-skills-in-use context.*

3. *Broader definition of language skills* to be taught—inclusive of listening, use of public-address systems, combinations of graphic and verbal presentations of ideas, and library know-how.

4. Greater emphasis on those *kinds of language skills that have utilitarian applications.*

5. More attention to the *analysis of what makes linguistic competence and* to the deliberate *teaching of those components*—e.g., specific reading skills for science, direct and deliberate vocabulary building.

6. *Wider use of mechanical gadgets,* such as tape recorders, opaque projectors, mechanical aids for improving reading skills, and public-address systems.

7. More attention to *remedial work,* for able students as well as students with difficulties.

8. Greater concern with the *individualization of instructional method.*

9. More emphasis on *developing well-rounded individuals* rather than on creating narrow competencies.

10. *Informality* more often the rule in the classroom.

11. Greater use of "free reading" lists and other arrangements whereby students get acquainted with a *wide range of literature* rather than intensive, whole-class study of a very limited list of traditional classics.

12. Broader definition of "classics" to include much *good contemporary literature*.

13. Wider use of the *non-textbook type of reading material,* such as inexpensive pocket-book editions of the classics that children may keep as their own, and periodicals.

14. More extensive use of *school and classroom libraries*.

15. *Closer integration* of work of English department with guidance, social studies, art, etc.

16. More teaching to *further individual goals and needs*.

17. More concern with *aiding children to grow from where they are*—in terms of skills and tastes—to their own, unique, highest potential.

18. More concern with *provision of experiential background* to make teaching of skills more realistic.

19. More *flexibility in quantity of subject matter* to be taught.

20. *Greater variety of elective English courses,* which may be taken in place of, or in addition to, the standard English courses—e.g., business English, journalism, and creative writing.

21. More concern with achieving a *balance between* emphasis on English to develop an acceptable, basic *cultural background* and English to develop *utilitarian communication skills*.

22. More concern with *English as a spoken language*.

23. More specific teaching of *communication skills that will make learning more efficient* in school and out—e.g., notetaking, study techniques for a variety of types of printed material, library science.

24. Greater concern with developing *individual creative talents*.

25. Greater endeavor to help students draw *generalizations from literature* which will be a guide for better living—less assumption that transfer from the specific to the general concept will be automatic.

26. Greater *reluctance to accept inhibiting factors on the creative powers of teachers*—such as too specific courses of study, dependence on omnibus and omnivorous texts, examinations developed by non-local agencies, and college entrance requirements.

We may say, in summation, that the goals and the reasons for offering or requiring English have kept pace with a changing world as evidenced by the enrichment of the English curriculum. However, probably greater changes have taken place in methods and teaching aids than in goals and approach, particularly in the relatively traditional situations.

These changes and trends—such as (*a*) a new flexibility in grading, grouping, and achievement standards, (*b*) individualized and remedial instruction, (c) the attempt to understand the student through his writing, (d) the development of listening skills, and (e) the use of new tools including resource people, television, and audio-visual aids—are significantly increasing the power of English teaching.

One of the most interesting innovations in the elementary-school program has been the growth of foreign language instruction. In a recent report, "enrollment figures given by Mildenberger showed Spanish leading with 222,000, then French with 47,000, and German third with 2500." [2:253] In spite of an increasing interest in a foreign language program at the elementary-school level, however, considerable disagreement exists over the relative merits of such a program. Typical of the "debates" is the one between Girard and Smith in the May, 1955, issue of the *NEA Journal.* [15:270–271] Girard favors the inclusion of foreign language in the elementary-school curriculum on such grounds as these: language study contributes to international understanding; an early start assures a better mastery of language; increasing availability of materials and a flexible time schedule in the elementary school facilitates inclusion; language can be correlated with other subjects; and many parents want it. In opposition to these claims, Smith contends that language study would only add to the already heavy load of the elementary teacher; time and money could be spent to better advantage; it is fallacious to conclude that language study promotes international peace and understanding; teachers are not prepared; and only a very small per cent of the population has any real need to use any of the languages. (NOTE: A number of articles in the April, 1955, issue of *Education* are devoted to the pros and cons of the issue.)

In analyzing the present status of foreign languages in the curriculum, Miel [33:139–148] makes the observation that the number taking foreign language in high school is decreasing while the number is increasing in the elementary school. She summarizes a number of developing practices in the elementary curriculum (a tendency to select languages already taught in high school, beginning instruction at the fourth-grade level, and use of the aural-oral approach), offers some cautions, and indicates a number of problems. She concludes with the recommendation that *"a program of comparative language study be set up as a part of general education* at the elementary school level." [33: 147]

SCIENCE AND MATHEMATICS

With the advent of sputniks and other evidences of Russian scientific progress, growing concern has been expressed over the alleged neglect of science and mathematics in the curriculum. It has been charged that the schools are no longer providing complete offerings in these subjects, that gifted students are bypassing mathematics and science for easier subjects, and that teachers are inadequately prepared to teach them.

With regard to the fear that science and mathematics are losing ground in the curriculum, a note of optimism appears in the October, 1957, issue of the *Phi Delta Kappan:* "For the first time since 1910, the percentage of students enrolled in high school mathematics and science courses is showing an increase, according to U.S. Office of Education figures." The report continues with the information that total enrollment in these courses is the highest in our history and that more and more schools are offering such courses ("Keeping Abreast in Education," page 37).

After studying the records of "the 1953 and 1956 winners in the Annual National Honor Society Program" (numbering 294 and 327 winners, respectively), Ahrendt [1:109–110] found that honor students allotted over 40 per cent of their high school work to mathematics and science and that 58 per cent of the students planned to follow scientific or technical careers.

For those who are interested in the curricular status of mathematics today, Schult has provided concise answers to a number of questions, such as the following: Are mathematics curriculums keeping pace with developments and applications in mathematics? What proportion of high school students studies mathematics? How are gifted students being identified and challenged? Is instruction being adjusted to the way pupils learn? What new media for learning are being used? How well are high schools and colleges cooperating in working out mutual problems? Are students being made aware of opportunities in mathematics?

Mathematics Today   by VERYL SCHULT

From the *NEA Journal*, January, 1957, pages 24–26. Reprinted by special permission of the *Journal*. Veryl Schult is Supervising Director, Department of Mathematics, Washington, D. C., public schools.

* * *

Much new and "modern" mathematics is being developed at a very rapid rate. New fields of research are opening, and opportunities for scientific discovery in mathematics appear to be unlimited.

Is mathematics in the schools keeping up with developments in pure mathematics and with the exciting fields of applications of mathematics —econometrics, sociology, psychology, genetics, electronic computation . . . ?

Let's look at the record.

Are Mathematics Curriculums Adjusted to Today's Needs?

Grouping on the basis of ability or preparation is rather generally accepted in mathematics, although the IQ of a student is often found to be less dependable than his GQ (Gumption Quotient).

In the 22nd yearbook of NEA's National Council of Teachers of Mathematics on *Emerging Practices in Mathematics Education,* many curriculum patterns were reported, such as the integrated mathematics program at Phillips Exeter Academy; one in Pasadena, capitalizing on the interrelationships of the many areas of mathematics; the sequential program based on developing mathematical concepts in the Florida program; and one differentiated according to needs, as in Los Angeles.

Other schools are experimenting with various curriculum patterns, such as the four-track program in

Washington, D. C., and the four-year sequences in Bethlehem, Pennsylvania, and Janesville, Wisconsin, which are offered as alternates to the college-preparatory sequences.

Many evidences of dissatisfaction with present curriculum content are being voiced, and interesting experiments in the reorganization of mathematics content are going on. For example, the University of Illinois is administering a project in selected secondary schools for the improvement of mathematics by experimenting with a mathematics curriculum in which the structure of mathematics itself and meanings and understandings are the basis of the content, and applications play a secondary role.

Many voices are being raised to de-emphasize plane geometry and stress its analytic aspect, to include some algebra in the teaching of deductive units, to de-emphasize deductive solid geometry but keep its measurement and spatial aspects, and to integrate the various branches of high school mathematics. (Textbooks to carry out such ideas are now appearing.)

Establishment of a truly modern curriculum in college-preparatory mathematics is the objective of a study now being made by the Commission on Mathematics of the College Entrance Examination Board.

Students planning to major in subjects other than mathematics in college are finding that the mathematical requirements of most fields have risen sharply in recent years. For example, social studies majors must now be prepared to understand statistics and probability, and business administration majors will have to cope with the complexities of high-speed computation machines and modern methods of data processing. Architects, foresters, farmers, pharmacists, premedical students, and radio-TV technicians and managers need mathematics in their careers.

The student who does not go to college is in a very similar situation. Much of modern industry requires that its skilled and unskilled labor be acquainted with the essentials of arithmetic, algebra, and geometry.

Are Many Pupils Studying Mathematics?

A 1956 Office of Education pamphlet reports that approximately two-thirds of high school pupils take algebra.

In the last twenty years, the actual total number of pupils taking geometry in any one year has decreased. About one-fourth of the public high schools do not offer plane geometry, but in those that do, enrollments in plane geometry are equal to one-third of the pupils in the tenth grade.

One out of ten pupils does not have an opportunity to take eleventh- or twelfth-grade mathematics because they are not offered in his school, and about one-third of the high schools do not offer trigonometry, solid geometry, and advanced algebra.

Figures were not given for courses other than the so-called college-preparatory courses except for ninth-grade general mathematics. However, the number of schools offering various types of basic, applied, or consumer mathematics courses is increasing.

Are Gifted Students Being Identified and Challenged?

Throughout the country there are many kinds of extracurriculum activities which are stimulating talented students in mathematics—contests, clubs, science-mathematics fairs —and much is also being done in the curriculum itself.

In Portland, Oregon, the high schools, with the assistance of Reed College, offer their High-School Mathematics Program for Superior Students—an outstanding experiment in enrichment and stimulation through seminars for exceptionally able students.

As an outgrowth of the School and College Study of Admission with Advanced Standing, the Advanced Placement Program of the College Entrance Examination Board is another thriving exploratory project.

Under this program, able and ambitious students in certain high schools are able to take college-level courses. If these students get satisfactory grades in these courses and in examinations, many of them may enter colleges and universities with credit and advanced placement.

Is Instruction Adjusted to What We Know About How Pupils Learn?

In 450 B.C., Sophocles said, "We must learn by doing the thing; else how will we know it unless we try?" But it took many centuries to evolve a laboratory method of learning and teaching, and other such effective methods. Mathematics is a science, and today is often taught in a laboratory setting.

There is general agreement that we really learn only what we understand —thus the present stress on concepts and meanings in most modern textbooks. For instance, in arithmetic, pupils in general do not "borrow" from another column (since the number is never paid back, it would be a lend-lose proposition) but they "change" a unit to an equivalent number of smaller units.

Junior high school pupils do not manipulate numbers to find exact square roots until they have studied the binomial theorem which puts meaning into the process.

Textbook problems are now the kind that seem important to pupils, and in some cases, as in Wichita, Kansas, and Richmond, Virginia, teachers and pupils have cooperated in finding out what kind of problems the people in their community are solving. Contrast such kinds of problems with the following from *Columbian Complete Arithmetic* of 1894: "If three men contribute equally to the purchase of a grindstone four feet in diameter, how many inches must each man grind off in order to receive his share?" Or from Graham's *Arithmetic* of 1824: "If a lion can eat up a lamb in 15 minutes, a bear in 20 minutes, and a wolf in 30 minutes, in what time will it be devoured by all three eating together?"

Are New Mediums for Learning Being Used?

Many student-made, teacher-made, and commercial materials have found a useful place in classrooms.

Films and filmstrips are enriching many classes in mathematics. Radio has been a successful teaching device, and for many years its use in Cleveland has been outstanding.

There have also been numerous television experiments in teaching mathematics.

Washington University in St. Louis taught a five-unit course in mathematics by television during the fall semester of 1956–1957. Each kinescope lecture was telecast twice daily over a commercial station and repeated on a closed campus circuit three times the following day. Students worked independently, and department assistants were available to give individual help during the day and from eight to ten in the evening.

Algebra is being taught during this school year by a combined TV-correspondence study course for six Nebraska high schools, through the Extension Division of the University of Nebraska, which also offered a high school credit course, "Arithmetic for Everyday Use," on TV last summer.

What's Happening in the Evaluation of Learning in Mathematics?

A quick look at the recent commercial mathematics tests shows that they are quite generally including concept-type questions, estimation questions, and tests on quantitative thinking which require little computation but which evaluate thinking and understanding.

Are Colleges Cooperating with High Schools in Working Out Mutual Problems?

One of the many fine examples of college and high school cooperation is that between Seattle schools and the University of Washington. The executive officer and the staff of the mathematics department at the university work with the director of mathematics and the mathematics teachers in the high schools in planning work for the superior students and in counseling high school students interested in further study of mathematics and science.

The School and College Study, in which three Eastern preparatory schools cooperated with three large universities, set a pattern for coordinating the work of grades 11, 12, 13, and 14. The success of this project has encouraged more work in this direction.

An interesting experiment under the Science Teaching Improvement Program (STIP) of the American Association for the Advancement of Science is the study on the use of science counselors. For this experiment, two experienced high school teachers, hired by the university science or mathematics department, are working with approximately one hundred science and mathematics teachers in a given area, providing in-service training and increasing the cooperation between staff members of the universities, the state departments of education, and secondary schools.

The Universities of Nebraska, Oregon, and Texas, and Pennsylvania State University are serving as the cooperating universities for the school year 1956–1957.

What Other Help Is Being Given?

In the changing secondary-school curriculum, high school teachers are being asked to teach some kinds of mathematics for which they had no preparation in college. Also, many of the new freshman college courses in mathematics require a high school preparation different from the kind that students have been receiving.

To meet the needs arising from this situation, the number of summer institutes for teachers of mathematics is growing rapidly.

Industry is spending money and time to help teachers solve their problems. Industry is financing fellowships and scholarships for teachers, institutes, conferences, workshops of all sorts, contests, and materials to bring the workaday world into the classroom.

The next yearbook of the National Council of Teachers of Mathematics, *Insights into Modern Mathematics,* available in March, 1957, will serve as another means of acquainting teachers with the background mathematics for the proposed new content in secondary and college mathematics.

Are Students Made Aware of New Opportunities in Mathematics?

* * *

The *Guidance Pamphlet in Mathematics for High School Students,* published by the National Council of Teachers of Mathematics, contains important vocational information. The Mathematical Association of America is now preparing a new edition of its *Professional Opportunities in Mathematics.* This publication evaluates some of the professional opportunities open to a young person upon completing an under-

graduate major program in mathematics.

Exciting new fields continue to open up for students trained in mathematics. For instance, it is estimated that in the next three to five years, there will be a demand for 60,000 persons with training in mathematics from a B.A. to a Ph.D. to operate electronic computing machines.

The popular Business-Industry-Education (BIE) days sponsored widely by schools and communities are bringing information to students from many scientific fields and pointing out the necessity for mathematics in a growing number of interesting careers.

One and one may usually give two, but this does not mean that all of mathematics is as static and definite as this fact. Quite the contrary. And never before has there been so much experimentation, interest, cooperation, and activity in mathematics, and such a determination to have the teaching of mathematics meet the needs of the age which it serves.

Additional observations concerning present trends in mathematics have been made by Rosskopf. [42:135–138] Because of current dissatisfaction, a two-track program has been developing: one for the non-college-bound students and the other for those needing preparation in technical mathematics. Attempts are also being made to break down the divisions between the different branches of mathematics. There seems to be general agreement on the need for "meaningful teaching of concepts rather than show-and-drill teaching." [42:138]

Despite the commendable developments in present-day mathematics programs, as pointed out by Schult and Rosskopf, and the growing prestige of the subject in the light of international developments, there is still little room for complacency on the part of mathematics teachers. The following indictment of the mathematics curriculum by Howard F. Fehr, President of the National Council of Teachers of Mathematics, is reported in the June, 1957, *Phi Delta Kappan:* "Most secondary school mathematics programs, including textbooks, are out of date. They teach nothing discovered in the past sixty years and are utterly out of step with the age of the atom and automation" ("Keeping Abreast in Education," page 382).

The Commission on Mathematics of the College Entrance Examination Board has pointed out that those who plan a mathematics curriculum must keep three points in mind:

1. We do not know exactly what careers our students will follow;
2. We do not know exactly how the mathematical needs of various occupations will develop in the years ahead;
3. Although much mathematical instruction will be directed at future usefulness, mathematics for its own sake is a valuable part of the general education of any future citizen.*

The Commission then concludes that "our mathematical curriculum must emphasize general principles, ideas, and techniques which have wide application and educational value, and that we must avoid a narrowly vocational approach."

In analyzing the present status of high school mathematics, the Commission makes this observation: "The present curriculum in high school mathematics was largely developed fifty to seventy-five years ago as a college preparatory course. The only major new idea that has entered this curriculum since that time is the development of 'General Mathematics' courses for non-college students." ** The Commission then proceeds to outline some needed changes in point of view, topics, and content. (Copies of materials, prepared by the Board, are available on request. Write to: Executive Director, Commission on Mathematics, College Entrance Examination Board 425 West 117th Street, New York 27, N.Y.)

While there has been considerable concern expressed over the static nature of mathematics programs at the high school level, modern de-

---

* College Entrance Examination Board, The Commission on Mathematics, "Objectives of the Commission on Mathematics of the College Entrance Examination Board," p. 3. (New York: College Entrance Examination Board, July 1, 1956.) (Mimeographed.)
   ** *Ibid.,* p. 4.

velopments in arithmetic curricula at the elementary school level present a brighter picture. Arithmetic programs are reflecting a changing educational philosophy, "increased knowledge of child development," and a clarification of purposes to meet the needs of a changing culture. Based upon considerable research activity,* some completed and more underway, increasing recognition is being given to meanings, rather than repetitive drill, to the readiness concept, to the importance of quantitative terms in other subjects, to the solution of problems related to the experiences of children, and to mental arithmetic. These, as well as other trends in arithmetic, are discussed in the article by Junge that follows.

The Arithmetic Curriculum — 1954 by CHARLOTTE JUNGE

From *The Arithmetic Teacher*, April, 1954, pages 1–6. Reprinted by special permission. Charlotte Junge is Professor of Elementary Education at Wayne University, Detroit.

The modern arithmetic curriculum is an outgrowth of various influences which have been operative over a period of years. Some factors have been in the picture for more than thirty years, others are of more recent origin—or are being recognized more recently as having significance. Among the more prominent of these influences are the changing philosophy of education, increased knowledge of child development, clarification of the nature of human learning, a rethinking of the purposes of instruction in arithmetic, and changes in our culture. As a result of these influences arithmetic curric-

ulums are becoming much more realistic about what children need in arithmetic and what seems appropriate and within children's capabilities at various age levels. Considerable research evidence has been accumulated on the nature of the learning process in arithmetic, the nature and the place of meanings in arithmetic, and upon the comparative value of various methods of instruction. These researches have significance for the teacher and curriculum maker, and although the research is not as complete as is to be desired, every advantage should be taken of the findings thus far in

* For example, see these three articles from *The Arithmetic Teacher:* William A. Brownell, "Meaning and Skill—Maintaining the Balance," 3:129–136 (October, 1956); John Jarolimek, "Quantitative Relationships in Social Studies," 4:70–74 (March, 1957); James Curtin, "Arithmetic in the Total School Program," 4:235–239 (December, 1957).

planning sound progress in arithmetic for children of elementary-school age.

Trends in the Organization of the Curriculum

The psychology of arithmetic, as indicated by recent research, stresses the point of view that arithmetic should not be viewed as a number of discrete, unrelated elements to be taught incidentally or through repetitive drill, but rather as a closely knit system of ideas, principles, and processes. Accordingly the real test of learning is not facility in figuring, but an intelligent grasp of number relations and the ability to apply these to quantitative situations with proper comprehension of both their mathematical and practical significance. Instruction in arithmetic aims at developing meaning and understanding and in helping the child see sense in what he does. This means teaching arithmetic with attention to the number system, for meaning in arithmetic inheres in the system itself.

The meanings in the number system are dependent, one upon the other. The simple, fundamental meanings are acquired first and the more complicated ones grow from these. The instruction of the learner must be continuously related and interrelated in larger and more significant patterns. This makes organization in the teaching of arithmetic an inescapable necessity.

Now, what does this mean for the curriculum maker in arithmetic? It means just this—that if arithmetic is to be taught with meaning and understanding as basic goals, then it must be taught with attention to the number system and to the relationships which exist within that system. This means a continuous course, a systematically organized course for even the first grade. It means that basic concepts must be thoroughly developed first so that the superstructure of facts and processes may be built upon them later.

The term "systematic instruction" should not be misunderstood. It does not mean formal or abstract. It means simple, systematic, and regular learning provided for in the schedule. Arithmetic is a subject which more than any other subject in the curriculum is organized and sequential. Accomplish what you can through incidental teaching, but never let it be supposed that in first grade or any other grade, a satisfactory course in arithmetic can be provided without being planned and systematically pursued.

Furthermore, the research in learning indicates that all learning is dependent upon previous learning and serves as a basis for future learning. Each new concept which the child meets in arithmetic is interpreted by him in terms of his previous experiences. Modern arithmetic curriculums recognize the importance of sequence in learning and are so planned that what a child learns today leads easily and naturally into what he learns tomorrow, the learnings at one grade level merge carefully with those of the next level, and basic principles continue as ever expanding threads of understanding throughout the whole of arithmetic.

It is interesting to note that present curriculums are as concerned with the sequential development of the "intangibles" in arithmetic as they are with the development of concepts and understandings. Many good programs give emphasis to the development of desirable habits and attitudes about arithmetic, to the steady development of ways of thinking about quantitative situations, to giving children progressively more mature ways of analyzing and solving problem situations. Growth in habits of neatness and accuracy of recording, of persistence in seeking solutions, in the use of initiative and the development of independence are stressed for it is recognized that such things develop as a result of planned instruction just as much as an understanding of the multiplication facts.

Arithmetic, when regarded as a system of quantitative thinking, is probably one of the most complicated subjects which children have to face in the elementary school. It is difficult because it is abstract. A great mistake was made in earlier arithmetic curriculums in rushing children too rapidly from one idea to another, in moving too rapidly from concrete situations to abstract applications. One of the basic principles which governs the construction of arithmetic curriculums today is that learning is a slow process and a relatively long time should elapse between a child's first introduction to a process and his mastery over it. Time must be allowed for meanings to develop before the children are expected to employ them in highly habituated reactions. In programs aimed at the development of understandings, *time is one of the dimensions of learning*.

In the learning of any concept or skill there are various degrees of understanding. Not all relationships can be learned at one time, and then, too, the significance of such relationships depends, in part, upon the experiences which accompany acquisition of these relationships. Curriculum builders have recognized this by spreading the learning of any one concept over a wide range of time instead of concentrating it all at one level. Consequently, skills and processes formerly taught at later levels in the elementary school are being extended over a longer period of time. For example, basic concepts which relate to multiplication and division, the ideas of equal groups, appear early in the work of first grade but no formal teaching of these concepts takes place until the third and fourth grades, and long division with two- and three-place divisors is the work of the fifth grade. The child in kindergarten and first grade is provided with many experiences which deal directly with ideas of measurement and fractions, the basic concepts are expanded in third and fourth grades, and the more difficult aspects of computation are taught in fifth and sixth grades.

This spreading of topics in arithmetic over several grades is a direct reaction to earlier programs which had a tendency to move arithmetic into the upper grades of the elementary school, thus throwing a heavy burden on both the teacher and the children of these grades. One of the main outcomes of the present emphasis on meaningful arithmetic has been this improvement in gradation of arithmetic materials and the development of programs which recognize the fact that maturation of ideas, skills, and concepts requires instructional programs so organized as to contribute to the steady development of understanding of and insight into mathematical relationships as the child advances from level to level in the school.

Closely related to this curriculum plan which spreads learning over several grades is the concept of readiness. Readiness to learn is an important consideration in all learning at all levels. The concept of readiness was formerly considered to be synonymous to mental maturity and related to grade placement. However, it is now recognized that readiness in arithmetic is a function not only of mental maturity but also of previous experiences, methods of learning, interests, attitudes, and purposes. Readiness is the concern of all teachers at all grade levels. It is not something to be waited for but something to be developed in the child by carefully planned learning experiences. Futhermore, the level at which a child may profit from opportunities to learn varies in the case of individual performances. A child is ready for different kinds of learning at different ages.

Reflection of this readiness concept is found in present-day curriculums in various ways. First of all, readiness to begin arithmetic is encouraged by providing many wide experiences with number in the kindergarten and first grade and an environment so stimulating that there will be a constant need for the use of number and quantitative ideas. Little pencil and paper work is done at this level and the emphasis in instruction is upon discussion, the use of real materials, and the solution of quantitative situations, which arise normally in the classroom, through the use of concrete and pictorial materials. These programs reflect the idea that readiness for arithmetic is built into the individual best by a process of rich, first-hand experiences, plus reflective thinking about these experiences. The quality of the concepts developed in this way, the degree to which they are understood, is dependent entirely upon the *quality* of the first-hand experiences and the quality of the thinking about those experiences.

Furthermore, present curriculums recognize that readiness is a consideration throughout all of the arithmetic in the elementary school, and to this end they provide readiness activities in connection with all new concepts in the curriculum. For example, activities which build a readiness for multiplication are incorporated in textbooks and curriculums long before the children begin to work systematically in this process. Exercises which build a background for understanding the addition of fractions, computation with decimals, and the use of formulas are woven into the curriculum long in advance of the actual work on them. Thus the children proceed smoothly from one step to the next in learning. Recently a sixth-grade boy commented to me about his teacher. "I like the way Miss S. teaches. She just doesn't throw things at you, she leads up to them gradually so they aren't hard when you get to them!" Obviously, Miss S. was a teacher who built the readiness background carefully before undertaking a new concept with the children.

Undoubtedly one of the most difficult and perplexing problems faced by curriculum makers in arithmetic is the wide range of differences among individuals in any one class. Psychology indicates that children within a class differ one from the other in mental ability, in the rates at which they learn, in interests, in the kinds of difficulties they encounter, in their responsiveness to corrective and remedial measures, as well as in their achievement. Psychologists also point out that while

children differ in their rates of progress and their accomplishments at any one time, they also show a high degree of similarity in the order in which different developments appear and are consolidated. The total picture is one of growth rather than one of unique stages and differences are a matter of degree only.

In an attempt to meet these individual differences, curriculums today include suggestions and materials to be used in challenging the gifted child in arithmetic as well as recommendations for types of re-teaching activities which may be used with the child who is achieving below the level of his classmates. In addition to this a study of curriculums and textbooks (which often constitute the curriculum in a school) reveals a tendency to keep children in any one class moving forward on an even front.

This means all the children in the group work on the same skill or process, but at different levels. One finds keyed exercises which refer children having difficulties to simpler exercises on the same topic while children who have achieved understanding carry on activities at a more advanced level. For example, in a class working on the subtraction of fractions, some children may be working with concrete materials, others may be using diagrams and recording solutions with numbers, and still others may be working at the abstract level solving problems involving this skill. All children are working on the same process, but each is proceeding at his own level of thinking.

The preceding paragraphs indicate that curriculums today recognize the importance of vertical integration in the development of understandings in arithmetic. It should be pointed out that the importance of horizontal integration is also recognized. While most educators agree that arithmetic must be taught as a separate subject, they also agree that it is most important that arithmetic be integrated with the other areas in the curriculum. Consequently, curriculums and textbooks carry many activities and suggestions of ways that arithmetic may be made to function in the social studies and science, in music and physical education, in reading and the other language arts. It is pointed out that many times the comprehension of materials in these other areas is dependent upon an understanding of quantitative terms and concepts. Upon occasion materials from the social studies or science may be used during the arithmetic period to introduce new concepts already learned, or as a source of problem material in connection with the concepts being learned. Similarly, curriculum guides suggest that teachers of the other curricular areas take time to develop the meanings of the quantitative ideas wherever they occur. Horn [1] in discussing this topic says, "The frequency and difficulty of the demands made upon arithmetic in attacking problems in other fields suggests that instruction in arithmetic can make important contributions to facilitating the work in these fields." He also states that "no one can seriously question the fact that a considerable amount of arithmetic is learned in connection with the study of problems in other areas. Indeed if the arithmetical demands in other fields are met, marked contribution from these fields is inevitable not only to the motivation for learning arithmetical abilities but also to their development and maintenance."

Trends in Content of Curriculums

The overall objective of arithmetic is to teach children to think quantitatively and to help them apply this ability in the solution of the problems of daily life. This objective has definite implications for the content in arithmetic. First of all, it indicates that arithmetic curriculums will not only stress the ability to compute but will also include an emphasis on the number system and number relationships. It also indicates that these skills and understandings will be developed best if they are presented in situations which are real in the lives of children.

A study of curriculums developed within the last five to ten years reflects these two emphases. Almost without exception arithmetic guides

[1] Horn, Ernest, "Arithmetic in the Elementary School Curriculum," The National Society for the Study of Education, *Fiftieth Yearbook*, Part II (1951), pp. 10–11.

and textbooks include content aimed at developing an understanding of the number system, the four processes with whole numbers and with fractions, and the rationale of arithmetic. Research has indicated that curriculums and methods of teaching which emphasize rational procedures appear to be the most economical route to speedy and accurate computation. The research also indicates that learning acquired in this way is more lasting and that it is more functional—children are better able to apply it in the solution of problems in new situations.

This emphasis upon the development of meaning and insight is as much a part of the curriculum of grades one and two as it is of the upper grades. Or, perhaps, it should be stated the other way around! When the meaning theory of teaching first made its appearance in the literature, there was a tendency to develop understandings of the simple, basic processes with children, but to resort to "telling" when teaching the more complicated skills. This latter situation seldom exists at the present time. Meanings are consistently taught from grades one through six in the elementary school with no break at upper grade levels.

Educators, in preparing curriculum materials for the elementary grades, draw heavily upon a knowledge of the life and needs of children in these grades and upon the extensive research concerning children's interests and activities. They try to insure that the content will be genuine and lifelike and that the children using the curriculum materials will come to see arithmetic as a very normal part of their everyday life. The problem of content in today's arithmetic classes relates to the type of situations familiar to children at that age level—to the games they play, to allowances and to saving, to buying and selling, to travel and to sports. Children are helped to solve arithmetic situations which arise in their home and school life and to collect and discuss current materials which show the application of arithmetic in the world today.

In addition to this many books and curriculums include items designed to help children learn something of the history of arithmetic, of the number system, of weights and measures. It is important that children see that arithmetic is not only a science, but also a cultural subject with a long history, and understand something of the contributions made by great civilizations to our present-day arithmetic. This attention to the historical aspects of arithmetic is commonly found in curriculums in third grade and above.

Closely related to this is the inclusion in some curriculums of appreciation units which not only provide activities which will help children see the important role of arithmetic in society, in sciences, and in industry, but which also include number games, puzzles, number tricks, and magic squares. It is plain to be seen that arithmetic is becoming a much broader and more interesting subject than it was formerly.

There are two areas of arithmetic content which have been brought more sharply into focus in the most recent school programs, and which are important enough in the total program to deserve special mention. First of all, greater attention is being given in all grades to development of abilities in problem-solving. Verbal problems are included as a part of the work at all grade levels—even the first—and effective problem-solving helps are systematically provided. These problem-solving activities aim at helping the child understand and see the relationships between what he wants to find out and the known facts. They seek to help the child develop his own way of solving problems and to leave him with a method of attack on quantitative situations. Consequently, modern programs in arithmetic encourage the use of problems to introduce new concepts, for practice on concepts which have been developed, and for evaluation and testing of concepts learned. Problem-solving is assuming a role of major importance in programs based on the development of meanings.

The second area of content receiving special attention at the present time is that of mental arithmetic. In all grades, from grade one on, attention is given to oral arithmetic, to mental computation, to the develop-ment of the ability to estimate, to round numbers, to judge the reasonableness of answers, and to use standard reference units in interpreting quantitative statements. Research indicates that most computations in daily life are done without pencil and paper and that if children are to use arithmetic effectively in their daily life then they must learn to compute mentally. Many programs include a well organized program in estimating, judging the reasonableness of answers, and oral arithmetic. Indications are that consistent attention to these skills develops a keen number sense, a healthy self-reliance, and the power to think with numbers.

Summary

In this discussion an attempt has been made to discuss some of the more significant trends in the organization and content of arithmetic curriculums today, and to show the relationship of these trends to research in education and psychology. The research in these areas must form the basis for any significant reform in curriculum and instruction in arithmetic. We are long past the time in educational method when rule of thumb and uncontrolled speculation are adequate for improving the learning process. Fundamental advances in the quality of instruction at any level in any school will depend upon the careful translation of the results of research into specific working ideas for method and curriculum.

In analyzing the mathematics required for high school graduation, Layton [24:315-319] concludes that, compared with English and social studies, mathematics and science occupy a less favorable position. Without doubt recent world events, focusing attention on the highly technical skills needed in the competition for outer space, will have a favorable effect where the mathematics program and mathematics requirements are concerned.

Occupying a dominant position in the world today is *science*. There are at least two apparent reasons for this: science affects every aspect of everyday living, and science is vital to military survival. Currently, the demand for a scientific emphasis in the curriculum for survival purposes at times reaches almost phobic proportions. As a result, two polarities of opinion concerning the place of science in the curriculum soon become obvious. One group decries an educational emphasis that might produce scientific robots devoid of general culture and value judgments; the opposing group warns that a neglect of science in the curriculum could lead to our annihilation by a superior, scientifically trained enemy. While these philosophical cross currents eddy back and forth, the schools continue to teach science with more or less discernible trends that have been described by Hurd. Basing his conclusions on an analysis of more than eighteen hundred articles, research studies, and the like, covering the past fifty years, he has summarized general trends in such categories as the following: objectives, psychology of learning, criteria for selection of content, laboratory and classroom methods, teaching materials, types of courses, and evaluation procedures. (The reader should also consult Mallinson and Buck's review of research in science, on pages 212-220 of this book.)

Mid-century Trends in Science Teaching   by PAUL DEH. HURD

From the *California Journal of Secondary Education,* May, 1953, pages 244-250. Reprinted by special permission. Paul DeH. Hurd is Associate Professor of Education, Stanford University.

Within the past half century of secondary-school science teaching many changes in philosophy and curriculum have occurred. Some of the developments turned out to be only "fads" or bursts of enthusiasm. Other developments more deeply rooted in clear-cut philosophical beliefs and backed by acceptable psychological concepts persisted. Over a period of years these "new" ideas become evident in the thinking and practices of teachers and a trend is established.

Statements of trends in education must always be made with certain reservations. A consideration of some of these factors is essential to a proper interpretation of trends. First of all, trends are apparent not only in time but also in the extent to which they exist in classroom practices. Whatever is a "trend" today has usually been a part of the educational literature for many years. "Traditional" practices always exist side by side with "newer" practices.

Definite trends are often difficult to describe as there is a tendency on the part of educators to verbalize newer procedures more than they actually exist in classroom practice. Almost every innovation in education is supported by many who state "this is what I have always done."

At other times trends are difficult to recognize owing to a tendency in education to attach new labels to older concepts or practices. At one time science teachers placed great stress upon the "scientific method," later upon "scientific thinking"; some questioned the use of the term "scientific" which then became "critical thinking"; today it is more likely to be in the plural—"scientific methods," or just plain "problem solving." The creator of each new term is certain that he is referring to something different from previous writers. Very often he is, even when he uses identical terms. The preponderance of literature on a topic and the sequence of events leading up to the development of a new concept have also to be considered in the determination of an actual trend.

Several other factors must also be taken into consideration when predicting educational trends. As an idea or practice approaches a point of general acceptance there is a tendency for fewer articles to appear in the literature concerning the idea or practice. For example, between 1900 and 1910 there were many more articles upon the importance of teaching science principles than there have been in any decade since then. However, in practice more courses are organized around science principles today than at any time in the past. In contrast, research studies upon phases of science teaching begin to reach a peak *after* the practice has become generally accepted. The largest number of research studies upon the particular learning values to be derived from laboratory work were in the period from 1930 to 1940; the philosophical discussions were most prominent at the turn of the century. Briefly, the greatest volume of opinionated literature precedes new educational practice; research upon the issue follows the practice.

From an analysis and synthesis of over eighteen hundred articles, research studies, committee reports, and yearbooks covering a fifty-year period, certain trends seem to be evident in science teaching.

These trends have been classified

into a number of broad categories in order to bring related ideas together. Some overlapping of ideas will be noted from one category to another. In a broad sense the degree of overlapping gives some indication of the strength of a developing trend. For the most part, in this article, the trends are presented without comment unless a statement is required to clarify or to give a more specific interpretation of the idea. Whether a statement represents a status, trend, or prediction is partly dependent upon one's evaluation and interpretation of his own experience. It would be more accurate to interpret the statements of "trends" as avenues along which science teaching is presently developing rather than as any specifically immediate or remote goals.

Trends in the Point of View of Science Teaching

Science should be regarded more as a "way of life" or a "philosophy of living" than as exclusively subject material and method. Science teaching should be directed toward human betterment not only materially but culturally as well. Current social and economic problems are a proper concern of science teachers. Cultural trends must also be immediately reflected in the nature and content of the science course. Science should be studied in terms of its implications for contemporary society and its role in human affairs. The development of a recognition and understanding of the interaction of science and hu-

man experience is an important purpose of science teaching.

Every effort must be made to introduce systematically the concepts and ideas of science which are essential to human adjustment. An understanding of science, its purposes, principles, concepts, and methods, is an essential part of the general education of *all* students. Those who plan to specialize in science need to acquire a thorough background in the methodology and the broader cultural and philosophical aspects of science.

With varying degrees of emphasis these points of view provide the guidelines for science teaching from the first grade through at least the second year of college.

Trends in the Objectives of Science Teaching

The objectives of science teaching grow out of one's point of view on the general nature of science teaching. Today's objectives are not so much new as they are a change in emphasis. A primary purpose of science teaching is to provide the type of experiences which will help students solve the personal-social problems encountered in contemporary living. Human adjustment is the major goal of science teaching.

There is a growing emphasis upon various problem-solving techniques useful in everyday living and a decreased emphasis upon the scientific method *per se*. The so-called scientific method is in reality an experimental laboratory procedure best suited to problems that can be solved by an exactness of measurement. This method is regarded as not highly suited to most human problems. However, such problem-solving procedures as a recognition of reliable sources of data, how to interpret data, and many other techniques are needed by and valuable to students in a wide range of problematical situations. Of equal value to the student is the acquisition of scientific attitudes or critical habits of thought.

College preparation as an objective of high school science teaching is slowly dying out. The data obtained from many research studies have failed to substantiate the point of view that high school science improves a student's ability to do college science.

Changes in our mode of living point toward a type of science teaching which will enrich the leisure hours of students. In this regard many teachers believe that the stress should be on creative activities rather than on the more passive leisure activities. The development of an appreciation of science and the achievements of scientists are objectives of increasing importance in science teaching.

Trends in the Psychology of Learning

There is a growing recognition that the learning situations in science courses should be as much like those of everyday life as possible. Students learn how to solve their problems involving science concepts only through dealing with realistic everyday problems. The effectiveness of learning is indicated by the student's ability to use his learning in the solution of personal-social problems. Retention is best insured when the student is able to organize his knowledge into concepts, principles, or generalizations. Attitudes and appreciations are more likely to be achieved if they are "taught for" directly; they are not necessarily concomitant with the "taking" of science courses.

If a student is not able to utilize his accumulated knowledge in science either to solve his present problems or to furnish hypotheses to guide his attack on future problems he has essentially not learned.

Trends in the Criteria for the Selection of Science Content

Many teachers are of the opinion that much of the content in science courses is there simply because of tradition. Teachers and authors of textbooks frequently include topics for no other reason than that they are afraid they will be accused of leaving them out. Better criteria are being demanded for the selection of content.

The selection of content must always be a major problem in science teaching due to the continually expanding frontiers of science and the wealth of knowledge. There will always be the question of what in the total accumulated knowledge of science is of the greatest value to teach. The present educational concept is that areas of greatest human concern and which involve the betterment of man's existence and adjustment should provide the primary basis for the selection of content. The current literature in science education indicates that the following problems should receive greater attention in secondary-school science teaching.

1. Conservation
2. Racial understanding
3. World peace
4. Mental health
5. Human betterment
6. Consumer problems
7. Leisure and recreation
8. Atomic energy and its utilization

Some of these areas are not particularly new concerns of science teachers, but they are now being approached with a vigor not typical of the last ten to fifteen years.

Of equal importance is the concept that the selection of content for science courses should be tailored to the student and to the community in which the course is taught. Most of the specific material in science courses should be included for its significance in the everyday lives of students taking the course. Students should, therefore, have a part in the selection of the content. A "standard" content for each science course in the secondary school is neither educationally tenable nor desirable.

Trends in the Organization of Science Content

There is a tendency to organize the content of science courses around broad areas of human concern or around problems, such as conservation or the maintenance of physical and mental health. Less emphasis is being given to a direct organization around the major principles of science, the most common form of organization during the past twenty years. Principles grow out of a study of science concepts, they are not the direct object of study. Teaching units are best organized around personal-social types of problems rather than around classified subject matter.

In order to deal adequately with a curriculum organization of this type science courses are becoming broader in nature. General biology has become more general than formerly in terms of drawing its content from more biological areas. Physics and chemistry are being combined with many other sciences such as geology, meteorology, and astronomy to form courses in physical science.

There is a trend toward the integration of a wide range of science fields. Within the next few years one may expect high schools to teach Science I, II, III, and IV, rather than general science, biology, physics, and chemistry.

Trends in Laboratory Methods

There is a growing dissatisfaction with the results achieved from laboratory work in science. The performance of "experiments" has been found to be practically sterile of acceptable educational values. Student duplication, "cookbook" fashion, of experiments in which the answer is known beforehand is difficult to justify in modern education. The rigid following of a certain number of steps with the specified procedures required in high school science laboratories is actually unique. It is not typical of either the way scientists work or the way the average citizen solves his everyday problems. Many science teachers have been slow to recognize this condition.

Recently there has developed a trend toward a type of laboratory teaching which, for the lack of a better name, may be called a laboratory exercise. In these exercises students work out and learn many basic techniques of research, such as how to recognize variables, how to use equipment, how to devise alternative procedures for obtaining data, how to obtain data through controlled experiments, how to recognize common sources of errors, how to do rotation experiments, how to recognize the adequacy of data, and many other experimental techniques and skills. After a series of preliminary exercises the student works on a comparatively few experiments during the rest of the year. In these experiments the emphasis is placed upon having the student design his own procedures for the purpose of gathering data on a problem of some significance. The test of a student's growth in laboratory work is to be found in the fertility of his suggestions for designing experiments to gather pertinent and accurate data on a problem. Quantitative results, while important, are not the final measure of laboratory skill.

More and more we can look to "laboratory experiments" to be in the nature of junior research where the premium is upon the skill and the creativeness used in solving an actual problem. Many feel that the best way to enlist young people into scientific vocations is to let students experience the excitement and satisfaction that come with real discovery.

Cooperative planning of laboratory procedures by several students should be encouraged. This is the way scientists work on research problems today.

The most immediate step being used by many teachers for the improvement of laboratory work is the use of an increased number of controlled experiments in the course.

Trends in Classroom Methods

Trends in classroom and in laboratory methods are not sharply distinguishable. Good methods are always directed toward the achievement of the objectives of science teaching. There is a tendency to use more activities of a research type in science classes. Most of the work in and out of class is concerned with the gathering, organization, and reporting of data in terms of a specific problem. Inductive methods of teaching are the most widely used. Science educators agree that there is no *one* best method for all science teaching.

Students today use a variety of textbooks plus a great deal of commercial pamphlet material and government bulletins. Room libraries containing a wide selection of books and magazines are in accord with the research type of teaching activities.

Assignments are typically on a long-term basis of two or three weeks. During this time students are involved in the various phases of problem solving. Class activities are as varied as required to solve the problems.

Audio-visual aids are widely used but a greater emphasis is being given to direct experiences. It is the student who develops the bulletin board, museum exhibit, or working model, or who gives the demonstration, that potentially learns the most. The student who watches may or may not increase his learning or insight.

Group procedures and cooperation in learning activities are being increasingly used. Many teachers are convinced that a student's total learning is enhanced by sharing and working with other students toward common ends.

Trends in Textbooks and Reference Materials

Science textbooks are beginning to reflect many of the newer trends in science education. General science, biology, and physical science textbooks typically reflect more of the recent trends than do chemistry textbooks. Physics textbooks have maintained the same general organization for the past fifty years. Otherwise, secondary-school science textbooks have grown from classical outlines of subject matter to volumes of cyclopedic

proportions. To the authors this means a more flexible textbook adaptable to many types of teaching situations; to many teachers it represents a hopeless number of pages to be covered. However, few authors have deleted any of the traditional content of their field; the growth has been primarily by the addition of new material.

A majority of texts are now organized in part or whole around broad principles or generalizations of science. A smaller number are organized around significant problems directly related to man's experience.

The modern textbooks contain suggestions to students for further reading on a variety of maturity levels; suggestions and descriptions of related problems or projects; experiments, exercises, questions, and many visual materials all designed to increase the effectiveness of learning. The better of the modern textbooks are deliberately structured to aid in the achievement of many of the objectives of science teaching. Exercises in the use of methods of science and applications of the scientific attitudes are distributed throughout the text.

A wider use is being made of current science materials to augment the textbook. The most significant trend has been in the use of a wide range of free and inexpensive pamphlets, brochures, demonstration kits, and filmstrips distributed by industrial concerns. On the whole this material is educationally superior to that of a decade ago.

The workbook has replaced the laboratory manual in a majority of instances. Its effectiveness as a device for improving the learning of science concepts has not yet been clearly established. Its convenience in teaching is attested by its widespread use; in some states over 90 per cent of the science teachers use commercially written workbooks.

The "junior" museum, science fairs, nature trails, and nature camps are receiving considerable attention as motivating and teaching devices in science. Field trips, due to the many management problems, have declined in use.

Trends in New Types of Science Courses

The most conspicuous trend in the teaching of secondary-school science is to be found in regard to physics and chemistry. Both of these subjects have experienced a sharp decrease in enrollment over the past fifty years and the decline is continuing. A recent national survey revealed that only 47.8 per cent of the high schools in the United States continue to teach physics.[1] Emerging to replace these courses is a new type of course in which an attempt is made to integrate the various principles found in the many physical sciences. However, no generally accepted

name has yet appeared for this new type of course. A survey of the literature reveals the following titles:

Generalized Science
Consumer Science
Senior Science
Applied Science
Basic Science
Practical Science
Industrial Science
Girls' Science
Popular Science
Physical Science
World Science
Advanced Physical Science
Applied Physics
Advanced General Science
General Physics
Descriptive Physics
Advanced Science
Vocational Science

Without exception these courses are described as better suited to the needs of all the students, and at the same time they represent an integration superior to the traditional physics and chemistry.

Photography as a separate science course has developed rapidly within the last decade; in many schools the enrollment exceeds that of physics. Other non-vocational physical science courses found in many schools are electronics, radio, aeronautics, aviation physics, and electricity. Within the next decade one may expect that the significant material within these courses will be incorporated into a "physical science" course and the remaining content delegated to club ac-

[1] Philip O. Johnson, "The Teaching of Science in Public High Schools," *Bulletin 1950, No. 9* (Washington, D. C.: Federal Security Agency, 1950), p. 5.

tivities. It seems apparent that many science educators and school administrators are hesitant to continue the more specialized courses in science at the secondary level. Many of these courses served their purpose as part of the war effort.

Biology now leads all sciences in the percentage of high school students enrolled in science. Some schools are offering an elementary biology in the ninth or tenth grades and advanced biology in the tenth or eleventh grades. Generally in these cases the physiology, hygiene, and first-aid courses are absorbed by the biology course.

Conservation as a distinct course is offered in some of the smaller high schools. About 10 per cent of the high schools offer some other type of biology than the usual course, such as botany, zoology, laboratory techniques, genetics, personal science, and consumer problems in life science. These courses are more typically found in larger high schools. Again the trend is to reduce the number of specialized courses.

Twenty-five years from now one may expect to find a general biology sequence in the ninth and tenth grades and a physical science sequence for the eleventh and twelfth grades and both required of all students. At the present time there is only sporadic support for a two-track system in science teaching, particularly if the division is to consist of general education and specialized courses. There is a trend to include more science materials in a wide range of shop, industrial, or vocational courses.

Trends in Evaluation

It is generally accepted that tests in science should give some indication of the growth of students in the attainment of *all* the objectives of science teaching. Most classroom and standardized tests in current use measure achievement in only a few objectives, usually knowledge acquired, vocabulary, some application of principles, and ability to solve mathematical problems involving science materials.

Newer instruments of evaluation are being developed to give indications of the students' "power" in (a) the use of critical methods of thinking in attacking both science and everyday problems of living; (b) the ability to apply the "scientific attitudes" to problems where these attitudes are applicable; (c) the application of science concepts and principles to novel situations. When the "ideal" test in a science course is developed nearly every item and situation on the test will be completely new to the student. The test will be designed almost wholly for the purpose of determining the student's "power" to utilize his science learning in attacking personal-social problems.

Summation

Within the next few years it may be expected that a large number of major changes will be made in the high school science curriculum. The curriculum of the last decade was geared to a wartime situation. A new type of curriculum that is better adapted to the conservation of human resources is indicated. This curriculum should be structured to increase man's adjustment to his physical and biological world and ultimately lead to human betterment. It seems desirable that the entire program of science teaching should be re-examined before the tremendous impact of increased enrollments now in the elementary school reaches the secondary level.

NOTE: Is it possible that the race for space supremacy that has developed since the appearance of Hurd's article may once more retard the use of science for human betterment? The chain of events that can take place within a period of only four or five years serves to illustrate the kaleidoscopic nature of the world in which we live.

Recent pronouncements concerning the role of science in the public schools have been colored by the Russian threat to national security. Morris Meister, principal of the Bronx High School of Science, attempts to cut through the confusion of issues by pointing out that there are identifiable characteristics which have always manifested themselves in the potential scientist. He offers three suggestions for school practice: (*a*) the promotion of better utilization of present staffs of science teachers, (*b*) attention to the problem of increasing the supply of qualified science teachers, (*c*) increased motivation of students through direct contact with science-related institutions and resources. He concludes with the thought that although the quest for more scientists must begin with the schools, "it would be a tragic error to assume that the school alone is responsible for the present poor yield." The reasons for our present scientist shortage are instead deeply imbedded in our culture.*

In making a study of science courses designed for purposes of general education, from a nationwide sampling of 800 high schools covering grades 9–12, inclusive, Flannigan [14:62–63] reached a number of conclusions. General education science courses, usually for the junior and senior years, are increasing. Although few schools allow such courses to be counted toward a science major or to fulfill graduation requirements in science, more than six out of ten such courses "are ac-

* From American Council on Education, *Vital Issues in Education,* edited by Arthur E. Traxler, pp. 26–33 (Washington, D.C., 1957).

cepted by colleges for entrance credit." Most of the courses are not designed for slow learners.

What is the status of science in the elementary school? "Science has long been a stepchild in the elementary school" is a generalization appearing in a recent issue of the *Review of Educational Research.* [2:252] (A more optimistic note concerning the status of science education in the elementary school appears in the report by Mallinson and Buck, pages 212–220 of this book.) Another publication states that the role of science has, over the years, assumed a *more* important place in the elementary-school curriculum. A summary of the developments in this area has been published by the Association for Supervision and Curriculum Development (Maxine Dunfee and Julian Grunlee, *Elementary School Science: Research, Theory and Practice,* Washington, D.C., 1957).

FINE AND PRACTICAL ARTS

In each of the large subject-matter areas, the trends noted in a given state or geographical area may or may not be indicative of gradual changes taking place all over the country. However, one area often can be singled out because it has been especially forward-looking in developing curriculum trends.

In an editorial introducing a "Symposium on Creative Arts and Crafts in Secondary Education" Bush points out that arts are no longer considered fads and frills and that the cleavage between the *fine* and *practical* arts is disappearing.

Editorial: The Arts and Secondary Education — A Creative Potential   by ROBERT N. BUSH

From the *California Journal of Secondary Education,* April, 1953, pages 182–183. Reprinted by special permission. Robert N. Bush is editor of the *Journal* and Professor of Education, Stanford University.

The arts are rapidly coming into their own in modern education. Fewer and fewer persons cry out against them as fads and frills, and recognized leaders in increasing numbers stanchly support them when they are attacked. The main reason for the prominent place being assumed by the arts in education is the stronger position that they now occupy in community, business, and industrial life. This is but another example of the reflection of a change in community life that laggardly makes its way into school practice.

For centuries, "art" was divorced from the everyday practical life of the people. Much bitter truth is lodged in the stereotype of a queer Bohemian character on the verge of starvation producing his works for the contemplation and amusement of the wealthy, powerful classes. The so-called *fine* arts and the *practical* arts remained unnaturally apart for a long period of time. Not until about the turn of the present century did business and industry begin to realize the need for the creative talents of the artist in the fashioning and marketing of their products. We cannot detail here the many influences that united to bring about a marriage of form and function in modern industrial production, but we see everywhere about us the result of a tremendous creative upsurge that has revolutionized the houses in which we live, the automobiles and airplanes in which we ride, the clothes we wear, and the household furnishings we use. Few aspects of modern life have escaped the influence of the twentieth-century artists. They have made a profound impact upon contemporary living, and the end is not yet in sight. As the physical frontier has closed in they have opened new nonmaterialistic vistas. Now widely recognized is the contribution of the creative arts and crafts to the integra-

tion and enrichment of the human personality, a central objective of education in our democracy.

The question that now confronts the secondary schools is no longer whether or not the arts should be included as a basic part of the general education of all youth in school, for that has already been decided in the larger cultural context. What remains is the working out of the details by means of which this shall be accomplished. It should not be assumed that this is unimportant, for as with many affairs of life, it is in the execution of the detail that the main goal is either obscured or brought sharply into focus. In a democracy especially the ends tend to intertwine and bury themselves in the means.

The symposium this month covers the field from junior high school through adult education. It is interesting to note at each level an insistent demand for expanded activities that outruns either the facilities or the available teaching personnel. The senior high school faces special difficulties in fitting this important field into what appears to many to be an already overcrowded curriculum. The colleges and universities in their admission and graduation requirements are only tardily recognizing the academic respectability of the arts and still must be counted as a deterring force in the expansion of creative activities in the secondary schools. Nevertheless, each decade records an increasingly larger number and percentage of pupils in secondary schools who are enrolled in regular courses in arts and crafts.

One of the delightful features of the program of arts and crafts is the life given to the entire school program by the teachers and the pupils directly engaged in it. The "creative" approach, act, or urge, by whatever name it is called, is not confined to or indeed always found in art classes. A sterile, pedantic, and routine approach to learning may be found in art classes as well as in other subject fields. But there is often in the art subjects and among the art teachers an abundance of original, unorthodox, and spontaneous energy that attracts and motivates pupils beyond the ordinary routine and causes them to see relationships with and applications to other phases of their school activities and to living outside of the school.

One of the telling criticisms of schooling is its preoccupation with training the intellect to the neglect of the emotions, which are in these days so desperately in need of education and of discipline. The deep personal and social troubles of the twentieth century, the social scientists agree, lie in faulty human relationships, which spring in large part from aggressive, hostile feelings which human beings express toward one another. In this area of understanding, controlling, and educating the emotions lies one of the most pressing and challenging frontiers of education.

The artists are old hands at dealing with the emotions, for these are the raw products of their trade. Through such mediums as painting, carving, ceramics, metalwork, the pupils command many languages to express their feelings as well as their ideas — and in the process of ordering their materials they order and discipline their emotions. This constructive educational end cannot be accomplished as well in any other fashion, certainly not alone through verbal experiences.

Thus it is that in the arts we have added a powerful new educational tool that may enable us to see the essential unity of human experience and help us to integrate in our thinking and action the emotional, intellectual, social, and physical aspects of life.

Because he gives an over-all picture of "fourteen years of public school art" and indicates the influence of art in adult education, as well as in business and industry, Wedemeyer's "introduction" to the April, 1953, *California Journal of Secondary Education* is also included here. (In the Symposium, which he introduces, are included such articles as the following: Lucille Brown Greene, "Creative Art Teaching and the Gifted High School Student," pages 197–202; George N. Sorenson, "Fine Art Appreciation Through Art in Industry," pages 210–213; and Edward A. Adams, "Art Education and Industry," pages 225–228. It has been pointed out by a number of writers that art is achieving more prestige in public education because of the place it now has in business and industry.)

Symposium on Creative Arts and Crafts in Secondary Education — Introduction by ARCHIE WEDEMEYER

From the *California Journal of Secondary Education,* April, 1953, pages 184–185. Reprinted by special permission. Archie Wedemeyer is Director of Art Education, San Francisco Unified School District.

Contributions to this Symposium on Creative Arts and Crafts in Secondary Education are selected from widely distributed geographic locations in California.

The topics are based on the experiences of sincere and enthusiastic teachers who have distinguished themselves in unique, yet typical, situations in our system of secondary education.

Through fourteen years of public school art, into special programs for adults and professional training for artisans, we follow a strong thread of conviction—to develop each student in the greatest satisfaction of his abilities, to stimulate those inherent creative powers each possesses toward intelligent and wise application. The patterns are variable according to the nature of the community and the objective of the learner. What has happened in Elementary Art in recent years influences somewhat today's action in Secondary Art.

From kindergarten through the sixth grade we have universally accepted growth and development as a factor more important in the art education of the young child than his painting or piece of clay. We have learned that the art experience can be used as a measure of progress, often more revealing than other objective growth evidence. The arts and crafts, because they encourage creativity and provide opportunities both personal and social, are an established part of the total elementary program. With the advent of accepting a child's art at his own level, there has been introduced a variety of materials and processes to provide for differences in the rates of learning and physical, mental, and emotional growth. Enrichment of the elementary art program and better understanding of how children learn are helping each boy and each girl in some satisfying personal expression. A desire for further art experience is being created.

In the junior high school the emphasis has moved from mastery of skills in drawing and painting to exploratory experience with many media. Experimentation with material that may be immediately applied to individual and group interests is stressed. A wide but well-guided range of energy-consuming processes so badly needed by the early adolescent is provided. Reality, close to the pupil's personal interests, becomes the substance of the activity.

In the senior high school, most students have elected preparation for future success upon what parents and counselors say they have the most aptitude for and upon what they already know about themselves. Competition for recognition becomes quite keen in all subject areas and at all levels of intelligence. Courses in arts and crafts are purely elective and fashioned for the two extremes—the student who is failing in "academics" and the student who is outstanding in art. In between are those courses offered to students who can find time to experience art for pure enjoyment. Often these three come together under the guidance of a superbly qualified art teacher. In whatever way the teacher has solved the problem of administering to these extremes, the processes continue on an original exploratory basis. Increasingly, technical skills and attitudes of appreciation are developed in accordance with individual differences and individual abilities.

Tremendous enrollments in adult art classes make us aware of values received in terms of satisfaction for our adult citizens. We carefully plan and provide these art classes because somewhere in the past we crowded out art opportunities by an inflexible system of programming for higher education.

Specialization above the twelfth year, in city college, state college, and professional art school, is attendant upon requirements of degree and demands of business and industry. The need for expert knowledge, special skills, and keen judgment in any phase of production is essential. We have a real concern about the quality of training and the type of student being trained for future placement in art education and in art production. From these special training programs come our principal brains, ability, and imagination. Out of these special training programs must come creative individuals with habits which will promote successful working and living relationships.

Real problems in American enterprise are neither scientific nor technical, rather are they related to the characteristics which human individuals possess. We have been most insistent in recent years that special art training incorporate those liberal art studies which help to widen the horizons of the specialist. . . .

In another editorial in a later issue of the *Journal,* introducing "A Symposium on Changing Conceptions in the Practical Arts," Bush [8:122] declares that practical arts have achieved increasing importance in the curriculum in response to the will of the people. He looks forward to the time when the fine line between "education for culture and education for work" will disappear. (In the same issue of the *Journal,* Matilla gives a very good history of development of the practical arts, pages 146–154. The entire February, 1955, issue of *Education,* placing considerable emphasis on *creativity,* is devoted to the subject of "Fine and Industrial Arts in the Elementary School." An earlier issue, September, 1953, deals with another of the arts, music.)

MORAL AND SPIRITUAL EDUCATION

Charges that the public schools are "godless" and evidence of moral deterioration in American society have given curriculum workers during the last decade much concern over the teaching of "moral and spiritual values." This concern is reflected by the rise in the publication of curriculum guides in this area in recent years, as reported by Merritt and Harap (see page 327 of this book, item 15). The problem is specifically related to the place of religion in the development of moral and spiritual values. Either to teach religion or to ignore the contributions of religion to our cultural heritage is untenable. The specific problem, then, becomes one of giving proper emphasis to religion in the development of moral and spiritual values in the school without disregarding a diversity of religious beliefs or infringing upon the religious rights of home and church or synagogue. Sister Janet has summarized the situation very well.

What Are We Doing About Spiritual Values and Character Education for Present-day Youth?

by SISTER MARY JANET, S.C.

From *The Bulletin of the National Association of Secondary-School Principals,* Vol. 40, No. 219 (April, 1956), pages 252–254. Reprinted by special permission. Sister Mary Janet, S.C., is Secondary-School Curriculum Consultant for the Commission on American Citizenship of the Catholic University of America, Washington, D. C.

Broadly defined, spiritual values are concerned with immaterial, unworldly, sacred things—the higher values of life. Included are the ideals and principles which are basic to American democratic society and, therefore, of primary importance in character education. In an era dominated by materialism, it is well to examine our status in relation to spiritual values. For simplicity, this brief summary outlines what we are doing to develop spiritual values (*a*) about things, (*b*) about persons, and (*c*) about God and religion.

First then, there are many learning experiences in schools which directly or indirectly influence the attitudes and habits of youth toward things— toward our country and its institutions, toward nature, toward property. Indeed a strong justification for universal education is its power to promote understanding of American democracy and to strengthen and perpetuate it. Through books and personal contact with its institutions, students learn to love their country's ideals and its bounty, to know and respect its incomparable documents of liberty, and to accept personal responsibility for its welfare.

They learn to respect and care for property, public and private, to be kind to animals, and to conserve the resources of the earth. They are led to appreciate beauty in literature, art, music, architecture, and nature, both through studying about them and through direct experiences which lead gradually to higher levels of taste and enjoyment.

Equally numerous are activities related to persons, for the development of human relationships that befit a democratic society is the constant concern of schools. This nation was conceived in recognition of the inherent dignity of the human person, a profoundly spiritual concept based on the common brotherhood of men under the Fatherhood of God. History shows it operating in the lives of great patriots of past and present. Projects in intercultural education have developed understanding and respect for all races, nationalities, occupations, and classes. The comprehensive high school in particular recognizes the dignity of youth of differing capacities and backgrounds and, in practice, teaches their mutual interdependence.

Youth are encouraged to accept responsibility for the common good by sharing in school administration and planning, and by cooperating with community projects such as charitable drives and safety campaigns. Completely guided, they choose and prepare for occupations consistent with their ability to serve the common good. Their natural idealism is satisfied by emphasis on the service concept which should prevail in the professions, in business, and in industry. All such experiences and many others are commonplace in the curriculum of the American high school.

My third point leads to a controversial but highly important matter. No one will deny that man's expression of dependence on his Creator represents the highest kind of spiritual value. In the church-related school, of course, fundamental religious truth is taught as such and is the foundation for character building. There is no controversy here. However, religious educators are constantly aware of pupils and graduates who do not live up to their religious beliefs, and today there is serious effort to devise curriculums which may relate religion more effectively to life. This is a large task!

But the task of the public school is even greater. There religion cannot be taught in general to all pupils because of diversity of beliefs. Neither can it be ignored if the school is to fulfill its function of promoting the democratic ideal. For America's ideals are rooted in belief in God and the unalienable personal rights which flow from the Creator. This concept constantly influences the conduct of our government, both national and state. Our coins proclaim to the world our trust in God. Chaplains are indispensable in the armed forces. Our presidents have continually relied on divine help and guidance; legislative sessions open with prayer. The Ten Commandments decorate the doors of the Supreme Court building; and, during sessions as the Justices enter, the Court Crier calls: ". . . God save the United States and this honorable court." God's place in our government is prominent and secure.

Neither are God and religion ignored in the public schools. There is considerable variation throughout the country, but I have witnessed activities regularly carried on in particular school systems: reading from the Bible without comment; grace before meals; religious songs; school assemblies opened with prayer, enriched by hymns, addressed by priest or minister; referral of pupils to clergymen for guidance; religious instruction on released time. This list is only a sampling.

Yet I believe more needs to be done. For it is a disturbing fact that none of these practices passes unchallenged, and some of them have made sensational court cases. In other words, there is no universal acceptance of God's place in the public school, and there is understandable insecurity among teachers and administrators. The Religious Education Association and the National Council of Churches of Christ are two organizations attempting to clarify the issue. Many cities and states also are carrying on various types of programs.

I cannot hope in a few words to resolve the conflicts. Yet I should like to present briefly a point of view—one that is theistic, but not sectarian. For there is a wide difference between the presentation of sectarian religion and the recognition of responsibility to God for our actions. Remember we are talking about the public schools of the United States of America, a country founded and continuously developed on a belief in man's complete dependence on God. Today it is this foundation which distinguishes us most sharply from the totalitarian state which recognizes no power higher than itself and scorns all individual rights. In spite of revolutionary changes wrought in society by society by technological and scientific advance, the basic ideals remain the substance of the American dream. Daily in the flag salute our pupils pledge allegiance to this nation, under God. It seems to me the public schools can make no mistake if they grasp other opportunities to strengthen this basic concept of democracy. I am a great admirer and a stanch defender of our public schools. I respect their God-fearing teachers and administrators. I believe that they will free themselves of their most serious critics in regard to the teaching of spiritual values if, without compromise, they allow the name of God to appear wherever it is called for in books and courses of study.

In harmony with the belief that the concept of God should receive more recognition in the public school curriculum, the San Diego City Schools have developed "A Guide to Moral and Spiritual Education in Elementary Schools," as well as a similar one for the secondary schools, in which belief in the concept of God is expressed in a forthright manner. The guides were prepared upon the recommendation of the School-Community Advisory Committee on Moral and Spiritual Education, with the approval of religious leaders of the community and the Board of Education. Both the "introduction" and the suggested activities for use in the classroom stress the importance of the concept of God in American education. For example, heading the list of "Guidelines" are "Existence of God: a Basic Assumption". . . and "Reverence for God.". . . [43:2] Again, heading the list of "Common Beliefs Related to Moral and Spiritual Values" are the following:

> That God is the creator of the
> heavens and the earth;

> That man is the supreme work of
> God's creation, and that man
> should honor and revere the name
> of God in thought and in speech. . . . [43:11]

In discussing the place of religion in moral and spiritual education, Caswell * expresses a different point of view from that of Sister Janet. At the outset, he maintains that those who charge the public schools

* Used by special permission from Hollis L. Caswell, "Are the Public Schools Irreligious?" *Bulletin of the National Association of Secondary-School Principals,* November, 1953, pp. 14–23. Hollis L. Caswell is President of Teachers College, Columbia University.

with being irreligious base their conclusions on a lack of evidence. Then he proceeds to furnish evidence, from his own widespread experience with professional groups and knowledge of teachers and teaching, that the public schools are universally friendly toward religion. Caswell also cites the content of textbooks and courses of study, as well as specific professional publications, as further evidence of a concern for religious values in public education. Out of the battle for a "single, nonsectarian, tax-supported public school system," which, Caswell warns, is apparently being fought again, arose two convictions: that a single school system could make a major contribution to needed national unity and that individual freedom in the realm of religion should be preserved.

The plan which provided for a nonsectarian, public school system and, at the same time, permitted churches to maintain their own sectarian schools has worked well. There are indications that both religion and education have fared better in America than in Europe, where churches have a dominant role in education.

Caswell concludes that the plan "will continue to work effectively so long as the following conditions prevail: first, that the large majority of people representing all classes and groups choose to send their children to public schools; second, that minorities who so desire may freely send their children to private schools; third, that public funds are used only to support public schools; fourth, that instruction bearing on religious beliefs is not injected into the public school curriculum; and fifth, that the public schools give appropriate emphasis to the common moral values in our culture, creating a friendly attitude on the part of pupils toward the role of religion in the life of the individual and of our nation." *

A practical approach to the problem of religion in public education was made in 1953 with the establishment of the Teacher Education and Religion Project by the American Association of Colleges for Teacher Education, a department of the National Education Association. The Committee, working with fifteen colleges and universities as pilot centers, has been attempting to develop ways of helping the prospective teacher "to understand, to appreciate, and to convey to his students the significance of religion in human affairs." The AACTE has published

* *Ibid.,* p. 22.

a book of essays, *Focus on Religion in Teacher Education,* and an annotated bibliography, *Religion in Education,* as an outgrowth of the project. (See the article, "Religion in Teacher Education," by A. L. Sebaly, national coordinator of the project, in the *NEA Journal,* May, 1957, page 317.)

The American Council on Education has also demonstrated in some of its publications a growing concern over the place of religion in the teaching of moral and spiritual values (*The Relation of Religion to Public Education,* 1947; *The Function of the Public Schools in Dealing with Religion,* 1953). In 1957, a Conference on Religion and Public Education was sponsored by the Council's Committee on Religion and Education. The proceedings of the conference have been summarized in the following report of which Nicholas C. Brown is editor: *The Study of Religion in the Public Schools: an Appraisal* (Washington, D.C.: The American Council on Education, 1958, 229 pages).

OTHER TRENDS

HEALTH, PHYSICAL EDUCATION, AND RECREATION

To summarize trends in these three areas in a book of general readings in curriculum development is a difficult, if not impossible, task. Scope and diversity of content present the main difficulties. Although teachers are now organized nationally as the American Association for Health, Physical Education, and Recreation—a department of the National Education Association—their *Journal* is still divided into three sections. In their study of trends in curriculum guides, Merritt and Harap combined health and physical education for classification purposes, but they found the two areas were covered by separate guides in 90 per cent of the cases (see page 327 of this book, item 16). There is also considerable overlap with other curriculum areas. For example, health education is often taught as a life science; recreation is an important objective of art, music, and speech activities. Furthermore, many objectives of these areas are partially achieved through extensive programs of student or extra-class activities. Another difficulty in pinning down trends in these areas is the multiplicity of topics and activities, such as camping, safety and driver education, alcohol and narcotics education, and fire prevention, to mention a few.

In the 1954 Yearbook of the AAHPER, designed to help those working with children of elementary-school age, La Salle has summarized a number of trends and problems in the chapter, "Looking Ahead." [25: Ch. 21] In *physical education,* there is now essential agreement on objectives, but there is a need to place more stress on mental hygiene values, to understand cultural values of different socio-economic and ethnic groups, to work toward specific attainable goals in achieving democratic living, to improve evaluative procedures, and to learn at what age children develop skills most readily. One problem is the increase of inter-school competition at the elementary level. In *health education,* encouraging progress has been made in many communities in developing health programs, but problems are still about the same as those of a generation ago. Although there has also been progress in the integration of school health activities with those of other health agencies, some communities have done nothing to coordinate health efforts. Further improvement is needed along these lines: better coordination of the health program within the school itself, motivation of health instruction in terms of children's interests, use of health education as a problem-solving tool rather than as a body of facts to be learned, relating health to other subject areas, and research on the way value systems of different social classes are related to health practices. In *recreation,* there is a need to develop constructive noon-hour, after-school, and weekend programs of wholesome recreation. More needs to be done to educate children to use out-of-school time constructively.

By way of summary, La Salle points out the need for research to secure information from related disciplines; the need to improve teacher preparation; the need to work for better facilities, instructional materials, and time schedules; and the need to integrate school and community effort.

Such factors as the incidence of mental illness and juvenile delinquency, plus the increase in leisure, are making everyone more aware of the importance of health, physical education, and recreation training. Current reports on developments in these areas are widely scattered and highly specific.

SOCIAL STUDIES

It may appear strange that the subject of social studies occupies a subordinate position under "other trends." The reason is that recent periodical literature has been lacking in amount and significance of reporting in the field of social studies as such. While this area still constitutes a major part of the program of studies, it is often reported on under more recent experiments in meeting the common needs of learners (see pages 225–252), such as "core," "life adjustment education," and the like.

Every teacher, irrespective of his or her speciality, is responsible for the development of good citizens. Hence, the social studies (or social sciences), with citizenship as a major objective, occupy a position of great importance in the curriculum. With such problems as increasing juvenile delinquency and persistent threats to national security making the headlines of the newspapers, even greater concern for an effective social studies program becomes evident on the part of both parents and teachers. This curricular prestige has not been achieved, however, without attendant difficulties. For instance, there is a popular, but mistaken, notion that mere memorization of the facts of American History produces good citizens. Still another problem relates to content of the social studies program. The difficulty is twofold. First of all, the social studies areas are so numerous and each is so comprehensive in scope that to draw content from all areas results in fragmentation and superficiality, overwhelming an already crowded curriculum. And second, there is the difficulty of concept involved. Quite often immature boys and girls are expected to deal intelligently with problems that confound the experts. Or at the other extreme, many would forbid the study of social, economic, and political issues of a controversial nature (and most of them are), keeping the students in ignorance of the problems they must help solve as adults.

In making an analysis of social studies requirements, based on a questionnaire sent to 118 public school systems in cities of more than 100,000 population, Jones [21:257–258] found that requirements are increasing in the high school. The subject most widely required is United States history, followed by civics or government, problems, and world history, in that order.

As chairman of a four-member committee of the National Council for the Social Studies, making a survey of the literature dealing with the social studies curriculum during the period of 1952–1955, McLendon [29:213–216] reported the following trends: "increasing offerings in history at the elementary and secondary levels"; continued emphasis on current events, especially those dealing with world or international affairs; and changes which reflect "contemporary social change and the interests of the American public." (NOTE: There is noticeable resistance to the trend toward the correlation of related areas under courses labeled "social studies" and a demand for a return to specific subject labels such as "history" or "geography.")

Basing his conclusions on the results of a survey of junior college bulletins, Crawford [9:261–273] found that the social studies that a junior college student might take could very well be a series of fragmented, unrelated subjects. He recommended the reduction of electives and the relation of offerings to specific aims growing out of the "needs and problems of youth" and proceeded to outline a suggested program.

NOTE: A valuable reference for the classroom teacher, as well as for committees working on the revision of a social studies program, is *Social Studies in the Senior High School,* Eunice Johns, editor, Curriculum Series, No. 7 (National Council for the Social Studies, November, 1953).

The two yearbooks of the National Council for the Social Studies for 1957 and 1958 reveal an interesting response to the pressures of contemporary changes. The first attempts the gargantuan task of analyzing the implications of great discoveries in science and technology in this century in order to help the teacher of social studies discharge his responsibility of helping his pupils to live in a world where each day science becomes more important.* The second places its stress upon the inter-relatedness of the social sciences and analyzes new viewpoints in the several social science disciplines. The underlying, unifying philosophic context is emphasized. "In a word, the social studies are *social* to the degree and with the depth and intensity that they treat man as a value-serving, a value-making, a value-choosing, and a value-pursuing creature. The ultimate concern of the social studies should be *oughts* which distinguish man from all other animate forms. These are its great moral-intellectual imperatives. It is *ought,* not *is,* which gives man his place 'in the great chain of being.' " **

The National Society for the Study of Education devotes its 1957 yearbook to an examination of the social studies in the elementary-

---

* National Council for the Social Studies, 27th Yearbook, *Science and the Social Studies,* Howard H. Cummings, editor (Washington, D.C., 1957).

** National Council for the Social Studies, 28th Yearbook, *New Viewpoints in the Social Sciences,* Roy A. Price, editor (Washington, D.C., 1958), p. 220.

school curriculum. It brings forth a series of proposals "regarded as valid by the student of child development, the student of the learning process, and the specialist in the social studies." Granted that they are good, the question is raised, "How can they become operative?" Two obstacles to effectiveness in operation are noted: (*a*) the stimulation of honest, free inquiry in a society in which the manipulation of the minds of others has been an accepted potent fact, and (*b*) the maintenance of curiosity exhibited by young children which declines over the succeeding years.*

DRIVER EDUCATION

A relative newcomer to the high school curriculum, scarcely more than two decades old, is driver education. The status of the program as of 1952–1953 has been reported by the Research Division of the National Education Association. Over-all statistics for programs, based on questionnaires to nearly 24,000 schools, are summarized as follows:

47 per cent of the respondents said they offered some type of driver education program.
82 per cent offered both classroom instruction and practice driving.
53 per cent of the programs were in rural areas.
35 per cent were in the "middle" states (Illinois, Indiana, Iowa, Michigan, Minnesota, Missouri, Ohio, Wisconsin).
53 per cent were offered by four-year high schools.
41 per cent of the programs were offered in schools with enrollments of fewer than 300 students. [36:95]

STUDENT OR EXTRA-CLASS ACTIVITIES

Because of the extent and importance of the student activity or extra-class program, especially at the secondary-school level, the subject is deserving of more consideration than the space allotted to it here would indicate. During the years 1951–1956, each April issue of the *School Review* included an annotated bibliography on extra-class activities, which revealed certain desirable developments and persistent problems. Some of the commendable changes taking place in the student activity program are as follows: encouragement of more widespread student participation; provision for more financial support by the board of education

* National Society for the Study of Education, 56th Yearbook, Part II, Nelson B. Henry, editor (Chicago: University of Chicago Press, 1957), pp. 306–314.

rather than making extra-class activities entirely self-supporting; attempts to reduce the costs to students; recognition of sponsorship of such activities as a part of faculty load; alleviation of emotionally charged, competitive features of the program; inclusion of such activities in the regular time schedule of the school; and protection of students from exploitation.

There are persistent problems, however, which remain to be solved—over-participation by a few and non-participation by many students; excessive costs for students, especially senior-year activities in high school; exploitation of students in such activities as weekend band reviews, essay contests, inter-school athletic contests; elimination of secret societies; and inadequate compensation for faculty sponsorship.

For a study of social clubs and student participation, see Hilda Taba, *School Culture* (Washington, D. C.: American Council on Education, 1955, 123 pages).

SUMMARY OF GENERAL CURRICULUM TRENDS

A comprehensive review of changes which have taken place during the past fifty years in three phases of curriculum development—formulation of objectives, selection of learning experiences, and organization of learning experiences—has been made by Tyler. This article also serves as a well-organized summary of this section on trends and offers an incisive analysis of causal factors influencing curricular changes.

The Curriculum—Then and Now   by RALPH W. TYLER

From the 1956 *Proceedings* of the Invitational Conference on Testing Problems, sponsored by Educational Testing Service, held at the Hotel Roosevelt in New York City on November 3, 1956. Reprinted by special permission of Educational Testing Service and the author. Ralph W. Tyler is Director of the Center for Advanced Study in the Behavioral Sciences, Stanford, California.

Any effort to review the development during the past fifty years of the school curriculum of the United States encounters a confusing complexity. This is not due alone, or even primarily, to the fact that we have no centralized control of education in this country, although it is true that the variations among the forty-eight states are easily marked. These local variations are less pronounced than are the differences of another sort.

One may analyze the development of curriculum theory, that is, the statements of rationale for the curriculum and the related discussions which seek to explain it and to make it more coherent and systematic. One may examine the work of the persons and groups who have designed courses of study and prepared curriculum guides. One may assemble reports of the curriculum in operation in certain schools to obtain a picture of what teachers are actually teaching at a given time in the few schools on which this kind of report is available. These three reviews will give quite different content, yet each is a significant aspect of the American school curriculum.

Another factor in the complexity of this topic arises from the unusually comprehensive definition of the term "curriculum" which is currently employed in American educational circles. The term is not limited in this country, as it commonly is abroad, to refer to the outline of the content to be taught, but is used to include all of the learning of students which is planned by and directed by the school to attain its educational goals. This inclusive definition covers the formulation of educational objectives, the planning, use, and organization of learning experiences, and the appraisal of student learning.

It also includes not only the learning activities carried on in the classroom and laboratory but also those at home or in extra-curriculum situations insofar as these are planned and directed by the school to attain its aims. The line drawn between the curriculum and other activities of the students is that which separates activities designed by the school to contribute to educational ends from those which are provided for recreation or for other purposes or are not part of the school's plan. It is true that the current definition of the curriculum is a more adequate one for thinking about, for planning, and for conducting an educational program; but it does mean that a review of the curriculum must include a larger range of matters than would be required if the definition were limited to the outline of content to be taught.

To bring my task into manageable size, I have chosen to focus attention on the development of curriculum theory over the past fifty years with occasional comments on the ways in which courses of study and curriculum guides diverge from the accepted rationale and with still fewer occasional comments on the discrepancies between teaching practices and curriculum theory. To simplify this complex review still further, we shall examine each of three major aspects of the curriculum in turn, treating the formulation of educational objectives, the selection of learning experiences, and the organization of learning experiences. Although the evaluation of the effectiveness of the curriculum is commonly included as an aspect of the curriculum itself, I shall not discuss it since the two following papers deal with the subject.

The Formulation of Educational Objectives

A major step in most theories of curriculum development is the formulation of the educational objectives of the school, that is, the goals to be attained by its educational program. To be sure, this is not an appropriate step in John Dewey's educational philosophy in which the direction of learning is guided by careful consideration of the quality of the learning experiences. Insofar as the learning experiences provide for continuity and interaction, in Dewey's terms the program is effective. His philosophy does not involve a distinction between ends and means. But the other chief leaders of American curriculum thought emphasize the importance of clear objectives as the basis for planning the learning experiences and appraising the results.

Since the turn of the century there have been several marked changes connected with the formulation of the objectives of the school. One of the most obvious has been the changed conception of the nature of educational objectives. The dominant educational psychology in 1900 was based on the theory of formal

discipline and expressed in terms of "faculty psychology." The mind had certain faculties such as memory and reason which could be trained or disciplined by proper exercise. The objectives of the school were stated in terms of the faculties to be trained, and the learning experiences were those exercises in which these faculties were engaged on content particularly rich in opportunities for memorization, reasoning, and the like. Certain subjects by the very nature of their form and content were superior means for cultivation of these faculties. Language, particularly Latin, for example, was a superior subject because the learning of it required the exercise of memory, while its grammatical structure provided exercise in orderly reasoning.

With the decreasing acceptance of the theory of formal discipline and the elimination of faculty psychology, the prevailing view became increasingly behavioral. Learning was then conceived as the acquisition of patterns of behavior which the student had not previously followed. Human behavior was defined quite generally to include all the reactions of an individual, his thinking, feeling, acting.

Educational objectives are now couched in behavioral terms. An objective is a statement of a kind of behavior pattern which the school seeks to have the student develop. In the first flush of behavioral concepts, roughly from 1918 to 1925, the objectives were commonly stated in highly specific terms, such as ability to add 2 plus 3, ability to use the indefinite article "an," ability to spell "believe," ability to recall the atomic weight of sulphur. This was a natural corollary to the prevailing associationist theory in the psychology of learning. Every number combination, for example, was viewed as a different stimulus to which the student was to learn an appropriate response. This extreme view led to the listing of nearly three thousand specific objectives for arithmetic, and nearly two thousand for English. A student had attained the goals of the curriculum when he had learned to make the appropriate responses to all of the specific stimuli, that is, when all of these innumerable objectives had been reached.

By 1925, this view of objectives had largely fallen of its own weight. On the side of the teacher it required keeping in mind far too many goals to be remembered, and on the side of the student, it denied the development of generalized behavior patterns which quite obviously were developing. The formulation of other theories of learning which took into account the phenomenon of generalized behavior provided terms in which educational objectives have commonly been stated since 1930. For example, in 1936 the Department of Superintendence of the National Education Association published a yearbook on "The Social Studies Curriculum." Among the objectives suggested were (pages 320–340):

1. Acquisition of important information
2. Familiarity with technical vocabulary
3. Familiarity with dependable sources of information on current social issues
4. Immunity to malicious propaganda
5. Facility in interpreting social science data
6. Facility in applying significant facts and principles to social problems in daily life
7. Skill in investigating social science problems
8. Interest in reading about social problems and in discussing them
9. Sensitivity to current social problems
10. Interest in human welfare
11. The habit of working cooperatively with others
12. The habit of collecting and considering appropriate evidence before making important social decisions
13. Attitudes favorable to social improvement

These obviously present a conception of generalized behavior. However, although they avoid the piecemeal aims of highly specific objectives, they may be as limited in their value for guiding teaching as the earlier statements of objectives in terms of faculties to be developed unless each of these thirteen objectives is clearly enough defined to have meaning for the teacher so that he can easily think of concrete illustrations of the general aims. The developments since 1935 in the conception of the nature of educational objectives have largely focused on defining in concrete terms aims which are expressed at a level of generality similar to those above. These efforts have been applied to defining the kind of behavior implied by such general terms as "understanding," "applying principles to concrete problems," "ability to interpret reading material," and to indicating the range of content to which each kind of behavior is to be applied. Thus, the objective "to develop understanding of the basic concepts of physiology" has been defined from the standpoint of behavior and of content. The behavior "understanding" is defined as "the ability to recall the concepts, to state them in one's own words, to give illustrations of them, to recognize illustrations given by others, and to compare and contrast related concepts." The content termed "the basic concepts of physiology" is defined by listing some two score concepts which these curriculum makers have selected as basic to this science. This kind of definition helps greatly to clarify the aims of the curriculum so that they can actually be utilized in planning and conducting an educational program in terms of the prevailing conception of the psychology of learning.

A second marked change in the objectives of the American school curriculum has been in the sources used to derive the aims. To some extent all of the five major sources have been used in every period of American history but at a given time certain sources are dominant in their influence while others are given only minor attention. Between 1900 and 1918, the judgments of subject specialists and the prevailing conception of the psychology of learning were dominant in formulating objectives. At the high school level, the Committee of Ten used sub-committees of mathematicians, historians, language scholars, and the like to outline the objectives of secondary school instruction in these fields. Although the prevailing educational philosophy had already emphasized knowledge and skill for the layman as a major aim of the American high school, this was given little attention in deciding on objectives. No studies were made of the needs of society nor of the needs of students to help in identifying appropriate objectives.

As a result of the success of job analysis in building vocational curricula during World War I, the process of formulating objectives from 1918 to 1933 leaned heavily upon job analyses, activity analyses, word counts, and other techniques for identifying the demands made on the individual by contemporary social life. At this time, curriculum makers also gave attention to the notions of educational psychologists as to what behaviors could be taught. However, during this period little attention was given to the prevailing social and educational philosophy regarding the characteristics of the good man and the good society. The opinions of subject specialists were given much less weight than in the previous period.

From 1933 to 1945, studies of children and youth served as a major source of suggestions for objectives. With an emphasis upon the responsibility of the school for meeting the needs of children and youth, curriculum commissions drew upon child study data and reports of adolescent studies to derive objectives. This largely coincided with the prevailing emphasis in educational philosophy and to some extent the work of educational psychologists was used. But the use of studies of social demands was notably less than in the decade previous while the opinions of subject specialists played a very minor role.

Since World War II, the shift in emphasis among the five kinds of sources has been marked. Primary attention is currently given to the opinions of subject specialists, particularly in mathematics and science. Very little weight is currently given to studies of the learner, but the specialists are asked to outline what they believe to be important potential contributions of their fields which will be of value to laymen as well as persons planning to specialize in the field. In this respect the emphasis is different from that in 1900. Today some attention is also being given to an examination of social demands, and to a lesser extent to the current conceptions of the psychology of learning. Much less use is made today of stud-

ies of the learner than was true fifteen years ago. In general, the shifts which have taken place in the primary sources used to derive educational objectives most closely parallel the changes which can easily be seen in the statements of objectives appearing in courses of study and in curriculum guides. Because the actual practice of teaching depends so largely on the habits and outlooks of the thousands of American school teachers, the shifts in practice are not so easily discerned.

A third marked change has been in the range of objectives which the American schools have not only accepted for themselves but have actively championed. At the turn of the century there was a sharp difference between the claims made regarding the schools' general contribution in promoting citizenship and character and the working objectives of the curriculum which were focused on knowledge and skills and intellectual discipline. The development of many basic attitudes, values, interests, and habits was recognized as a primary function of the home and church, and for those habits, attitudes, and skills relevant to work the employer was expected to play a strong role. The school today commonly lists the whole range of educational goals required for the induction of young people into effective adulthood. It includes objectives relating to home life, personal-social relations, civic life, occupations, and the like. It includes not only knowledge and intellectual abilities but interests, attitudes, social and recreational skills. Frequently, too, there is no indication of relative weighting. Developing social skills and a cooperative attitude appear to be viewed as jobs as important for the school as developing understanding of basic concepts of science and the social studies or the acquisition of the skills involved in reading.

Since the level of learning required of people today is a high one, a major problem in education is to select wisely among all the possible goals the important tasks which the school can do well and to concentrate its energies effectively. Since the total educational job is very great, the home, the church, the employer, and the other potential educative agencies of the community need to be encouraged and strengthened to take their share while the school concentrates on the things it can do best, and in many cases the things that only the school can do. Hence, the present shift in school objectives is toward a more discriminating selection, toward the kinds of learning which involve intellectual skills, which require sequential experiences to reach the necessary level of competence, which involve concepts and principles that are not apparent on the surface and for this reason are not likely to be learned through the guidance of laymen. This shift is likely to reduce the great range of objectives, and to diminish the emphasis upon social adjustment and similar goals which fail to recognize the importance of individuality and individual creativity in responding to experiences and in solving problems. The increasing emphasis upon understanding and thinking as kinds of objectives, with lessened stress upon attitudes and habits as primary goals, may help to revive the conception of the individual who controls his feelings and actions in terms of his knowledge and thought rather than one who simply seeks to express "acceptable" attitudes and feelings and to do the "proper" thing. This is a shift in objectives which will be interesting to observe.

The Selection of Learning Experiences

Among the changes taking place in the learning experiences provided by the American schools, those in the prevailing notions of the nature of learning experiences are particularly significant. At the beginning of this century, the term was not used. Exercises, assignments, examples, problems were the words commonly employed to designate the learning tasks set for students outside of the class session, while the term "recitation" was used to refer to the oral responses expected of the student in the class. No mention was made of the student's mental reactions in the class, although it was clear that he was expected to pay attention, that is, to watch and listen to the teacher's presentations. When I began to teach more than thirty-five years ago, we had to file lesson plans for each week in advance. These plans outlined the content to be covered, what the teacher expected to do and the out-of-class assignments to be made. The focus of planning was on the teacher.

John Dewey and other educational leaders gave wide publicity to the increasing psychological evidence that learning could be most readily interpreted in terms of what the learner was doing. It was his reactions that he learned—not the teacher's. The teacher's role was to stimulate, guide, and reward the learner as he carried on the behavior which the school sought to teach him. This view placed attention upon the activity of the learner as the basic factor in attaining educational goals. By 1925, both writings of theorists and curriculum guides were commonly using the term "learning activities" to refer to the basic elements of the teaching-learning situation. Courses of study were listing reading activities, listening activities, study activities, and laboratory activities in outlining the day-by-day program of the school.

By 1935, curriculum writers were pointing out certain limitations in the concept of learning activity. For example, two students might both be reading an historic account of the California "Gold Rush," yet each might be carrying on quite different mental reactions and making different emotional responses. One might be thinking of the excitement and challenge involved in the long wagon haul the pioneers made in crossing the country, thrilling himself as he imagined the Indian encounters. The other might be thinking of the rough, lawless life of the early mining community, wondering why people would leave the comforts of civilization to live in such trying conditions. In terms of the course of study, both were engaged in the same learning activity but each was having a different experience and to that extent was learning something different. This kind of analysis led to the adoption of the term "learning experience" to refer to the reactions of the student in the situation. In 1936, Dewey's book on *Education and Experience* clarified this concept further by emphasizing the notion that "experience" involves the interaction of the individual with the situation. This interaction involves some mutual effects, the individual modifying his reactions in terms of the demands of the situation and he also modifying the situation through his reaction to it. Today, almost all curriculum writers use the term "learning experience" and they seek to plan the learning situation so as to give direction to the experience the student has, that is, to his internal perception of the situation and his own interaction with it. This requires consideration of what the learner brings to the situation, what it will mean to him, how he is likely to respond to it mentally, emotionally, and in action.

Beginning with James and Thorndike and exercising increasing influence in recent years is the conception of the learning situation as one which should provide for certain essential conditions of learning. Thorndike's earlier work emphasized two conditions—exercise and effect. Current curriculum guides mention such conditions as motivation, opportunity for practice, guidance of desired behavior, provision of satisfaction when desired behavior is elicited, and the like. Hence, some of the current courses of study are pointing out the need to consider these conditions in selecting the learning experiences for a particular class group from a larger list of suggested ones.

A second marked change in learning experiences can be found in their range. Although the Sloyd movement had influenced forward-looking American schools in the late 1800's to introduce manual training, not as vocational training but as a means of "learning through the hands," most of the learning exercises employed at the turn of the century were verbal ones. Listening and reciting, reading and writing represented the ways of learning the "academic subjects," except for the laboratory periods in high school science. Even the laboratory exercises were heavily verbal, with detailed instructions in the manual and a formal plan for writing up each "experiment." Map work in geography and field work in biology were strongly recommended by the writers of the period from 1905–1915. Most courses of study advised having children make maps and locate points of geographic interest on them. At this time, too, high school botany courses typically required the student to collect and identify fifty or more plants.

By 1910, high school agriculture was widely offered in rural areas. These were first courses to introduce the project, or "student initiated" enterprise, which, it was hoped, would help him to understand and to apply the knowledge he was gaining in the course. The use of projects spread to other fields and to the elementary school, thus providing a much wider range of learning experiences than schools had commonly used. The writers who urged the introduction of projects conceived of them as involving a range of experiences as broad as life itself, but in the actual use of projects in the schools, activities involving the construction of objects have been predominant. Many teachers think of a project as making, growing, or producing some physical object. The extended inquiry which Dewey thought had largest potentialities as an educational project is rarely found. The intellectual learning experiences are frequently quite minor to the physical manipulations required to complete a "construction project."

During the depression, with its great reduction in opportunities for remunerative work for youth, many secondary school leaders recommended the addition of work experience to the high school program. Although only a small minority of high schools introduced work experience as part of the curriculum, some developed well-planned programs which involved using a wide variety of work activities as means for attaining educational objectives related to science, social studies, mathematics, and English as well as vocational fields.

The greatest impetus to extending the range of learning experiences has been the technological developments in communication. Lantern slides were in use at the turn of the century but were not found in many schools. At best they served only to extend the number of pictures which could be employed, to add concreteness, or to give variety to the teacher's presentation. The perfection of the motion picture, however, made it possible to analyze movements, to show time and space relationships much more graphically, and to increase the sense of reality in dealing with many subjects which require vicarious treatment. The addition of the sound track heightened the sense of reality and added another dimension of analysis. The sound-slide film gave some of the features of the sound motion picture in a more economical form, but it lacked the distinctive assets of motion. The television set made possible instantaneous viewing of events in a fashion much like the motion picture but with a further sense of the reality of the event, due to the viewer's realizing that it is taking place at the same time he is seeing it. These technological developments have gone far in removing the physi-cal limitations to providing as wide a range of learning experiences in the school as those of life outside. But much of the comprehensive, effective development of these potentialities lies ahead. They still represent a small percentage of the learning experiences provided by American schools.

The selection of learning experiences so as to provide for individual differences among students is another respect in which changes have taken place in the last fifty years. Attention to individual differences has been accentuated by two factors: the psychological studies which have identified the extent of differences among schools, among classes, and among students in the same class; and the increased visibility of individual differences brought about by the enrollment in the school of children from heterogeneous ethnic groups and social classes. There are few teachers now who fail to recognize a variety of differences among the students in their classes—differences which affect interests, meanings, efforts, and outcomes in schoolwork.

Typical devices to provide for differences among students have involved adaptations in the time given for completing learning exercises, or variations in the exercises themselves, or both. The first type of adaptation requires a plan for students to work at varying rates. Among the early developments were the San Francisco, Dalton, and Winnetka plans, all of which involved organizing the school day into two parts, one for group activity and the other for individual work. These plans also required the development of a series of assignments with full directions on paper so that the students could work as individuals on different assignments at the same time. As a student took an assignment it became his "contract" which he undertook to finish before he went on with another assignment in the same field. He might, therefore, complete his assignment much earlier or much later than the average.

Adaptations of the learning experiences themselves were first found in courses of study which marked some of the exercises as those to be required of all students and others as optional for the better students. By 1915, this was common among American schools. By 1925, a number of cities had introduced "ability grouping" in which the course of study was differentiated in such fields as reading and arithmetic into three levels — the superior, the average, and the slow sections. These three courses of study differed in the time provided for learning exercises and to a lesser extent in the nature of the exercises. In reading, the amount of material dealing with personal and social activities of children was greater in the slow sections, while the adult material was greater in the superior sections. In arithmetic, more concrete objects were counted and compared in the slow sections than in the others.

The use of individual projects was also a means of adapting to the individual student's interest and ability. This was recommended in courses of study as early as 1915. Learning exercises carried out by small groups (two to ten students) were first employed in the late 1800's to compensate for inadequate laboratory equipment. The apparatus was insufficient to provide opportunity for every student working individually to carry out the assignment. By 1930, small group projects were being used by many schools as a manageable means of providing for individual differences. The projects themselves could differ in the rigor of their intellectual demands and the division of labor among the students in the small group could adapt further to the abilities and interests of the individual. Unfortunately, all too often the slowest learner was given some handwork which involved little if any new learning. By 1950, with the publication of research on the psychology of small groups, educational writers were recommending the use of small group projects as a means of heightening motivation and increasing the amount of meaningful learning activity. Since 1948, the attention of educational leaders has focused increasingly on the "education of the gifted student." This has led to emphasizing learning experiences which require greater understanding, or skill, or effort than those usually provided in the course of study. It has also stimulated some schools to develop learning experiences that can be carried on as independent work.

The most typical development in the past twenty years found in courses of study to provide for individual differences has been the listing of a large number of suggested learning experiences from which a given teacher may select ones particularly appropriate for his class as a whole or for groups or individuals within the class. The uniform lesson plan so common when I started to teach is almost unknown now. Most curriculum guides include a discussion of how to select from among the large number of learning experiences suggested in the course of study those which are likely to be most effective for students with varying backgrounds and abilities.

The Organization of Learning Experiences

Important educational objectives involve patterns of behavior of such complexity that they can be developed only gradually over considerable periods of time. For example, the ability to read critically and to make comprehensive interpretations of what one reads is not acquired in a few brief lessons. To understand the basic principles of science and to use these principles in explaining the biological and physical phenomena

round about us require a variety of related experiences extending over many hours. If the development of such complex behavior patterns as these is left to isolated or unrelated periods of learning, adequate achievement is impossible. Hence, a major phase in building a curriculum is to work out an organization of the many, many learning experiences required so that the student develops these complex behavior patterns gradually, day by day, and relates them to others so as to have an increasingly unified understanding, and a well integrated command of essential skills.

The purpose of organizing learning experiences is to maximize the cumulative effect of the large number of learning experiences required to develop complex behavior patterns. Three criteria are commonly considered as standards to be met by a well organized curriculum, namely, continuity, sequence, and integration. Continuity refers to the reiteration of the desired behavior through the many learning experiences used. Sequence refers to the gradation of the learning so that each subsequent experience not only builds on previous ones but goes beyond in order to require a higher level of skill, or a broader or deeper degree of understanding. Integration refers to the relation of what the student is learning in one field to what he is learning at about the same time in other fields. A broader and deeper understanding is facilitated by comprehending the relation among the various concepts, facts, and principles being studied, and a more adequate command of basic skills is achieved as the relation of these skills to one another is seen.

One surprising fact about curriculum development in the last fifty years has been the limited attention given to the theory of curriculum organization. Other than the common-sense notions of these criteria and of such rule-of-thumb principles as "learning experiences should proceed from that which is known to that which is unknown, from the simple to the complex, from the easy to the difficult," no new formulations have been made since the time of Herbart and of James. This is an area crying for substantial theory to be tested in practice and to provide a guide for practice.

At the more specific level, developments in reading and in the foreign languages have been most marked. In reading, continuity and sequence are commonly achieved through carefully controlled vocabulary development, adding new words gradually and systematically, and through the control of sentence structure in the reading materials, beginning with simple declarative sentences and moving gradually to compound and complex ones. Integration is sought both by relating the reading material to the common activities of the children and by introducing work-type reading in the other subjects on a gradual basis. A similar scheme of organization is commonly followed in the foreign languages.

In arithmetic, the development of skills is usually facilitated through an organization which begins with learning experiences involving addition and subtraction, then multiplication and division, then common fractions and decimal fractions. No explicit scheme of organization for concept development in arithmetic can be found in the current courses of study. The content of arithmetic problems has changed greatly since 1900. Beginning about 1920, studies were made of the kinds of problems commonly encountered by children and adults. Typically, arithmetic courses now order the problem content in terms of frequency of occurrence of the problems outside of school and in terms of the age level at which this kind of problem is commonly encountered by children.

The typical high school curriculum in mathematics has changed little in the past fifty years so far as organization is concerned. Tenth-grade geometry builds little, if at all, upon algebra. Advanced algebra and solid geometry in the eleventh grade have little sequential relationship to tenth-grade geometry, and trigonometry in the twelfth grade does not provide a clear sequence for the eleventh-grade work. The so-called "modern mathematics program" which is now getting under way with the sponsorship of the mathematical organizations should provide a much better organized curriculum for high school mathematics.

In organizing the so-called content fields, like the sciences and the social studies, major attention has been given to the ordering of content rather than to behavior. At the beginning of this century science was not commonly taught in the elementary school, while in the high school botany was most frequently offered in the tenth grade, physics in the eleventh, and chemistry in the twelfth. By 1920, general science was offered as the introductory science course in more than one-fourth of the high schools and now it is taught in almost all schools in the eighth or ninth grade, with biology in the tenth, and physics and chemistry, where offered, being placed in the eleventh or twelfth grades. The content of general science is usually selected to relate to the scientific phenomena most commonly observed by children. The content of biology is usually chosen to explain the human body, the maintenance of health, and the conservation of natural resources. The organizing notion here is to begin with phenomena which are common in the student's environment and in which he is likely to be interested. The advanced science courses, physics and chemistry, deal with the more abstract principles, which are thought to be less common and more difficult. The organization of these two courses has not greatly changed in the past fifty years. These illustrations in the field of science in-dicate the attention given to organizing the content dealt with in the learning experiences, but no similar effort has been made to organize the behavior, that is, the skills and abilities to be developed.

This is also true for the social studies. The changes taking place in their organization have been changes in the ordering of content. The most common sequence of content in the social studies is to begin with the community, then the state, then the nation, and finally the world. There is little evidence to indicate that this is sequential in terms of difficulty in learning.

Thus far, we have been reviewing the continuity and sequence of learning experiences in the content fields. The problem of integration, that is, how to relate learning experiences so as to aid the student in seeing the relations between what he is learning in one field and what he is learning in another, has been attacked most commonly through changes in the structure of the curriculum. In 1900, the elementary school curriculum was composed of ten or more specific subjects like reading, writing, spelling, arithmetic, geography, history, nature study, hygiene, music, drawing. Now, the typical course of study includes reading and the language arts, arithmetic, science, fine arts, health. This reduction in the number of subjects has been accomplished by building a more closely related series of learning experiences in language, in which reading, writing, and spelling are involved; in social studies, where geography and history are interrelated; and in the fine arts, where music, drawing, and painting are brought together.

In the high school, the broad fields of English, mathematics, science, social studies, foreign language, and fine arts have frequently replaced more specific subjects, and in some cases the core curriculum has been developed which provides a large structure for learning experiences that occupy from one-third to one-half of the high school student's day. Since these larger structures are usually planned as courses rather than several separate sub-courses, there is opportunity for better integration. Typically, however, the only principle of integration which has been explored is to bring together the content and skills needed to deal with each of the student "problems" which provide basic units of the course. This principle does not always provide for the necessary continuity and sequence nor for all of the more helpful relationships among the fields which are involved. In many cases, a particular problem involves knowledge or skills from certain fields in only a minor degree and does not suggest the more significant ways in which these fields are related.

It is clear after reading the works of curriculum theorists and examining courses of study that the past fifty years have not been a time of great development in the organization of learning experiences. In this respect, curriculum changes have been relatively few. The careful, systematic work done in the field of reading is a shining exception. The arousal of interest and stimulation of thought among secondary-school teachers who have worked on the construction of core curricula suggest the great intellectual resources available under effective leadership to attack fundamentally and systematically the problem of developing a better organized curriculum.

Summary

This review of changes in the curriculum of the American schools during the past fifty years has touched several high spots, but it has not presented possible explanations for the kinds of changes noted. It is probable that many of these developments can be understood in terms of the tasks which the American schools were facing at these different periods and the ideas prevailing in the field of psychology which school leaders found when they sought from scholars assistance in attacking critical school problems.

In the period prior to World War I, the elementary school was steadily growing to include a larger per cent of the children of age six to fourteen. The critical task was to teach the three R's to children of immigrant parents and those from the working classes. This required a re-examination of the psychology of reading and arithmetic, for the usual background of interest in and experience with language and children's stories could not be taken for granted, nor could early experiences with number concepts in the home be assumed for all children. It is not surprising that in this period long lists of specific objectives for these subjects were worked out and that special attention was given to children's interests and abilities in devising learning experiences.

World War I ushered in a fifteen-year period when the economy developed rapidly and workers were in demand. No wonder that job analyses and other forms of analyses of social life were used to identify more definitely the demands which the individual would be expected to meet and to use this source in setting objectives. From 1930 until World War II, the great depression increased rather than decreased the number of youth in school because of the limited opportunities for employment. But the same limitations in jobs made the analysis of social demands a less relevant source for educational objectives than a study of youth themselves to find needs and potentialities that might justify educational effort when no great social demand was apparent. This period also was a difficult time for many secondary schools because youth saw no future and had no interest in deferred educational values. In their eyes schoolwork had to be justified immediately in terms of its interest and meaning to them. Hence, the devising of learning experiences of immediate interest and relevance to students and their organization around student problems helped to meet this pressing problem.

Since World War II, the insatiable demand for technically trained people has focused attention on the opinions of subject experts as a source of objectives and has given greater emphasis to knowledge and skills. The current demand for highly competent professionals and technicians has increased the interest of the schools in the education of gifted children and in devising a better organized curriculum to reach high levels of achievement. The shortage of teachers has furthered the demand for technological devices that increase the range of learning experiences, such as television and the sound motion picture.

Throughout the fifty years, the schools have been pressed by continuing conditions which create critical problems that cannot be solved without further curriculum developments. The first of these is the rapid change in technological development and social life which requires a continually increasing level of education on the part of our people. The second is the increasing proportion of children and youth who are sent to the schools for education. The third is the dislocation in other educational institutions, the home, the church, the neighborhood which rapid social change has engendered. The educational needs of today and the immediate future are greater than ever before. American education has done an amazing job in getting almost all children and youth in school and providing schools for this immense number. The schools have been astoundingly successful in building confidence on the part of the public in the capabilities of education in building our civilization. The time has come, however, to recognize realistically the magnitude of the job; to

identify the objectives which the schools can best attain; to encourage the home, the church, and other institutions to undertake the tasks appropriate to them; to devise learning experiences clearly relevant to the school's proper objectives; and to work out an organization of the curriculum which aids the students in attaining a high level of educational competence. These steps still lie ahead of us.

6

RESOURCES FOR TEACHING
AND LEARNING

TEXTBOOKS

What takes place in the classroom *is* the principal part of the curriculum; therefore, the resources and procedures used by teachers constitute major determinants in the achievement of educational objectives. Inasmuch as resources may be classified as either material or human, it may be further concluded that the teacher and the textbook are the two chief factors in formal education. Despite recent developments in multiple types of teaching-learning materials, both of a formal and informal variety, "printed materials, especially in the form of textbooks, continue to be the core of instructional materials in this country." [3: 120]

Since textbooks do constitute such an important material resource in the curriculum, careful selection becomes vitally important. Rogers [41:42–48] has pointed out a number of difficulties encountered in textbook selection: participation of lay groups in selection, objections to textbooks on the basis of alleged subversion (see page 197, for example), time lag between production and use, questions of mechanical make-up, and questions of suitability of a book for students in a particular school.

A "spotlight report" in *Better Schools,* addressed primarily to laymen, describes the state-adoption systems in operation, discusses inadequate budgeting and charges of subversion, and indicates that "the textbook is not the whole school."

Another Spotlight Report: Right Choice of Textbooks
Is Important   from BETTER SCHOOLS

From *Better Schools,* March, 1957, pages 7–8, published by the National
Citizens Council for Better Schools. Reprinted by special permission.

The textbook has been called the child's "other teacher." As an individual interested in school improvement you therefore have a stake in how schoolbooks are selected quite aside from the fact that you, as a taxpayer, pay for them.

This does not mean that laymen should go rushing to take over the job of educators in picking out textbooks. One of the commonest methods of selection is by teachers—and who knows better than the teacher what is needed for a particular classroom in a particular grade?

But the layman nevertheless has a legitimate interest and there have been cases where school authorities invited lay groups to review textbooks and teaching materials. There have been other cases where citizens' committees have decided on their own to undertake such studies—and have come out better informed about what their schools are trying to accomplish.

* * *

At least one community, Ferndale, Michigan, set up a continuing committee with the following objectives:
• To check the adequacy and use of materials at all instructional levels.
• To help evolve a policy for the guidance of the school staff in treating controversial issues.

• To review, at the request of the board or superintendent, specific instructional materials whose suitability may be questioned.
• To review from time to time local policies concerning instructional materials.
• To make such recommendations to the board and superintendent as the committee and the community believe appropriate.

* * *

A few years ago textbooks were getting more attention than they are now, but this was because of a few situations which made the headlines because somebody said this or that textbook was subversive. These controversies have largely died down now. One reason is that the books in question, written against the emotional background of the depression of the 1930's, are out of date or out of print. Of course, then or today, no single textbook can satisfy all shades of American thought. Even an unbiased, wholly objective book can be subjected to criticism by a biased person who hoped to find his pet bias in it.

But if textbooks are the child's "other teacher," they should not be neglected by parents and workers for schools just because excitement happens to be lacking. Learning about the textbooks used in your community will in itself give you background about school affairs and will have by-product values as you discover what part the teachers play in selections of the books, whether they are satisfied with the selection system, and what can be done about it.

Systems for selection of textbooks have changed considerably over the years. In early colonial days students used whatever schoolbooks they could get—often those their parents used. The simplest were the hornbooks which merely listed the alphabet and some numerals and included a spiritual message from which children learned to read. Gradually, bound volumes became more plentiful, and eventually many of them appeared. Through the years the forty-eight states have practiced many different methods of selection and buying.

This variety in method allowed such curious results as one state having the same textbook in the hands of every fifth-grader and another state supplying two wholly different sets of books to two schools in the same town.

Three Major Adoption Systems

Practices are still not uniform today—and perhaps should not be—but in general they are reduced to three major systems, two of which still allow considerable latitude at the local level, where the teacher has to operate.

Free or open systems of textbook selection are used in a majority of states. Under this plan, regardless of whether books are bought by the state or the district, each school unit is free to select its own books for its own classes.

A multiple-choice system is the next most popular plan. Under this, the state department of public instruction selects a list of approved books, and the local unit may choose among any on the list. This sometimes allows wide latitude, but still not a totally free choice. But if committees of teachers making selections don't have as wide a choice because of prior screening, neither do they have as much work to do in combing lists. Both methods have their advocates, and sometimes a combination of methods is used, such as multiple choice in elementary schools and open choice in high schools.

The third plan, "single" or "exclusive" textbook adoption, is one in which the state department of education selects all books, one for each class, so that all classes in the state at the same level use the same book. This is used by only three states for all schools. Even in these three states, Alabama, Florida, and North Carolina, there are some variations, but they classify themselves as single-textbook-adoption states. Two other states use this system for elementary schools only, California and Arizona. Its chief advocate is California, which prints its own textbooks. California has a highly mobile population, and therefore regards uniformity of textbooks in various communities as an important advantage. . . .

* * *

Budgeting Calls for Sharp Pencils

A point at which laymen, including citizens' committees and school board members, as well as administrators, can take hold of the textbook problem is during the regular budget sessions. But it is not an easy point.

It may be astonishing to discover the fact that the school child of today has 20 per cent fewer books than did the child ten years ago. The figure comes from an annual survey conducted for the American Textbook Publishers Institute.

* * *

A reason for the decrease is budgeting. It may seem simple to budget for textbooks, but the publishers argue that it isn't. You estimate increased enrollment and increased cost of book production, and there you have it. School boards and superintendents have tried that.

But, say the publishers, you have forgotten something. Books, on the average, last about four years. Therefore, most schools figure on spending about one-fourth of the total cost of all their textbooks each year for replacements. But if the same method of figuring textbook expenditures is applied to rising enrollments, the new students end up with just one-fourth of the books they need.

For instance, in a school of 100 students, each child may have five books costing a total of $12. The school replaces one-fourth of these each year at a cost of $3 per child. Therefore,

to arrive at the budget for textbooks, the number of children (100) is multiplied by the per-pupil expenditure ($3) for a $300 budget allowance. However, if enrollments jump to 110, the formula doesn't work. It gives a total of $330, where actually an expenditure of $420 is required. The extra 10 pupils require an investment of $12 each to give them the books they need.

* * *

Because so many schools have failed to grasp this simple economic fact, the American Textbook Publishers Institute has prepared detailed information on the subject. A free booklet, "Budgeting for Textbooks," is available from the Institute, 1 Madison Ave., New York 10, N.Y.

One way of handling the problem of financing textbooks for new schools has been getting more attention recently. Some school districts, in issuing bonds for new buildings, have included the cost of textbooks in this capital outlay. You'd have to check your state laws on such a practice—but it's being done successfully in more than one state.

What's Between the Book Covers?

No great hue and cry seems to exist this year about the content of the books—what's between the covers of the texts. But this sort of thing has come up before, and it can happen again. Perhaps there are some guidelines to go by out of past experience.

In the first place, it seems to be reasonably obvious that the textbook publishers, a group of pretty diverse and intelligent individuals, are in business to make money. Competition being as keen as it is, no one of them is knowingly going to print a bad textbook, nor an anti-social one. He doesn't want to lose money or to have his competitor's product show up better.

Yet American textbooks are not perfect, as the publishers themselves will be quick to admit. These books, like other creative efforts, are often a compromise between the ideal and the possible. Human fallibility enters here.

* * *

One of the chief charges made a few years ago was that some given textbook advocated a change in the existing social order. This sometimes took on great proportions in an aura of high excitement. In a way it provided a parallel to the old saying that "for want of a nail the shoe was lost, for want of a shoe the horse was lost, for want of a horse the rider was lost, for want of a rider the battle was lost—all for the want of a horseshoe nail."

The parallel here is that somebody would find a passage in a textbook which could be made the basis of a dispute. On the basis of that passage aroused opponents would condemn the whole textbook, then broaden the attack to all textbooks within the school system, then to the school system itself.

When a social change was concerned, often the charge would be that the textbook was advocating the change, and therefore the school system which used the book also was advocating the change. On examination it would be found that the text was merely recording a change which already had occurred.

* * *

This discovery didn't necessarily satisfy the critics, some of whom wanted social changes ignored or opposed. An easy "out" for publishers would seem to be extra care in taking a wholly factual, middle-of-the-road position. But then they were subject to the criticism that their books were namby-pamby and lacked vitality and interest.

An example would be a textbook reporting on the growth of government activities during the last generation. An up-to-date book which touches the subject can hardly avoid reporting that growth did occur. But some critics will want this reported as government interference, and others as government participation and aid. How can the textbook publisher satisfy everyone? The fact is, he can't—but if criticisms are considered in the light of prejudices, and if critics will remember that the publisher is a businessman rather than a conspirator, we will perhaps achieve a more objective evaluation of textbooks.

The only satisfactory way for citizens to find out how good their textbooks are is to judge for themselves how well they perform the job they were designed to do. They are generally carefully designed to serve to-day's schools. The schools and their curricula, which generally have grown out of what the public has demanded, are the determining factors in the nature and function of textbooks.

Textbook Is Not the Whole School

It should be remembered that the textbook, important as it is, does not constitute all there is to schooling.

The teacher is of far greater importance. A good teacher can take a dull textbook and bring it to life for her pupils. A poor teacher can give assignments out of a fine textbook and still not achieve the results of the good teacher.

* * *

There are many supplementary teaching tools—too many to cover in a discussion of textbooks alone—which help determine the effectiveness of teaching and textbooks. Numerous instructional aids do not depend on the printed word.

The most effective classroom instruction makes full use of all the teaching tools that can contribute to better learning. Each has a function

which it can perform most effectively—and all are important. Experiments have been under way for some years to produce an "instructional package" which will include textbooks, films, and other audio-visual materials, all carefully designed to augment and supplement each other. Possibly this is the direction improvement in teaching materials will take in the future.

Meanwhile, the many materials available to the teacher have been likened to the different instruments in an orchestra, each one of which contributes to the harmony of the whole. Certainly, an awareness has spread during the past few years that there need be no competition among the different kinds of teaching materials. Each has its place and our classrooms should take advantage of the great variety available in order to improve instruction and increase the rate of student learning.

* * *

The citizens who own the schools need to know which of these are being used and how. Only on the basis of such knowledge can they judge all teaching materials, including textbooks.

In discussing a course of action for "the battle of the books," Haefner [18:227–228] observes that investigations of textbooks are not new, for criticisms always occur during a period of crisis; that attacks manifest "the age-old struggle against freedom to teach and freedom to learn"; and that "critical examination of teaching materials can be a wholesome and desirable democratic process." Since charges are often too serious to be ignored, Haefner suggests that it is important to make a study of the pattern, the motives, the logic, and the methods used in attacks on textbooks.

As a simple guide to those charged with the responsibility for textbook selection, Mellott (editor-in-chief, textbook department, John C. Winston Company, book publishers) discusses the following factors to be studied: "organization, content, method, illustrations, and general appearance." [31:158–159]

Although criticisms of *methods* of teaching reading have made the headlines in recent years, there also appears to be some dissatisfaction with the *content* of elementary school readers or "textbooks." Thompson [46:11, 14, 16, 18] maintains that the problem is "not only '*Can* Johnny read?' but 'What makes him *want* to read?'" She observes that, compared with the McGuffey readers, the material in modern readers lacks imagination and discrimination. Very few selections have been written by "authors of established literary reputation." In the same vein, Rafferty contends that "we are teaching trivia." He contrasts the old and the new readers in the following bit of satire:

Ulysses and Penelope have been replaced by Dick and Jane in the textbooks of our schools. The quest of the Golden Fleece has been crowded out by the visit of Tom and Susan to the zoo. The deeds of the heroes before Troy are now passé, and the peregrinations of the local iceman as he wends his way among the stodgy streets and littered alleys of Blah City are deemed worthy of numberless pages in our primers. The Stone Age and sterile culture of the Pueblo Indians loom large in our curriculum, but the knightly Crusaders are ignored. Jackie pursues his insipid goal of a ride in the district garbage truck with good old crotchety Mr. Jones, while the deathless ride of Paul Revere goes unwept, unhonored, and unsung. It is interesting, and certainly significant, that modern education has deliberately debunked the hero to make room for the jerk. The lofty exception to the rank and file, whom all of us could envy and emulate, has been compelled to give way to the Great Mediocrity, the consensus of all that is harmless and safe and banal among us.*

According to Nila Banton Smith, "More challenging materials are needed. Children of today are sophisticated; much of the material they are supposed to read in school is below their level of intelligence and understanding." **

---

* Quoted by special permission from "Suffer, Little Children," by Max Rafferty, Superintendent of Schools, Needles, California, published in the *Phi Delta Kappan*, December, 1956, p. 90.

** National Education Association, Department of Elementary School Principals, "Reading for Today's Children," *The National Elementary Principal*, Thirty-fourth Yearbook Number (Washington, D.C.: the National Education Association, September, 1955), p. 8.

A frequently used supplement to the textbook is the workbook. The workbook is a type of instructional material the effectiveness of which is often discussed pro and con. According to Hurd (page 158), it is widely used in science. After reviewing the debate over workbooks or "consumable texts," Madden [28:94–95], by means of several penetrating questions, suggests how a teacher of large classes or an inexperienced teacher, for example, may use a workbook profitably if he avoids excessive use, uses it to supplement the text and to promote better understanding, and considers needs of pupils of primary importance.

AUDIO-VISUAL MATERIALS

According to an observation in a recent issue of the *Review of Educational Research,* "a vast amount of research has accumulated during the past thirty years, demonstrating conclusively that A-V instructional materials, properly used, can make significant contributions to learning over a wide range of conditions and subject-matter content." [3:148]

To what extent are classroom teachers using audio-visual materials? What are some of the obstacles to more widespread use? Answers to these and other questions have been provided by the Research Division of the National Education Association. Four of the serious barriers to effective use of audio-visual materials, reported by 623 school districts, are "(*a*) Classroom teachers as a whole are not interested in using audio-visual material (49 per cent), (*b*) it is difficult to obtain sufficient funds for equipment and materials (39 per cent), (*c*) the district lacks a central agency to get the materials together and to coordinate the work (26 per cent), and (*d*) adequately trained leaders are not available for employment (16 per cent.)" * Further analysis of the reasons why classroom teachers are not interested indicated lack of suitable instructional space as the number-one problem and lack of money as second in importance. "Concluding impressions" of the above report have been summarized in these words:

In some ways, this report shows that real progress is being made in audio-visual education. More departments of audio-visual education are being established, more equipment and materials are available in the classroom, more

* From "Audio-Visual Education in Urban School Districts, 1953–54," *NEA Research Bulletin,* Vol. 33, No. 3 (October, 1955), p. 123 (Washington, D.C.: National Education Association). Quoted by special permission.

classroom teachers are prepared to use the materials, and more teachers are using them.

On the other hand, some problems that call urgently for attention stand out from the data. More time, better timing, more central coordination, better-adapted classrooms, more and better training, and behind all the needs, better financial support—these represent work yet to be accomplished in audio-visual education.*

While there may be partisans for a particular type of instructional material—the textbook or audio-visual materials, for example—the National Citizens Commission for the Public Schools (now the National Citizens Council for Better Schools) offers some pertinent suggestions for harmonizing extreme viewpoints.

The Harmony of the Whole

by THE NATIONAL CITIZENS COMMISSION FOR THE PUBLIC SCHOOLS

From *How Good Are Our Teaching Materials?* published by the National Citizens Commission for the Public Schools (now the National Citizens Council for Better Schools), January, 1955, pages 53–54. Reprinted by special permission.

The wealth of teaching materials available to the schools today might be compared to the many instruments in an orchestra. The teacher, as the director, calls on each one as it is needed to contribute to the harmony of the whole. No single instrument is complete in itself, nor can it be criticized intelligently as a separate entity. Any evaluation of it must consider how well it performs its part of the entire program.

There is no place within this cooperative effort for competitive jockeying for primacy. It is the skillful use of all materials in their rightful place that leads to better learning.

Both textbook partisans and exponents of audio-visual materials are coming to a fuller realization that both are vitally important and neither is all-sufficient.

Efforts are now being made to integrate audio-visual and textbook learning more fully. Experiments with films and filmstrips designed as an integral part of textbooks are already in progress. A complete and carefully planned instructional materials package with textbook, tests, recordings, films, supplementary pamphlets, etc., has not yet been developed. Nevertheless, it suggests the way in which, ideally, many class-

* *Loc. cit.* Quoted by special permission.

room tools should be integrated to serve the schools most efficiently.

Knowledge of the role each should play is still incomplete. Experience and research, however, are fast expanding our understanding of how the new aids can supplement and sharpen traditional tools.

In order to evaluate instructional materials intelligently, laymen must be aware of the objectives their schools seek to achieve. (See the Commission's working guide, *What Should Our Schools Accomplish?*) Then it will be possible to determine how well the instructional materials are adapted to helping the teacher reach these objectives. It is not enough to know the formally stated goals of a school. Citizens should become better acquainted with the individual teachers and learn what each one seeks to accomplish in his own classroom. For the job that the teacher is trying to do really determines what materials are needed and demonstrates their effectiveness or lack of it.

When citizens understand this relationship of instructional materials to classroom goals, they understand far better why the teacher urges that he be given visual aids for certain parts of the course, textbooks to serve other purposes, supplementary reading materials and other instructional equipment. They are also able to judge the value of these materials far better when they understand their specific purposes.

Academic freedom is less important as professional liberty for the teacher than as freedom for children to learn. So it is with instructional materials. They are important not so much because they help the teacher teach as because they help the learner learn. Their purpose is to help students learn better, faster, and more accurately. Wherever they succeed in this purpose their importance cannot be overestimated.

When laymen understand the nature and purpose of the whole range of classroom tools they will almost invariably give them whatever support is needed.

This is the best insurance any community can have that these instruments of instruction will serve the community's common interest, its children.

FREE AND INEXPENSIVE MATERIALS

A category designated as "free and inexpensive materials" is beginning to assume increasing importance in the modern school with its emphasis on the use of a great variety of instructional resources. In a recent issue of the *Review of Educational Research* [3:180–181] it is reported that free and inexpensive materials are widely used, but that there is concern over their quality and adequacy. Consequently, the report concludes with these recommendations: more cooperative research by workers in colleges and universities and in business and industry to study preparation and use of such materials; and more help for teachers, both pre-service and in-service, in discovering and using such materials.

CURRICULUM RESOURCE CENTERS

Of inestimable value to curriculum workers, especially teachers and their classes, are resource centers for instructional materials. The development of such centers in city and country school systems, in institutions of higher learning, and in state departments of education has taken place at an accelerated pace during the last two decades. At first these resource centers were thought of "more as repositories of materials than as workshops and places of learning" [3:193]; but the workshop movement has been instrumental in bringing about a greater emphasis on the laboratory function of such centers for both teachers and students. While the desirability of integrating more closely various types of centers has been recognized, resource centers are still classified and operated as separate libraries, museums, audio-visual centers, and curriculum laboratories (or libraries). [3:184–196]

The importance of the librarian in charge of the materials center is stressed by Lieberman. [27:71–76] He maintains that there are two features of curriculum development today: (*a*) "shared leadership" and (*b*) "diversity of materials." The need for the "materials specialist" or school librarian to work with curriculum committees "to improve the instructional program of the school" cannot be overemphasized.

RESEARCH FINDINGS TO AID THE CLASSROOM TEACHER

Directly related to the improvement of instructional materials and procedures is the utilization of research findings in the classroom. Too often the results of research either are not readily available or are not directly applicable to classroom situations. (These problems, as well as others relating to the application of research to the classroom, are discussed at length in Part Three of this book.) In order to make the findings of research more accessible to teachers, the NEA Department of Classroom Teachers and the American Educational Research Association, another NEA department, have been publishing a series of pamphlets, entitled "What Research Says to the Teacher." (See the Bibliography on page 287 for a complete list of titles.) As a further service to teachers, the *NEA Journal* publishes condensations of these reports from time to time. Strang's article on "homework," pages 220–224, is an example. The *Journal* also includes concise, readable summaries of research studies like the one by Shane below. Basing his conclusions on some 800 studies, he attempts to answer the forty-nine questions about language arts most frequently asked by teachers.

What Research Indicates About Teaching the Language Arts
by HAROLD G. SHANE

From the *NEA Journal,* October, 1955, pages 402–404. Reprinted by special permission. This article is a condensation of *Research Helps in Teaching the Language Arts,* edited by Dr. Shane, a booklet published by the Association for Supervision and Curriculum Development, a department of the NEA. Harold G. Shane is Professor of Education, Northwestern University.

Recently the Association for Supervision and Curriculum Development, NEA, sent forms to over a thousand teachers studying in five major universities, asking them to indicate the questions they would like to have answered by findings in language-arts research. The responses were sorted and grouped, then submitted to over twenty authorities, who listed some eight hundred available research studies which would help answer the forty-nine questions most frequently asked by the teachers.

Most of these eight hundred studies have been located and reviewed during the past eighteen months. This article is a highly condensed summary of some of the research findings which it is hoped will be of interest to readers of the *NEA Journal.*

Reading

Readiness for reading can be determined successfully, the research indicates, but no *single* measure is sufficiently accurate to permit conclusions pertaining to an individual child. Readiness for reading can be fostered by providing suitable experiences, and these experiences are especially important for children with meager backgrounds and those speaking a foreign tongue in the home. Research shows that the "right" time to begin reading varies with individual children. In general, however, a *mental* age of approximately six and one-half years appears to be the optimum one for success.

Phonetic analysis has been shown to be helpful in reading—but with the important qualification that it should be functional rather than rote.

A mental age of seven or above is necessary for rudimentary insight into phonetic principles, the research indicates. Some type of systematic approach involving phonetics is recommended by a number of researchers, but they differ as to when, in what form, and to what degree such word analyses are desirable. The sheer variety of phonetic combinations is in itself a problem, and apparently neither children nor adults make effective use of diacritical markings in determining pronunciation.

Most experimenters report success in ventures aimed at improving speed of reading. Improved motivations, the use of teaching aids, and information on one's own progress have been found to increase speed. A child's IQ and his vocabulary directly determine the extent of his comprehension in reading.

While research reports agree that reading programs should be modified because of individual differences in children, they disagree as to whether ability grouping is desirable. The causes of reading disabilities have been identified in various studies. Among the more common causes are physical deficiencies, meager environment, low IQ, and psychological problems.

Children's reading interests tend to follow definite patterns, varying from grade to grade with sex, age, and IQ. Comic books, however, are a prevalent "childhood disease," with nearly everyone reading them in the first eight grades. Even in high school the comic book accounts for 25 per cent of the magazine reading!

Research indicates that our bases for evaluating progress in reading should be broadened to include greater attention to reading in relation to socio-emotional adjustment, home conditions, maturity level, intelligence, and physical health.

Handwriting

Readiness for *writing,* as indicated by investigations, is influenced by elements similar to those which determine *reading* readiness — mental age and perceptual acuity, for example. Apparently premature stress on correct letter forms may stifle *creative* written expression, but there is little or no conclusive research on how to stimulate creative writing.

With respect to the mechanics of writing, manuscript forms are now taught through grade 2 almost universally in the United States. Most schools begin teaching cursive forms in grade 3. Reports conflict as to which form permits greater speed, but manuscript is apparently easier for young children to learn. Investigators declare that, contrary to much current opinion, the change from one form to another does not create any particular problem for children.

Ironically, research indicates that illegibility in handwriting increases with age, being three and one-half times *greater* in adult penmanship samples than in elementary-school specimens! The letters *a, e, r,* and *t* tend to be most troublesome.

As many as 9 per cent or 10 per cent of children today tend to be left-handed and for a variety of reasons: genetic, instructional, environmental, and so on.

Spelling

Many spelling lists are now available to the teacher as a result of research studies. Like spelling books, these carefully constructed lists vary appreciably both in content and in the grade-placement of words. Research indicates that radio, television, and similar influential cultural elements are changing and enriching word acquisition in childhood.

Most research studies indicate that spelling should be taught methodically. However, there is a lively controversy between the proponents of "functional" and "formal" spelling instruction. Each side cites research findings to back up its claim that its methods are the better. The actual issue is not whether to teach spelling but the degree to which spelling instruction should be structured.

Visual defects do not apparently characterize poor spellers, the studies show. Spelling ability correlates with the IQ and to an even greater extent with a child's vocabulary. There is also a positive relationship between visual discrimination, phonetic ability, and achievement in spelling.

English Usage

Investigations have demonstrated that strict grammatical usage, as often taught in school, is out-of-date in the sense that it is more fastidious than the everyday brand used in normal speech. It has also been shown through research studies that formal grammar should not be introduced at too early an age and that teaching sentence diagraming has a limited value in improving actual language usage.

Some researchers feel that their findings point to the need to teach a smaller number of usage skills more thoroughly. It also has been noted that children tend to omit rather than misuse punctuation in informal writing.

Children's Literature

Children's reading interests have been investigated repeatedly and likes and dislikes rather clearly established by age, sex, and intelligence. Among the findings is the fact that the *story* in a book rather than its *format* attracts children.

A considerable amount of research points to definite (although presumably unintentional) examples of stereotyping and prejudice toward racial groups portrayed in children's books. On the other hand, large numbers of books have been cited as suitable for strengthening intercultural understanding and sympathy. Bibliotherapy, the use of books as a means of helping individuals with personal and psychological problems, is becoming recognized in both psychiatric and educational journals as useful.

Listening

Especially in recent years, listening has become a recognized phase of the language arts, if one is to judge by the substantial body of current research pertaining to it. The keen interest in listening seems most appropriate, since research has established, in a forty-two-state survey, that elementary-school children are expected to listen during 57.5 per cent of the school day.

Various kinds of listening skills have been identified through research, as have factors influencing listening ability—IQ, reading-comprehension scores, degree of fatigue, and the listener's vocabulary, to name a few. Evidently the ability to listen and comprehend is as varied as the ability to read with comprehension.

Foreign Language in the Grades

An extraordinary surge of interest in the teaching of foreign languages below grade 7 is evident in recent publications. In 1954, for example, approximately 80 per cent of the programs of foreign-language instruction in elementary schools had been begun during the preceding thirty-six months. Surveys show that Spanish is the most popular tongue, with French second, and German a lagging third.

As yet, there is not much research in elementary-school foreign-language teaching, but the advocates of such instruction feel that although aural-oral work in a second language can be started, under normal circumstances, at the five-year-old level, reading and writing in it are better introduced in the middle grades.

Conclusion

A review of research studies in the various language-arts areas strongly supports the view that many of the perennial questions discussed by teachers can be answered, at least in part, by an examination of the painstaking and often fascinating reports in research journals. There is a wealth of information in this educational storehouse for those who will seek it.

Although research reports provide a wealth of information, they often raise as many questions as they answer and challenge the teacher, in his daily work with children, to find new and better ways of achieving the goal of creative teaching.

An adaptation and abridgement of significant research studies in the three R's—reading, writing (legibility and fluency), and arithmetic—which is attracting considerable attention is *Research in the Three R's,* of which C. W. Hunnicutt and William J. Iverson are editors (New York: Harper & Brothers, 1958). Research findings in the first R, reading, attempt to answer such questions as the following: What is the relationship between effective reading and such factors as eye movements, intelligence, readiness, and phonetic training? Does reading in the various content fields pose special problems? How can readability or difficulty of material be determined? (Dale and Chall include a usable formula on pages 194–213 of the Hunnicutt-Iverson book.) What are the sizes and rates of growth of children's vocabularies? (Rinsland describes how he developed a vocabulary list for elementary-school children on pages 213–223. He derived his list from a comprehensive study of over 200,000 samples of children's writings.)

Research findings in the second R, writing, deal with such factors as manuscript and cursive writing, analysis of spelling difficulties, improved methods of teaching spelling, and improvement of language usage. (See, for example, "What Grammar Should Be Taught?" by Fries, on pages 322–330.)

Research in the third R, arithmetic, covers such problems as drill versus meanings, readiness for number concepts, and grade placement of formal instruction in arithmetic.

For teachers who are especially interested in research in the language arts, there are several very good references on the subject. McCullough * has made an excellent survey of research in reading, dealing with such problems as vocabulary, comprehension, speed, and tastes and appreciations; "grouping for instruction"; and evaluation of "growth in reading skills." An extensive bibliography is also included. Emmett A. Betts ** has reviewed the research on phonics, including an extensive bibliography. Betts also served as editor of the "Spelling Number" of *Education* for January, 1956. In an article on spelling in that issue, Betts (pages 310–325) has indicated the reasons for spelling difficulties, included an informal spelling inventory, and given several suggestions for helping children improve their spelling. The entire issue of the April, 1958, *Review of Educational Research* is devoted to "Language Arts and the Fine Arts." Since methods of teaching are inseparable from curricula, the teacher may find the March, 1958, *Phi Delta Kappan,* which is subtitled "What Research Says about TEACHING and LEARNING," quite helpful. Included are excellent summaries of findings of research related to such topics as the learner and learning, individual differences, lecture versus discussion, problem-solving, critical thinking, and directive and non-directive methods of teaching.

---

* Constance M. McCullough, "What Does Research Reveal about Practices in Teaching Reading?" *English Journal,* 46:475–490 (November, 1957).

** Emmett Albert Betts, "Phonics: Practical Considerations Based on Research," *Elementary English,* 33:357–371 (October, 1956).

Although the following references would not be classified as summaries of research, they do offer some helpful suggestions to the language arts teacher. In *The Reading Teacher's Reader* (New York: The Ronald Press, 1958), Oscar S. Causey has organized a collection of articles and reports which covers such subjects as the following: the nature of the reading process, effective methods and procedures, the place of phonics, word recognition and vocabulary building, emotional factors in reading, and the value of audio-visual materials. In the September, 1955, *National Elementary Principal* (Thirty-fourth Yearbook Number, subtitled "Reading for Today's Children"), there is a sampling of current, worthwhile *practices* in reading. The issue is actually the second in a series of yearbooks on reading, the first appearing in 1938. Several pertinent topics are covered, such as developing reading readiness, individualizing group instruction, reading in various subject matter areas, selection of textbooks, and interpreting the reading program. Jewett * has given a concise summary of fifteen trends in high school English teaching.

The U.S. Office of Education, with the assistance of the Research Committee of the National Council of Teachers of Mathematics, made an analysis of research in the teaching of mathematics during the calendar years 1955 and 1956. Data from 123 studies, classified by three grade levels—college, high school, elementary—were received. A summary of findings for the high school and elementary-school levels, plus recommendations for future research, follows.

Summary   by KENNETH E. BROWN

Reprinted from *Analysis of Research in the Teaching of Mathematics 1955 and 1956*, pages 21–23. Published by the U.S. Department of Health, Education, and Welfare, Office of Education, Bulletin 1958, No. 4 (Washington, D.C.: U.S. Government Printing Office, 1958). Kenneth E. Brown is Specialist in Mathematics in the U.S. Office of Education.

High School Level

Several of the studies on teaching high school mathematics placed emphasis on understanding concepts. The means of securing understandings varied from the use of cardboard strips to pupil discovery and

---

* Arno Jewett, "National Trends in Teaching High School English," *English Journal*, 46:326–329 (September, 1957).

experimentation. The teaching methods, no matter whether they involved physical aids or a grouping within a class, seemed to be beneficial to some extent when used by the advocate. Like the chalk board, the device itself seldom teaches, but when used by skilled teachers it helps instruction. Surveys seem to indicate that the chalk board is the most frequently used aid in mathematics teaching and the lecture-recitation the most popular method.

The research evidenced considerable activity in the study of the content of high school mathematics courses. The research varied from a listing of some practical problems for a course to a control experiment involving teachers in several states. No doubt the research on the frontiers of mathematics education is most valuable; but for implementation to take place, research will need to determine what specific changes can be put into effect with the present teachers. For example: How much modern mathematics and which modern mathematics can present teachers incorporate in their classes? How much change can be made in the content of high school courses and still give security not only to the teachers but to the parents? These and similar questions remain unanswered.

Research has shown that a combination of scores on an aptitude test and an achievement test, and previous mathematics marks is a good predictor of success in high school

mathematics; but research has not shown what motivates pupils to pursue the study of mathematics. Research indicates that high school mathematics teachers are a dominant force in causing high school pupils to pursue the study of mathematics. Research has not shown, however, why these teachers are outstanding in their ability to influence pupils.

Elementary School Level

Several studies were reported on the use of physical devices in the teaching of elementary-school mathematics. Although some devices seemed to be helpful when used by the experimenter, none of the devices made outstanding contributions.

Teachers indicated that some of the physical devices are desirable but that they lack the money to buy, or the time to make, them; also that for effective teaching they needed instruction in using the aids.

Many of the studies were concerned with ways to teach arithmetic so that the concepts in operation will have more meaning to the pupil. These studies varied from teaching division as successive subtraction to teaching arithmetic with the aid of a computing machine. But in each case the purpose was to emphasize the meaning of the operation. Investigations in this area usually involve patterns of thinking done by pupils in problem solving. Although the research indicates that meaning should be emphasized in arithmetical instruction, it has not determined how much drill should be merely repetitive or how much it should include repeating the operation in a meaningful social situation.

Recommendations for Future Research

The research in mathematics education reported for the years 1955–1956 indicates that many persons have attacked small problem areas. Some of these areas of investigation are of minor importance. A casual reading of the summaries of research in the appendix reveals student studies of inferior quality with very little contribution to the teaching of mathematics. Little of the research was that of a team approach to the solution of a critical problem in this area. Even the studies of individual faculty members differed materially in their quality and contribution to mathematics education. Some of the investigations resulted in the compilation of teaching material or detailed experiments which were never published or were published in very abbreviated form. Such research has little impact on mathematics education.

This report on research in mathematics education lists certain unanswered questions and problems in mathematics education where there has been little research. However, it should not be assumed that these are the most critical issues in the teaching of mathematics.

Research reflects three important needs in mathematics education. *First, the identification of the crucial problems.* (These problems might be identified by state groups of teachers or by national committees. In any case, they should be identified to give direction to research.) *Second, greater coordination of effort in attacking the identified problems.* (Many of the problems are too large to be solved by a single individual; teamwork will be necessary.) *Third, publication and wide distribution of research.* (Unpublished research has little impact on classroom practice.)

Future advancement in the teaching of mathematics will depend upon the extent to which we identify the crucial problems, coordinate our efforts to solve them, and make the results known to the classroom teacher. [ED. NOTE: The above recommendations for future research are equally pertinent to all subject matter areas.]

Glennon and Hunnicutt have organized and presented research findings in an attempt to answer some thirty-seven questions concerning the teaching of arithmetic. The questions range from such general ones as *What do we know about readiness for arithmetic?* and *What is the relationship of personality traits to achievement?* to such specific inquiries as *Should children add up or down in column addition?* and *What method for dividing by a decimal?*

The authors have made a valuable summary of the field and offer the following admonition for its interpretation: "Although most of the answers provided are research-based, there are some answers that are not strictly and rigorously research-centered. However, it should be remembered that all modern educational practices were at one time, or still are, the result of speculative inquiry. Also, in the last analysis all curriculum problems are value problems." *

In a further attempt to encourage teachers to make more application of research findings to the classroom, some of the periodicals include non-technical summaries of research as a regular feature. An illustration of this type of summary is the non-technical review of research in science, appearing in the October, 1954, *Journal of Education,* by Mallinson and Buck. They have reviewed the present status of the science program in three areas: (*a*) the curriculum (objective, content, materials); (*b*) teaching and learning of science (objectives, students' interests, audio-visual aids, evaluation techniques); and (*c*) the training of science teachers.

Some Implications and Practical Applications of Recent Research in Science Education

by GEORGE G. MALLINSON and JACQUELINE V. BUCK

Reprinted from the *Journal of Education,* October, 1954, pages 23–26. Permission is granted by the *Journal of Education,* published by Boston University, School of Education. George G. Mallinson is Dean of the School of Graduate Studies, Western Michigan University, Kalamazoo. Jacqueline Buck is Mrs. Mallinson.

In science education, as in every other area of education, a great many investigations have been undertaken in order to solve many of the related problems. For the most part these individual investigations are merely "drops in the bucket," and a large bucket at that! But, during the years, the "bucket" is being filled gradually, and a survey of the accumulated "drops" reveals much progress toward solving the problems.

Few science teachers, however, have either the time or the publica-

* Vincent J. Glennon and C. W. Hunnicutt, *What Does Research Say About Arithmetic?* Association for Supervision and Curriculum Development, a department of the National Education Association (Washington, D.C., 1958), p. ix.

tions available to read thoroughly all the research that has been produced in the field of science education. Yet nearly all of them are interested in learning some of the implications and practical applications of these studies. Hence, this review is an attempt to provide science teachers with such information, namely a nontechnical summary of the findings of recent research studies in science education.

Obviously in a report of this type it would be a tremendous task to cite individually all the several hundred contributing investigations as well as discuss their methods and findings. Further, it would serve no useful purpose. Hence, such citations will be left to the more technical, detailed reviews of research in science education.

For convenience, the studies have been summarized under the following major headings: (*a*) the science curriculum, (*b*) the teaching and learning of science, and (*c*) the training of teachers.

The Science Curriculum

The history and growth of science education. According to historical studies the place of science in the secondary-school curriculum has been well established for many decades. However, the nature of science instruction in the secondary school has been, and is, changing constantly. In the early days of education, science was considered to be a "mental discipline" course. This meant that

young men who were being trained for the professions (and at that time they were about the only ones who attended secondary schools) were taught science because of its value in "training the mind," not because of its practical applications.

In harmony with this philosophy of science education, the "traditional" science courses such as botany, zoology, astronomy, geology, chemistry, and physics established themselves in the secondary schools. It was believed that these "college courses in miniature" served admirably the primary function of the high school, namely, preparing students for college. The non-college student failed to profit from such courses and so many ultimately dropped out.

In contrast, the present era of education is chiefly one of "general education." This implies that the high school is being designed for the education of *all* students, regardless of their future occupational plans. Hence science programs are being modified to meet with the prevailing philosophy. Recent studies indicate that science educators are attempting to develop courses that will offer *all* students a background in science that will enable them to interpret adequately the scientific age in which they live as well as provide them with foundations for later specialization in science.

This change to the general education philosophy is slow, and sometimes painful. Nevertheless the transition is evident in that today about

50 per cent of the students in the average high school are enrolled in one or more science courses. The largest enrollments by far are in the general education courses, namely, general science and general biology, the latter being offered in about 95 per cent of all high schools. In addition, there is evidence of the steady growth of a new general education course, general physical science. The traditional courses in physics and chemistry, however, are offered in less than one-half of the high schools in the country. Further, in many of the schools in which they are offered they are taught in alternate years. The smallest of all science enrollments are of course in the more specialized courses such as physiology, earth science, and botany.

The history of elementary-school science roughly parallels that outlined for secondary. However, science was introduced much later to the elementary school than to the secondary and it is still in a state of flux. For many years there was little or no science instruction at the elementary-school level, except as it was taught incidentally with other subject-matter areas. Few adults of the current generation can recall receiving science training in the grades except for occasional lessons in "nature study" in which they may have learned to identify birds or leaves or wild flowers. When it was introduced, elementary-school science seems to have grown more or less from the top down. Instead of being developed in terms of what was desirable for elementary-school children, elementary-school science courses were miniature editions of those taught in high school. However, the importance of an organized program of science in the elementary school, designed with the elementary-school approach, is currently well recognized. Research workers at the elementary-school level are devoting efforts to identifying the elements of science that will enable young children to interpret, at their levels of maturity, the science experiences with which they come in contact. There are still many problems with respect to this type of instruction in elementary-school science, but at least it seems to be "here to stay."

Objectives of science instruction. Since the objectives of science teaching determine to a large degree the science curriculum, research on curriculum is generally accompanied with research on objectives. Research in the history of the development of the elementary-school science curriculum indicates the changes that have taken place in the objectives of science at this level. The evidence shows that the memorization of facts for mental discipline is of no more value as an objective at the elementary-school level than at the secondary. However, many studies do show that there are three major objectives of science instruction that apply to all levels, including the elementary. They are the development of the abilities to (*a*) understand and apply important scientific facts and principles, (*b*) think critically, and (c) attack scientific problems using rational techniques. Much research has been carried out successfully in identifying the important facts and principles, the elements in critical thinking, and the techniques of problem solving. However, research in science education has much to accomplish in finding the best methods for attaining these objectives.

Course content. While there is still much "traditional" subject matter in courses in high school science, the contents of these courses are shifting gradually from an array of logically-organized facts to the study of problem areas that are focused on the experiences that students face at this age level. Research shows that this newer organization of learning experiences is more functional, as well as more interesting to the student than the older one. Further, this newer approach provides him with information that ramifies into his daily experiences rather than merely providing a list of facts, about 90 per cent of which are forgotten within a year after the course is completed. These functional materials actually increase in usefulness with time since they are continually reinforced as students face related experiences from day to day.

The program of elementary-school science is changing more rapidly than the secondary. Since elementary science is relatively new and less bound by tradition, teachers are often freer to "break loose" and organize the instruction around cores of material that are important and interesting to children. In harmony with these efforts, there has been a great deal of research concerning definite grade placement of science topics and concepts in the elementary school. However, all studies seem to indicate that any attempt to allocate, for example, concepts of botany to the second grade, concepts of electricity to the third grade, or concepts of zoology to the fourth grade is unrealistic. Research evidence indicates unequivocally that learning is continuous, and that learning patterns vary from child to child. Hence, concepts in any area of science may be feasible elements of content at any grade level, depending on the complexity with which they are developed, and the learning experiences that are used to develop them.

Textbooks and supplementary materials. A comparison of science textbooks of several decades ago with modern ones is akin to contrasting the "flapper" fashions of the roaring twenties with the current clothing styles. Studies of modern textbooks in science indicate that they are more profusely illustrated, have much more color, are built around problem areas to a much greater extent than the older ones, and have a greater diversity of end-of-chapter activities. However, there is much room for improvement. Many of the suggested activities are out-of-date, while most of the suggested experiments are still

designed around cookbook procedures rather than around problems
that stimulate students to think and
to experiment inductively.

In addition, the levels of reading
difficulty of many textbooks, both elementary and secondary, are often
above the levels of the students for
whom they are designed. Few books
provide for growth in reading ability
from the beginning to the end of the
year. Also, only a few textbooks bear
witness to having technical vocabularies that have been selected by careful research techniques.

Within the last few years some publishers have prepared science units in
pamphlet form for use in the science
classroom. Many teachers have used
these in addition to using magazines,
comic books, commercial pamphlets,
and government bulletins in science
courses. Research studies have shown
that all these have great value in motivating students and for supplement-
ing the textbook. However, in the
few studies in which the effectiveness
of these materials has been compared
with that of textbooks, it has been
found that textbooks provide the
foundational materials just as well
and with less effort from the teacher.
Thus these materials seem to be well
named—"supplementary."

Integration with other courses.
Within recent years much has been
written about the core curriculum
and integrated courses. However,
there is little research that deals with
the integration of science with other
school subjects. The research that is

available tends to indicate that while
it is possible to integrate science materials with materials from other
areas, there seems to be no significant
evidence of any substantial increments in achievement. This is apparently one area in which more
research is needed before definite
conclusions can be drawn.

The Teaching and Learning of Science

*Teaching the objectives of science
education.* A great many studies have
been conducted to determine the effectiveness of current teaching methods, and to develop new methods of
instruction that will be helpful in
reaching the desired goals of science
instruction. Several conclusions can
be drawn. First, nearly all these studies indicate that all the major objectives of science instruction can be
accomplished, but any significant accomplishment demands planned and
directed efforts. That is, *it is possible*
to develop in children the ability to
recognize and apply scientific principles, to think critically, to develop attitudes of openmindedness, to be free
from superstition, to suspend judgment, and to attack scientific problems using rational techniques. However, one cannot expect that these
desirable outcomes are concomitants
of the teaching of facts or of incidental efforts. Rather, conscious effort
must be put forth to develop them.

Second, the exact method by which
these objectives are taught seems to
be relatively unimportant. No one

method seems to be superior to any other. The most effective method will differ depending on factors such as the age level of the students, the topic being studied, and the personality of the teacher. Again a variety of teaching methods seems to be of greater effectiveness in achieving the objectives of science instruction than one method alone. Hence, discussions, experiments, demonstrations, and projects all are helpful when used judiciously.

Science interests of students. Currently one hears much about "meeting the needs and interests of the child." In science education numerous studies have been conducted in an attempt to identify students' interests. These studies have been motivated chiefly by two considerations. Some workers have attempted to identify interests for the purpose of organizing courses of science instruction around the areas of greatest student interest. Others have attempted to identify students with high interest in science in an attempt to guide them into science courses and hence help to alleviate the great shortage of scientists and science teachers.

However, neither of these considerations has been instrumental in achieving especially fruitful results. With respect to the former consideration, findings indicate that children's interests are in general too unstable to be useful in developing the foundations of curricula. A young child may watch a Western movie on TV today and hence want to be a cow-

boy. Tomorrow when he watches Captain Video, he will want to be a space cadet, and day after tomorrow, when his class visits the fire department, he will have a great desire to become a fireman. Thus the span of attention on any single activity tends to be short and is directed by ephemeral experiences. Obviously, this example applies to an elementary-school child, but similar conclusions can be applied to a somewhat lesser extent to high school students. Studies show that interests are seldom stable until at least late adolescence. Hence, any attempt to organize the foundations of courses around interest is obviously impractical. At best interests seem to be most suitable as "jumping off points" for the introduction of meaningful activities.

With regard to the second major purpose, the results are again rather disappointing. The instability of interest just cited may cause the process of guiding students into careers in science to be misguidance. Thus an attempt to direct students into science courses strictly on the basis of the results of interest tests or questionnaires is of dubious value, and may even be most undesirable.

Audio-visual aids. An area in which much research has been undertaken is audio-visual aids. Many studies have been conducted for determining the most effective uses of films, filmstrips, recordings, radio and TV programs, and other aids. All these studies seem to emphasize the merits of using audio-visual aids in teaching science. Yet as a group they indicate that no one aid is significantly better than any other, and that the use of a combination of aids is superior to the exclusive use of one. In addition, in the elementary schools, audio-visual aids have great value in assisting teachers who may lack subject-matter background in science.

Evaluation techniques. Perhaps one of the most difficult, and yet one of the most essential, phases of any instructional program is that of evaluation. To measure effectively and thoroughly all the outcomes of a program of science instruction (or for that matter any type of instruction) is virtually an impossible task. Yet evaluation of some type is necessary. For that reason investigators are constantly attempting to develop new methods of evaluation, and are trying to improve the older methods.

Studies indicate that one of the most widely used techniques of evaluation is the standardized achievement test. Unfortunately, even though science educators agree that they are attempting to teach scientific attitudes and problem-solving techniques, as well as the knowledge of facts, current measuring devices measure little more than factual attainment. Studies show, however, that it is possible to measure the development of scientific attitudes and problem-solving techniques. Hence, a major problem facing science educators today is that of devising measures of these outcomes that may be used feasibly in the classroom. It

would seem that test organizations might well serve the needs of teachers by preparing tests that do measure such objectives, rather than publishing endlessly what has already been shown to be unsuitable.

In addition to teacher-made tests and standardized tests, research shows that other evaluation techniques are sometimes used. In the elementary school especially, observational techniques are often utilized; and in the secondary schools, projects, reports, and experimental work are often used in evaluating the outcomes of learning. However, it is evident that this is one of the areas of science education where a great deal of study still needs to be done.

The Training of Teachers

Present status of science teachers. In the last analysis, without regard for equipment available, time allotted, or course organization, the success of any science program depends on the teacher. And, of course, the work of the teacher to a large extent depends on her status and training.

Investigations dealing with the status of science teachers indicate, unfortunately, that the position of science teacher is far from being professionalized to the extent that is desirable. Few science teachers teach science exclusively, a great number of teachers teach one class in science only, and many of our science courses in present-day high schools are taught by people who have had little or no science training. Hence, it would seem that the improvement of science instruction may depend, in a large part, on the extent to which science teaching can become increasingly professionalized.

Competencies of science teachers. Consistent with the findings of studies of the status of science teachers are the findings of studies concerned with the competencies of science instructors. Research indicates that there is great inequality and lack of uniformity in the types and amounts of scientific training that science teachers have had. Most beginning teachers start their work in small schools where they usually teach generalized courses, or a number of different specialized courses. Yet their college training in science is not designed for such teaching. For the most part, prospective science teachers possess competencies in one or possibly two specialized areas of science. Few have had broad-field courses that will enable them to teach the generalized courses in science. In addition, test results indicate that while they may have a knowledge of specialized facts of science, most of them lack the ability to generalize and to apply their scientific knowledge—the very competencies one hopes to develop in students.

The above statements apply, of course, to secondary-school science teachers. Yet, the situation with respect to elementary-school teachers is even more discouraging. Here many teachers have no formal science training at all, while most have had

limited amounts. As a result, elementary-school teachers often avoid teaching science.

Training programs for science teachers. One major cause of the situation just described is the failure of state certification agencies and colleges to evaluate and standardize their requirements. Studies of such requirements indicate a great diversity among the requirements of various states for teacher certification and among various teacher-training colleges for graduation. It is obvious that the states and colleges need to investigate the amount of science background that is desirable in the preparation of science teachers at both the elementary and secondary levels. Much attention needs to be paid also to the type of training that is desirable. A survey of the opinions of administrators with respect to the types of training that they would like their teachers to possess reveals that the vast majority of them prefer a teacher with extensive training in many fields, rather than intensive training in one area. Currently colleges are failing to provide such training. Even if requirements for training teachers were changed immediately, the situation of teachers in the field would not be improved. Some research has been done with respect to the problems of present teachers—research designed to set up in-service training programs in science for the elementary level. As one might expect, the primary problem of these teachers is the lack of subject-matter background. Other problems deal with the lack of equipment and lack of knowledge about ordering ready-made equipment and constructing and using home-made equipment. Hence, some workshops and other types of in-service training programs have been established in an attempt to assist elementary-school teachers with these problems. Research indicates that it would be advantageous for school systems to organize more of these less theoretical, more practical types of in-service programs.

Summary

While it would serve no purpose to summarize the studies already summarized there seem to be two observations that are justified by the foregoing discussion:

1. Many of the studies could be improved immeasurably in quality. One gets the impression of efforts to produce results rather than to produce *valid* results. The ordinary safeguards of research are frequently disregarded.

2. The number of status studies seems to be sufficient. A vast number of the problems of science education have been identified. However, there is a conspicuous lack of studies that deal with efforts to seek solutions. More of these studies are needed.

HOMEWORK

One of the recurring issues with respect to instructional procedures is what to do about homework. In a condensation of a more complete analysis of the problem in the series, "What Research Says to the Teacher," Strang reports on students' methods of study; improvements in study hall and supervised study procedures; variations in homework practices; problems of family relations, mental health, and lack of guidance; relation of scholarship to homework; and factors affecting any decision concerning homework. (The reader may also wish to refer to the special feature on homework in the September, 1957, *NEA Journal*, pages 365–374.)

Guided Study and Homework   by RUTH STRANG

From the *NEA Journal*, October, 1955, pages 399–400. Reprinted by special permission. Ruth Strang is Professor of Education, Teachers College, Columbia University. This article contains some of the practical suggestions found in *Guided Study and Homework* of the series, "What Research Says to the Teacher," published by the Department of Classroom Teachers and the American Educational Research Association of the NEA.

According to modern theories of learning, the pupil should want something, perceive something, do something, and get satisfaction from the learning experience. All of these elements are usually present in effective study methods.

Role of the Teacher

In helping students study more effectively, the classroom teacher's role is obviously far different from the too prevalent practice of making an unexplained and unmotivated page assignment in a single text. Such an assignment makes no provision for the wide range of reading ability in every grade and gives pupils no practice in setting their own goals.

Ideally, teacher guidance in study involves understanding the individual students—their stage of development, their idea of themselves, their readiness for a certain kind of learning; providing concrete challenging materials and suggesting timely topics and realistic practical problems; promoting inter-personal relations that furnish incentives for learning; encouraging student initiative in setting meaningful goals, finding worthwhile problems, and discovering learning aids.

How Students Study

Students' reports of the way they study indicate that certain methods are used more often by good students than by poor students. One of the most extensive surveys of this kind in grades 4 to 12 reported the ten most significant methods of study characteristic of high scholarship:

1. Have a clear notion of the task before beginning the work of a particular study period.
2. Make complete sentences while writing.
3. Seek to master all the material as progress is made from lesson to lesson.
4. Study and understand the meaning of a chart or table.
5. Try to interrupt work at a natural break in the printed material, such as at the end of a chapter.
6. Do not take notes while reading.
7. Work out concrete examples to illustrate general rules and principles.
8. Have on hand the materials required.
9. Use facts learned in one class in preparing for another.
10. Read each topic in a lesson until it is clearly understood.

Improved Study Halls

Dissatisfied with the role of policeman and with the function of merely maintaining quiet, many teachers in recent years have enlisted students' interest in governing themselves in study halls.

Schools have successfully developed honor study halls managed by the students, usually through the student council. The success of this plan depends on building the attitude that being a member of the honor study hall is a responsibility, an achievement, and an honor. Students who wish to become members are approved by a joint committee of students and faculty; they agree to observe the study-hall rules of quiet, independent work, and cooperation with the students in charge.

The honor study hall shifts the focus from control by outside authority to development of inner controls through social motivation.

While the students are studying, the teacher is on hand to observe their study habits, discuss progress with individuals, and provide enough encouragement and suggestion to help them understand and overcome their own difficulties. If the teacher recognizes a common difficulty, he may give appropriate instruction and practice to the whole group.

Supervised Study in the Classroom

Some schools have abandoned the traditional study hall in favor of supervised study in each classroom. Investigations have suggested that supervised study be an intrinsic part of any unit of work extending over several days or weeks. The planning should include thoughtful attention to ways of studying the work of the unit.

Skillful supervised study provides instruction in how to study a particular assignment; practice under supervision; and an opportunity to complete unfinished work, engage in voluntary leisure reading, or engage in some other worthwhile ac-

tivities. As assignments become more creative and emphasize problem solving and research, the classroom, library, and laboratory become the most effective places for study.

Variations in Present Practice

Surveys of present homework practice report wide variations. The range is from no homework even for older students to an excessive amount even for young children.

Assignments often are vague. Some teachers still do not acquaint students with the specific skills and abilities a given assignment requires. Frequently the students do not know why they are to read the chapter.

They are not told whether they are to learn specific isolated facts, to get the main idea, to relate details to the main ideas and to get the author's pattern of thought, to draw inferences and conclusions, to answer questions in the book, to raise their own questions, to relate the content to what they have previously learned, to relate the content to other experiences they have had, or to apply what they have learned to practical life situations. Teachers should clarify these points and should vary assignments so that pupils will build a repertory of study skills.

Tests and Assignments

The kind of homework given and the kind of studying done are influenced by the kinds of examinations students are expected to pass. If tests stress merely the recall of facts rather than the power to use information, students tend to focus their attention on details. If tests call for problem solving and the ability to use facts, students are more likely to read to see relationships, to draw conclusions, and to make generalizations rather than merely to memorize.

The kind of studying done also depends a great deal on the nature of the assignment. Exercises that can be done mechanically encourage copying, while an assignment that calls for initiative, imagination, and individual effort rules out copying and challenges the students to work effectively.

Homework and Family Relations

The help a pupil gets at home is often of doubtful educational value. Some parents mean well but confuse the child by using methods different from those used in school. Others nag their children and put too much pressure on them. At times parents' help consists of practically doing the child's homework for him.

Ideally, parents help the child by pointing out principles involved, giving illustrations of them, and making suggestions for the pupil's own study.

Mental Health Aspect

Excessive tension and a sense of pressure are often associated with homework. If a pupil is not able to resist the appeal of television or outside activities, he may begin to think of himself as lacking in purpose and

will power. Late hours spent in study and failure to complete assignments may make a conscientious pupil depressed and anxious.

For mental health, children and young people need to engage in worthwhile out-of-school tasks suited to their individual capacities. Whenever homework crowds out social experience, outdoor recreation, and creative activities, and whenever it usurps time that should be devoted to sleep, it is not meeting the basic needs of children and adolescents.

Lack of Guidance

The individual differences of students are often not recognized. Intelligent students enjoy doing challenging intellectual tasks. Others, largely because of parental ambition, have too high a level of aspiration; they are carrying programs unsuitable for them.

For these students, homework may be an excessive addition to the school day; it may decrease the interest and vigor with which they engage in school activities. The resulting fatigue, frustration, and dissatisfaction with school should be attributed to poor guidance rather than to homework *per se.*

Homework and Scholarship

Some evidence of the effect of homework on scholarship has been reported by schools that have reduced or abolished homework and then observed the results. In some secondary schools where homework had been abolished or limited, the sum total of achievement did not seem to have been affected.

One principal asked the parents' cooperation in experimenting with a reduction of homework. Instead of assignments in three subjects, pupils were given homework in only two, and the time to be spent in home study was limited to one hour daily, with weekends free. He asked the parents to observe any evidence of less strain and tension, the relative eagerness with which their children went to work on their homework, their use of free time in worthwhile activities, and any improvement in sleep and general health.

In their reports later in the year, more than three-fourths of the parents reported favorable results from this reduction of the homework load. Almost 90 per cent said they would not want to return to the larger amount of homework.

Any decision regarding homework should take into account many factors—home conditions, the amount of homework given, its relation to the time for study at school, and the stimulating quality of the curriculum which may lead to study activity at home. A re-evaluation of the curriculum and teaching procedures might lead to improved supervised reading and study in school and to home study that would be a worthwhile learning experience for the student.

NOTE: A list of *sources* of curriculum materials, which teachers and other curriculum workers may find helpful, is included following Part Two, pages 288–290.

7

PROGRAMS FOR MEETING
COMMON NEEDS OF LEARNERS

GENERAL EDUCATION

The major function of the American public-school system is to provide for the educational needs of *all* boys and girls. These needs fall into two categories: common needs and special needs. The basic program in terms of common needs is often referred to as "general education" or "common learnings." That there is considerable confusion over the meaning of "general education" is well illustrated by Oliva. [38: 235-238] He identifies four definitions of "general education" along with the philosophical exponents of each: (*a*) required subjects—essentialists; (*b*) the great books—perennialists; (*c*) activity curriculum (elementary) or core curriculum (secondary)—pragmatists; and (*d*) the social-problems core in high school—reconstructionists.

A further distinction is made between "general" and "liberal" education by Morse. [34:395-399] *Liberal* education is subject-centered, deals with a fixed body of content, stresses reflective thinking more than behavior, and is intellectual and traditional in outlook. *General* education is more concerned with the learner than the subject matter, stresses individual development, and emphasizes "behavior and social usefulness," as well as intellectual development.

That unresolved issues with respect to general education are not new can be deduced from an excellent discussion of the subject by Judd [22:5-16] over twenty years ago. His definition of general education as "education which everyone must have in order to live intelligently in a modern community" [22:14] is still apropos. (For further evidence of difficulties in defining and organizing general education, the reader is referred to a series of articles in *The High School Journal,* October, 1953, to May, 1954, inclusive, devoted to the subject of "General Education in the Secondary School.")

Whenever general education is defined in terms of a preconceived body of subject matter, as is often the case, the objectives of general education become obscured. Furthermore, it becomes impossible to secure agreement on the part of two or more people as to what is the content of most worth.

FUNDAMENTALS

Closely identified with the subject of "general education" is that of the "fundamentals." Perhaps the two terms are synonymous in the minds of some people. Conceptions of the "fundamentals" vary considerably. Some think of them in terms of the three R's; others, as the required, so-called "cultural" subjects; and still others, as all the facts, skills, understanding, and attitudes needed for successful living. Russell discusses both the narrow and broader definitions of "fundamentals" and furnishes evidence of how well the schools are teaching them.

The Fundamentals in Schools Today   by DAVID H. RUSSELL

From David H. Russell, *The Fundamentals in Schools Today,* Field Service Leaflet No. 4. (Berkeley, California: Department of Education, University of California). Quoted by special permission. David H. Russell is Professor of Education, University of California, and President of the American Educational Research Association for 1958–1959.

*   *   *

What Are the Fundamentals?

Parents, taxpayers, and school people all want the school to teach "the fundamentals." Many want "fads and frills" left out of the curriculum, hence the problem of the difference between a "frill" and a "fundamental." Is the child's health a fundamental? Should he have some knowledge of science? Does he need to be very sharp in "mental arithmetic" or, if a choice must be made, is it more important that he understand ideas of time and space and our number system? The fundamentals for a ten-year-old city boy of today are probably not the same as they were for a farm boy of fifty years ago. Probably the "readin', 'ritin' and 'rithmetic" of the Little Red Schoolhouse are not the only fundamentals for the modern child.

Not all parents and teachers will agree, but here is a list of suggested *fundamentals for 1955* that many people interested in schools will accept:

1. The child must know some of the important *facts* basic to his living —facts of language, social living, science, health, and other areas which men have developed in past years and are continuing to use and explore today.

2. The child must have *skills* basic to modern living—skills such as those involved in seeing, speaking, listening, reading, writing, arithmetic, maintaining health, and getting along with others.

3. The child must have *understanding* of himself and of his environment. Facts and skills useful in everyday life are of little value unless the boy or girl understands reasons for them. At different ages children need to develop, among others, concepts of home, family, community, country, democracy, and interdependence, for these are "fundamental" ideas in the modern world.

4. The child must develop the *habits and attitudes of good citizenship.* Knowledge of facts, skills, and understandings is important as they are combined into actual behavior.

Parroting of the "right words" is not enough. Love of country is something to be exhibited in behavior, not just talked about. All children need help in practicing social and moral behavior associated with citizenship in a democratic state.

5. The child must develop *abilities in clear thinking.* The facts, skills, and understandings of the first three fundamentals above contribute the materials for clear thinking. The child must acquire not only old customs and permanent habits of good citizenship, as in (4) above, but the ability to solve new problems, to think critically about current affairs. He must be able to distinguish between fact and opinion, between the important and unimportant, in a world of many opinions and propagandas.

These five fundamentals are a large order, you will say. They are, and they are certainly too much for the school alone; help must come from home and community. But stated simply, they mean that most of us want the child to *know,* to *act,* and to *think.* Are the old-fashioned three R's included? They certainly are, but by themselves they aren't enough. More knowledge of the world, skills in working with others, ability to think through one's problems—these too are "fundamentals" in 1955.

Does the child completely master these fundamentals at the sixth grade or tenth grade or twelfth grade? Of course not. Most adults are still learning some of them. But every child in a good modern school is *working toward* these goals. Children differ greatly but by the third grade they have acquired many skills in listening, reading, and working with others. They know many facts about their immediate environment and have some understanding of themselves and what a "good citizen" is. Similarly, at all other levels the child is broadening and deepening his knowledge and improving his working methods and thinking abilities. He gradually achieves competence in each of the five fundamentals.

Is the Modern School Teaching the Fundamentals?

Not all modern schools are teaching these fundamentals as well as they should, but nearly all of them are trying to do so. "Readin', 'ritin', and 'rithmetic" skills are easier to teach than are some of the other fundamentals, and we have the most evidence about them. Some school programs are handicapped where teachers are untrained, classrooms overcrowded, and materials meager. How can the teacher successfully develop principles of health or safety if every day the school plant violates them? Many teachers, like other adults, do not think clearly in solving their own problems, nor do they read critically as they scan their daily newspapers; and so it is too much to expect that they will obtain high levels of performance in the fifth fundamental above. These same teachers, however, may be doing a fine job in developing skills or in

promoting warm human relationships that help the child understand his place in the group. Out of the very variety of school life and differences in teachers, children over the years develop each of the five fundamentals.

Compared to the school of grandfather's day, the modern school is doing a good job on the fundamentals as the term is herein defined. As a matter of fact, the school of fifty or a hundred years ago wasn't a very efficient organization. Illiteracy then was high; for example, mass circulation magazines like *Saturday Evening Post* or *Reader's Digest* were unknown. The educational status of the men drafted in 1917 in World War I was far below today's record. A couple of generations ago, the schools failed about 30 per cent of the children enrolled and sent only 5 per cent of them to high school and only 2 per cent to college. Today it is common to have 95 per cent of youth fourteen to eighteen years of age enrolled in high school. Thus they are at least receiving an opportunity to profit from schooling, an opportunity which, in a democracy, should be available to all youth.

The modern school is more efficient in teaching the fundamentals listed above because of certain changes over the last two or three generations. These include the following:

1. The modern school is teaching much more than the old school. Instruction in health, science, music, and the other arts, for example, was

largely unknown fifty years ago, but is a regular part of the modern curriculum. Children may learn group skills on the playground and science concepts in camps run by some school systems. True, sometimes today's school may attempt too much, but at least it is not restricted to the narrow curriculum of an earlier day.

2. Today's school provides a greater variety of teaching-learning activities. Children differ greatly in their learning capacities and, accordingly, in the ways they learn most efficiently. Hence the modern school offers such activities as field trips, construction, reading, discussion, using audio-visual devices, and opportunities for creative activities. This does not mean that writing or computing is neglected. Rather, these varied ways of learning reinforce one another and, by aiding understanding and clear thinking, they improve the final product.

3. School people know more about children and so can help them better. Literally thousands of research studies have been made of children and adolescents. Just as parents join child-study groups, teachers study child and adolescent psychology in preservice and in-service professional training and apply more of it in their teaching.

4. The scientific study of educational problems makes teaching and learning more efficient. School people now have results of careful studies, some involving years of work and thousands of dollars, which give direct help on such topics as the most useful words in spelling, the hardest operations in arithmetic, and the best ways of solving problems. As in medicine and engineering, there is a lag between research discovery and classroom application, but more and more the results of research are being put into practice in the modern school.

Because of these and other developments, children tend to learn more efficiently than ever before. The next sections give specific evidence of this fact.

What Does Research Say About the Three R's?

Some of the criticisms mentioned in the first section of this leaflet take the form, "Why aren't the schools as good as when I went to school?" Psychologists tell us that memory is selective, that we remember the good things we want to remember, so other bases of comparison are probably needed as well as our imperfect memories alone. The relative efficiency of schools a generation or two ago and today is a question of fact; therefore, it should be checked by fact, not opinion. Accordingly, one thoughtful approach to the problem is to turn to research findings:

There are available probably a hundred studies and summaries of research done carefully enough, without bias and with other scientific safeguards, to warrant the term *research* on pupil achievement "then and now." In making such studies, the same tests have been given in the same way to comparable groups of children. These conditions are not readily met because some test items of fifty years ago, such as *brougham* in spelling or using *rods* in surveying, are not much used today. Furthermore, in the upper grades in school today, one is testing nearly 100 per cent of the children of a given age, whereas two generations ago perhaps only 10 per cent of that age group were in the same grade, due to failures and drop-outs. Despite these difficulties, the scientific studies show that achievement today is usually as good as or a little better than it was when grandfather, or even father, was a boy. What are a few specific results?

An early study in the 1920's by Caldwell and Courtis compared achievements of children then with those of children about a hundred years ago. After giving the same tests and marking them in the same way, the research men found that the children in the more modern school made only from one-third to one-quarter as many errors in spelling as the children of the earlier day. In certain questions in history such as "About what year did the first colonists come to New England?" the early group scored 59 per cent correct as compared with 71 per cent correct for the modern group. More recent comparisons may be cited. A group of high school seniors in 1941 scored 11 per cent higher than a similar group of seniors in 1919 on tests of mathematics, English, and practical information. A group of sixth

graders in 1948 had better scores in vocabulary and paragraph reading than a similar group in 1931, although on the average the 1948 sixth-graders were younger than 1931 children at the same grade level. One California city recently found that the graduates of the elementary school were three-tenths of a year ahead in reading and seven-tenths of a year ahead in arithmetic over their counterparts of sixteen years earlier. One of the most impressive sources of evidence is the results of testing thousands of young men during the draft for the Second World War. These tests reveal a much higher educational level than in the First World War and especially good results in certain states which support education more adequately than others.

The results, in one large California city, of accurately given tests of mental ability and achievement in two of the three R's illustrate the need of careful interpretation in making comparisons of "then and now." The city is one in which the school population has been changing. Here are the test results for over 2,000 eighth-grade youngsters for each of the years indicated:

	1935	1947	1953
Chronological Age	15–0	14–0	13–10
Mental Age	15–3	13–10	13–4
Reading Age	15–1	13–10	13–11
Arithmetic Age	*	13–3	13–11

* Data not available. All ages are reported in years and months.

At first glance, one might say that the eighth-grade youngsters in 1953 were not doing as well in both reading and arithmetic as they were six or eighteen years previously. It is true that they did not score as high on these tests as the corresponding children did in 1935, but it is also true that a different population of eighth-graders is involved. The 1953 children are over a year younger in chronological age and nearly two years younger in mental age than the 1935 group. In relation to their mental ages, the 1953 group is doing considerably better than the previous groups in both reading and arithmetic.

The results in the three R's and related areas indicate, then, that children in today's schools are usually achieving as well as or slightly better than children of twenty-five or fifty years ago. Exact comparisons are often hard to get, but the evidence is incontrovertible. Some individual children may be having trouble with their reading or arithmetic, and some specific schools where the nature of the population has changed may not have as high absolute scores as they did. Nevertheless, generally speaking, children are achieving as well as or better than they did a generation ago.

What Does Research Say About Other Fundamentals?

The import of the evidence about the three R's given above is clear, but facts about the other fundamentals such as children's understanding, habits of citizenship, and thinking abilities are hard to find. There are two reasons for this difficulty: (*a*) comparisons with children's knowledge of science or health concepts fifty years ago, or with their citizenship behavior or thinking abilities, are almost impossible to make because schools of the earlier time did not try to teach or measure such educational products; (*b*) it is difficult to get good tests or other measures of these more "intangible" aspects of human behavior.

Although there are difficulties in obtaining first-class evidence, a few examples of research findings may be given. In the study mentioned above, Caldwell and Courtis found that, compared to children of about a hundred years earlier, modern children tend to make lower scores on tests of pure memory and higher scores on thought and meaningful questions. Another study of the success of high school graduates in college found that, compared to students from traditional high schools, students from thirty so-called progressive high schools did slightly better in marks, study habits, and independent work and were much more active in campus activities such as student government and dramatics. In another study, Wrightstone discovered that students from modern high schools were somewhat more honest, more cooperative, and better able to get along with others. In another investigation involving large numbers of children in New York

City, compared to children in traditional schools, children in modern "activity" schools made slightly lower scores in reading speed and in arithmetic but higher scores on "self-initiated activities" and "experimental" and "quality of cooperative" behavior. In another city, Gray found few differences in oral reading and speed of reading between 1916 and 1948, but the pupils in 1948 had much larger comprehension scores. These samples of the many available studies suggest that, in specific skills, differences between "then and now" are slight but that the modern school does a better job in helping children understand and think.

* * *

Since *reading* is one of the fundamentals around which much controversy has been raging, it is interesting to take note of Gates's excellent exposé of a number of fallacies in Flesch's book, *Why Johnny Can't Read*. At the same time, Gates has described how the public schools actually do teach reading effectively.

Why Mr. Flesch Is Wrong   by ARTHUR I. GATES

From the *NEA Journal*, September, 1955, pages 332–334. Reprinted by special permission of the National Education Association and the author. Arthur I. Gates is Professor Emeritus of Education, Teachers College, Columbia University.

The problem of teaching children to read well has been a formidable one ever since it was first undertaken. It is quite similar to the task of keeping children in perfect health.

In reading ability as in health, some children are excellent, the majority are "normal" but not perfect, and a few are poor. In health some children still "do poorly" despite several centuries of study by the professional groups and nearly a century of very intensive scientific research; in reading, despite a couple of centuries of study by professional teachers and more than a half century of research by psychologists, educators, and others, some children still do poorly.

Recently, a popular writer, Rudolf Flesch, whose doctor's degree in adult education represents no considerable experience or training in the teaching of elementary-school reading, has proclaimed a solution to all the problems of reading. "It's very simple," he writes. "Reading means getting meaning from certain combinations of letters. Teach the child what each letter stands for and he can read" (pages 2, 3).

Mr. Flesch describes and defends his method of teaching reading in his book, *Why Johnny Can't Read*.

His method requires children to learn to recognize words by a complex and synthetic procedure of building up word parts.

Children are first taught to recognize, name, and sound the letters, to sound each of a large number of phonograms, such as *lk, nt, ffs, ngs, ear, ur, ai, dge* and *dgi.* They are expected to learn to locate these word parts in each of several hundred words and to combine or blend them into whole words. There are several hundred words on eighty-seven pages of exercise material, including such forms as *quizzical* and *peevishly.*

This elaborate program is to be taught before the child does any reading. Flesch insists that any child can do it readily enough, although at points he implies that it would take several months. In fact, he recommends that parents undertake to teach their children at home before they enter the first grade.

Flesch's program is one of the most extensive and difficult of the many phonetic schemes that have been presented during the last two centuries. Although few are so elaborate and difficult, systems of this kind have been studied both by teachers in the practical situation for a century and more recently by investigators using scientific procedures.

In the course of these experiences and studies, numerous difficulties of such a method of teaching reading and spelling have been observed. Some of these are:

1. Many children find learning a phonetic scheme of this kind at the age of six, or earlier, very difficult. Indeed, there are some who become utterly discouraged by it.

2. The phonic procedure recommended by Flesch tends to get children into the habit of recognizing words piecemeal. This habit not only does not work well on unfamiliar words for many children, but it also tends to interfere with the quick perception of words.

3. The Flesch type of phonic instruction does not give children guidance and instruction in many other techniques which make for efficient, quick, and accurate word recognition. Modern basic programs and modern texts on teaching reading provide instruction for securing the whole array of techniques and the whole range of clues which have been found to be useful in quick and accurate recognition of words.

4. The method tends to make such demands on the child's attention as to cause neglect of the meaning of the material. Children tend to become mere word-callers.

Mr. Flesch declares (on page 42 of his book) that the child who has been taught phonics "has never in his life read a single word by just taking in its general shape and guessing what it might mean. But our schools, as I said before, train our children in just that—word guessing." This is a completely misleading statement.

He maintains that phonics has been thrown out bodily from instruction in reading in America's schools. This is not true.

He says (pages 79–80) that children are shown words and expected to memorize them as words, and therefore know only those that are in a small vocabulary. He maintains that they are given little or no instruction or guidance in developing techniques in working out the pronunciation and recognition of unfamiliar words.

The fact of the matter is that practically all authorities recommend, most basal textbooks embody, and substantially all teachers give instruction in the useful clues for word recognition. Definite instruction is given in employing these clues at times when they seem to be most useful and when the children can successfully learn them.

By placing the American system in a false position, it is of course easy to attack it. Most teachers and all students of reading instruction would vigorously disapprove of the methods which Flesch falsely ascribes to them. In many instances he has attributed to investigators and writers the very views they have severely criticized.

The typical procedure in American schools is to start children out by teaching them to recognize a few words as sight words. They study these words as they would learn to recognize postage stamps, insects, and other small objects. These words are immediately used in stories and other continuous material. Thus, the child from the beginning is able really to read and get the thought of sentences, paragraphs, and longer selections.

Usually, after only a few words have been learned, the teacher begins work in word analysis and word-form study. She shows pupils how to look at words from left to right, and to develop a sharp eye for the distinctive features of each word. She draws their attention to frequently reappearing parts in words, such as syllables, phonograms, and letters. She teaches them to locate, recognize, and sound individual letters, frequently appearing syllables, and phonograms.

In brief, the classroom teacher introduces a program of word study and word analysis designed to give the child greater skill in both visual and phonetic analysis as well as in the use of context and other clues.

The modern teacher encourages children to use the meaning of connected discourse to recognize particular words. For years preceding their entry into school, children have learned to recognize and understand the *spoken* word in this manner. Indeed, their skill in figuring out the meaning of individual words, phrases, and sentences from the torrents of words which fly about them in their early years is one of the most remarkable and important intellectual achievements of childhood. It is merely good common sense to teach them how to use these remarkable skills as aids in recognizing words and their meaning during reading.

Teachers' manuals and textbooks published since 1930 strongly recommend, furthermore, that the child be taught not only to recognize letters, phonograms, and syllables, and to sound and blend them, but also to acquire the habit of trying, after an initial survey of the word, to locate those features which are most helpful in recognizing and pronouncing that particular word.

Most teachers' manuals and textbooks describe an extensive program in word study and word analysis, including definite work in phonics. Teachers are urged to note the phonetic elements and the letter sounds which children themselves point out in different words and to help them decide whether they are the more useful or the less useful clues. The program is carried forward with the expectation that the children will become more exact in their recognition of different kinds of clues; more thorough in their knowledge and use of individual letter sounds, phonograms, and syllables; more expert in studying words to ascertain what sorts of attacks are most useful; more versatile in shifting from one approach to another; and generally more competent in the phonic and visual analysis skills.

In each succeeding grade, increasingly definite and exact instruction is given in distinguishing long and short vowels and in utilizing the structural elements—prefixes, suffixes, root words, derived forms, and contractions. As a pupil gets into the higher grades, even more encouragement is given to him to use the quicker clues to recognition, resort-

ing to the more detailed studies only when this is necessary.

Beginning late in the third or fourth grades, the dictionary is introduced, including the diacritical marks, and more exact identification and use of letter and phonogram sounds. Skills in dividing words into syllables are highly useful at this more advanced stage when the majority of the unfamiliar words will be words of many syllables. In these grades certain rules, found by careful experimentation to be helpful rather than merely puzzling, are introduced.

The modern teacher and the textbook writer, therefore, have many types of information which enable them to be more effective in selecting and emphasizing the most useful— and avoiding futile instruction on less useful or misleading—rules, conventions, and procedures. Anyone who examines a textbook on the teaching of reading, or the manuals accompanying basal series, or courses of study published by cities, counties, and states, can scarcely fail to see that Flesch's charge that nothing is taught but "looking at words and guessing wildly" is completely untrue and misleading.

On page 38 Flesch insists that phonics has been driven out of spelling as well as out of reading.

This is an entirely false statement, as anyone can easily discover by looking over any modern series of spellers. One will find a much broader and more thorough program in the study of phonics and other phases of word structure than Flesch himself suggests.

Rudolf Flesch assumes that once the child is taught to sound out the individual words, the job of teaching is done. He illustrates the merit of the idea in the following statement (page 103): "But the fact is, and I testify to it, that those children [they were Czech children] read what was in the paper. They were perfectly able to pronounce words they had never seen before. . . . Needless to say, that six-year-old child hadn't the slightest idea of what the word meant."

He suggests no procedures for developing the most subtle and difficult techniques involved in efficient, intelligent reading—the mental techniques required to secure the meanings of words or to vary the rate and type of comprehension to meet the various purposes of reading. He seems not to be concerned with teaching children when and how to read slowly and exactly, as when full and accurate comprehension of every detail is needed, or more rapidly when grasping the general ideas is adequate, or to skim selectively at high speed when surveying a newspaper or catalog.

He gives no suggestions for reading for such different purposes as merely to get the main ideas literally compared with reading to evaluate or criticize; or reading for temporary understanding compared with reading to retain permanently; or read-

ing to note all the main points as contrasted with reading to select only those ideas which are specifically needed.

Flesch's concept of what must be done to teach children to become efficient, versatile, intelligent readers is an incredible oversimplification of the problem.

Flesch misrepresents many other phases of modern American teaching of reading, such as remedial instruction, reading-readiness testing, and the character of supplementary reading material. He also endeavors to arouse popular acceptance of his phonic scheme and distrust of typical school programs by an incredible misrepresentation of facts concerning the results obtained by both.

Flesch states repeatedly that the schools taught children to read far better prior to 1930 than they do today, that reading disabilities were rare then, that "there are no remedial reading cases . . . practically anywhere in the world except in the United States" (page 2), and that if we "teach children phonics, . . . there won't be any sex differential in their achievement, as there is none in England, in Germany, in France, and in the rest of the world" (page 114).

These statements are flatly contradicted by the hard facts. For example, in 1925 a careful study conducted by Percival showed that one pupil in six in California and other representative schools was required to repeat the first grade and that 99.1 per cent of these were rated as failures in reading, despite phonetic training. One child in every five was a repeater in the second grade and 89.7 per cent had failed in reading.

Scores in reading tests given in 1921 and repeated in 1947 in Lincoln, Nebraska (reported by D. A. Worcester and Anne Kline, University of Nebraska), were far better in 1947 in every grade tested. In fact, in speed of reading, the pupils in grades four to seven in 1947 exceeded the pupils of 1921 by one grade. The average 1947 grade five excelled all higher grades. The 1947 score for grade five was 93.1; the 1921 score for grade five was 78.9; for grade six, 78.4; for grade seven, 90.5; and for grade eight, 90.4.

In grade three, there were 237 children with a very low score (below 30) per thousand in 1921, and only 41 in 1947. Very superior reading for third-grade pupils, indicated by a reading-rate score of 100 or better, was achieved by 6 per 1000 in 1921 and by 106 per 1000 in 1947. *The strikingly superior test scores were obtained despite the fact that the children in 1947 were from six to eight months younger than were those in the same grades in 1921.* Similar studies in other schools have mainly shown less great superiority, but the results with almost no exception show that children are better readers today than were their peers prior to 1930. Flesch's statement to the contrary

notwithstanding, reading problems exist and remedial reading is provided in some form in practically all European nations. In England, research carried on by Cyril Burt, F. J. Schonell, and many others since 1920 has produced estimates of reading backwardness about the same as those made in this country. Boys have been found to have difficulty more frequently than girls in England, Norway, and other countries, just as in the United States.

Before believing Flesch's assertion that England has found formal phonics a panacea for the problems of reading, one had better read Fred Schonell's scholarly volume, *Backwardness in the Basic Subjects* (London: Oliver and Boyd, first edition 1942, second edition 1951), John Duncan's *Backwardness in Reading* (London: George C. Harrop, 1953), and the article on "Backward Readers" in the *Times* (*London*) *Educational Supplement* of August 14, 1953. At almost the time Flesch praises the British phonic instruction, Duncan, after prolonged study, declares it is "unsuitable for any pupil," especially the slow learner, and advocates an approach very similar to the one outlined in this article. Schonell subscribes to the same general view.

The *London Times* article declares that a major source of reading difficulty in England is the use of a type of phonics which Flesch advocates, a method characterized as "barking at print." The article states: "When such children reach the modern school, we think they can read, but they can't. They only make noises at print."

Flesch doubtless realizes that in order to persuade teachers and parents to accept his panacea he must somehow explain how a few score psychologists and educators who have been investigating the nature and teaching of reading for several decades could be so wrong, as he declares they are.

In a confidential tone to parents and teachers he proceeds to discredit these investigators by such statements as: "They [the reading investigators] *are* firmly committed to the application of the word method, and it would be inhuman to expect from them an *objective* point of view" (page 8). (Italics mine.) "Our 'scientific' educators simply don't *want* to know the truth" (page 68). "I say, therefore, that the word method [which he ascribed to these investigators with utter falsity] is gradually destroying democracy in this country" (page 132).

And finally, Flesch, a Viennese lawyer who came to this country in 1938, reveals what he regards as the real explanation by the statement: "I am not one of those people who call them [the reading 'experts'] un-American or left-wingers or Communist fellow travelers" (page 133) —a statement which clearly implies that there are many persons who do.

Inasmuch as investigators in England and other countries have reached conclusions similar to ours, the conspiracy must be international. It must, indeed, include educational theorists and curriculum and other specialists, as well as teachers and school administrators. Close reading of Mr. Flesch's book, in fact, makes it apparent that his aim is to discredit American education in general. And no attack has yet appeared which is more flagrant in its misrepresentation of the facts.

See also Riesman's comments concerning *Why Johnny Can't Read,* on pages 403–404 of this book.

LIFE ADJUSTMENT EDUCATION

Another curricular term that has provoked confusion and controversy is "life adjustment education." Perhaps it is unfortunate that the word "adjustment" was ever used in the first place. For many people it has the connotation of mediocrity or chameleon-like conformity. An accurate definition of "life adjustment education" is found on the inside cover of the report of the Second Commission on Life Adjustment Education: "Life adjustment education is designed to equip all American youth to live democratically with satisfaction to themselves and profit

to society as homemakers, workers, and citizens. It is concerned especially with a sizable portion of youth of high school age (both in
school and out) whose objectives are less well served by our school than
are the objectives of preparation for either a skilled occupation or higher
education." [10:cover] The remainder of the report, too long to du-
plicate here, summarizes educational developments in twenty-nine
states, 1950–1953.

"Life adjustment education" is not to be confused with the "activity
program." The former originated with a national conference of vocational educators who believed that the needs of an estimated 60 per
cent of all high school youth were not being satisfactorily met in
school. The latter program began with the child-centered, progressive
education movement of the early thirties.

CURRICULAR DESIGNS FOR GENERAL EDUCATION

REQUIRED SUBJECTS

One of the first problems in the development of a general education
program is to decide upon what type or types of organization or design
of teaching-learning experiences to use.

The oldest, and still the most common, approach to the organization
of general education is in terms of required subjects. In an editorial in
which he discusses "Required Courses in High School," Bush expresses
a philosophy in harmony with modern trends in secondary education
when he says: "A sound principle, it seems, would be to have the *basic
requirements* as set forth at the highest levels by the people—through
the legislature and the State Board of Education—stated in terms of
fundamental objectives to be achieved. The details of how these shall be
achieved—the curriculum pattern—is the domain of the professional
educator." * (Other articles in the February, 1955, *Journal* deal with
such subjects as "Programs of College-Bound Students," "Legal Requirements for Graduation in the United States," and "The Role of the
Legislature in Prescribing Instruction for Secondary Schools.")

The curriculum developed around the "required subjects" is familiar

* From an editorial, "Required Courses in High School," by Robert N. Bush, in the
California Journal of Secondary Education, February, 1955, p. 65. Quoted by special
permission. Robert N. Bush is editor of the *Journal* and Professor of Education, Stanford University.

to all. Gradually, changes in this traditional curriculum are taking place. The most notable divergence from a separate-subjects type of organization is discussed in the following section.

CORE

A point of view gaining impetus is that the essence of what is to be learned is not the specialized content of isolated subjects, but rather the common elements of related subjects. Carried to its logical conclusion, this point of view has led to the development by many individuals and groups of a "core" curriculum. (The word "core" has unfortunate connotations. In the usual sense it suggests the part of the fruit to be discarded, but in this case it is the part to be retained.) When the educator speaks of the *core curriculum* or the *core program,* he is making use of an established word to express an evolving concept. He is also examining, within the framework of this concept, established ideas and practices, in an effort to meet emergent demands for a new general education. In other words, the term "core" is comparatively new to education, but it is old in our language. Likewise, many types of core programs are new to school practice while their basic principles are old to teaching and learning.

In making a status study of the "core" during the school year 1950–1951, the Office of Education asked high school principals to respond to four different interpretations of the core:

Type A—Each subject retains its identity in the core; that is, subjects combined in the core are correlated but not fused. For example, the teaching of American literature may be correlated with the teaching of American history. The group may be taught both subjects by one teacher or each subject by the appropriate subject teacher.

Type B—Subject lines are broken down. Subjects included in the core are fused into a unified whole around a central theme; e.g., "Our American Heritage" may be the central theme for a core unifying American history and literature, and possibly art and music.

Type C—Subjects are brought in only as needed. The core consists of a number of broad preplanned problems usually related to a central theme. Problems are based on predetermined areas of pupil needs, both immediate felt needs and needs as society sees them. For example, under the theme, Personal-Social Relations, there may be such problems as school citizenship, understanding myself, getting along with others, how to work effectively in group situations. Members of the class may or may not have a choice from among several problems; they will, however, choose activities within the problems.

Type D—Subjects are brought in only as needed as in Type C above. There are no predetermined problem areas to be studied. Pupils and teacher are free to select problems upon which they wish to work. [48:8]

Concerning the four core concepts, Wright makes this observation: "According to the interpretation of core given by most writers in the field, A and B are unified studies—core-type but not true core. Types C and D meet the criteria for core. Both are concerned with the problems of youth; they are pupil-centered rather than subject-centered." [48:7]

While it may be impossible to define the word "core" to everyone's satisfaction, it is possible to define and to understand some of the bases for the concept. It is also possible to identify some of the needs that have given rise to the demand for a new kind of general education.

Most of the literature on the subject in this area deals with programs and practices of the secondary school. It is at this level that the need is most apparent, for the elementary school has essentially a core program. The pupil passes from the comparative integration of this program to the comparative fragmentation and complexity of the secondary-school program.

Perhaps no present-day educator has made a more thorough study of the core program than Alberty. In the following article, he describes the principal characteristics of "a sound core program" and dispels a number of misconceptions about it.

A Sound Core Program — What It Is and What It Isn't

by HAROLD ALBERTY

From the *NEA Journal*, January, 1956, pages 20–22. Reprinted by special permission. Harold Alberty is Professor of Education, Ohio State University.

In recent years, many attempts have been made to clarify the concept of the core, as that term is applied to the high school curriculum. Yet probably no other term in the field of educa-

tion is surrounded by so much confusion and so many misconceptions. It is literally true that there is no commonly accepted meaning of the term which makes it possible for administrators, teachers, and laymen to communicate intelligently concerning it.

Some of the fairly common definitions are: a group of required subjects, a combination of two or more subjects, a large block of time in which learning activities are planned cooperatively, any course taught by "progressive" methods.

Added to this confusion is the fact that many terms such as the following are used synonymously with core: common learnings, general education, unified studies, self-contained classrooms, basic courses, fused courses, and English-social studies.

As a consequence, when one is told that a certain school has a core, it is unsafe to draw any conclusions whatever concerning the nature of the program.

In my opinion, the conception of core most likely to transform and improve general education in the high school is this: a group of structured problem areas, based upon the common problems, needs, and interests of adolescents, from which are developed teacher-student planned learning units or activities.

Following are some of the principal characteristics of an effective adolescent-problems core program based on this conception.

1. It deals with the area of general education and hence is directed primarily toward the development of the common values, understandings, and skills needed for effective democratic citizenship.

2. Since it provides for general education, it is required of all students at any given level.

3. It utilizes a block of time sufficiently large to deal with a broad, comprehensive unit of work, with homeroom and guidance activities, and with individualized instruction.

4. It is based upon the common problems, needs, and interests of youth as ascertained by the teaching staff and the core teacher in cooperation with his students. It draws freely upon all pertinent resources, including logically organized subjects or fields of knowledge.

5. It has a clearly defined but flexible scope and sequence based on pre-planned problem areas derived from the major values of democratic living and the common problems, needs, and interests of students.

6. Instruction is based upon learning units derived principally from the established problem areas, which are planned, carried forward, and evaluated by the teacher and the students.

7. It is supported and reinforced by a rich offering of special-interest activities—both formal and informal—designed to meet the particular needs of students and to develop their unique capacities, interests, and talents.

The foregoing presentation is intended as a frame of reference for discussing what I believe to be certain misconceptions concerning a sound core program. Some other investigator might interpret one or more of these as not being misconceptions at all but rather as the only true interpretation of the core. Therefore, the misconceptions about to be discussed can be so regarded only against the backdrop of my own interpretation.

Misconception No. 1. The core concept is new and has had very limited application; hence, programs based upon it should be regarded as highly experimental, if not radical and dangerous.

As a matter of fact, the various elements of the adolescent-problems core as defined above have been in successful use for many years.

(*a*) The practice of setting aside a significant portion of the school day for general education is commonplace, as attested by the practices of most high schools and colleges.

(*b*) The problem approach and the utilization of direct, firsthand experience as starting points for learning have proved their effectiveness over a period of at least half a century—even before Dewey established his famous laboratory school in 1896. It was the very heart of the revolution in agricultural education which began about 1910. In 1923, Ellsworth Collings documented experimentally the desirability of a complete break with the subject-centered curriculum. Good elementary schools have used effectively the problem and direct-experience approach to learning for many years.

(*c*) The value of utilizing the broad unit-of-work approach was documented by the early followers of Herbart and later by Morrison, Miller, Thayer, and others. By 1930, the techniques of unit teaching were well known and practiced by many high school teachers.

(*d*) The use of student-teacher planning grew out of the success of the socialized recitation, which had its beginning in the early decades of the century. Its value has been well documented by studies in group dynamics in both education and industry.

(*e*) The success of teaching the so-called fundamentals through broad comprehensive units of experience has been documented over and over. Collings could again be cited as a pioneer in this field. His results have been verified in scores of experimental studies.

Thus it is evident that the features of a sound core program have long since passed the experimental stage.

Misconception No. 2. The core program is progressive or modern while the subject-centered special-interest program is conventional or even traditional.

This misconception gets us into great difficulties because it tends to create a cleavage between teachers working in the core program and those in the special-interest areas when they need to work together more effectively.

There is no valid basis for this misconception because the techniques of curriculum development and instruction open to the core teacher are, for the most part, equally applicable to the special-interest teacher. For example, the science teacher may base his course on problems, needs, and interests of students. The program will, of course, have a narrower scope than the core, since he is dealing with a restricted field of knowledge.

He may organize the course in terms of comprehensive units of work, using the logic of his field only as a way of determining scope and sequence. He may emphasize teacher-student planning if he regards the logical system of knowledge of his field as a guidepost rather than as a mandate to "cover ground." He may also perform a highly important specialized guidance function.

The difference between the two types of program is to be found in the fact that the core program deals with the area of general education, and hence finds its scope and sequence in the broad areas of living, while the special-interest areas deal with a content determined by the *particular field*. Both types of learning experience are essential to a well-rounded education.

Actually a good core program cannot be developed without the help of the subject specialist: in planning resource units or guides, in core classroom teaching at points of need, and in teaching his special field with constant reference to what goes on in the core so as to reinforce and enrich the core program.

Misconception No. 3. The core has no definable content. It is largely

process, or methodology. Its values lie in the way the students learn. Almost any content is satisfactory, so long as the students share in planning, and are achieving certain democratic values held by the teacher.

This view is held by many teachers and some authorities who find their orientation in the more radical theories of the "left-wing progressives" in education and who hold that any attempt to define scope and sequence in advance of classroom teacher-student planning is a violation of the creative process. It places too much emphasis upon the utilization of the immediate felt and expressed wishes, wants, and desires of the students in the group.

Programs designed around this misconception have done much to bring the adolescent-problems core into disrepute because it is difficult, if not impossible, to explain to inquiring parents just what Johnny is learning because the teacher himself won't know until *after* the year's work is finished. It is likewise difficult if not impossible for special-interest area teachers to plan their own programs or their participation in the core because of the highly tentative nature of the program. And it is difficult for administrators and supervisors to anticipate resources which will be needed.

It is my contention that the core program, based on a more realistic approach to education for effective citizenship, should have a content as capable of definition as that of a field of knowledge. The content can be derived: (*a*) from careful studies of problems of youth which grow out of their own basic drives and from the pressures and tensions of the environment which impinge upon them; and (*b*) from the democratic values to which we as a people are committed.

Such a definition of scope might well eventuate in a series of problem areas in the basic aspects of living from which cooperatively planned learning units would be developed. The sequence of learning would be determined largely by each individual core teacher and his students.

Misconception No. 4. The core is merely a better way of teaching the required subjects.

Clearly this misconception has some kinship with the one explained immediately above. There is, however, an important distinction. Proponents of this point of view hold that the core is a *method of teaching* which has for its aim the mastery of the conventional subjects—usually English and the social studies. To the other group, the principal aim is the attainment of the values which inhere in the process of living democratically.

The program which eventuates from this misconception is known as unified studies, English–social studies, and multiple-period classes. It is taught by one teacher, in a block of time larger than one period.

Obviously there are certain advantages to such an arrangement. The teacher gets to know the students bet-

ter and hence has the opportunity to develop a more effective homeroom guidance program. The student is likely to see interconnections among the subjects that are unified. However, it can be justified only as a transition from the conventional separate-subject program to the more vital adolescent-problems core.

Misconception No. 5. The core, once firmly established, will gradually absorb the entire curriculum and eventually result in the complete destruction of all subject fields.

This view is the result of a lack of understanding of the fundamental differences between education directed toward the development of the ideals, understandings, and skills needed by all for effective citizenship and education directed toward the development of the unique interests, abilities, or talents of the individual. The former is the distinctive province of the core; the latter can best be accomplished by teacher specialists in appropriately equipped shops, laboratories, and studios. Each of the two aspects of education has its distinctive functions; each reinforces the other.

The prevalence of this misconception is probably accounted for by the fact that the adolescent-problems core draws upon all pertinent fields of knowledge in dealing with common problems of living and calls for the assistance of the specialist in determining the potential contributions of such fields of knowledge. What it neglects to take into account is the need for courses or experiences designed specifically to meet the special needs, problems, and interests of students.

Misconception No. 6. The core is more suitable for the below-average or dull student who has difficulty in mastering the conventional subjects than for the bright student who expects to go to college.

There is no evidence known to the writer that indicates that the adolescent-problems core is peculiarly adapted to any *one* class of students. Current practices reveal its successful use in schools with selective enrollments as well as in schools with more heterogeneous populations. As a matter of fact, the core, with its emphasis upon broad units of work, affords the opportunity to provide for individual differences *within* the unit, so that students of all levels of ability may find stimulating experiences.

The so-called Eight-Year Study of the Progressive Education Association, conducted in the 1930's, provided ample evidence that graduates of high schools utilizing the adolescent-problems core succeeded as well in college as did graduates of conventionally organized high schools.

Misconception No. 7. The core is better adapted to the junior high school than to the senior high school.

It is difficult to understand the logic back of this familiar misconception, for no one would seriously argue that

the problem-solving approach becomes ineffective at the senior high level. The nature of the pertinent problems, of course, will change as the students develop, but that means only that the school should adapt instruction to the student's maturity level.

Surveys of core-program development indicate that 85 to 90 per cent of all the cores are to be found in the seventh and eighth grades. In only a small number of schools is the core extended to the senior high school level.

Probably many educators are convinced that the core program is actually better adapted to the junior high school, but the present situation is due to additional factors.

Traditionally, the seventh and eighth grades were regarded as part of the elementary school, where most or all of the instruction was given by one teacher. Consequently, many principals who reacted against the extreme specialization of the early junior high schools saw the core as a way out which would have the sanction of tradition.

On the other hand, the traditional requirement of sixteen Carnegie units for high school graduation has tended to be a barrier to the extension of the core to the senior high school.

Finally, the teacher-certification problem has added to the difficulty of extension.

It is far easier to state the misconceptions concerning a sound core program which serve as blocks to its development than to suggest ways to remove the blocks.

All that the writer hopes for is that this analysis may stimulate thinking about a conception of curriculum development which has the potentiality for improving our present programs of general education in the high school.

By way of further clarification of the core concept, Harvill [19:215–217] discusses the nine "ingredients" of the core, summarizing his remarks in these words: "Perhaps the most distinctive separate ingredients of the core are its time allotment, its increased emphasis on the process of democratic living and learning, its possibilities for improved guidance, and its moderate experimental approach which brings freshness and variety to the teaching process." [19:217] (NOTE: In two prior issues of *Social Education,* January and April, 1954, Harvill outlines the advantages of core organization and gives origins of the concept.)

"How *effective* is the core program?" is a question that may very well be asked. That there should be some skepticism about the outcomes of the core program is to be expected. For instance, Fawcett [13:71–80] does not believe that necessary skills in mathematics can be taught in a core program.

After analyzing national surveys and reports on experiments with the core program in the junior high schools, Van Dyke drew the conclusions expressed in the following article.

How Effective Is the Core Curriculum in the Junior High School?
by L. A. VAN DYKE

From a summary of a presentation by L. A. Van Dyke, printed in the *Bulletin of the National Association of Secondary-School Principals,* April, 1954, pages 165–172. Reprinted by special permission. L. A. Van Dyke is a Professor of Education at the State University of Iowa, Iowa City, Iowa.

. . . In summary, the evidence now available in answer to the question, "How Effective Is the Core Curriculum in the Junior High School?", is sketchy and inconclusive. It is the opinion of the writer that the following are the most important facts which have some bearing on the question:

1. The number of junior high schools in the United States using a core curriculum is not large. There are approximately four hundred junior high schools, out of a total of nine

thousand, attempting a core program. Approximately seventy-five schools use a Type C or Type D program exclusively in which conventional subject lines are discarded and the scope is based on problems related to the needs of students. [See Wright's definition of the four types of core on pages 240–241.]

2. A large majority of junior high schools undertaking any type of core program begin rather cautiously with the correlation of two or more subjects. English and social studies are most frequently used in determining the scope and sequence of the core.

3. There has been some net increase in the number of schools undertaking a core program in the past three or four years. These increases, however, are limited to eight states.

4. The few experimental studies which have been attempted to show the relative success of core and conventional curriculum programs in providing for the acquisition of skills and knowledge suggest that students in core classes achieve as well as or slightly better than students in conventional courses in the same school. Measures of the statistical significance of the relative gains made on standardized tests generally show that differences are not significant. The gains are, however, more often in favor of the core than the non-core group.

5. Teachers of core classes who have reported on their experiences with these classes in professional periodicals are generally favorable toward them. The values most frequently mentioned are: (*a*) aiding pupils in making a successful transition from the elementary to the secondary school, (*b*) improved provisions for guidance, (*c*) improved social adjustments by pupils and fewer behavior problems, (*d*) greater student interest in learning activities, and (*e*) improved rapport between teacher and pupils.

6. Librarians report much greater book circulation, particularly of non-fiction materials, after the inauguration of the core program. They also report increased circulation in literary-type materials.

7. Principals of schools with a core program also are favorable in their evaluations. They emphasize the same advantages claimed by core teachers.

8. Some administrators and teachers have had unfortunate experiences with the core curriculum in the junior high school, and a few schools have discontinued it after a trial run or have made it optional rather than required. The total number and percentage of these schools, however, are small. Problems causing the most difficulty are: (*a*) lack of teachers trained for core instruction, (*b*) lack of suitable rooms and equipment, and (*c*) lack of suitable instructional materials. Some teachers report that the core makes excessive demands on their time and energies.

After analyzing "fifty-four doctoral dissertations, twenty master's theses, and six school system or university research projects" dealing with the core, Wright makes three suggestions for needed research: (*a*) more "evaluative studies should involve the type of program that uses the problem-solving approach in genuine problem situations"; (*b*) "more attention needs to be given to the development of successful instructional practice and to making information available on techniques for overcoming problems that arise"; and (*c*) state-wide surveys "can contribute materially to knowledge in this area." [49:3–4]

In her conclusions on "problems and practices," Wright summarizes the advantages of the core and suggests the key factors in the development of a core program.

Conclusions   by GRACE S. WRIGHT

Reprinted from Grace S. Wright, *Core Curriculum Development: Problems and Practices*. U. S. Department of Health, Education, and Welfare, Office of Education, Bulletin 1952, No. 5 (Washington: Superintendent of Documents, Government Printing Office, reprinted, 1955), pages 98–100. Grace S. Wright is a specialist in the Secondary Education and Curriculum Coordination sections at the U. S. Office of Education.

1. As curriculum committees study ways of providing for the personal and social needs of youth and of making instruction more meaningful, increasingly they try the core curriculum.

2. Adoption of the core pattern of organization sets both a physical and psychological stage for curriculum change. The longer block of time releases the teacher from the limiting effects of the usual forty-minute period. Activities planned for his classes no longer need be contained within the walls of the classroom. Organization of instruction on a problem-solving basis seems more nearly feasible to a teacher who has two or, at the most, three classes a day than it does to a teacher with five classes. Likewise, when the total number of pupils a teacher must know is reduced by half, as it is in the core pattern of organization, the possibility of knowing his pupils better is doubled. When homeroom or study-period time is added to the time a teacher spends with a group of pupils, as is frequently the case, his ability to help them is further increased. Possibilities for growth are limited only by the vision of the staff and its willing-

ness to seek constant improvement.

3. Most schools which introduce the core pattern of organization begin with the unification of English and social studies in a modified core approach (Types A or B). Some never progress further. For one reason or another—loss of leadership, rigid requirements for subject-matter teaching, public disapproval, or sheer ignorance of how to proceed—progress is halted before the staff reaches a pupil-problem basis of operation. In other schools, however, the unification of subjects is only the first step. Pupil-teacher planning, the substitution of democratic leadership for teacher-domination, the opportunity given by the lengthened period to know better a group of boys and girls, carry the classroom program forward. Strong principal leadership encourages teachers to work together on next steps. Thus a true core curriculum (Types C or D) is evolved.

4. The principal is the key person in promoting the development of the core curriculum. Unless the principal is enthusiastic about the possibilities of the core approach, and gives active support to its development, the school's program will be modified but little. Even a master teacher can have small influence outside his own classroom if the principal is merely permissive in his attitude. Principals who have worked in schools which have had a flourishing core curriculum are almost without exception convinced of its worth. They desire it for the school they serve, and if the approach is accepted by the staff, they give it their enthusiastic support.

5. If the chief obstacle to the further development of the core curriculum is the lack of qualified teachers, as high school principals have pointed out, then the greatest eventual hope for the core rests with teacher-education institutions. Only a few such institutions so far have accepted responsibility for the preparation of teachers of core to the extent of actually designing special programs, but there is what seems to be the beginning of a trend.

6. Advancement of the core curriculum in the years immediately ahead depends upon the reorientation of teachers now in service. Most of these teachers were trained as subject specialists. To many of them, therefore, the techniques of cooperative planning, of counseling youngsters, and of practicing democracy in the classroom are new and untried. The typical high school principal initiating a core program provides a program of in-service education. Most of the principals reporting in this study provide for discussion or workshop groups meeting at regular intervals throughout the school year.

7. Provision of a conference period during the school day for core-teacher planning is a characteristic feature of the most successful of the Types C and D core programs. Principals so schedule their classes that all core teachers in a grade have the same period free for working and planning together. Such a period is

an excellent in-service device, continuing year after year, provided the principal lends his support through frequent participation, or if other leadership is present to promote growth.

8. By providing opportunities for teachers to work together in in-service education programs and in conference-time planning, the core curriculum is a potential force in promoting better staff relationships.

9. Because the core program increases public interest in the school, it can help to promote better school-community relationships. Retrenchments in some localities due to lack of understanding of and sympathy with core on the part of some members of their staffs and the public are causing administrators increasingly to involve the public as well as all of

the staff in discussions and study of the type of curriculum the schools should offer. Whether the result is the core curriculum or some other type of program, the closer working together of school people and the public they serve should help to improve school-community relationships.

10. Programs of evaluation of the core curriculum are needed to provide evidence that the claimed outcomes are realized. Many of these outcomes concern intangibles difficult to evaluate. When educators can point to improved social attitudes, better civic behavior, equal or improved competence in basic skills, plus information or knowledge of the type needed by everyone, a wide acceptance of the core curriculum will be assured.

NOTE: A number of references will provide practical suggestions for curriculum workers who are interested in developing a core program. Those who are interested in the teacher-education aspect should consult *Preparation of Core Teachers for Secondary Schools,* prepared by a Committee on Preparation of Core Teachers with Harold Alberty as chairman, Association for Supervision and Curriculum Development, National Education Association, 1955. Curriculum workers planning to initiate a core program in their own schools may profit from the experiences of others by consulting such references as the following: (*a*) *Education,* January, 1953, is a "Core Program in Action" number. (*b*) Lucile Lurry, "Core Program Development Through Action Research," in the December, 1955, *School Review,* pages 469–476, cites six projects of action research, describing one in detail. (*c*) Irene Taub, "Ten Years with the Core Curriculum," in the January, 1955, *Social Education,* pages 66–70, outlines the core developments in Farragut Junior High School, New York City. (*d*) Myrtle Toops, *Working in the Core Program in Burris Laboratory School* (Col. Pub. No. 154, Ball State Teachers College, Muncie, Indiana, February, 1955, 60 pages), explains how the core program has developed at Ball State. (*e*) Maurice Wollin, "Supervision in the Core Program," in the May, 1955, *High Points,* pages 43–53, offers practical suggestions on implementation of the core with specific references to New York City.

8

PROGRAMS FOR MEETING
SPECIAL NEEDS OF LEARNERS

OVERVIEW

In the preceding section, types of curriculum organization or design for meeting the needs *common* to *all* boys and girls have been discussed. If the public school is to fulfill its function completely as an educational institution in our society, it must also recognize and provide for the unique needs, interests, and abilities of every child. This function is important from both an individual and a societal viewpoint.

In his discussion of "The New Illiteracy," Whyte [47:33–35] stresses the point that *conformity* is becoming "the dominant cultural movement in the United States" and proceeds to clinch his argument with examples from various aspects of American life—industry, advertising, corporations, suburban life, school curricula, and parental attitudes. Whyte does not stand alone in his fear that we are becoming a nation of conformists. For a further discussion of "the trend toward standardization of taste, style, thought, and behavior," the reader is referred to the article by McNally (page 300). The fact that our society appears to exist in a perpetual state of insecurity—a condition that places a premium on conformity and maintenance of the status quo—serves to give further support to the concern expressed by Whyte and others. These evidences of an unbalanced social outlook would indicate a need for the school to give greater recognition to the unique qualities of its pupils. Thus, in the face of certain disturbing trends that would make

253

education even more of a mass, lock-step affair (pyramiding enroll-ments, larger classes, recommendations for the use of TV to replace teachers, etc.), there is no room for complacency about meeting the educational needs of American children and youth today.

Concern about meeting the special needs of pupils is not new. Well established practices in providing for individual differences are already operative at two levels, the administrative and the instructional. Ad-ministrative procedures include the following: comprehensive programs of student activities, elective subjects, special and remedial classes, pro-motional policies (social promotion, acceleration of brighter pupils, re-tardation of slow learners), homogeneous grouping, and counseling on the basis of educational and vocational goals. Within the classroom, the teacher has made provisions for individual differences by means of sub-grouping, differentiated assignments, and the use of a variety of learn-ing activities and materials.

Inasmuch as provision for individual differences is still a major prob-lem in the classroom, each teacher must decide on the procedures that he can use most effectively in his particular situation. Effective class-room organization is one important factor to be considered. Here Wrightstone has provided helpful suggestions to the teacher in his sum-mary of "What Research Says about Class Organization for Instruction."

What Research Says About Class Organization for Instruction
by J. WAYNE WRIGHTSTONE

From the *NEA Journal*, April, 1957, pages 254–255. Reprinted by special permission of the National Education Association. J. Wayne Wrightstone is Director of Educational Research for the Board of Education of the City of New York.

Most teachers have weighed the pros and cons of various methods of organizing classes for instruction. Although many questions still re-main unanswered, research can be helpful in the consideration of these methods.

Organizing the Elementary-School Classroom

Research has some answers as to how well various plans meet the wide range of abilities and achieve-ment among elementary-school pu-pils.

Nonpromotion. The traditional practice of failing "poor" students offers a temptingly simple solution. There is evidence, however, that children do not learn more by repeating a grade. Nor does nonpromotion produce greater homogeneity; in fact it leads to greater diversity of mental abilities in a class. Often it undermines the personality of the nonpromoted pupil.

Ability grouping. Experts disagree about grouping youngsters according to ability, whether the criterion is IQ, reading level, or marks given by classroom teachers.

One procedure organizes classes in a school on three levels of ability. Usually this reduces the range of achievement and frees the teacher from making many adaptations to individual pupil differences. The actual reductions in range are about 15-17 per cent when classes are divided into three ability levels, and only 7-10 per cent when there are two ability groups.

Opponents of "ability grouping" point out that it produces relatively small change in the range of individual differences and that many differences in academic achievement continue. Opponents say that personal and social learnings are as important as academic learning, that children should not be labeled by ability grouping, and that the plan often concentrates "problem" children in the same class.

Advocates of this method, on the other hand, base their stand on the help it gives to the classroom teacher. Thus far, research indicates that so-called "homogeneous grouping" is seldom very satisfactory.

Ungraded primary. Attempts are made to narrow the range of pupil differences by having ungraded classes. In these classes, children share similarities of achievement, especially in reading, rather than mere chronological equality. At the end of six semesters, most children have been found to have better social and academic adjustment than their peers in a graded primary plan. At the end of the three-year primary period, there is likely to be less retardation in the ungraded group.

On the other hand, there are two persisting problems: some parents and teachers do not understand the plan, and there are difficulties in accurately rating pupils for their initial placement.

Subgrouping within a class. There is extensive use of subgrouping within a single class. This plan provides flexibility and ease in making changes according to the purposes of the teacher and pupils.

Some subgrouping plans are organized for direct instruction in a specific skill, such as reading. Others are organized on the basis of children's interest, such as committees in social studies, science, or library activities. Still other subgroups are organized to handle classroom problems involving social living—committees on room decorations, class plays, and services to school or community.

Organizing the Secondary-School Classroom

Methods of organizing instruction at the secondary level have similarities to those used in elementary schools. They also have important differences.

Ability grouping. The findings of research studies indicate that groupings do not actually reflect great uniformity of ability. Even disregarding the lack of precision of the tests, there are differences in reading ability among students grouped by intelligence scores. Neither does homogeneity in mathematical ability necessarily mean significant uniformity in language ability.

Departmentalization. For years, secondary schools have practiced departmentalization. In addition, there are many instances of two- or three-track plans within such subject fields as science, mathematics, and English. This technique of grouping, according to ability and achievement, reduces somewhat the range of individual differences.

School curriculum. There are many opportunities for student grouping simply by organizing the curriculum in terms of vocational aims. The commercial students are separated from the college-preparatory; the future industrial workers are separated from the general non-college academic students. And there are distinctions among the curriculums between those which are terminal and those which are foundational.

All the curriculums, moreover, permit adaptations to individual abilities and interests.

Core curriculum. Research indicates that students in the core-curriculum plans achieve as well in subject-matter mastery as students taught by separate subjects. In addition, they rate higher on measures of personal adjustment and social participation. Also the morale of core classes is usually higher, and students say that they receive more help on personal problems.

Differentiated instruction and supplementary assignments. The evidence shows that all plans of differentiated instruction have educational values, but that none is convincingly superior to the others. Current practices in this area include common assignments with differentiated rates of learning, minimum and maximum assignments with differentiated achievement level, and common objectives with special assignments for each student.

Laboratory types. Laboratory types of instruction include unit plans, individual projects, and contract plans. These are characterized by self-instructive materials and tests to show mastery of a whole unit or sequence of skills. They help the teacher adapt instruction to the individual differences of students.

Extracurriculum activities. Groupings in which students participate according to their interest and ability in voluntary activities, such as school publications, dramatics, and science clubs, are valuable in stimulating individual student development.

Adapting Instruction to Individual Needs

Research indicates some general characteristics of pupils with high and low ability which have implications for teaching and class organization. For example, children with high ability can engage in independent activities and respond well to long-range assignments that require a high degree of mental organization. Children with low ability, on the other hand, learn best when supervised with short-time units and specific assignments. Classroom teachers can adjust instruction and organization to meet these variations without using grouping.

Characteristics of Effective Class Organization

An effective class organization, according to research, is characterized by flexibility, independence, and control. *Flexibility* permits change as conditions in the classroom and purposes of instruction demand. *Independence* provides for individual initiative and action on the part of teacher and pupil. *Control* is essential for the smooth and orderly functioning of any plan of grouping.

Class organization should be flexible so that the teacher can modify the grouping to meet new needs or situations. More than one basis for grouping may operate at the same time. For example, there may be specific instructional groups, interest groups, and friendship groups all working in the classroom at the same time.

Class management concerned with individualizing instruction is directly related to the degree of independence of the children. Children need to learn to work independently in many ways with many materials. Being able to do this involves knowing how to proceed independently with an assignment and how to follow systematically from one activity to another. This, in turn, requires the ability to understand and follow directions as well as such study and library skills as locating needed books, using reference materials, finding information, and taking notes.

Some techniques for carrying on independent work should be taught to the class as a whole. Others may be taught to a particular group for a particular type of assignment.

Control is an important characteristic of good classroom management. The social climate of the classroom is important in developing effective control. The teacher's personal attitudes influence the emotional and social climate of the classroom. Thus, pupil-teacher rapport reveals the degree of warmth and interest that the teacher has for the children.

Research studies have shown that authoritarian methods of control induce pupil attitudes of self-concern and of competition with others. Democratic leadership, however, causes other pupil attitudes to emerge, such as concern for the welfare of the group, for the individuals within a group, and for effective working relationships among group members.

NOTE: English teachers will find helpful suggestions, based on research, in the article by Olive S. Niles and Margaret J. Early, "Adjusting to Individual Differences in English," *Journal of Education,* December, 1955.

Within the past decade, educators are beginning to recognize the fact that the school has a twofold responsibility in making provision for individual differences among its pupils: to meet the individual needs of normal children and to provide for special needs of exceptional children. Since the foregoing literature has dealt adequately with provisions for individual needs of normal children and since the current emphasis is on the special needs of exceptional children, the remainder of this section will be primarily concerned with the latter group. In their study of trends in the production of curriculum guides, Merritt and Harap noted "a recent upsurge of interest in the education of the exceptional child" (item 25, page 328).

Because the term "exceptional children" is relatively new to educational literature, it becomes necessary at the outset to determine what distinctions are made between normal and exceptional children. Two definitions follow.

Dunn describes an *exceptional* pupil as *"one who deviates from the average in mental, physical, social, or emotional characteristics to such an extent that he is unable to profit adequately from the regular high school curriculum alone, and requires special educational services in order to have educational opportunity equal to that provided the usual pupil."* [12:4]

A more analytical definition of *exceptional* children appears in *School Life:* " 'Exceptional' children and youth are those who have unusual educational needs because of blindness, partial loss of vision, deafness, impaired hearing, crippling conditions, special health problems, speech defects, mental retardation, mental giftedness, or serious social and emotional maladjustments." [45:6] Some have objected to listing the gifted and the defective, for example, under a single classification. It should be noted that neither of the above definitions implies that any two groups are alike nor that they should have the same educational fare. What is implied is that each group has special needs that must be met by a tailor-made program, not one suitable for the usual pupil nor any other special group.

Educational provisions for exceptional children have been taken care of by means of special programs and special schools. There is a general belief that such children should remain in regular schools with normal children whenever possible, even though a variation in program be necessary. Some writers, moreover, have warned that mere physical proximity does not insure true integration with nor acceptance by normal children.

GIFTED PUPILS

The group of exceptional children that appears to be receiving most emphasis in professional literature at the present time is the *gifted*. Who are the "gifted" children? The Metropolitan School Study Council defines the gifted children as those who "are recognized as the top 10 per cent of the general public school population in terms of mental ability. This 10 per cent usually includes all pupils with an IQ of 120 or better." [32:3] Birch and McWilliams state: "By the *gifted* we mean the most intelligent 1 per cent of the whole population. . . . By the term *superior* we mean the most intelligent 15 per cent of the whole population." [6:1] In a bulletin, entitled *The Superior Pupil in Junior High School Mathematics,* published by the U.S. Office of Education, McWilliams and Brown describe "superior" pupils as "the rapid learners in academic subjects. They are the pupils in the upper 20 per cent in general intelligence whose abilities lend themselves readily to intellectual pursuits." [30:3] It should be noted that all of the above definitions of the "gifted" or the "superior" pupil have one thing in common: They limit giftedness to intellectual ability or to the ability to do academic work, or both. No recognition is given to special aptitudes or abilities, such as those exhibited by artists or musicians, for example. Witty believes that the definition of giftedness needs to be broadened (page 275). Recently, some writers are referring to the "academically talented" rather than to the "gifted" pupil.

Although gifted children are now in the spotlight, many contend that their needs are still being met more in words than in deeds. In the article that follows, Terman and Oden upset certain misconceptions about gifted children and stress the need to identify them early in life and to give them proper guidance.

Major Issues in the Education of Gifted Children
by LEWIS M. TERMAN and MELITA H. ODEN

From the *Journal of Teacher Education,* Vol. V (September, 1954), pages 230–232. Reprinted by special permission of the executive secretary, National Commission on Teacher Education and Professional Standards, National Education Association. The late Lewis M. Terman and Melita H. Oden have both been associated with Stanford University. Terman as Professor Emeritus of Psychology and Oden as Research Associate in the Department of Psychology.

Of the many unresolved issues in the education of gifted children, we have chosen five for brief discussion in this symposium. These are: (*a*) democracy and the IQ, (*b*) the educational lock step, (*c*) early identification of the gifted, (*d*) educational opportunities that are feasible, and (*e*) needed guidance and counseling.

Democracy and the IQ

This is a very old issue, but it was the late Professor Bagley who first brought it to the fore and who did more than anyone else to prejudice the minds of educators against offering any kind of special opportunities for the gifted. He wrote with particular scorn of training the gifted for leadership, and proposed instead that the important thing was to teach the average people when and where to tell their would-be leaders to get off. To argue, as Bagley did, that all children should have the same kind of school training, at least through the grades, seems to us no less absurd than to argue that all children should have the same kind of medical treatment. Yet the Bagley point of view not only survives; it is in fact fairly widespread, though it is losing ground.

The Educational Lock Step

This refers to the belief that for the sake of normal social adjustment the gifted child should be kept with others of his own age, and that only such opportunities should be provided for him as are possible under this limitation. The doctrine is based on the belief that the social maladjustment caused by acceleration outweighs any of its advantages. The truth is that the evidence from every serious investigation of the problem shows this view to be largely false. Our data show there is a marked tendency for children of very superior IQ to be more mature both socially and physically than children of average ability. This is not to say that every child should complete high school and college as early as his IQ would permit. The gifted child who is already maladjusted or exceptionally immature socially should be allowed little acceleration or none, but the facts obtained in the thirty-year follow-up of our large gifted group prove conclusively that children of 135 IQ or higher who are accelerated one, two, or even three years are usually more successful in later life than equally bright children who are held in the lock step. If you don't believe it, see Chapter 20 in *The Gifted Child Grows Up*. Acceleration is especially desirable for those who plan to enter a profession that calls for years of graduate study. Other advantages are that the accelerated find their schoolwork more challenging and that earlier graduation enables them to marry earlier (which, on the average, they do).

Early Identification of the Gifted

Thirty years ago if you wanted to know who was the brightest child in a classroom, your best single chance of finding out was not to ask the teacher but to take the name of the youngest child in the room. But in these days where tests of intelligence and school achievement are so easily available, one might suppose that nearly all of the gifted would be identified at an early age. Such is not the case. There are still millions of children who leave school without ever

having had any kind of standardized test. Even where tests are used their results are so frequently misinterpreted that some of the gifted are likely to be overlooked. One reason why early identification is important is that acceleration by grade skipping is most feasible in the lower grades. Another reason is that the earlier the gifted child is identified the better his later education can be planned for.

Educational Opportunities That Are Feasible

Under current conditions of teacher shortage and overcrowded classrooms, about the only kinds of special opportunity that are readily feasible for the gifted are three: (*a*) segregation in special classes; (*b*) parallel classes for fast, medium, and slow learners; and (*c*) acceleration.

The pros and cons of segregation have long been debated. Our belief is that segregated classes at their best are very good indeed, but that they are rarely at their best. Parallel classes are a great help, but they are possible only in the larger schools. Acceleration, on the other hand, is always possible and in the majority of cases is desirable whatever other special provision may be made. As for the curriculum enrichment that is so often praised as the ideal solution for the gifted, it is indeed fine in theory but it is very difficult in practice. Under the conditions that presently prevail it can hardly be regarded as a panacea. We believe, nevertheless, that teachers should be alerted to the desirability of special assignments for the gifted in their classes and that they should be instructed by school supervisors and principals in the kinds of enrichment that are possible.

Needed Guidance and Counseling

In 1953 the National Manpower Council, composed of twenty nationally eminent persons, reported after extensive investigation that 40 per cent of the young men and women in the United States who are potentially good college material either do not enter college or, if they enter, do not continue to graduation. What causes are responsible for this appalling wastage of brainpower at a time when there is an acute shortage of well trained minds in nearly every field of science, teaching, scholarship, and business?

There are doubtless many causes, but we believe that two of the most important are: (*a*) frequent failure to identify the gifted; and (*b*) when they *are* identified, failure to provide the kind of counseling service that is so badly needed in high schools and colleges. Of the more than 1,450 members of our gifted group (all of them in the top 1 per cent in general intelligence), nearly 15 per cent did not enter college and 30 per cent did not graduate. It is true that the schooling of some was cut short by the great depression, which began shortly before or shortly after most of them reached college age. We are quite certain, however, that many more of them would have gone to college if there had been adequate counseling service in the high schools they attended. As a matter of fact there was little or none at all in most of the schools. The result was that nearly two hundred did not enter college and more than four hundred did not graduate. The situation has improved in the last twenty years, especially in the educationally more progressive cities, but we are reliably informed that in both amount and quality the counseling available in most high schools is far below what is needed.

Counseling at the high school level is necessary not only to insure that more of the brighter students will get the amount of training they should have, but also to insure that each will get the kind of training best adapted to prepare him for later specialization. This means *vocational* counseling, not for the purpose of encouraging the student to choose once and for all the occupation he will enter, but rather to discover the broad general fields where his abilities and interests lie. One of the most valuable single tools for this purpose is Strong's Vocational Interest Test, especially the form designed for men. This test reveals more clearly and accurately than any other what the student's patterns of interest are like; for example, whether they resemble most closely the interest patterns of successful men in the physical sciences, engineering, medicine, law, architecture, journalism, or some of the thirty other occupations for which the test can be scored. The thing that counts is not so much the score in a particular occupation but rather the patterns of interest that are disclosed. To interpret the great variety of patterns that are found calls for skill and experience, but when properly used the test is so valuable that every boy should be given a chance to take it before the end of his senior year. If the Strong test had been available and could have been taken by all the men in our gifted group when they were in high school, at least 10 to 20 per cent might have made a better choice of career.

In a study of 673 boys and girls in the Connecticut schools in grades 2 to 12 with IQ's of 120 or above, Cutts and Moseley found that bright children will, if left to their own devices, follow the path of least resistance, occupying themselves with that which is easy and interesting rather than with something that is "difficult and irritating." As a result, the researchers make this comment: "We do not subscribe to the theory that the nastiest medicine is, on that account, most efficacious. A subject is not 'good' for a pupil just because it is hard. But the experience of working long and hard to achieve a desired goal is good. How is the teacher to help a bright child shift his opinion of a subject from 'like the least and work hardest' to 'like best and work hardest,' or, if this is not possible, still to divorce the ideas of dislike and hard work?" [11: 172]

Just what provisions *are* being made for the gifted pupils in our schools today? A condensed summary of current educational practices appears in the following article by Strang.

The Mental Diet of Our Gifted Children   by RUTH STRANG

From the *NEA Journal*, May, 1955, pages 265–267. Reprinted by special permission. Ruth Strang is Professor of Education, Teachers College, Columbia University, New York City.

In a world where it is increasingly necessary for Americans to meet quantity with quality, our schools cannot be content to intone, "Forward! March! Two-three-four," to students who, intellectually speaking, have wings on their feet.

Fortunately, many of our schools are making a specific effort to meet the needs of the gifted and talented.

This is being done in a variety of ways, some of which will be described briefly in the paragraphs that follow.

Providing a "Lush" Environment

Some gifted children will be stimulated to use their ability in a class that offers challenging experiences. Even without being previously identified, some will read widely, engage in research projects, and do creative work needed in attaining the group goals. A stimulating classroom will bring out their abilities.

Making Rapid Promotion

In the far more common situation, skipping one or two grades in elementary school may be the only attempt to meet the needs of the able learner. Of course, the decision to have a bright pupil skip a grade should always be made on an individual basis, taking into consideration his social, physical, and emotional maturity, the lack of environment opportunities, his own attitude, and the attitude of his parents and teachers.

For obvious reasons, this is the poorest kind of acceleration. It does, however, have the advantage of enabling the able learner to get started in a profession earlier than he otherwise would. And there is evidence in Terman's and in other follow-up studies that such acceleration, made on an individual basis, need not cause social or emotional maladjustment.

Far better than skipping a grade, however, is the kind of acceleration in which the pupil is placed in a rapid-advance class, in which he completes three years' work in two years, or four years' work in three.

For example, in Western High School, Baltimore, pupils enrolled in the advanced college preparatory program complete their regular academic work in three years. In their fourth year they may take a college-level year while still in high school and, on graduation, be admitted to advanced standing in college.

Another form of acceleration, possible in a large high school, is the Kenyon Plan for speeding the progress and enriching the program of able high school pupils in eleven subject fields.

In the Newton (Massachusetts) High School this work has been carried on in English, French, mathematics, biology, and physics. Under such a plan the able pupils tackle more difficult concepts than pupils in regular classes, and use problem-solving methods.

The plan is flexible enough to allow a pupil to transfer to a regular class if he so wishes. Studies are now being conducted to determine the effects of several kinds of rapid advancement during high school and college years.

Adding More Subjects

Within the framework of the ordinary public school, it is possible to include one or more additional educational opportunities in the gifted pupil's schedule. Since he can carry the regular program with ease, an extra class in art, music, foreign language, shop, typewriting, advanced science, creative writing, dramatics, or home economics may be added.

This plan, while inadequate by itself to meet the needs of gifted children, has several advantages: it increases their range of interests and useful skills; it may foster mental health by providing more creative outlets; and it may contribute needed leadership in these fields.

Subgrouping Within the Regular Class

Subgroups of gifted children can do advance study, work on a special project, or explore a common interest. Activities such as these give children of different abilities opportunities to make their special contribution in the small group.

Success with such grouping requires a wide range of suitable reading and other instructional materials, physical facilities that make comfortable grouping possible, and a skillful teacher who is concerned with the group process as well as with subject matter. Although others may disagree, it has been my observation that, if these conditions exist, this method of flexible, multiple subgrouping within a regular class is one of the best ways of meeting the needs of all the pupils.

Providing Supplementary Instruction and Guidance

There are several other ways of giving special instruction and guidance to gifted pupils in regular classes. One of these may be illustrated by the plan in the Bedford, Ohio, public schools, which employ a coordinator of education for the gifted. Such pupils are identified and taken out of their regular classes for special educational experiences.

A second way is the Long Beach, California, plan of having the counselors in each school identify gifted pupils, interview these pupils and their parents, and discuss with teachers ways in which the staff may better meet the pupils' needs in each class.

In addition, Long Beach schools give the gifted children in the sixth grade an extra period a week in the library during which they are introduced by the librarian to biographies, travel books, or other kinds of reading. Each of them selects a book and reads parts or all of it during the week. The following week they meet again to discuss informally what they have read. The pupils having this experience are most enthusiastic about it.

Modifying the Regular School Program

A more fundamental modification of the regular school program has been carried out and evaluated in the

Colfax Elementary School in Pittsburgh. The able learners spend half the day in regular classes with pupils of their own age, where they have an opportunity to work together in music, art, and physical education. During the rest of the day the intellectually superior are grouped together in a workshop type of program, where they not only work on problems and projects at their own pace but also get instruction in the basic elementary-school subjects.

An evaluation of this program, carried out with sixty-seven children in the fourth, fifth, and sixth grades, showed that the gifted children were not rejected by the other children because they were together in the workshop group. Nor did they reject or accept children in regular classes any more than they did in their own more homogeneous group.

As might be expected, when free to choose those with whom they would like to work and play, either in school or outside of school, the gifted students tended to choose children of somewhat similar ability. However, there is possibly more danger of cliques when intellectually gifted children are in regular classes than when they are working with their intellectual peers part of the day.

Under this plan, the mental-age differences between the gifted and the children in the regular classes were much greater than the differences in achievement in reading and arithmetic. This suggests that achievement tests do not measure the actual learnings of these children. Furthermore, when these children are removed from the group, the average children get much more effective teaching.

Another plan of providing special instruction for the gifted in the ordinary public school requires still more modification of the regular school program. One of the most thoroughly evaluated programs of this kind is the well-known major-work classes of Cleveland, Ohio, which have been in operation for over twenty-three years. These classes are organized in the elementary school for children with IQs of 125 or above.

The children in the major-work classes meet together for their regular academic program, which is enriched through pupil-initiated projects, research type of study, and opportunities for small groups and individuals to communicate the results of their study in interesting and effective ways. Part of the day they are with the regular class and have special teachers in physical education, music, and other school activities.

A thorough evaluation and follow-up study of pupils who had been in these classes showed that in comparison with a control group those who had been in the major-work classes were significantly superior in social responsibility, leadership honors and awards, hobbies and talents, vocational ambitions, critical thinking, and the reading of nonfiction books and magazines. A larger proportion of the major-work pupils were going on to college and into the professions.

Sending Gifted and Talented Pupils to Specialized Schools

In large cities, certain high schools are particularly geared for pupils with special gifts or talents.

For example, the Stuyvesant High School, New York City, features science education. Admission is based on an IQ of 110 or above on a group test; "a satisfactory score on an English and mathematics test"; and the recommendation of teachers and the principal of the lower school. Once in high school, there is progression of experience in honor classes for pupils who demonstrate superior learning ability. A specialized school may also furnish a high type of liberal education, as does the High School of Science in New York City. Philadelphia, Baltimore, Cincinnati, and other cities have had these specialized schools for many years.

Finally, there are a very few schools for gifted children only. Best known of these are the elementary school and high school connected with Hunter College in New York City. These schools represent grouping of gifted pupils for the purpose of providing specially qualified teachers and conditions in which the pupils are highly stimulated by other gifted minds and by challenging work and appropriate methods and materials of instruction. They may go as far and as fast as they are able without wasting time listening to explanations and doing assignments unnecessary for them.

Under the most favorable conditions—with good physical conditions, adequate materials of instruction, and gifted teachers skillful in group-work methods—the educational needs of gifted children may be best met, it seems to me, in regular public-school classes plus some additional classes and extra-class and community activities.

Under fairly favorable conditions, a program that partially segregates the gifted seems most desirable, combining the values of a degree of grouping for better learning with the value of being with pupils of varied abilities and background.

Under very poor conditions, special classes or even special schools may be necessary to help gifted children develop their potentialities for their personal satisfaction and best service to society.

Certainly it is democratic for the public schools to provide the educational experience all children and youth need.

By and large, a good deal more has been provided thus far in the way of special training for children of limited capacities than for children who have the potential of becoming the nation's future leaders, great scientists, and creative artists.

Strang's article has just presented a clear, concise summary of provisions for gifted pupils. Discussing the various practices in the education of gifted children, Witty makes an analysis of each, weighing their relative merits. His discussion of the controversial practice of acceleration is especially good.

Practices in the Education of the Gifted   by PAUL A. WITTY

From *Frontiers of Elementary Education III*, pages 47–54. Proceedings of a Conference on Elementary Education. Compiled and edited by Vincent J. Glennon, Professor of Education, Syracuse University, and published by the Syracuse University Press, 1956. Reprinted by special permission. Paul A. Witty is Professor of Education and Director of the Psycho-Educational Clinic at Northwestern University.

One of the most significant milestones in psychology and education is associated with the making of practical tests for the measurement of intelligence. Another significant phase of psychological progress is in a related field—the development of child-study techniques designed to reveal the nature and needs of children.

The name of L. M. Terman is conspicuous in both areas,[1] for he and his associates originated the Stanford-Binet intelligence tests and employed them widely. Psychologists were at once attracted to the extreme cases; for example, the very bright and gifted children whose abilities were unusual and conspicuous. L. M.

Terman, Leta Hollingworth, and the writer identified groups of such children and ascertained facts about their physical development, their social status, and their educational attainment. The results of these studies of children at or above IQ 130 agreed closely.

Contrary to popular thought, gifted children were shown on the whole to be somewhat above the average physically and socially. They were superior to their classmates of similar age in size, strength, and general health. The idea that they were physically retarded, unsocial, spectacled, "booky" misfits was disproved.[2]

The academic development of

[1] L. M. Terman and M. Merrill, *The Measurement of Intelligence* (Boston: Houghton-Mifflin Company, 1938). L. M. Terman and others, *Genetic Studies of Geniuses* (Stanford, California: Stanford University Press), Vols. 1, 2, 3, 4.

[2] L. S. Hollingworth, *Gifted Children* (New York: The Macmillan Company, 1926). L. S. Hollingworth, *Children Above 180 IQ* (Yonkers: World Book Company, 1942). Paul Witty, "A Genetic Study of Fifty Gifted Children," *39th Yearbook of the N.S.S.E.*, Part I, 1940. Parts of this article have appeared in *Nursing Outlook*, "Gifted Children Our Greatest Resource," and *Teachers College Record*, December, 1955.

gifted pupils was not typically one-sided. Although they were generally superior, they did their best work on tests of reading and language; their poorest attainments were in handwriting and spelling. Their superiority in reading was especially noteworthy. Forty-five per cent of Terman's group and one-third of the writer's group learned to read before entering school. Sometimes the precocity was very great.

In every investigation, extreme rapidity of learning proved to be a characteristic of the gifted child. His attainment in school subjects was sometimes phenomenal. In several studies it was reported that by the time the gifted pupil was ten years of age he had, on the average, knowledges of pupils in classes two or three grades above his own. Yet, he was seldom accelerated or offered an enriched program of study. Almost without exception, studies made during the period 1920–1945 showed that the schools were making little special provision for gifted children. As one writer stated:

The gifted, the potential leaders, discoverers and creators . . . are usually left to develop their own skills in their own way and in terms of personal initiative alone.[3]

It is clear, then, that the gifted child requires a curriculum enriched and developed according to his particular needs. That he seldom is the recipient of such educational provision is generally known.

Neglect of the Gifted

Although there is a renewed interest in the education of gifted children, surveys show that only a beginning has been made in caring for them. There are, of course, many reasons for the neglect of the most able pupils. Among these reasons is the indifference of some school administrators and teachers to the problem presented by gifted pupils. It is, of course, generally recognized that the preservation and advancement of civilization depends to a large extent upon contributions made by gifted individuals.

Although there is now in the elementary school a somewhat more general provision for the gifted, the neglect of this group is still great. And the neglect appears to be even greater in the secondary school than in the elementary school. It appears that many gifted pupils "languish in idleness" throughout the four years of the high school and fail to develop the ambition or work habits essential for profitable college careers. It is estimated that in many states not more than 50 per cent of the total number of gifted pupils who graduate from high school go on to college. Moreover, probably a third or more of gifted young people leave college with an inadequate amount

[3] C. C. Miles, *Manual of Child Psychology*, edited by L. Carmichael (New York: John Wiley and Sons, Inc., 1946), p. 931; revised 1954, p. 1028.

of education to qualify them for the best use of their abilities. That many gifted students are not challenged sufficiently by their college courses, too, is suggested by studies of the educational status of the gifted youth in college. L. M. Terman reports that the overlapping of educational attainment, objectively measured, is so great that in certain colleges about 20 per cent of the gifted sophomores and 15 per cent of the gifted freshmen reach or exceed the median scores of seniors. Reasonably, he proposes that we "quit accrediting college courses and credit instead the individual student." [4]

The need for more adequate stimulation and guidance of the gifted throughout college and in graduate schools is suggested by C. Gilbert Wrenn. This investigator reports a follow-up of the top 16 per cent of a group of 1938 Minnesota high school graduates.[5] Nine years after high school graduation, "only 45 per cent (of this top group) had received baccalaureate degrees, and 8 per cent had earned advanced degrees. In approximate figures only 4 per cent of the high school graduates with IQs of 125 and above had earned advanced degrees."

The recent resurgence of interest in gifted or "rapid-learning" pupils has included emphasis on stimulating leadership in science. A number of articles in educational periodicals have been devoted recently to the promising student of science. For example, R. H. Knapp and H. B. Goodrich [6] stressed the need for early identification and guidance of capable students. It has, of course, been demonstrated that there is a great waste of such pupils' ability.

The National Manpower Council estimated in 1951 that one-fourth of our eighteen-year-old youth had IQs 110 or above. Of this fourth, 60 per cent did not enter college and 20 per cent did not complete high school. Of the 40 per cent that entered college, only about one-half graduated.

Many potential discoverers and creators are in our classrooms today. These, like other gifted students, are frequently neglected. Our primary responsibility is to identify promising children and youth and provide opportunities merited by their ability and interest and necessary for their full development.

Provisions for the Gifted Pupil

Most educators stress the desirability of offering gifted pupils broad and diversified educational opportunities. Some recommend widespread adoption of acceleration, and others

[4] L. M. Terman, "The Gifted Student and His Academic Environment," *School and Society*, XLIX (January 21, 1939), pp. 65–73.

[5] C. Gilbert Wrenn, "Potential Research Talent in the Sciences Based on Intelligence Quotients of Ph.D.'s," *Educational Record*, XXX (January, 1949), pp. 20–22.

[6] R. H. Knapp and H. B. Goodrich, *Origin of American Scientists* (Chicago: The University of Chicago Press, 1952).

endorse acceleration only as a temporary expedient and partial solution to the problem. If acceleration is practiced to excess, there is a fear that the gifted pupil will become maladjusted socially.

As early as 1933, Witty and Wilkins summarized the literature on acceleration and found that moderate amounts of acceleration seemed justifiable for the gifted.[7] J. W. Trusler later recommended more frequent grade-skipping for pupils of IQ 125 and above.[8] This recommendation seems to be in accord with suggestions drawn from genetic studies which show that acceleration in the elementary school up to two full grades is not associated with undesirable later adjustments in the gifted. Recently Pressey studied some relationships of acceleration to success in college and concluded: "The evidence was practically unanimous that younger entrants were more likely to graduate, had the best academic records, won the most honors, and presented the fewest disciplinary difficulties."[9]

It should be pointed out that the use of acceleration has not been popular among American educators.

Several studies reflect the doubt shown by administrators, supervisors, and teachers concerning the practice —particularly at the high school level.

An excellent summary of studies in this field has recently been written by D. A. Worcester who stresses these values of acceleration:

1. First of all, acceleration recognizes the facts of life. Children do differ from each other markedly. Some develop much more rapidly than do others. Usually those of greater academic potentialities are also more mature socially and emotionally and fully as well developed physically.

2. Failure to accelerate involves dangers. There is evidence to show that gifted children who are held back with those of their C.A. (chronological age) are more likely to develop behavior and personality problems than are those who are accelerated. There is danger, also, of promoting lazy and careless work habits among those who are educationally beyond their classmates but who are held back with them.[10]

The time when acceleration is best practiced has not been investigated carefully. But it has been generally shown that acceleration of one or two years is not associated with undesirable results in the case of the gifted. Worcester states:

[7] Paul Witty and LeRoy Wilkins, "The Status of Acceleration or Grade-skipping as an Administrative Practice," *Educational Administration and Supervision,* XIX (May, 1933), pp. 321–346.

[8] J. W. Trusler, "Pupil Acceleration in the Elementary Schools," *Grade Teacher,* LXVII (October, 1949), pp. 16–17 and 96–98.

[9] S. L. Pressey, "Educational Acceleration: Appraisals and Basic Problems," *Bureau of Educational Research Monographs,* No. 31 (Columbus, Ohio: Ohio State University, 1949).

[10] Dean A. Worcester, *The Education of Children of Above-Average Mentality* (Lincoln: University of Nebraska Press, 1956), pp. 33–34.

This writer advocates early entrance, with a provision for later acceleration for those who were not identified for early entrance and for those whose capabilities have become so developed that they are no longer working efficiently in their present group. The senior high school–freshman college years seem to offer one of the best possibilities for later acceleration.[11]

The School-College Plan (Ford Foundation), involving Andover, Exeter, Lawrenceville, Harvard, Yale, and Princeton, was developed to avoid duplication in the offerings in college and in the preparatory school.[12] As a result, a recommendation was made that superior students of good emotional stability, health, and social adjustment be permitted to take the normal eight years of high school and college in seven years. Another Ford program, The Program for Early Admission to College, is now ending its second year of operation. Four hundred students were admitted, in September, 1951, to twelve colleges prior to their graduation from the high school. Another four hundred were admitted in September, 1952. It appears already that the adjustment of the students to the advanced work and to other requirements was satisfactory. However, it is too early to evaluate this program.

The School and College Study of Admission with Advanced Standing, under the executive directorship of William H. Cornog of Philadelphia, is studying ways to develop curricula for high school pupils of high ability which will lead to advanced standing at college.[13]

It is possible for a pupil of high ability to be accelerated as much as two years in the Baltimore schools. The bright pupil has an opportunity to complete the three years of junior high school work in two years at the Robert E. Lee School. He can enter the advanced preparatory courses at one of three high schools. In this way, pupils save the equivalent of a year in college. This program has been in operation for approximately fifty years. Colleges such as Cornell, Oberlin, Smith, and Goucher accept these accredited pupils into their sophomore classes.

Several studies suggest that special classes for the gifted provide opportunities that are associated with salutary development. Since the educational outcomes of such classes have not been fully evaluated, it is impossible to pass final judgment upon the wisdom of following this type of provision generally. At best, such provisions could probably care for only a small proportion of the nation's gifted children.

Enrichment, too, is indispensable in the education of the gifted. Yet, in the past three decades few enrichment programs have been developed

---

[11] *Ibid.*, p. 36.

[12] Morris Meister, *Science Teacher*, XX (April, 1953), pp. 107–110.

[13] William H. Cornog, "School and College Study of Admission with Advanced Standing," *Bulletin of Information* (November, 1952), pp. 1–17 (Philadelphia 4, Pa.).

in our schools. At the present time there is a renewed interest in the formation of special classes and schools in which enrichment of experience is planned for gifted pupils. The manner of providing enrichment of education for gifted children will perhaps become a local responsibility in every school system. In large cities, it may be feasible and desirable to group the gifted for instruction; in smaller communities, the gifted child may be given an enriched program in regular classrooms supplemented by individual instruction and guidance. Close cooperation with the home should help to assure the most wholesome growth of the gifted child.

During the past eight years a marked resurgence of interest in special classes for the gifted has developed, and many programs for gifted pupils are being initiated. Of course, much of this work is influenced by the earlier contributions from cities such as Cleveland, Ohio; Los Angeles, California; Allentown, Pennsylvania; and others.

One of the characteristics of some special programs is the emphasis given to the social development and adjustment as well as to other "developmental needs" of the gifted child. For example, programs for the gifted in the Cleveland Major Work Classes today include varied social experiences.

Similarly, in the Hunter College Elementary School, careful planning assures well-balanced growth of each child. Examples, too, may be drawn from the work of regular classroom teachers who attempt to expand and enrich the social experience of the gifted. These efforts include opportunities for the pupils to participate in workshops, the development of group projects, class excursions, creative expression in which groups of talented children take part, and recreational activities of many kinds. In some cases, the parents of the gifted participate in planning and carrying out such projects.

Enrichment Within Regular Classes and Counseling Services

There has been a reawakening of interest in providing for the gifted in regular classes. For example, Marion C. Sheridan has suggested some ways by which an English teacher can enrich the curriculum for superior students in a regular class. The activities proposed include independent reading, creative pursuits, and projects related to the mass media of communication.[14]

In a rather comprehensive article presenting activities for the gifted pupil throughout the elementary and secondary school, Buck R. Rex describes procedures suitable for use in guiding the work of the gifted in regular classes. This presentation stresses the work of consultants, committees, creative pursuits, and ways

[14] M. C. Sheridan, *NEA Journal,* XLI (December, 1952), pp. 566–567.

of planning and evaluating the endeavor at various levels.[15] It is generally conceded that one desirable means of providing for the gifted within the heterogeneous class structure is through differentiated assignments. However, with constantly expanding enrollments, it is becoming increasingly difficult for a teacher to provide opportunities for the different levels of ability in the regular classroom.

Claude L. Reeves, assistant superintendent of the Los Angeles schools in charge of secondary education, expresses the view that the gifted can be helped greatly through counseling. Such a program requires the services of a coordinator in counseling who works with pupils, their teachers, and parents from the elementary grades through high school. Programs of this type, differing chiefly in details, have been started in San Diego, Santa Barbara, Long Beach, Berkeley, and Ventura.

Several recent articles describe techniques for guiding gifted children. Ruth Strang has emphasized the need for early identification of the gifted and for continuous help in meeting their problems. Some of the common problems are cited as well as some procedures which may be employed by counselors. The significance of the home is also stressed.[16]

Enrichment in the Special Fields

The writer, in collaboration with Samuel W. Bloom, has described programs in science for the rapid-learning pupil.[17] The programs include the outstanding endeavor in the Bronx High School of Science, the Forest Hills High School (New York), the Monroe High School in Rochester, the Evanston Township High School (Illinois), the New Trier Township High School (Illinois), and the work in Baltimore, in New York, in Phoenix, and in Los Angeles and other California cities.

Various other types of opportunities are being offered the gifted pupil in the field of science. Morris Meister, Principal of the Bronx High School of Science, New York, stresses the fact that the High School of Science is a school in which science is being used as one of the tools by which a more liberal education is obtained. The high school is organized "around a purpose that is meaningful and attractive to the students." A specialized high school can thus provide a more flexible curriculum and offer a larger number of electives. The program in the High School of Science

---

[15] B. R. Rex, Jr., *Exceptional Children*, XIX (December, 1952), pp. 117–118.

[16] Ruth Strang, *The Personnel and Guidance Journal*, XXXI (October, 1952), pp. 26–30.

[17] Paul Witty and Samuel W. Bloom, "Science Provisions for the Gifted," *Exceptional Children*, XX (March, 1954), pp. 244–250, 262. "Conserving Ability in the Sciences," *Exceptional Children*, XXII (October, 1955), pp. 10–16, 46.

has been fully described elsewhere.[18]

Paul Brandwein has described a program in Forest Hills, New York, for *The Gifted Student as Future Scientist*. In this provocative book, he discusses the problem of meeting the needs of the potential scientist and sets forth a curriculum designed to meet these needs.[19]

In *Exceptional Children* (September, 1955), the writer, in collaboration with Samuel Bloom, describes the curricula of additional schools whose work in the field of science is outstanding. Attention is directed to the role of the teacher as a crucial factor in the successful stimulation of gifted children and youth. Emphasis is placed on the problem of training adequate numbers of teachers and the difficulty of holding capable teachers, especially in fields such as science, under prevailing conditions in our schools. The problem of teacher training is clearly one of the primary issues in the education of the gifted.

Expression is blocked in some children by strong emotion or by insecurity traceable to deprivations at home. In communities which offer children only very meager opportunities, the expression of intelligence may be different from that found in more fortunate areas. Moreover, there are children whose abilities in art, music, or writing, though rare and distinctive, can be recognized by performance.

Perhaps it is desirable to broaden our definition of the gifted and to consider any child as "gifted" whose performance, in a potentially valuable line of human activity, is consistently remarkable. Abundant opportunities should be offered in both home and school for the release and expression of such abilities.

There is an increased tendency to think of the gifted in terms of this broader definition. In an experiment, now under way in Portland, Oregon, teachers' judgments and the results of standardized mental and educational tests are used for screening and examining children of high ability, with a view to enrichment of their school programs. "Children are also screened for exceptional talent in the areas of art, music, mechanical comprehension, creative writing, creative dance, creative drama, and social leadership." [20]

The authors of *A Survey of the Education of Gifted Children* state:

---

[18] Morris Meister and H. A. Odell, "What Provisions for the Education of the Gifted Students?" *Bulletin of the National Association of Secondary-School Principals*, XXXV (April, 1951), p. 30.

[19] Paul Brandwein, *The Gifted Student as Future Scientist* (New York: Harcourt Brace and Company, Inc., 1955).

[20] Clifford W. Williams in *A Survey of the Education of Gifted Children*, Supplementary Educational Monograph, No. 83, by Robert Havighurst, Eugene Stivers, and Robert F. DeHaan (Chicago: University of Chicago Press, November, 1955), p. 88.

There is a threefold importance in looking for a variety of talent in children. First, such discovery points out to teachers that there are other bases besides intelligence for talent in children. Second, it calls attention to more children than a single talent-criterion does. Third, it encourages the teacher to use a variety of avenues of approach to children, whereas a single measure of giftedness narrows her approach.[21]

The method used for the identification of the gifted will vary with the type of school or with the objectives of the program. The intelligence test is the generally established and most widely used method for identifying gifted children.[22]

Concluding Statement

The foregoing discussion should not lead one to minimize the significance in a democracy of attempts to provide more adequately for children who are gifted in abstract intelligence. These children often have other special gifts and aptitudes, too. But we are also interested in other types of giftedness.

Educators at all levels of instruction must divest themselves of the belief that gifted students can get along by themselves and that it is undemocratic to give them special education suited to their particular needs. And we must also dispel the fear sometimes expressed that the gifted may become selfish through too much consideration, for "it is precisely this group of individuals of great ability who, in the long run and as a group, will be the least selfish, the least likely to monopolize the good things in this world, and by their inventions and discoveries, by their creative work in the arts, by their contributions to government and social reform, by their activities in all fields, will in the future help humanity in its groping struggle upward toward a better civilization." [23]

It appears that one way of advancing social welfare is to provide educational opportunities for all gifted pupils in accordance with their ability and promise. Such a program would necessitate early identification of gifted children and continuous study and guidance of them throughout their home and school careers. For some of them, it would require the provision of scholarships in order that they might complete high school or college. For others, it would necessitate subsequent guidance and aid so that they might in larger numbers acquire specialized training and graduate degrees—thus receiving the special preparation needed for outstanding accomplishment in science and other areas so important to the advancement and welfare of modern society. It is to be hoped that the fu-

[21] Robert J. Havighurst, Eugene Stivers, and Robert F. DeHaan, *A Survey of the Education of Gifted Children, op. cit.,* p. 6.

[22] Paul Witty (ed.), *The Gifted Child* (Boston: D. C. Heath and Company, 1951).

[23] Rudolph Pintner, "Superior Ability," *Teachers College Record,* XLII (February, 1941), p. 419. See also the writer's article in *Teachers College Record,* 1956.

ture will bring an even greater in-   greatest resource—gifted children
terest in the full development of our   and youth.

   That provisions for gifted children are still inadequate is indicated in
the "conclusions" of Witty and Bloom in their discussion of "The Education of the Superior High School Student," which follows. (The
same point is made in "The Plight of the Gifted Child," *Look*, November 26, 1957, pages 40–44, 46–47.)

Conclusions   by PAUL A. WITTY and SAMUEL W. BLOOM

From "The Education of the Superior High School Student," *Bulletin
of the National Association of Secondary-School Principals*, January, 1955,
page 22. Reprinted by special permission. Paul A. Witty is Professor of
Education and Director of the Psycho-Educational Clinic at Northwestern University; Samuel W. Bloom is a teacher of science in the Monroe
High School, Rochester, New York.

Our educational system has recently been severely criticized for its
failure to teach the skills effectively.[1]
Studies seem to show that our pupils
are perhaps better prepared today in
the fundamental skills than they were
in schools of the past. Despite the
commendable work of good schools,
it has become clear that there is a
great neglect of exceptional pupils. In
fact, surveys suggest that our superior pupils are the most neglected
of all groups in special education. It
is true that some schoolmen have attempted in recent years to care more
adequately for the superior high
school pupil. In far too many schools,
however, superior pupils are con-

sidered adequately served if they have
a wide choice of electives and the opportunity to participate in extracurricular activities. Of course, these
provisions are inadequate to meet
the needs and foster the full development of gifted pupils. Many conscientious teachers do provide individually appropriate experiences
for the superior student within the
regular classroom. However, with
teacher-pupil load constantly mounting in size as it is today, even the
most conscientious teacher may neglect the gifted. Nevertheless, it is re-
assuring to note that a large number
and variety of efforts are now being
made to offer guidance and stimula-

[1] H. J. Fuller, "The Emperor's New Clothes," *Scientific Monthly*, LXXII (January,
1951), pp. 32–41. See also: A. E. Bestor, Jr., "Aimlessness in Education," *Scientific
Monthly*, LXXV (August, 1952), pp. 109–116; J. E. Hawkins, "The Education of
Future Scientists," *Vital Speeches*, XVIII (April 15, 1952), pp. 395–400.

tion for the superior secondary-school student. Unfortunately these efforts are widely scattered. Too, they constitute only a beginning in meeting a great need. It is hoped that the future will bring a greater appreciation of our responsibility and a widespread inclination to develop more suitable curriculums for the gifted high school student.

NOTE: Mathematics teachers are referred to bibliographical reference No. 30, page 286, for suggestions concerning classroom procedures to be used with gifted pupils.

MENTALLY RETARDED AND SLOW LEARNERS

With the advent of the movement in education to provide for individual differences in school children, attention was first focused on the slow learners. Their attributes, their needs, and appropriate learning activities for them have been for a long time the subjects of study and discussion. Now that gifted children are becoming the major concern of educators, the former "wave" of literature about slow learners has perceptibly receded. Another trend might also be noted. Whenever slow learners are now discussed, the discussion is usually in terms of two categories: the mentally retarded, with IQs ranging from 50 to 70, comprising about 2 per cent of the school population; and the slow learners, with IQs of 70 to 90, making up about 18 per cent of the school population. [7:16] Chief concern at the present time seems to be for the mentally retarded group.

Reininger [40:310–314] makes a number of suggestions for a program that is suitable for mentally retarded children: objectives, identical with those of normal children, which stress an adjustment to physical, social, and personal environment; use of the same building and facilities along with normal children; a curriculum that emphasizes "development of attitudes rather than acquisition of information"; functional reading, speech, arithmetic, and science; social experiences in geography, history (stressing biography), and a study of obvious problems to develop effective citizens; art and music for enrichment and emotional development; suitable activities and environment to promote physical and mental health; and methods which stress concrete learning and experience units.

A comprehensive and well-documented survey of the literature on curriculum practices for the mentally retarded has been made by

Wolk.* Although there has been considerable research on the mentally handicapped during the past ten years, little actual research has been done in relating the curriculum to the needs of mentally retarded children. Wolk reviews the research on the characteristics of the mentally handicapped. She shows that their needs are not primarily academic. They are, rather, directly related to the social situations which will be met after leaving school.

OTHER EXCEPTIONAL CHILDREN

To make generalizations about educational provisions for all of the various groups of exceptional children is, as yet, difficult. That the movement to educate exceptional children has only recently begun to gain momentum has already been intimated. Hill, basing his conclusions on data from the U. S. Office of Education, points out that "during the past five years special education has made its greatest strides in the junior and senior high schools of the United States." [20:149] However, Hill, as well as Dunn [12:8], indicates that "the vast majority of such services are still found in the elementary school." [20:150] "In only one category, the mentally gifted, do high schools appear to be making more provisions than elementary schools," according to Dunn. [12:8] (NOTE: The entire January, 1955, issue of the *Bulletin of the National Association of Secondary-School Principals* is devoted to the subject, "The Education of Handicapped and Gifted Pupils in the Secondary School.")

In the Biennial Survey of Education in the United States for 1952–1954, the same conclusion as in the 1947–1948 report is drawn that "there is no doubt . . . that many exceptional children are still going without the special instruction they should have. Despite the growth that has taken place, special education needs to be developed much further before all who require it will be served." [44: "Foreword," iv] Significant findings of the report include the following:

1. During the 1952–1953 school year, the number of children enrolled in the nine types of special education programs covered by the present survey was 497,216. Special schools and classes for exceptional children (within the nine types covered by this survey) appear to be reaching about 18 per cent, or roughly one in five, of the pupils in need of such services. The percent-

* Shirley Mae Wolk, "A Survey of the Literature on Curriculum Practices for the Mentally Retarded," *American Journal of Mental Deficiency*, 62:826–839 (March, 1958).

age is lower for children in rural areas, and higher for those in urban areas, but even in urban areas is below 40 per cent.

2. Programs for children with speech handicaps enrolled 306,747, or nearly 62 per cent of all exceptional children enrolled. . . . [44:17–18]

While the schools still have a long way to go before they make adequate provisions for all groups of exceptional children, certain "basic principles of special education" are beginning to emerge. These have been well summarized by Dunn.

Basic Principles of Special Education   by LLOYD M. DUNN

From "The Exceptional Pupil—A Challenge to Secondary Education," *Bulletin of the National Association of Secondary-School Principals,* Vol. 39 (January, 1955), pages 10–11. Lloyd M. Dunn is Associate Professor of Education and Co-ordinator of Special Education, George Peabody College for Teachers, Nashville, Tennessee. Reprinted by special permission.

1. A basic principle of special education is that exceptional pupils have the same fundamental physical and psychological needs as the usual pupils. This positive philosophical point of view emphasizes that these persons also have the same general developmental patterns which are common to all children. They also have many of the same feelings and desires. Thus, a crippled student differs primarily from his non-handicapped classmates in that he has orthopedic disability. The implication of this concept is the need for a mental health approach to working with handicapped pupils.

2. In view of the common needs, problems, and similarities of all adolescents, in so far as possible the educational program and activities for exceptional pupils should be a part of, and apart from, the high school program for the usual pupils. Some pupils may require special classes for academic instruction for part or all of the school day; others may be enrolled in regular classes. In either case, whenever the student is able to compete on relatively even terms with others in the school, the opportunity should be provided. Thus, the mentally retarded pupils should have the opportunity to share with the rest of the student body in recreational activities, physical education, and the use of the lunchroom. For academic instruction, they will need special class instruction from an especially trained teacher.

In the past few years, many misunderstandings have resulted from various interpretations of special education. There are those who believe that special classes, schools, and services segregate the pupil and do irreparable harm to his personality. Of late, this extreme point of view has become more and more untenable.

Research, experience, and recent educational thought concur on the thesis that a pupil can be more cruelly segregated in a program where he is not accepted by his classmates than in one where he is only physically separated from some of the school group. Many handicapped youth will need additional services, not to provide a superior education, but rather to provide equal opportunity to his rightful democratic heritage—an education at public expense. Integration for integration's sake is therefore not advocated.

3. Another basic concept of special education stresses the team approach. A complete diagnostic, treatment, and education program for many handicapped pupils requires the services of personnel from a number of disciplines. Close cooperation among educational, medical, social, and psychological specialists is essential to the total growth and development of pupils with exceptional conditions.

4. A fourth basic concept of special education is school success. To attain this goal, especially in the case of the atypical student, diagnostic and guidance services are needed. There is need for a careful appraisal of the achievement and capacity of the pupil along with a report of his physical condition. With this information, the school is better able to plan a program suited to the student. To provide success experiences the school must take the student where he is, and advance him at a speed which will insure optimal growth in keeping with his potentialities and interests. For some junior high school students this may mean a program of reading instruction at the grade three level or below. For others, it will mean special emphasis on a study of atomic energy. For still others, especially those with hearing losses, it may require special emphasis on speech and language development. If "exceptional" students are to find success in high school, educators must adopt a clinical and individualized approach to the study and instruction of each student.

In the June, 1957, *Review of Educational Research* [2:283] the following trends in the readiness of the school to adjust the curriculum to individual differences are indicated: to assume responsibility for exceptional children; to reconsider administrative possibilities that had been dismissed because of "earlier writings"; to try various techniques and provisions instead of just one program for everyone; to attempt various ways of integrating exceptional children into regular programs; and to provide for better sequential articulation by involving more staff members in the development of the program for exceptional children.

SUMMARY

The purposes and functions of public education have often been well stated, but just what the American people expect of their schools has not yet been made clear. Because the schools have assumed more and more responsibilities, many of which were once discharged by other educational agencies, the time is overdue for some important decisions to be made. First of all, the people must decide what functions have priority in public education. Secondly, educators themselves must decide what schools can do best.

The schools have not stood still, either in philosophy or practice, during the past fifty years. From institutions stressing training of the mind, the mastery of subject matter as an end in itself, and preparation for the next higher school, today's schools have developed functional curricula designed to improve the behavior of boys and girls and to deal with practical personal and social problems of contemporary society.

The elementary schools are developing flexible, informal, and cheerful environments for learning and providing a balanced program of experiences in social living, basic skills, and expressive arts.

At the high school level there has been a growing concern for meeting the needs of *all* youth. Beginning as selective, college-preparatory schools, enrolling but a small percentage of youth of secondary-school age, modern high schools have become comprehensive schools, enrolling 75 to 80 per cent of eligible youth and providing programs as varied as the needs and interests of boys and girls they serve. Elective subjects and extra-class activities meet special needs; general education subjects provide for common needs. In spite of renewed interest in the core curriculum, much remains to be done to develop a more effective program of common learnings.

Curriculum organization or design is still largely in terms of separate subjects. Some subjects have undergone considerable change in content and organization during the past half century. English has been expanded to include all the language arts—reading, writing, listening, and speaking—with increased stress being placed on language for use. Foreign languages have lost ground in the high school but have been gaining enrollments at the elementary-school level. There has been a tendency to combine related subject matter areas into broad fields, such as "social studies" or "general science," for example. Mathematics and science are enjoying added prestige and increasing enrollments because of the international situation. While mathematics problems are becoming more functional, textbooks and content are still very much out-of-date. The high hopes for a science curriculum that would promote human betterment appear to be overshadowed by the desire to serve military survival purposes. The arts, both fine and practical, are gaining acceptance along with the more venerable academic subjects, largely because of their importance in business and industry. Increasing emphasis upon health, physical education, and recreation and their many subfields is noticeable.

Because of added emphasis on citizenship in a time of national insecurity, social studies requirements are increasing. The trend toward integration of related areas in the social studies is sometimes offset by agitation to return to specific subjects, such as geography or American history. Among miscellaneous trends is the renewed interest in the teaching of moral and spiritual values.

Resources for teaching and learning have undergone marked changes during the last generation. From the recitation method with its emphasis on memorization of the textbook, the schools have moved toward varied individual and group activities related to the interests and needs of pupils and the problems of society. The textbook is still largely the child's "other teacher," but it has been supplemented and enriched by many other resources. Research, especially in reading, has supplied much useful information in curriculum planning, but findings are not yet utilized by teachers as much as they should be.

Meeting the common needs of all pupils through programs of "general education" or "common learnings" occupies a major portion of the time and energy of educators. Such concepts as "general education" and "fundamentals," however, result in considerable confusion and disagreement among both educators and other citizens. Despite voices to the contrary, the "fundamentals," narrowly conceived as the three R's, are being well taught in present-day schools. This is especially true of reading, which has often been the main target for critics.

The core type of organization is gaining adherents, especially at the junior high school level, although there are still many misconceptions about the core and the percentage of schools which have introduced a true core type of program is still low.

Currently there is renewed interest in provisions for individual differences, with the gifted pupils receiving most recognition. While there is much discussion of acceleration, segregation in special classes, and enrichment programs, very few schools have actually done much about identifying and meeting the needs of gifted boys and girls. Unfortunately, the insecurities and international pressures of the times tend to awaken reactionary forces and demands for conformity precisely when the contributions of individual initiative and leadership are most needed.

Bibliography

1. AHRENDT, M. H. "Mathematics and Science." *NEA Journal,* 46:109–110, February, 1957.
2. AMERICAN EDUCATIONAL RESEARCH ASSOCIATION. "Curriculum Planning and Development." *Review of Educational Research,* 27:237–304, June, 1957.
3. ———. "Instructional Materials." *Review of Educational Research,* 26:111–197, April, 1956.
4. ———. "The Educational Program: Adolescence." *Review of Educational Research,* 24:1–104, February, 1954.
5. BARLOW, MELVIN. "Modern Secondary Education from the Standpoint of a Vocational Educator." *California Journal of Secondary Education,* 29:39–43, January, 1954.
6. BIRCH, JACK W., and EARL M. McWILLIAMS. *Challenging Gifted Children.* Bloomington, Ill.: Public School Publishing Company, 1955.
7. BLAHA, M. JAY. "How Shall We Select and Develop Appropriate Learning Experiences for the Slow Learner in the Senior High School?" *Bulletin of the National Association of Secondary-School Principals,* 38:16–18, April, 1954.
8. BUSH, ROBERT N. Editorial: "The Practical Arts in Secondary Education." *California Journal of Secondary Education,* 29:122, March, 1954.
9. CRAWFORD, W. H. "A Broad-Fields Social Studies Program." *Junior College Journal,* 25:261–273, January, 1955.
10. CUMMINGS, HOWARD H., *et al. A Look Ahead in Secondary Education.* Report of the Second Commission on Life Adjustment Education for Youth. U. S. Department of Health, Education, and Welfare, Office of Education, Bulletin 1954, No. 4. Washington, D. C.: Superintendent of Documents, Government Printing Office, 1954. 105 pages.
11. CUTTS, N. E., and NICHOLAS MOSELEY. "Bright Children and the Curriculum." *Educational Administration and Supervision,* 39:168–173, March, 1953.
12. DUNN, LLOYD M. "The Exceptional Pupil—a Challenge to Secondary Education." *Bulletin of the National Association of Secondary-School Principals,* 39:3–11, January, 1955.

13. Fawcett, Harold P. "Mathematics and the Core Curriculum." *Bulletin of the National Association of Secondary-School Principals,* 38:71–80, May, 1954.

14. Flannigan, Norman A. *A Study of High School Science Courses in Grades 9–12 Designed for General Education.* Doctor's thesis. Ithaca, N. Y.: Cornell University, 1954. 210 pages. Abstract: *Dissertation Abstracts,* 15:62–63; No. 1, 1955.

15. "Foreign Language in the Elementary School?" *NEA Journal,* 44:270–271, May, 1955. (See also the October, 1956, *NEA Journal,* 444–445.)

16. French, Will. "The Role of the American High School." *Bulletin of the National Association of Secondary-School Principals,* 39:1–62, February, 1955.

17. Goslin, Willard E. "What Shall We Teach?" *Junior College Journal,* 24: 511–519, May, 1954.

18. Haefner, John H. "The Battle of the Books." *NEA Journal,* 42:227–228, April, 1953.

19. Harvill, Harris. "Nature of the Core Curriculum." *Social Education,* 18: 215–217, May, 1954.

20. Hill, Arthur S. "The Growth of Special Education in Secondary Schools." *Bulletin of the National Association of Secondary-School Principals,* 39:149–154, January, 1955.

21. Jones, Evelyn. "Analysis of Social Studies Requirements." *Social Education,* 18:257–258, October, 1954.

22. Judd, C. H. "What Is General Education?" *Bulletin of the Department of Secondary-School Principals,* 21:5–16, October, 1937.

23. Krug, Edward A. *Curriculum Planning* (Revised Edition). New York: Harper & Brothers, 1957. 336 pages.

24. Layton, W. I. "The Mathematics Required for Graduation from High School." *The Mathematics Teacher,* 47:315–319, May, 1954.

25. La Salle, Dorothy. "Looking Ahead." *Children in Focus—Their Health and Activity,* Chapter XXI. 1954 Yearbook. American Asssociation of Health, Physical Education, and Recreation. Washington, D. C.: The National Education Association, 1954.

26. "Let's Attack the Problems . . . Not the Schools." *Ladies' Home Journal.* October, 1954, pages 54–57, 184–187.

27. Lieberman, Irving. "The Backbone of Curriculum Development and Implementation: Instructional Materials." *Proceedings* of the Northwest Association of Secondary and Higher Schools, 40th Year. (December 2–5, 1956.) Portland, Oregon. 76 pages.

28. Madden, Richard. "Workbooks! Tool or Crutch?" *NEA Journal,* 45:94–95, February, 1956.

29. McLendon, John C. "Significant Trends in the Social Studies Curriculum." *Social Education,* 21:213–216, May, 1957.

30. McWilliams, Earl M., and Kenneth E. Brown. *The Superior Pupil in Junior High School Mathematics.* U. S. Department of Health, Education, and Welfare, Office of Education, Bulletin 1955, No. 4. Washington, D. C.: Superintendent of Documents, U. S. Government Printing Office, 1955. 57 pages.

31. MELLOTT, MALCOLM E. What to Look For in Choosing a Textbook." *NEA Journal,* 44:158–159, March, 1955.

32. METROPOLITAN SCHOOL STUDY COUNCIL. *How to Educate the Gifted Child.* New York: Metropolitan School Study Council, 1956. 58 pages.

33. MIEL, ALICE. "Does Foreign Language Belong in the Elementary School?" *Teachers College Record,* 56:139–148, December, 1954.

34. MORSE, H. T. "Liberal and General Education—Partisans or Partners." *Junior College Journal,* 24: 395–399, March, 1954.

35. NATIONAL CITIZENS COUNCIL FOR BETTER SCHOOLS. *What Should Our Schools Accomplish? A Guide to Goals and Curriculum in the Public Schools.* New York: National Citizens Council for Better Schools, October, 1955. 84 pages.

36. NATIONAL EDUCATION ASSOCIATION. "The Status of Driver Education in Public High Schools, 1952–53." *NEA Research Bulletin,* Vol. 32, No. 2, April, 1954.

37. ———. Department of Classroom Teachers. *What Research Says to the Teacher.*

   No. 1. Teaching Reading, June, 1953.
   No. 2. Teaching Arithmetic, October, 1953.
   No. 3. Teaching Spelling, January, 1954.
   No. 4. Teaching Handwriting, August, 1954.
   No. 5. Personality Adjustment of Individual Children, October, 1954.
   No. 6. Learning Process, December, 1954.
   No. 7. Evaluating and Reporting Pupil Progress, March, 1955.
   No. 8. Guided Study and Homework, July, 1955.
   No. 9. Teaching High School Mathematics, October, 1955.
   No. 10. Teaching High School Science, April, 1956.
   No. 11. Reading in the High School, September, 1956.
   No. 12. Science in the Elementary School, April, 1957.
   No. 13. Class Organization for Instruction, April, 1957.

38. OLIVA, PETER F. "Which General Education?" *Educational Forum,* 18:235–238, January, 1954.

39. POOLEY, ROBERT C. "What about Grammar?" *Journal of Education,* 136:195–197, April, 1954.

40. REININGER, RUTH E. "A Curriculum for the Educable Mentally Retarded Preadolescent." *The Elementary School Journal,* 56:310–314, March, 1956.

41. ROGERS, VIRGIL M. "Textbooks under Fire." *The Atlantic,* February, 1955, pages 42–48.

42. ROSSKOPF, MYRON F. "Trends in Content of High School Mathematics in the United States." *Teachers College Record,* 56:135–138, December, 1954.

43. SAN DIEGO CITY SCHOOLS. *A Guide to Moral and Spiritual Education in Elementary Schools.* Revised 1956. 72 pages. (Also a corresponding guide: *A Guide to Moral and Spiritual Education in Secondary Schools,* 1956, 55 pages.)

44. *Statistics of Special Education for Exceptional Children 1952–53.* Biennial Survey of Education in the United States, 1952–54. Chapter 5. U. S. Department of Health, Education, and Welfare. Washington, D. C.: U. S. Office of Education, 1954. 78 pages.

45. "Teachers of Exceptional Children." *School Life* (Official Journal of the Office of Education), 39:6–7, 10–11, January, 1957.

46. THOMPSON, DOROTHY. "Why and What Should Johnny Read?" *Ladies' Home Journal,* October, 1956, pages 11, 14, 16, 18.

47. WHYTE, WILLIAM H., JR. "The New Illiteracy." *The Saturday Review,* 36: 33–35, November 21, 1953.

48. WRIGHT, GRACE S. *Core Curriculum—Problems and Practices.* Department of Health, Education, and Welfare, Office of Education, Bulletin 1952, No. 5. Washington, D. C.: Superintendent of Documents, U. S. Government Printing Office, 1955. 104 pages.

49. ———. *The Core Program—Abstracts of Unpublished Research; 1946– 1955.* Circular No. 485. Washington, D. C.: U. S. Department of Health, Education, and Welfare, Office of Education, June, 1956. 70 pages.

Sources of Curriculum Materials

A Bibliography of Bibliographies of Instructional Aids to Learning, by Robert D. Marshall. (Curriculum Bulletin No. 157.) School of Education, University of Oregon, Eugene, Oregon. 1955. 42 pages.

A comprehensive and carefully selected list of catalogues of free and inexpensive materials. Contents: General bibliographies of teaching material, audio-visual materials, pamphlets and inexpensive books, commercial catalogues; special subject bibliographies; audio-visual magazines, pictorial magazines, and special sections appearing regularly in general magazines.

Bridges for Ideas: 1. "Tear Sheets for Teaching" 2. "Bulletin Boards for Teaching" 3. "Felt Boards for Teaching" 4. "Lettering Techniques" 5. "Using the Consultant." The Visual Instruction Bureau, Division of Extension, The University of Texas.

CRS Audio-Visual Catalog. Children's Reading Service, 1078 St. John's Place, Brooklyn, N. Y. 1957. 63 pages.

An annotated list of phonograph records, filmstrips, tape recordings, and rhythm band instruments (Kindergarten-Senior high school).

Current Curriculum Materials from Representative School Publications. Association for Supervision and Curriculum Development, NEA, 1201 16th Street, N. W., Washington, D. C., 1957. 78 pages.

A list of curriculum bulletins, courses of study, and other related publications from the U. S. Department of Health, Education, and Welfare; state departments of education; and school systems in various parts of the United States, Hawaii, and Canada. An annual listing of publications placed on exhibit during the Annual Conference of the ASCD, NEA.

Educators Guide to Free Films, 6th edition, by Mary Foley Horkheimer and J. W. Diffor. Randolph, Wisconsin: Educators Progress Service, 1957. 625 pages.

An annotated list of free films from industrial, government, and philanthropic organizations. Completely revised annually.

Educators Guide to Free Slidefilms, 9th edition, by Mary Foley Horkheimer and J. W. Diffor. Randolph, Wisconsin: Educators Progress Service, 1957. 204 pages.

An annually revised professional, cyclopedic service. Of the 674 titles in the 9th edition, 131 are listed for the first time.

Educators Guide to Free Tapes, Scripts, and Transcriptions, 3rd edition, by Walter A. Wittich and G. H. Halsted. Randolph, Wisconsin: Educators Progress Service, 1957. 184 pages.

Annotated and revised annually. The 3rd edition lists 57 free tapes, 177 free scripts, and 96 free transcriptions.

Educators Index to Free Materials, 56th edition, by John Guy Fowlkes and P. T. Cody. Randolph, Wisconsin: Educators Progress Service, 1957. 174 cards.

The *Index* is an annually revised annotated list of free charts, films, maps, and exhibits of significant educational value. The sources include departments of the federal government, state agencies, chambers of commerce, travel bureaus, private foundations, and major industrial concerns.

Elementary Teachers Guide to Free Curriculum Materials, 14th edition, by Patricia Horkheimer Suttles. Randolph, Wisconsin: Educators Progress Service, 1957. 319 pages.

"This guide is a complete, up-to-date annotated schedule of selected free maps, bulletins, pamphlets, exhibits, charts, and books." Indexed by titles, subjects, and sources. Revised annually.

Free and Inexpensive Learning Materials, 8th edition. George Peabody College for Teachers, Nashville, Tenn. 1957. 264 pages.

All material listed in this catalog has been examined and evaluated. The 8th edition lists 4,255 items, most of which cost no more than fifty cents each. Criteria for selection: accuracy and recency of subject matter, freedom from exaggeration, good organization, timeliness of subject matter, lack of bias in subject matter, easy-to-read format.

Instructional Materials for Elementary Schools. The National Elementary Principal. 35th Yearbook. Vol. 36. September, 1956.

List of Outstanding Curriculum Materials, 1951–1954, by Marcella Lawler and others. Washington: Association for Supervision and Curriculum Development, NEA, 1955. 35 pages.

National Directory of Safety Films. National Safety Council, 425 North Michigan Avenue, Chicago, Illinois, 1956. 68 pages.

A comprehensive listing of 1,200 35mm and 16mm motion pictures, filmstrips and slides on safety and related fields of fire prevention, first aid, and civil defense.

Pamphlet Review Service. World Affairs Council of Northern California, 421 Powell St., San Francisco, California.

Vol. II, No. 1, September 1957: "Together Toward Peace." 18 pages.
Vol. II, No. 2, November 1957: "Asia and the West." 30 pages.

A listing and review of new and inexpensive junior and senior high school aids on current world problems. Five issues published bi-monthly during the school year. Each issue is devoted to one topic.

Selected Bibliography for Curriculum Workers. Association for Supervision and Curriculum Development, NEA, 1201 16th Street, N. W., Washington, D. C.: NEA, 1957. 77 pages.

Books, booklets and bulletins relating to education and allied fields such as art, audio-visual education, special education, and human relations.

Sources of Free and Inexpensive Educational Materials. Field Enterprises, Inc., Educational Division, Merchandise Mart Plaza, Chicago, Illinois. 1958.

An alphabetical list of names and addresses of organizations and agencies which supply free and low-cost educational materials. The following types of materials are listed by subject: pamphlets, pictures, post cards, maps, posters, charts, teaching units, courses of study, science experiments, exhibits, films, filmstrips, slides, handicraft kits, supplies, tools. Particular attention has been given to the needs of elementary and secondary school teachers and of librarians.

Fearon Publishers, 2450 Fillmore St., San Francisco 15, Calif.

Handbooks on various subjects: science activities, blackboard games, paper sculpture, holiday art, map and globe activities, exhibiting children's work, etc.

PART THREE

The Curriculum: Its Process and Direction

9

THE PROCESS OF CURRICULUM

DEVELOPMENT

INTRODUCTION

Basic to all curriculum planning is an understanding of two things: a knowledge of what the curriculum really is and a knowledge of the process by which the curriculum has become what it is. In Part Two an attempt has been made to describe the public-school curriculum now in operation and to clarify a number of concepts about it. In the preceding pages forces affecting the curriculum have been discussed and some of the modes of development have, no doubt, been suggested. However, a more thorough description and analysis of the process of curriculum development, together with future implications, are necessary for a complete understanding of the issues and problems with which the public schools must cope today.

Like any other social process, curriculum planning requires proper orientation of those who would engage in it. At the outset, curriculum workers must have a clear picture of the society in which the schools operate—a society marked by accelerated changes, an economy of plenty, urbanization, standardization, and mass communication. Nor can we forget that today we live in a world that "is in our back yard." These, and other facets of our society, are described in a series of articles in *The National Elementary Principal* under the caption, "Background for the Instructional Program." In the fifth and last of the articles, McNally briefly summarizes recurrent themes in preceding presentations, indicates other social trends having educational significance, and suggests how groups or individuals might use these challenging facts and insights in the development of the instructional program.

What Shall We Teach . . . and How?

by HAROLD J. MCNALLY

From *The National Elementary Principal* for May, 1957, pages 6–11. Reprinted by special permission. Harold J. McNally is Professor of Education, Teachers College, Columbia University.

Public schools are established and maintained to contribute to the welfare of the society they serve. The role of the schools in serving society can be defined without great difficulty —when the varieties of work done in that society are relatively few, when each individual's role is clearly defined and relatively unvarying, when the society remains reasonably stable in its institutions and values from one generation to the next, and when much of the teaching of the values and behavior appropriate to that society is painstakingly done in the home. This was the case in our country a century and a quarter ago. Children had limited vocational choices, lived in closely-knit family groups which gave them social, moral, and vocational instruction; and grew up to travel, dress, play, work, and even think in much the same patterns as those of their parents and grandparents. A straightforward program of reading, writing, arithmetic, and history which emphasized nationalism and moral values served to discharge the school's responsibility adequately.

The problem of what shall be taught in the public schools of today's United States is considerably more complex. Schools today are being asked to assume many of the responsibilities formerly borne by other institutions. William Carr's article in this year's series contains a delightful listing of the subjects which we are urged, exhorted, enticed, or required to add to an already-crowded curriculum. On the other hand, tradition encourages us to cling to a curriculum which seems oddly impervious to the impact of contemporary epochal discoveries, to world-shaking events, and to inexorable and profound changes in our society. How can we gain a perspective that will help us to modify our content and method to serve today's distinctly different world, and at the same time preserve basic values and avoid acceding to whims and riding current educational fads to unwise extremes?

In his important role of instructional leader, the principal needs such a perspective. The theme articles in this year's volume of *The National*

Elementary Principal have been an attempt to present some vistas in that perspective. A number of specialists who are students of the social scene have presented highlights of today's society which have significance for what we teach. While we recognize that these do not by any means constitute a comprehensive or thorough analysis, they do provide a background against which we may raise certain provocative questions, questions which should be raised as the principal and his staff consider whether what they are teaching is suited to the needs and demands of the world in which their pupils are living.

In this article, I have attempted to do several things. First, I have sought for common or recurring strands in the year's theme articles. Second, I have tried to identify in these articles other facts or insights which appear to have considerable educational significance. Third, I have raised some questions as to what these facts, insights, and recurrent themes mean for the educational program. And, finally, I have tried to suggest some ways in which a principal might use these materials in the exercise of his instructional leadership.

Change — The Order of the Day

In this year's theme articles, one motif stands out above all others: *change.* Time and again the authors refer to the fundamental changes that have taken place and are taking place in today's world. Kenneth

Cooper quotes an Indonesian as saying that his country is living in thirty different centuries at the same time. Thomas Carskadon reports that whereas muscle power accounted for two-thirds of all productive power in the United States a century ago, today — only three generations later — it accounts for only 1 per cent of the power doing America's work. Again, we are told that in the past half-century our leisure time in the United States has nearly doubled and seems likely to increase still further. And so it goes. Crowded into the lifetime of people still living have been more fundamental changes, perhaps, than have taken place in any thousand years of human history heretofore.

Not only is this change rapid; it is accelerating. Within a relatively few years, we have broken through the sound barrier, split the unsplittable atom, put an earth satellite into production, flown non-stop around the world, projected pictures of events as they happened onto screens thousands of miles away, seen Jules Verne's *Nautilus* become a reality, built jet aircraft that streak across the entire United States between lunch and dinner, and conquered almost all of the dreaded killer diseases of mankind. Every year it takes less time to accomplish the impossible. In a recent article in the *Saturday Review,* an eminent medical authority, Lawrence Kubie, made the incredible statement that within the foreseeable future we shall discover how to prolong a human being's life indefinitely![1] Consider these changes against the fact that they are happening in a society in which the population is increasing in unprecedented numbers. Ralph Tyler stated that it is now "possible to say that approximately half of all the adults who have ever lived in the world are still living." In other words, the world won't stay put. Already, many of the things you and I learned in school are either obsolete or downright untrue.

What does this mean for the school program of today? Much of our current school program educates children for today's world, assuming that it will be substantially the same when these youngsters are adults. This was once a valid assumption. But when the only thing one can be sure of is that the future will be vastly different, what kind of education does one provide for those who will inherit the future? What kinds of learnings have value and relevance in a rapidly changing world? How can we deal with history so that children will be able to set today's kaleidoscopic cultural shifts in the long perspective of human progress? What values can we try to develop with today's children that will serve as stable guides in a world of apparent impermanence and protean values? How much more important are questions like these than whether we should teach about Indians or Eskimos in the third grade!

The final fact worth noting about change is its all-pervasiveness. It touches all segments of our life and is worldwide. The facts of change are obvious, tangible, omnipresent, and irrefutable. How do we, or how should we take account of this in planning educational content and method? Margaret Mead suggests that we exploit "the unused capacities of childhood" and "accord the imagination of childhood . . . recognition and underwriting." She maintains that our educational program should provide for more diversification of experience.

Leisure—for Whom? for What?

A second strand that ran through many of the articles was the fact that the leisure time of the members of our labor force is increasing, and will continue to increase. This fact was noted by educators years ago, and for three decades we have talked glibly about "worthy use of leisure." Yet as a nation and as a profession we have not recognized the fateful implications of this development; or if we have, we have not faced up to them.

"Future historians," says Shirley Cooper, "will doubtless point to leisure time for the common man as one of the outstanding achievements of this age." With increasing life expectancy there are already many whose total "working years" are less than half their total life. Probably the majority of our working force

[1] Lawrence Kubie, "Hidden Brain Power," *Saturday Review,* Volume 39 (Oct. 13, 1956), p. 26.

now work only about half their waking hours. Millions seek ways to kill time outside their working hours; after retirement they kill time until time mercifully retaliates.

Yet not all share equally in this increased leisure time. It is primarily the less "educated" non-professional groups who have inherited this new leisure. In professional, executive, entertainment, and other service occupations, there are many who have all too little leisure; paradoxically, this group is probably better prepared to use leisure constructively.

What can we do in our schools to help make leisure the blessing we have envisioned, rather than the catastrophe it could become? How should our educational program today differ from what it was when the 60- to 70-hour week prevailed? I have heard it said that education for retirement should begin in the kindergarten. Whether in kindergarten, fifth grade, or tenth grade, what kind of education should it be? Do ascetic, intensified academic programs for gifted children contribute to this objective? Do we teach our pupils recreational activities which are rewarding and practicable throughout life? Do we help children catch the excitement of learning so that the days, and life itself, are not long enough for all the enchanting things they want to do? Or does their schooling result in aversion to learning, so that they become skilled in avoiding it, and seek the opiates of vacuous, effortless, unstimulating

entertainment? What kinds of recreation recreate? What do the answers to these questions mean for educational planning and practice in elementary schools? I fear we haven't grasped the seriousness of this question, for leisure is something we are accustomed to thinking of lightly. It is time for us to get serious about it.

Mass Communication—A Mixed Blessing

Wilbur Schramm and others of our authors dealt with the changes and problems of communication in this jet-propelled society. To cope with the flood of printed, typed, telephoned, telegraphed, broadcast, and televised information, today's school product has to be educated in far more of the communication arts than has been usual in the teaching of the first two of the three R's. Carr speaks aptly of "the pressure of the press, the radiance of the radio, and all the props of propaganda" which assail today's citizen at every turn. What are our schools doing to teach discriminating reading, listening, and viewing? There is much evidence that great masses of our populace are the easy dupes of the unscrupulous advertiser, the shrewd and unprincipled demagogue, and the eloquent hate-monger. Has your staff discussed curriculum content and method that will help children to analyze and identify propaganda of the domestic as well as the Russian variety? Are the children in your school learning how to evaluate television programs? Have they learned to spot slanted news in the daily press? Do they learn to differentiate the demagogue's specious reasoning and unsupported generalizations from documented fact? Are they being helped to know half-truths and unsupported allegations in advertising? These are questions a staff should not neglect, for these learnings should start in the elementary school.

An Economy of Plenty

A fourth development mentioned by a number of our authors is the astonishing productivity of the United States. Our overworked superlatives just don't do justice to the fact, quoted by Carskadon, that:

The United States, with little more than 6 per cent of the world's population and less than 7 per cent of its land area, now produces and consumes well over one-third of the world's goods and services, and turns out nearly one-half of the world's factory-produced goods.

What account have we taken of this in our schools? Are the children in your school going to be better consumers of this fantastic flood of fabulous fabrications because they were your pupils? Are they learning the difference between "cheap goods" and real bargains? Are they developing standards of taste? Are they learning to resist high-pressure salesmanship which, as one wag put it, "Gets people to spend money they don't have to buy things they don't want to serve needs they don't have"? Are they discussing how this mar-

velous productive capacity could be used to help mankind, or are they being taught that this is a weapon with which to win the next war? Or is it treated as a "hat trick," a magnificent curiosity?

The World IS In Our Back Yard

Another aspect of this productivity is the almost unbelievable disparity between the United States and other nations. This fact is part of the international understanding so urgently required of Americans, and needs to be seen in relation to other aspects of our place in the international picture. Do our children learn of the delicate economic, political, and military interrelationships in the world today? Do we know enough about these things ourselves? If we were to examine our teaching in social studies and current events in the light of Vera Dean's article, how would that teaching look? What are we teaching of the proud and important history of the countries of Africa and the East? Are our children being helped to realize that they may live to see the locus of the world's great power once again among those people who are now referred to as "underdeveloped"? Are we able to help children see America's policies and actions from India's or Egypt's vantage point, as well as from our own? Do we help them (as in Edward Steichen's impressive and moving photo epic, *The Family of Man*) to appreciate the bonds that unite all peoples, or do we teach them the divisive peculiarities, the "queerness" of "for-eigners"?

What should we be teaching about sovereignty? About colonialism? About race and prejudice? About the United Nations? Ignorance or narrow dogmatism with respect to the issues involved here could mean the death knell of America's world leadership within a generation. Great forces are astir among the long-dormant peoples of the East and of Africa. Earl Mazo, commenting on Vice President Nixon's recent visit to Africa, said: "He (Nixon) is convinced now that within twenty-five years the "Dark Continent" will be the decisive area, that it will hold the crucial balance of power in the world."[2] Our children should be learning of these people with understanding and respect.

Some Other Items

All the above "strands" seemed to run through this series of fascinating articles. In addition, some other developments which were referred to in only one or two of the articles are of considerable importance.

Urbanization. The development of the "urban region," and the fact that the United States has become a predominantly urban nation has far-reaching implications for education. Philip Hauser reminds us that: "Any reexamination of the instructional program . . . might well inquire into the adequacy of that program . . . in preparing students for the changes in social organization and in thought and action characteristic of urban existence." What can schools do to help children and adults live satisfyingly in "the lonely crowd" of these great impersonal centers? How can we educate for the role diffusion characteristic of the specialization of today's urban life? Tyler suggests that the way we handle education for group membership may help answer these questions. How can we help individuals develop a sense of responsibility for their own fates and a feeling that they can influence social and government processes? John Dawson tells us that democratic government is supported by people seeking opportunity to act as responsible persons. What should we be doing in our schools to help children learn desirable avenues for exercising their citizenship responsibilities in a responsible manner? How can we help children grow into men and women who will rise above petty partisanship and narrow vested interests, and realize that to act in the interest of the larger society of which they are a part is to act in their own best interest in the long run? The practical answers have to be found in our schools and classrooms.

Changes in family life. Growing out of and influencing these and many other changes has been a basic change in family functioning and relationships. Divorce is prevalent. For

[2] *New York Herald Tribune,* March 2, 1957, p. 10.

various reasons, parental supervision of children has decreased, resulting in what Fred Hechinger calls "the creation of a new category of young- sters, the 'door key kids.'" Parents are uncertain about their authority roles with respect to their children. Many of us can remember when din- nertime was determined by Dad's homecoming hour, not by the chil- dren's television program. Fewer real tasks and recreations are engaged in together by family members today. As families grow up, the children tend to disperse, and often live hun- dreds of miles from their parents and from one another.

Of what, then, does "worthy home membership" now consist, and how can the school educate for it? What should be the division of responsibil- ities between home and school? For how much of the education of "the whole child" can the school be ex- pected to assume responsibility? What techniques of home-school co- operation will foster children's best growth?

The trend toward standardization of taste, style, thought, and behavior. Mass communication, mass produc- tion, and population mobility—all re- ferred to in this year's theme articles —have resulted increasingly in our wearing the same styles of clothes, listening to the same TV comedians, singing the same songs, reading the same best-sellers, living in identically designed homes, eating the same

frozen foods—and there are those who have aspired to get us all to hold the same beliefs. Kenneth Cooper pointed out the need for encourag- ing diversity in the face of all these pressures toward conformity. "The cultivation of idiosyncrasy," as Ben- jamin [3] called it, should be one of the major goals of our schools, for we sorely need such unique kinds of persons as Francis Bacon, John Stuart Mill, Thomas Jefferson, Henry Ford, Arturo Toscanini, Albert Einstein, Emmett Kelly, Marian Anderson, and Jonas Salk. How can we focus individualization in our schools on such an objective? All too often "in- dividualization" has meant special attention to some pupils so that all may be elevated to the norm, which is by definition mediocrity.

Cooperation and competition. It is a rather common assumption that we live in a highly competitive so- ciety. Schools which stress coopera- tive activity and minimize competi- tive activity are sometimes criticized on the grounds that they are "not facing reality," not preparing chil- dren for a competitive society. Rob- ert Isenberg points out, however, that a careful analysis of our business and industrial structure and of our activities as social beings indicates that, actually, cooperation is a more potent factor than competition. Our success in most of the things we do depends upon our ability to cooperate. What does this mean for anyone—

[3] Harold Benjamin, *The Cultivation of Idiosyncrasy* (Inglis Lecture) (Cambridge, Mass.: Harvard University Press, 1949).

parents or teachers—working with children? Are we actually more "realistic" when we work to develop techniques of cooperation than when we stress competition? Do we need to reexamine the use of competition as motivation for learning? Do we need to learn how to help children develop a kind of "beat your own record" competition?

The need for social invention. Perhaps the root implication of our theme articles, hinted at here, implied there, and stated clearly in a few instances, is our desperate need for social invention. Dael Wolfle asks urgently what society will do with all our material inventions and advances, and asserts that these are "questions (which) affect all mankind, and the answers that are arrived at should result from the thinking of other men, and not of scientists alone." Harold Rugg says, in effect, "create or perish." But our creation must be social as well as technical inventions. And our social inventions will inevitably involve moral value decisions. They will deal with the control and government of our technological advances and, as Dawson maintains, government in a democracy is the result of decisions of the people. In our curriculum planning, how shall we provide for the cultivation of Rugg's creativity (which Mead maintains we have hardly tapped in today's schools), of the values Wolfle pleads for, of the responsible citizenship which Dawson says is necessary to maintain ac-

countable democratic government? These questions will not be answered by philosophers or "authorities" in high places. They can be answered only by thousands of principals and teachers in public schools throughout the land.

So What?

Granted, you may say. Of course these are important questions. But what am I to do about it all? Each reader will have to answer such a question for himself, of course, but several possibilities come to mind.

Since 1950 the number of local principals' associations has increased substantially. Could not these articles serve as texts for group discussions at some of the meetings of these locals? One can envision round-table discussions, each table discussing the implications of an article's content. Consultants from outside the field of education as well as from within it could be enlisted to help in such discussions. Annual meetings of principals' state or county organizations might use a somewhat similar pattern. Plan such work conferences so that all who attend will have opportunities to participate actively and do some rigorous thinking.

These materials could also be used with local curriculum committees, particularly (but by no means exclusively) by committees which are concerned with the social studies and the language arts.

Perhaps the most obvious use of these excellent papers is in staff meetings in local schools. If your staff committee for the planning of such meetings thinks well of the idea, copies of the year's theme articles (which are to be gathered together in a special publication) could be obtained (single articles could be mimeographed) and placed in the hands of each teacher. They could then be made the subject matter of discussion at some staff meetings, where principal and staff would appraise the curriculum and methods in the light of the ideas developed in one or more of the articles and related readings. In this respect, it would probably be better to focus on one area, such as *communication* or *leisure,* use the theme article as a point of departure, and have various interested staff members assume responsibility for doing related readings chosen from those suggested in the article or from other sources related to the topic. In larger school systems, central office resource personnel can be called upon to help out.

One question which is often raised by elementary-school principals is, "What can we do to infuse some vim, vigor, and vitality into our Parent-Teacher Association?" Why not involve them in discussions of these issues? Instead of a painful harangue or limping stage pageant, garnished with coffee or punch and cookies, let parents jump in with both feet and discuss some of these same problems and issues. If such discussions are well planned (as any PTA meeting should be and as many are not), not only are the participants likely to be interested; some good ideas may be harvested for use in the school program.

For those parents who are interested in delving more deeply into these topics, parent or parent-teacher study groups might be formed, which would hold meetings extending over a semester or a year. Such groups should have a goal, such as being asked to submit to the faculty any recommendations growing out of their deliberations. In such case, it should be clear that they are responsible for *suggestions,* not *decisions.* These activities with parents are valuable public relations, helping parents gain insight into the problems faced by teachers and principals, and letting them see at first hand our efforts to provide an improving and appropriate education for their children.

It may not seem strange for me to suggest that these materials might be used as subjects of discussions with college students in education, particularly those who are preparing themselves for leadership positions (such as principalships and supervisory posts) in which they will have responsibility for leadership in curriculum improvement. Where they are not used as primary texts, they will certainly constitute valuable supplementary reading in discussions of curriculum content and organization.

Finally, these articles, and others like them, should be read and meditated upon by each of us individually. The game we are playing is "for

keeps." It may be impressively un-
original to say it, but the education
we give to the current generations is
likely to affect profoundly the course
of human history.

The ideas and developments dealt
with in this series of articles deserve
our thoughtful consideration. In an
earlier issue our Editor said: "For if
these things are true, then they have
real significance for education. They
are not just interesting bits of information; they are guides to sound
educational planning and practice.
But they become truly valuable only
as they make their way into the thinking of many people. Between the
covers of a magazine they are simply
accessible; within the minds of men
they come alive."

That's a challenge if I ever saw
one!

Reviews of curriculum trends have made it clear that the program of
the public schools is not static. Neither is the process of development.

Twenty-five years ago, curriculum revision in large city school systems was a major-production affair. The entire professional staff was organized into committees, consultants were called in, innumerable group
conferences and staff meetings were held, and eventually production
committees were set up. After a year or so of intensive meeting, planning, and writing, the presses worked overtime producing courses of
study to serve as blueprints for instruction during the next ten years.
Curriculum revision was over, and everyone could go back to the usual
business of keeping school.

Today, curriculum planning takes place by evolution, not revolution.
It is a continuous process, not an all-out, once-every-ten-years affair.
Recognition of the transitory nature of the results of curriculum planning is probably indicated by the decline in *printed* curriculum guides,
revealed in the study by Merritt and Harap (item 6, page 326). No
longer do the products of curriculum development appear as a permanent document prepared by the experts. Now, pupils, parents, and the
public take part in the continuous development of the school program.
Although today there are permanent curriculum committees, making a
continuous study of the school program, which are drawn from the total
school system, the primary unit for curriculum revision is the building
principal and his staff.

A concise, over-all review of trends in "organization and procedures
for curriculum improvement" is presented by Passow in the June,
1954, *Review of Educational Research:* "(*a*) Widest possible participation in planning, testing, and evaluating by all persons—professional

and lay—who are affected by policy and action decisions; (*b*) assignment of the individual school to a more central role in curriculum activity; (*c*) use of groups for initiating, planning, executing, and coordinating improvement efforts; (*d*) fusion of supervision, in-service education, and curriculum activities to concentrate personnel and process for the improvement of instruction; (*e*) experimentation with procedures and devices for more effective involvement; (*f*) extension of kinds and uses of consultative services from many sources—central office, state department, universities, and colleges, for example; (*g*) use of cooperative research in field situations for improving practices; (*h*) teamwork from many levels in cooperative enterprises; and (*i*) development of more effective and widespread leadership." *

PARTICIPATION

In the resumé above of trends in the process of curriculum planning, more widespread participation (not by professional people alone) is indicated. However, there are still differences of opinion (and practice) as to *who* should participate in curriculum planning and as to what the role of each participant should be. A good introduction to the problems involved in more widespread participation in curriculum improvement is provided in the following editorial by Van Til.

Editorial: Curriculum Improvement — Who Participates?

by WILLIAM VAN TIL

From *Educational Leadership*, Vol. XI, No. 6 (March, 1954), pages 335–337. Reprinted by special permission of the Association for Supervision and Curriculum Development and the author. William Van Til is Professor of Education and Chairman, Department of Secondary Education, New York University.

Who should participate in improving the curriculum? To the modern democratic educator, the answer does not seem to be difficult. All who are affected should participate. Parents and other members of the lay public, teachers and administrators, children and youth. So it seems that our ques-

* From the American Educational Research Association, "The Curriculum: Organization and Development," *Review of Educational Research*, 24:221 (June, 1954). Quoted by special permission of the Association and of the author. A. Harry Passow is Associate Professor of Education, Teachers College, Columbia University.

tion is answered. You need read this issue no further.

But if the answer is as easy as this, why isn't the curriculum everywhere throughout the nation improved through the participation of all affected? What should be done everywhere seems clear enough. Follow the principles of good group process. Have everybody in for study and agreement. Carry out the mandate of all. Selah!—the result is curriculum change supported by everyone.

This happens mostly in Fairyland. Why?

The Road to Agreement Is Rocky

Successful group work is a difficult business. Many group members have difficulty in accepting and even more difficulty in living by the basic principles of group process. Stuart Chase summarized these principles well in *Roads to Agreement*. Successful agreement involves genuine participation with everyone getting into the act. It involves the release of group energy into constructive channels. It involves clear communication among all and a mutual understanding of semantics and logical traps. It involves willingness to consider the facts first, as in the scientific method, despite thirst for theoretical controversy. It involves the participants' feeling secure while afloat on the risky seas of group consideration.

The people who must come to accept and live by such principles, if agreement is to be achieved, come from highly varied economic, social,

religious, and political backgrounds in an age of anxiety and in a culture in conflict. They perceive each other quite differently. Their personality patterns are deeply set.

Impossible, then, to achieve roads to agreement? Not at all. As American folksay puts it, in this country the impossible just takes a little longer to achieve. Not impossible. But not easy either. Not to be exorcised by the voodooism of a single socio-drama at the opening of a conference, useful as socio-drama is.

Plenty of People Are Included in "All"

If all who are affected should take part, everyone in the school community should be in on the improvement program. Here's a tough one too. Everyone is quite a few people, even in Crossroads, U. S. A., as well as in a Los Angeles or New York City area surrounding a school. If we settle for representatives, there is a problem of proper balance among groups. If we settle for samples, there is a problem of achieving a fair sample. Granted that fair representation can be achieved, many who are affected will be left out. Without personal participation in planning, they may feel uninvolved and may regard their representation as merely nominal.

But assume we can get fair representation in planning sessions and, through ingenuity in reporting back and through use of instruments, some involvement of many others in a more distant and a less personal relationship. Assume planning sessions use group processes skillfully. Many agreements and shared actions will result. But agreement by all on everything is unlikely in as diverse a society as America.

Should total agreement be insisted upon as a prerequisite to action? Though the democratic and peaceable Quakers answer yes, some students of group action fear that the price of total agreement may be too high. The price may be long periods of inaction while the disagreement waits in the freezer, cooling off. Or the disagreement may be irreconcilable, as a democrat's difference in ideology from the authoritarianism called communism. Or the price may be obfuscation of real differences, specious agreement on generalities, with "operators" then free to interpret supposed consensus as they will. So some regard total agreement as strictly for the totalitarians.

The Question of Highest Loyalty

The knottiest problem of all may be the proper responsibilities and relationships of those who make up "all who are affected." Specifically, what are the responsibilities and relationships of the professionals and the public? Who decides what? Discussion of this is usually between those who compare education to medicine and those who say that education should follow public mandates.

Those who use the medical analogy argue that educators, like doctors, must diagnose and treat rather than have laymen prescribe, else what avail the careful training and practical experience of the specialist? Those who urge following popular mandates say that since the schools belong to the people, educators should assume leadership yet always recognize that decision-making in education, all the way from broad-policy making to decisions on technical details of teaching phonics, belongs to the people. This latter position usually includes a democratic faith that the people will study the facts, will support full and free inquiry, and will judge well.

But another dimension should enter this discussion of responsibilities and relationships of the professionals and the public. The attempts to capture man's mind through capturing his children's schools never cease. Suppose the people of community X —not a minority but whatever you usually mean when you say the people—decide to reject free inquiry. Suppose the people of community X want indoctrination of a set of not-to-be-examined but claimed-to-be-good answers on certain economic, social, religious, or political issues. Yet the educators in school leadership positions in community X believe that there can be no freedom without freedom of the mind and consequently support the method of intelligence. The people of community X reject freedom of inquiry. The educational leadership of community X regards freedom of inquiry as fundamental. What, then, is the modern democratic educator's highest loyalty? What should a man do? (Or, reversing the question, suppose the educational leadership of community X, not the people, rejects free inquiry and sponsors some claimed-to-be-good imposition?)

Valid But Not Easy

Frederick Lewis Allen is responsible for the immortal statement,

"Everything is more complicated than it seems to most people." Apparently this applies to improving the curriculum through the participation of all.

The easy answer, "All who are affected should participate," remains valid. But it doesn't remain easy. And it doesn't answer some related problems.

NOTE: The entire March, 1954, number of *Educational Leadership* is devoted to the theme, "Curriculum Improvement—Who Participates?"

When one considers the roles of various participants in curriculum planning, he should probably begin with the state education authority. It has already been suggested that the state exercises control over local school programs by means of legislative enactments and state-wide textbook adoptions. In addition, the state may exercise a leadership function, as well as a restrictive one. Although the present trend is toward a local, "grass roots" approach to curriculum planning, the state can still exercise leadership in coordinating and facilitating local developments.

THE ILLINOIS CURRICULUM PROGRAM

One of the best examples of a state-wide effort to improve the curriculum is the Illinois Curriculum Program (ICP). The program was begun on September 1, 1947. Before February, 1952, it was known as the Illinois Secondary School Curriculum Program (ISSCP). Since 1952, all school levels from kindergarten through grade 14 have been included in the program.

In the very beginning ten underlying principles to guide the program were set up. These have never been changed. Some of these principles, briefly summarized, are as follows: The advisory body to set up governing policies of the program should be drawn from both lay and professional representatives of all state-wide organizations whose interests are involved; participation by any local school should be on a permissive basis; local schools should be provided at little cost necessary materials and "know-how" to secure needed data for school improvement; workshops should be provided for both lay and faculty personnel to work together for school improvement; "developmental projects in pilot schools" should be stimulated, with the state department and institutions of higher learning providing consultant service on a cost-free basis; cost-free publications—such as a guide, manuals, descriptions of successful programs—should be sponsored; initially, finances should be provided by legislative grants and free consultant services should be provided by institutions of higher learning, with local schools making contributions later to match benefits received; and some one person should be made responsible for implementing policy and programs agreed upon.

From the ten principles were developed six major purposes of the Illinois Curriculum Program: to coordinate all persons and groups interested in the curriculum on a state-wide and local level; to provide materials for local studies basic to local curriculum improvement; to encourage projects designed to improve school subjects and school services; to sponsor workshops where administrators, teachers, and lay citizens, assisted by consultants, can work together on mutual problems; "to prepare and distribute publications"; and "to facilitate improved school-college relationships." [18:1-7]

In December, 1954, the Steering Committee of the ICP outlined the following major series in a comprehensive program of proposed publications: (*a*) growth and learning; (*b*) techniques and procedures; (*c*) subject fields; (*d*) special fields; (*e*) student progress; (*f*) administration and supervision; and (*g*) curriculum and research. The first in the series to be published is the kindergarten bulletin: *School Begins with Kindergarten,* The Subject Field Series, Bulletin No. C-One, with Fred P. Barnes as editor. [7:vi]

LOCAL LEADERSHIP

At the local level, it is important to consider, first of all, the leadership function of the administration. Derthick outlines the responsibility of the superintendent in making effective use of each member of his "team" in curriculum development.

Venturing in Education—The Superintendent's Role in Curriculum Improvement   by LAWRENCE G. DERTHICK

From the *NEA Journal,* February, 1953, pages 90–91. Reprinted by special permission. Lawrence G. Derthick, formerly Superintendent of Schools, Chattanooga, Tennessee, is U. S. Commissioner of Education.

When the going got rugged Columbus had two words for it—"Sail on!" Either expressed or unexpressed these words have been the superintendent's motto since the first school administrator paced with misgivings the new and wobbly deck of school system management. We cannot despair, for the hazards of today, like the uncharted waters of 1492, are challenges to venturing.

Today we need to reconsider the superintendent's role as he works with others on curriculum improvement. It is here that this article centers attention.

The Curriculum

Most of us accept the idea that the curriculum is made up of the direct experiences offered to children under the guidance of the school. At that point we sit back with an air of satisfaction. But we haven't gotten very far.

We still must wrestle with the old question: "What knowledge is of most worth?" And just to make the task even more complicated, the world keeps rolling out new ideas, knowledge, and situations. We are reminded of the small boy in the Ding cartoon who, visualizing the march of economic and political events, exclaimed, "I'll never catch up!"

The school administrator's task is to strive for perspective in the midst of many curriculum issues. Standing apart for a moment from the knotty problems, we can see that four processes offer possible solutions: (*a*) better objectives, (*b*) better selection of content and experiences, (*c*) better organization of the curriculum, and (*d*) better instruction. All of these call for *more* evaluation: What are we trying to teach? Why are we teaching it? What success are we having?

The superintendent's job is to concentrate his energies on these processes. He cannot devote full time, but he will seek systematically to enlist, organize, and support those who can put forth the necessary teamwork.

The Classroom Teacher

The first member of the team is the classroom teacher. He (and I do mean she, also) is the one who determines the curriculum. Regardless of the study bulletins, guides, textbooks, and other gadgets, the curriculum is what takes place under the guidance of the classroom teacher.

Books, articles, and speeches have proclaimed the value of the competent teacher. No one has overstated the case. Few things in American life are more soul-stirring than to watch a real teacher develop the God-given qualities of children.

So we superintendents turn to classroom teachers with curriculum problems, and they have responded well in the past. They have served many hours upon curriculum committees. This is good, for they know the direct problems of instruction, and, by participation, they develop understanding of the curriculum agreed upon.

But often we have been unreasonable. We expect the same teacher to serve again and again upon committees with little chance to catch up between assignments. We do not pay enough attention to teacher load. Committee work following a full day of teaching may be necessary at times, but it shouldn't become a habit.

Too often we have asked committees to make bricks without straw. It isn't right to expect a committee, gathered around the table with blank paper and a few sharp pencils, to draft a new course of study. These committees need materials with which to work—sample units, books of reference, audio-visual materials, and reports on the effectiveness of content, experiences, and curriculum patterns. They need the advice of curriculum specialists and the guidance of scholars.

Such resources may come to the committee through expenditures by the local board of education, by pooled arrangements within a county, by services made available through the state department of education, by cooperation with a college, or by the efforts of teachers' associations. But little will happen unless the superintendent "thinks on these things."

The Child

Another player on the team is the child. To a considerable degree the school is and should be judged by what happens to the child. If we are to devise suitable curriculums we must know how children get that way; that is, how they learn and grow.

Childhood has certain inalienable rights. The values and experiences put before children must have significance for them. If every year is to be lived effectively, the curriculum must be planned with full understanding of the needs and nature of children at each maturity level.

But effective living and learning at each age does not mean whimsical living. The verb "learn" requires an object. One learns by learning something; that something is the curriculum. By a study of children we learn ways to make the curriculum effective.

We have learned from children that learning is an active process. What the school presents to its pupils results in worthwhile learning when pupils respond in worthwhile ways. In a good school children are doing things—with their muscles *and* with their minds. To appeal to the modern child the curriculum offers a variety of activities ranging from the "facts and more facts" (of the Dickens character, Mr. Gradgrind) to the less tangible moral and spiritual experiences.

Sometimes on curriculum committees, but more often in school situations, pupils can help plan the evolving curriculum. The use of their help is something to be encouraged—by the superintendent.

The Central Staff

Years ago the pattern of the central staff, in relation to instruction, was to employ experts who could *tell* classroom teachers how to teach. That day is gone. By labels (such as consultant) as well as by policy and practice we have developed advisers and resource people.

But the number is still too few. The 1952 AASA Yearbook showed that one in four of the city superintendents did not have any professional assistants; two in five rural superintendents were similarly handicapped. The median number in both cases was less than three. There is a deficiency in resource people and research workers to assist classroom teachers and principals.

We superintendents have been too thrifty in employing central office personnel. The superintendency is now a constellation of jobs which no one person can carry effectively alone. That old budgetary standard of 5 per cent for "administration" is a lame duck; it should be killed off. Besides, providing resources through the central office isn't "administration" when it directly improves instruction.

The Principal

To have an improving curriculum requires organization and constant vigilance to keep the organization flexible. Curriculum committees do not just happen and once in operation their vitality must be maintained.

The central core of the curriculum organization can be the principals. This is not always so. Sometimes the principals are left standing on the sidelines watching the parade between the classrooms and the central office.

If we superintendents really mean

that the principal is the professional head of a school unit and the community engineer of a district, then he must have a place in curriculum improvement. To say this does not mean "he's the boss"; it does mean that his talents and key position are to be brought into the curriculum process.

The Scholar

We have yet to find the best ways to bring the scholar into curriculum development. He elbows in through textbooks and some other printed materials. His influence needs to be felt more with regard to the selection and proper emphasis of content.

No classroom teacher can be a scholar in the many areas of human knowledge and experience. Yet every teacher can be *scholarly* in his approach to new problems and his use of information in the fields of his competence. To his own abilities should be added many contacts with the experts who know the up-to-date and truly significant knowledge and resources.

As superintendents, we must seek new ways to bring the scholar to the aid of the curriculum builders. In this way, we can be sure that the "fundamentals" are on solid ground.

The Parents

In recent years progress has been made in increasing the participation of parents and other laymen in curriculum improvement. By their demands for school services, parents have long been a factor in determining what the school teaches. Now the lay role is changing.

For one thing, the parents are getting in on the ground floor. They are discussing the objectives of the school, suggesting resources, and helping to select patterns of experiences. Such participation in non-technical problems not only improves the curriculum, but it also builds a core of community understanding.

Parents are finding that they must stand together in maintaining what they want, especially in meeting the attacks of misinformed or malicious critics. Often the criticism of how schools teach the three R's is but an effort to undermine school budgets and reduce taxes. Parents who have helped plan a curriculum are not easily misled by Pied Pipers.

And So, Mr. Superintendent

You and I face an age of stirring ventures. All the currents and cross-currents of the community touch our offices. The distractions are many. We may easily forget our professional leadership opportunities. We may overlook the human resources available to us in our staffs and in our communities.

Somehow you and I must get time beyond the daily grind to see to it that the curriculum is guided by constructive influences. Through the school's program the youth of America must learn *how* —not *what*—to think, to *distinguish* between fact and fiction, to *appreciate* the great moral and spiritual values, and to *hold close* to the democratic ideals exemplified by our republic.

In building better curriculums, all of us in the profession can place our confidence in the people. For as Jefferson often said, only through the education of the people can our democratic life be maintained and improved.

Since the trend now is to recognize the individual school as the primary unit for curriculum revision, the building principal is the one who ultimately becomes responsible for leadership in curriculum improvement. Hand has stressed the important role of the principal and "the grand strategy" he must use in order to bring about lasting improvement in school practices.

In Summary   by HAROLD C. HAND

From Harold C. Hand, "The Principal as a Leader in Curriculum Revision," *Bulletin of the National Association of Secondary-School Principals*, April, 1955, pages 386–398. Reprinted by special permission. Harold C. Hand is Professor of Education, University of Illinois.

For best results, the individual school should be made the unit for curriculum development. Unevenness both in the quantity and quality of curriculum development is always to be expected, even within any given department of a school. Lasting improvements in the curriculum are quite unlikely unless the principal of the school is regarded as the responsible leader in respect to all that is done in this regard within his school. The principal's effectiveness as such a leader will be in direct proportion to the extent to which he understands the grand strategy of curriculum development, and knows and is able to execute its basic supportive tactics.

The grand strategy of curriculum development is so to change the influences which play upon lay citizens, teachers, and pupils that those (influences) which lead these persons to support desirable changes in school practice will be stronger than those (influences) which induce them to oppose such changes.

The first and most basic tactic necessary to accomplish this strategy is to identify the influences which are at work and to assess the direction and the strength of the force in which each of these influences results. The second basic tactic is actively so to involve laymen, teachers, and pupils that through self-persuasion they will make the influences which play upon them supportive of desirable changes in school practices.

The influences in respect to which this tactic of self-persuasion through active involvement commonly needs to be applied include beliefs regarding who is actually attending high school; the suitability of the school program for youngsters over the full ranges of native endowment, socioeconomic status, and physical condition; equality of participation in the activities which comprise the school's informal curriculum; the extent to which school attendance is cost-free; the correspondence between one's views as to what the purposes of instruction should be and those which are being striven for and achieved; the correspondence between one's views as to the best way of organizing the instructional program and the way in which it is currently organized; the correspondence between one's view in respect to methods of teaching and those presently employed; and the extent to which proposed changes in school practice threaten one's security.

As said, the principal who understands the grand strategy of curriculum development and knows how to and is able to execute its necessary tactics is the one who gets durable improvements made in the practices of his school.

To do so, he must indeed be a perceptive, wise, and patient leader —and be so seen and accepted by the patrons, pupils, and teachers of his school.

It has already been intimated that the role of the curriculum "expert" or consultant from the outside has changed during the past twenty-five years. No longer is he the director of curriculum reorganization. He is called in only when there is a felt need for his services. Aikin suggests that "not until a principal and his teachers have struggled with their problem themselves will they accept or use assistance effectively from any outside source." [1:14]

THE TEACHER

It is now generally agreed that curriculum improvement is, in the last analysis, the result of improved practices by individual classroom teachers. This point cannot be emphasized too strongly. Improved instructional practices are the result of pre-service and in-service education programs for teachers. Thelen points out the limited usefulness of a number of approaches to curriculum development in typical in-service programs for teachers and, using "findings in the area of group dynamics," outlines necessary conditions for curriculum improvement.

Group Dynamics in Curriculum Improvement

by HERBERT A. THELEN

From *Educational Leadership*, Vol. XI, No. 7 (April, 1954), pages 413–417. Reprinted by special permission of the editor of ASCD publications and the author. Herbert A. Thelen is Associate Professor of Educational Psychology and Director of the Human Dynamics Laboratory, University of Chicago.

There are a number of approaches to the improvement of curriculum. Each has a limited usefulness, and each is correct as far as it goes. Thus one approach assumes that a "professionally minded" teacher, with some administratively provided consultant help, will bring about improvements in his teaching. Here the emotional support and reward typically come from the consultant; the teacher bucks teaching standards within the school, and, when the consultant is no longer available for support, the "improvement" either regresses or simply terminates. A second approach to curriculum improvement is through "working committees" on the faculty. Assuming that these committees are freed to deal with significant instructional problems, then there are usually two consequences. The first is that the teachers stimulate one another and possibly move toward better practice. The second is that each committee prepares a report of recommendations which are usually accepted without commitment by the faculty, and then buried. A third approach to curriculum improvement is through "cooperation" with the community. To the extent that the cooperation centers about practical problems of work-experience, planting gardens, helping in settlement houses, etc., it extends the range of experience for the students. To the extent that the teacher is creative and knowledgeable, this approach may contribute to education rather than to training only. To the extent that it provides a set of expectations from the "outside," there emerges a set of supportive forces which encourage new developments. A fourth approach is to send teachers to summer workshops to get "the word," and this leads to anything from a new direction maintained through the support of the "internalized" workshop group to all sorts of new problems of communication and of being out-of-step with the home group. A fifth approach is through studious application of a well formulated method, such as those of curriculum makers. This provides a set of methodological concepts on which a school department can depend, but it gives little guidance at the most important point: namely, in deciding just what the objectives should be.

Each of the approaches recognizes some limited but important fact: that individual growth of teachers is required for origination of new and better curriculum ideas; that the individual teacher must be supported emotionally by other people during the creative act and also in maintaining his new practices; that consultative aid can be helpful; that demands from the community help to externalize problems and give them enough objectivity so that one knows how to make choices; that methods of thinking about curriculum are useful.

It is my purpose in this paper to elaborate on these and some other conditions "required" for school-wide curriculum improvement. I shall present the discussion as a development of a general plan which a school might adopt; but I do this primarily to illustrate the required conditions, not to advocate this particular plan. It is my belief that if one examines successful efforts to improve curriculum he will find the conditions I am about to identify, even though the implementing plan may not formally provide for them.[1]

Conditions for Curriculum Development

1. Improvement is the result of changes in practices by individual teachers. Of the possible changes a teacher might intellectually diagnose as desirable, he is actually psychologically "ready" to experiment only

---

[1] For the remainder of this discussion I shall draw on *Groups At Work* (Chicago: University of Chicago Press, July, 1954).

with certain ones. These are the ones which do not involve more risk or frustration than the teacher can tolerate; and they are also the ones for which the teacher can see how to rectify the situation in case his experimentation turns out badly.

2. Because of the highly personal and creative involvement of the teacher, he needs the emotional support of a small group of associates. The group must be one in which he is free to verbalize his bright ideas, obtain criticism without feeling defensive, experiment with tentative notions, make demands for listening and reacting, and obtain help to make observations or plan materials needed for new activities. Such a group is essentially a psyche group or clique. Its members give it loyalty and protect each other from real or fancied attack.

3. These self-training cells or cliques must communicate ideas and recommendations for policy (both instructional and administrative) to each other and to the administration. This suggests that they must have the status of faculty working committees, and that there must be expectancy for reporting to the total group. For reporting to the total group to be appropriate, it is required that the total group have some over-all problems to be solved and that the individually guided work of the self-training groups results in some contributions useful to the solution of over-all school problems.

4. The over-all problems for the to-tal faculty must be "externalized"; that is, they must be seen as demands from the "outside." The reason for this requirement is that if the "school problems" are formulated as intra-mural concerns only, then the formulation of the problems will be used as the means for forwarding the interests of one group against those of another, and decisions will be based on power rather than on objective assessment of conditions. This is typically the case with legislative processes. There is, however, one important difference between legislation and curriculum improvement: namely, that decisions for the latter purpose bind the teachers to take action, whereas legislation requires no personal-emotional commitments.

5. The requirement that problems for the total faculty be seen as demands from the outside means, practically, that the demands come from the "community." For the "community" to be in a position to make demands on the school means that the school and community must be associated in purposes accepted by both. And the condition under which this is possible is one of cooperation on joint problems. The problems on which community agencies, groups, and individuals have interests which overlap those of the school are problems of training students to meet their needs. In other words, the legitimate overlap is in matters of youth welfare, work-experience, civic participation, social opportunities, and the like.

Such cooperation is between selected single teachers or groups of teachers with agencies or individuals in the community. The demand on the faculty as a whole is for policy to guide this cooperation. Such policy, arising from a wide variety of working relations on a variety of needs of students for training, should be based on professional study of how the training experience is to be inaugurated, supervised, and guided. This, then, is the first kind of "outside demand" or externalized problem to be solved by the faculty on the basis of relevant insights from the small teacher groups.

6. School-community training experience is directed at the immediate needs of children in their effort to live successfully in the community. Such training is not necessarily *educative* in the larger humanistic sense. This, then, poses a second kind of demand on the total faculty: to develop methods of teaching whereby the training experience is made educative. Roughly speaking, this is the usual definition of the job of in-service training, and our additional insistence on the community-based training activity is for the purpose of keeping the discussion of teaching methods "down to earth" and in line with objective reality conditions. In other words, the school-community operating relationship is needed to keep the school from simply floating off in its own little island culture that may have no relationship to "real" problems and that therefore may be

unable to provide any objective criteria for testing competing ideas about teaching.

The kind of teaching problems which the faculty would be studying can be illustrated in the following manner. Suppose, during training to be consumers, the students work in stores, have a hand in purchasing materials for their clubs or science department, test materials and products, and the like. The *educational* problem, over and above such practical need-meeting training, is to build on this experience some understandings of such general matters as the ethics of waste; the relationships among design, function, and beauty; the relationships among labor, materials, and management; the problems and significance of policies for distribution of goods and services; and the like. While only certain teachers would supervise any particular type of training experience, it is the responsibility of *all* teachers to illuminate the significance, values, social roles, and societal problems involved in these practical matters.

7. While not directly a condition for in-service training, the preceding design leads logically to a further opportunity. It is this: through the teacher's experience in the community and through his discussion with the children of the meaning of their experiences to them, a variety of practical suggestions should emerge for the improvement of the lot of children in the community. That is, the teachers will be in an excellent posi-

tion to form opinions of needed modifications in agency programs and other arrangements for children. In effect, the school can become an instrument for "feedback" to various agencies and groups about problems and conditions of child welfare. It seems to me that this possibility should entitle the school as represented by selected teachers and principal to a place on the community council or other official family of community institutions. By such means, two-way communication with the community is established: (*a*) the teachers initiate requests for assistance by the community in setting up training experiences outside the school; and now (*b*) the teachers report back to the official agencies of the community facts and suggestions about aspects of child welfare relevant to community programs.

Thus this over-all design, originating in an analysis of conditions required for effective improvement of curriculum by a school, results in a rationale for the "community school."

We arrive at three possible and complementary roles for the schools as institutions within the community: (*a*) collaborators with others in setting up and supervising training experiences; (*b*) professional educators working among themselves to improve methods for simultaneous training and education of children; (*c*) consultants to the collaborating agencies on aspects of their functioning related to the welfare of students.

The role of collaborator gives indi-

vidual teachers their "place" in the community. The "professional educator" role gives the faculty group as a whole its "place" among other groups in the community. And the consultative role, usually but not necessarily exercised through school officials as representatives of the school, gives the school as an institution its "place" in the community.[2]

Translation of this design into effective operating procedure will require many decisions about how to organize the necessary roles, obtain sufficient and appropriate communication, plan agenda for faculty meetings, and the like. The following recommendations in this regard seem most important:

1. The small working groups should be formed through voluntary selection of faculty members by one another. There should be no effort to force people into the program. As it moves along, a group standard of participation will develop, and this will provide the only pressure. If such a standard does *not* develop, then the program is missing the boat, possibly through lack of emotional support by the principal, possibly through too small a rate of reward by satisfaction in accomplishment.

2. The principal must be emotionally involved in the work. Probably he might serve best in the role of executive secretary to a faculty steering committee which plans agenda for the meetings of the total faculty. The principal's actions can be of great as-

[2] *Ibid.*, Chapter III.

sistance in scheduling classes so that self-training committees can meet, occasional expert consultation is available, the teachers are put in touch with appropriate citizens or agencies —such activities will do more than any amount of talking to maintain the program. The principal may find, however, that he has to work out some conflicts between his role as executive secretary on the one hand and as administrator and public relations man on the other.

3. In appraising the program and its accomplishments, evaluative criteria must be applied not only to changes produced but also to the adequacy of the processes of working together. If the conditions of cooperation and competition are realistic and steadily improving, then the proper evaluation is that the accomplishment is adequate. But the effects of actual changes should also be studied to sharpen up goals, and diagnose needed skills. (A faculty workshop might help if such needs become apparent.) The problems of evaluation will be comparatively easy to solve as long as the school keeps close interactive contact with the community.

OTHER PARTICIPANTS IN CURRICULUM PLANNING

In recent years, the schools have been urged to give pupils or students more voice in curriculum planning, especially at the classroom level. In the December, 1957, *California Journal of Secondary Education,* Alter [2:473–478] recommends "Ask the Graduates" as a worthwhile approach to curriculum improvement and summarizes the results of this procedure which has been used continuously in Beverly Hills High School since 1941.

As previously suggested, there is a definite trend toward increased lay participation in curriculum planning. Despite the trend, however, numerous fundamental issues concerning organized citizen participation have been raised by Hamlin in the October, 1953, *Review of Educational Research.*

Though organized participation is extensive and crucially important to the schools, there has been little research regarding it. Answers are needed to such fundamental questions as these:

1. What have been the effects upon the schools of citizens' organizations of various types?

2. What arrangements make for continuing and satisfactory, rather than sporadic and unsuccessful, participation by citizens' groups?

3. What relationship should exist between a citizens' group and the board of education, the administrator, the teachers, the non-academic employees, and the students of a school system?

4. What are the relative merits of independent and school-sponsored citizens' groups?

5. What are the results of different procedures in selecting individual members of citizens' groups?

6. How do citizens' groups working for better schools affect the thinking and actions of citizens generally?

7. What are the effects upon other groups in a community of school-sponsored citizens' committees? *

Not only is research lacking on important questions about lay participation in curriculum improvement, but Lieberman contends that "at the present time the public expects to decide many things which should be decided by educators." [23:122] Using lay control of teacher certification and lay determination of what should be taught as examples, he further points out how professional autonomy is being undermined. [23:87–156]

In spite of unanswered questions, undesirable features, or differences of opinion with respect to lay participation in curriculum development, such participation is taking place everywhere today.

In the introduction to his article, "Better Schools When Public Participates," Jensen suggests some of the values to be gained from public participation in planning educational programs.

Better Schools When Public Participates   by GLENN JENSEN

From the *Phi Delta Kappan,* November, 1955, pages 77–83. Reprinted by special permission. Glenn Jensen is Director of the Bureau of Class Instruction, Extension Division, the University of Colorado, Boulder.

There is no question but that, as a nation, we have today sufficient resources to organize and to maintain an excellent public education program. In those localities where education is facing a crisis, where a shortage of personnel and facilities exists, where an apparent lack of funds forces school administrators to provide a sub-standard program, and where unwarranted criticisms have arisen, it has been found generally true that in these communities the people have not been made fully

* From the American Educational Research Association, "Research on Human Relations and Programs of Action," *Review of Educational Research,* 23:346 (October, 1953). Quoted by special permission of the Association and the author. H. M. Hamlin is Professor of Education at the University of Illinois.

aware of the needs and problems of the schools nor have they identified themselves in any way with those problems.

Where Criticism Thrives

Some educators themselves have been responsible for impeding educational progress and community understanding. They have accomplished this by assuming that the function of educational leadership was fulfilled when they informed the people of the community of the purposes and the practices of the public schools, with patrons expected to approve. Evidence to the contrary, that this type of "leadership" is not doing the job, may be found when a study is made of the success of violent critics of the public schools—who have preyed upon those lacking understanding of the schools and of the import of the educational program. It is in communities exhibiting no leadership of any kind, or "leadership" of the kind mentioned, that critics of the public schools have been most successful.

In some communities contact between the school and the community consists largely of attendance reports, athletic events, commencement ceremonies, and other limited contacts designed to insure complacency. Parents rarely are invited to visit the school and the PTA is an ineffective organization. In such communities there is an absence of community participation and none is encouraged for fear the *status quo* may be disturbed. When additional support for the schools is needed it is necessary to resort to high pressure campaigns in order to "sell" the people on the school. These attempts at "selling" as a part of an intensive campaign are poor substitutes for community confidence based upon understanding through participation in school affairs.

Learning by Doing

We have long known that children learn by doing; that experiences gained in participation tend to increase knowledge, promote skills, and develop certain attitudes. More of us might consciously apply this same psychological fact in our efforts to bring about increased public understanding of the schools. Only recently have we begun fully to realize that those who are meaningfully involved in school activities tend to learn more about schools than those who are not. In fact, public school officials have no real alternative but to work with the people of a community and to reflect the will of these people. Only through enlightened public support won through widespread public participation can the schools find the strength to prosper. This active and aggressive lay participation is one of the most effective ways to help the people of a community understand their real stake in public education, and move to preserve it.

Most schoolteachers and administrators today realize that lay people are extremely valuable and helpful to the educational program as resource persons, as two-way channels of communication between the schools and the community, and as public-relations promoters. School leaders now are beginning to realize that if you want people to support a program you must be sure they understand its values and that they have shared with personal satisfaction in the planning and developing of that program.

* * *

NOTE: The remainder of the article by Jensen describes a number of specific programs from various sections of the country in which the public has participated—school improvement programs, lay craftsmen assisting vocational training classes, PTA participation in guidance programs, citizens serving as resource persons, businessmen helping with BE Days, and the like.

If laymen are to participate in curriculum planning, certain principles or guidelines are necessary to smooth, cooperative operation. A number of these have been summarized by Toy: a need for mutual respect and trust between educators and lay citizens; a need for citizens and schoolmen to "be clearly aware of their respective roles and responsibilities"; willingness on the part of both groups to cooperate; and the need for a group that represents the whole community. Such a group should begin with self-education, engage in "fact finding, not fault finding," cooperate with school authorities, and "maintain its independence of thought and action." [35:19–21]

NOTE: The National Citizens Commission for the Public Schools —now the National Citizens Council for Better Schools—of which Henry Toy, Jr. is president, has published a number of useful guides on the organization and operation of citizens' committees, such as *How Can We Organize for Better Schools?*

The trends toward increased lay participation in curriculum planning and toward the "grass roots" or local-community approach to curriculum improvement have already been noted. But the use of either procedure in large cities, where well-defined community lines are lacking, poses a real problem. In his report on a Work Conference on the Educational Problems of Great Cities, Polley describes one possible solution to the problem.

Community Approach to Educational Problems of Great Cities
by JOHN W. POLLEY

From *Teachers College Record,* December, 1953, pages 153–159. Report of a Work Conference on the Educational Problems of Great Cities held at Teachers College in August, 1953. The twenty-one participants—assistant superintendents, principals, and teachers—came from Baltimore, Buffalo, Minneapolis, New York, and St. Louis. Reprinted by special permission. John W. Polley is Professor of Education, Teachers College, Columbia University.

During the first two weeks of August, 1953, teams of school personnel representing particular physical areas within five great cities met to consider how educational problems look from the place where education occurs—the local community—instead of viewing it from the top down. This grass-roots approach was an attempt to find ways of increasing the effectiveness of education in great cities. Research in finance and adaptability, carried on under the leadership of Paul R. Mort, has shown that you get less education per dollar spent in a city of 100,000 and greater population than in smaller places.

The large city school system is the newest experiment in school operation in America. Fifty years ago the first school district was established which served more than a million people; that was the Greater New York school district. Great city school organization has been based on attempts to apply to large populations the popular structure long established in small school districts.

By the 1920's it was becoming apparent that large city school systems were too remote from the public. Extensive publicity campaigns became common. The procedure of taking the public into the confidence of administrative authorities grew over the decades that followed. Today in any large city a vast number of educational enterprises will be found involving the public.

Typically such enterprises deal with a total city-wide problem. Only a small fraction of the people interested in the schools can take any part. Great numbers of interested, able people are doomed to have their thinking and planning done for them. The resulting loss of interest and concern can only work to the detriment of the schools.

Staggering problems face our great city school systems. Any city with 500,000 inhabitants has a far greater population than many of our states. Increasing enrollments, shifts of population from old areas of the city to new, and the decreasing value of the dollar add up to vast problems.

Such special problems alone are

enough, but even before them come the day-to-day problems of running the school system—planning the educational program to meet the needs of boys and girls, helping teachers find satisfaction in their jobs, adjusting to needs and demands on the schools as society changes.

The lack of means to bring about a give-and-take relationship for exchanging ideas over the whole city, the existence of pressure groups (each intent on bringing about its own brand of action on some part of the program), and the multitude of problems peculiar to the various areas which make up the city add an unequaled variety and complexity to school problems in great cities.

The Work Conference on the Educational Problems of Great Cities was planned to explore the possibilities of a new approach to this complex array of needs. This approach places emphasis on communities within the city, working within the city-wide framework for schools, taking an increasingly active part in solving some of these problems. It places emphasis on principals and teachers using the freedom to act which they now possess within city regulations, trying out new means of working with the public. It calls for grass-roots thinking and planning and action.

Public interest in the schools centers on the spot where education takes place—individual schools all over the city. Problems are not so vast and complex at this level. Best of all, there are scores and hundreds of people whose interests and abilities can be tapped to help build good schools.

If several schools in a reasonably homogeneous community within a city work cooperatively on their problems, a variety of resources becomes available without the impersonality and complexity of the total city situation. Tie these resources and the ideas from such communities into the total city school program and added power and vitality become available.

The members of the Work Conference took a two-way approach to the problem before them. They examined techniques for bringing schools and community closer together. They also made plans for an area approach (that is, a combination of several schools working together) to the solution of school problems. Such an approach will enable each city to take advantage of the vast resources in the form of the personal abilities of principals, teachers, and citizens in developing the school program.

The group began by outlining the leeway for action already in the hands of administrators at the local level within their cities. They followed this by defining what leeway for action should exist. They stated in general terms how the leeway should be used. Three main areas were identified: curriculum; staff; and supplies, equipment, and the budget.

Throughout the two-week Work

Conference, the members and resource personnel emphasized the important part the public must play in planning the educational program. Accordingly, the members of the Conference spent some time in defining the sphere of the public in planning for schools. This they outlined in the form of "A Charter for Public Participation." The Charter or guide was based on the ideas expressed by members of the Conference on ways of avoiding possible difficulties which might arise from the planned relationships with the public.

Last, the group summarized in nine points the highlights of the Conference. . . .

CONTINUITY, FLEXIBILITY, AND DESIGN

One of the major problems of curriculum workers is to provide a continuity of learning experiences for children at every grade level of the public schools and, at the same time, to avoid undesirable duplications or omissions. This involves a broad description of the scope and sequence of at least the minimum essentials of education for all children at each grade level and in each subject or other type of curricular design. Obviously, the first step in the development of a coordinated program should begin at the state level. Consequently, state leaders in curriculum planning have developed curriculum guides to serve as a framework for curriculum planning in local school districts. Unlike the prescriptive and detailed courses of study of three decades ago, newer types of state guides leave much latitude for local initiative in curriculum planning. In addition to state curriculum guides, larger school districts have developed their own guides to meet specific local needs.

An analysis by Merritt and Harap of 796 courses of study published in 1951 through 1953 by 185 school systems throughout the United States reveals some interesting trends in the production of curriculum guides.

Summary of Trends in Curriculum Guides
by ELEANOR MERRITT and HENRY HARAP

From Eleanor Merritt and Henry Harap, *Trends in the Production of Curriculum Guides; A Survey of Courses of Study Published in 1951 through 1953* (Nashville, Tenn.: George Peabody College for Teachers,

1955), pages 40–43. Reprinted by special permission. Eleanor Merritt is a consultant, Curriculum Laboratory, Iowa State Teachers College, Cedar Falls, Iowa. Henry Harap is Professor of Education and Associate Director of the Division of Surveys and Field Services, George Peabody College for Teachers, Nashville.

1. The inclusion of the term *guide* in a majority of the titles indicated an increasing acceptance of the view that the proper function of the instructional bulletin is to serve as an aid, not as a prescribed course of study.

2. Compared with the preceding triennium, the output of curriculum guides increased 46 per cent, which indicated a growing emphasis on the cooperative production of instructional bulletins.

3. Unlike the customary teaching guides, eighteen brief handbooks issued by state and local school systems dealt chiefly with administrative matters as well as programs of instruction. In some instances these handbooks were prepared specifically for new teachers.

4. The output of teaching guides was approximately doubled in health and physical education, music, and science; tripled in guidance; and nearly quadrupled in special education and vocational education.

5. The proportion of teaching guides covering the whole range of twelve grades rose sharply, indicating an increasing acceptance of the importance of a continuous curriculum for grades 1–12.

6. The quality of typography of the teaching guides continued to show marked improvement. The present study showed a continuing decline in the proportion of printed guides and an increase in the proportion of mimeographed publications. The offset process gained in favor, particularly by city school systems.

7. Committee procedure in the administration of a program of curriculum development continued to receive common acceptance. Approximately four-fifths of the curriculum guides were produced by groups of teachers and administrators working together.

8. The teacher continued to play an important role in the leadership as well as in the production of teaching guides. The subject or production committee was headed by a teacher in the preparation of one-third of the published bulletins.

9. The school systems of the country appeared to be in the midst of a second cycle of revision of the curriculum guides which were produced since the end of World War II.

10. The trend toward dividing a subject into units of work showed a slight decline in the last three years. It was too early to conclude that this was indicative of the beginning of a conservative trend.

11. There were signs of a tendency to simplify the outline and form of

the unit of work. In a number of cases the pattern was less formal and more meaningful to the reader.

12. Several school systems published bound collections of units of work for a variety of subjects to serve as source material and for illustrative purposes. In addition, fifteen school systems published series of separate units of work with emphasis on topics of recent development such as *atomic energy* which were still in the formative stage.

13. The renewal of interest in the core curriculum reported in the last survey continued apace in the current triennium. With a single exception, all the newly published guides on the secondary level were confined to grades 7, 8, and 9.

14. Suggestions for the use of community resources were found in 65 per cent of the teaching guides, demonstrating that there was a growing tendency to push the schoolhouse walls farther outward into the community. In addition, about a dozen school systems prepared teaching guides, resource units, or books dealing specifically with life in the local community.

15. The recent emphasis upon the study or teaching of moral and spiritual values gave rise to the publication of several guides in this field during the last three years.

16. Although health and physical education were combined for purposes of classification, only seven guides treated both subjects in one bulletin. Actually, health and physi-

cal education appeared as separate guides in 90 per cent of the cases. The health guides were beginning to emphasize mental and emotional as well as physical health.

17. The treatment of home and family living as an integral phase of our culture continued to receive more emphasis. The correlation of homemaking with subjects such as art and music as well as with home experience gained increasing acceptance.

18. In the teaching of the English language, there was an increase of emphasis upon reading, writing, speaking, and listening rather than on form and structure; remedial reading on the elementary and secondary level; and the improvement of speech in all grades.

19. There was a sharp rise in the output of guides for the librarian or teacher of library practice. There appeared to be an increased emphasis upon the role of the library as an inseparable part of the total pattern of learning.

20. There was a sharp increase in the output of teaching guides in arithmetic for the elementary grades. The tendency to make number experiences more functional continued to increase. A marked trend toward experimentation and flexibility in mathematics for secondary schools with emphasis upon usefulness in life was shown in the last few years.

21. There was a sharp rise in the publication of teaching guides in elementary music during the last triennium. Increasing recognition was

given to the belief that music should be used to enrich and vitalize other subjects.

22. Science for the junior high school stressed aspects of everyday living such as *keeping well* and *weather*. On the senior high school level the guides were devoted to the separate treatment of biology, chemistry, and physics. Several systems published parallel courses for those who intend to go to college and those who do not.

23. The organization of courses in the social studies into large teaching units continued to have the increasing acceptance of curriculum planners. The sequence of the social studies in the first six grades was based upon the expansion of the horizons of the learner, beginning with home and school and culminating in a view of the world.

24. There was a marked increase of interest in the teaching of Spanish and French to children in the elementary grades in the last three years. A conversational approach to the teaching of language was emphasized in some of the guides.

25. The quadrupled output of guides over the preceding triennium was an indication of a recent upsurge of interest in the education of the exceptional child. Each publication was a specialized treatment with greatest emphasis upon the speech- and hearing-handicapped, the mentally retarded, and the mentally superior child.

26. The organization of the long-range program of curriculum development was taking hold in several of the larger school systems that maintained divisions of curriculum and in some smaller school systems that employed a curriculum director. These systems published several successive bulletins to give continuing guidance to the teachers.

While Merritt and Harap noted a trend toward the production of curriculum guides which stress curriculum continuity for grades 1–12, provision for proper articulation between different school levels is still a problem. In an attempt to bring about closer articulation between the elementary school and the high school, Swenson stresses the need for teachers and administrators: (*a*) to recognize the objectives common to all grades of the twelve-year school, (*b*) to discover principles of child development and learning which are applicable at all levels, and (*c*) to gain a knowledge of the total twelve-year program in order to provide for proper continuity and sequence of learning experiences. The achievement of the three objectives just described can take place only through appropriate pre-service and in-service education of teachers. [33:281–288]

Although the original proponents of the junior high school movement maintained a number of advantages for an intermediate school, provision for better articulation between the elementary school and the high school has often been given as a strong point for the junior high school. Yet, some argue that the junior high school has failed in its function of making possible a smooth transition of the elementary pupil from the elementary to the secondary school and that too often the junior high school has become only a miniature copy of its big brother, the senior high school. It has even been proposed by Schutter [31:51–54] that the seventh and eighth grades might very well be abolished in favor of a six-year elementary school and a four-year high school. Thus undesirable repetition would be eliminated, college entrance would be accelerated, and teacher and building shortages would be alleviated.

The most critical point of articulation in the American educational ladder is the transition from high school to college. In an editorial introducing a "Symposium on College Admission Requirements" in the January, 1953, *California Journal of Secondary Education,* Bush points out difficulties involved in the relationships between high schools and colleges—such as the tendency for lower schools to be considered as *preparatory* schools by higher schools and the prescription of courses for admission by colleges—and makes proposals for improving the situation.

Editorial: The High Schools and the Colleges

by ROBERT N. BUSH

From *California Journal of Secondary Education,* Vol. 28, No. 1 (January, 1953), pages 1–5. Reprinted by special permission. Robert N. Bush is editor of the *Journal* and Professor of Education, Stanford University.

The high schools are acutely sensitive about their relationships with the colleges and universities which hold great prestige and power in the educational family. Even though the high schools are maligned by employers for poorly preparing young employees for the rigors of business and industrial life and by the elementary schools for being too restrictive and subject-matter centered to provide for the needs of the pupils who come from the lower grades, they appear less concerned about such criticisms than when the colleges question the preparation of high school pupils for academic work. How the graduates of Midvalley High School fare in the English X examination at the university and the quality of their scholastic record as freshmen at the colleges to which they go, are among the most frequent ways in which the quality of the high school program is judged.

College admission requirements, the subject of the symposium in the *Journal* this month, have become a focal point of discussion in the broader field of school-college relations. One of the most vocal criticisms leveled at the high school is that while on the whole only a small, though increasing, proportion of its pupils go on to college, a major portion of its attention and resource is directed toward meeting the needs of this minor group. When so criticized for not providing an educational program more suitable to the needs of all of its students, the argument most frequently advanced by the high school is the restrictive demand of the admission requirements of the colleges and universities. The problem is accentuated by the fact that a single high school, however small, must provide a curriculum sufficiently broad to enable each graduate who plans to attend college to satisfy the course requirements for admission to any one of a variety of higher institutions. Requirements for admission and the ensuing academic standards vary so greatly from institution to institution that the high school is confronted with a bewilder-

ing complexity. The smaller the high school, the more difficult the task. And it must be remembered that the small is still the typical high school.

Can the purposes and views of the colleges and the high schools be so divergent as their discussions at times suggest? Are they not both interested in the best possible education for each student? What are the sources of the difficulties in their relationships?

Part of the problem is the perennial one that characterizes the relationships between any two educational units and stems from the nature of the hierarchy between them. Each lower school is a *preparatory* school for the next higher one. The chief interest of the higher school in the lower one is in this preparatory function. While the lower school is also interested in its preparatory function, its major concern is with what it can do for all of its students at the time. It is an unfortunate but tenacious practice for the higher to blame the lower school for what it considers to be glaring inadequacies in the preparation of entering pupils. This protective reaction is an easy psychological habit to fall into. "What can you expect from us," the middle school asks, "when we receive such poorly prepared students from the lower school?" It is unlikely that this tendency will ever disappear entirely, although its shrinkage may be anticipated as educators assume increased scientific and professional objectivity in their work. There is already a noticeable shift in the attitude of the high school toward the elementary school. Recognizing the facts of individual differences, the high school educator not only accepts, but expects pupils from elementary schools to vary in their capacities and attainment; he is willing to begin with them where they are and take them as far as possible in the allotted time. This attitude is beginning to be expressed toward high schools by junior colleges and to a limited extent by the state colleges. It may be expected that it will slowly permeate all educational levels.

Another source of difficulty in the relations between the high schools and the colleges clusters around the practice of the higher institutions to require a prescribed set of courses for admission. Whether or not with intent, this practice places the college in a position of powerful control over the curriculum of the high school. It is responsible for the cry of "dictation" by the secondary educator. Throughout the nation there is a marked trend away from requiring a set pattern of courses for admission to college. This is the result of the weight of a considerable body of research data which has failed to establish the superiority of any particular course pattern as preparation for successful college work and the insistent demand of the high schools that, knowing best their own pupils and situations, they should be freed from the external authority of the higher institutions. It is too early to determine whether or not this shift from course requirements will bring any fundamental change in the secondary school because it has been under way such a short time, and has not even been felt appreciably in some parts of the country. On the one hand are those who claim that the high schools neither use the freedom which they now have nor want more, but rather are pleased to have such an honorable and impenetrable defense for their lethargy. Others are of the opinion that specific course requirements for college admission constitute one of the greatest single blocks to the improvement of secondary education and that without their removal no fundamental progress can be made. In this regard the action of the University of California of December 6, 1952, as reported by Dr. Spindt on page 34 of this issue of the *Journal*, is of particular interest. [Ed. note: Briefly, the University will admit a student who has not followed the required pattern of subjects if he has a "B" average scholarship and if his program has "been previously filed with and approved by the Board of Admissions and Relations with Schools." This is an experimental plan for the years 1953–1959.]

Since the colleges and universities include older, more mature students than the high schools, select intellectually superior students, and have responsibility for the production of intellectually disciplined practitioners in the various professions, they appropriately take a more intellectual approach to education than either the elementary or the high schools. This partly explains the direction of their influence upon the high schools, for they reason that the best preparation for college will be under circumstances that are as nearly like those in college as possible. This means preoccupation with things intellectual in a curriculum that in content, organization, and presentation closely parallels that of the higher institution. Accordingly the colleges are inclined to be alarmed over such dominant trends in the curriculum of the modern high school as the increased emphasis upon the fine arts, crafts, and "practical" subjects, at the seeming expense, for example, of foreign language. Mathematics, physics, English composition, and Latin are considered to be much more appropriate college-preparatory subjects than, for example, typewriting, music, speech, and physical education, and consequently deserving of a favored place in the school program. That grades in some subjects correlate more highly with college success than do grades in other subjects should not lead to the assumption of a necessarily causal relationship. Moreover, the making of a whole man, whose intellectual, emotional, and physical components are developed harmoniously, is the objective of a truly liberal or general education, which is the concern of both the high school and the college. In this view, it may be that the colleges

themselves have been too one-sided in their programs and should perhaps be less disposed to make over the high schools in their own image. A better relationship would undoubtedly exist between the colleges and the high schools if the former would recognize that the pupils in the lower school are different from those in the college in their maturity, needs, and purposes, and that therefore the program, even for the college-bound student, may need to be of a different character from that offered by the colleges.

A distinction should be made between the problem arising at the transition from elementary to secondary school and that appearing at the end of secondary education where the situation is more emotionally laden. In the first instance, practically all of the students are required by law to continue in school, and the secondary institution is required by law to accept from the lower school all but a few who are clearly unfit. More vigorous, albeit hidden, selective processes begin to operate even before the end of secondary school and become openly recognized and competitive by the beginning of college. Those who are to attend institutions of higher learning must be selected. Since this is a critical decision from the standpoint both of the individual and of society every effort should be directed toward improving selection procedures. We have increasingly made clear our national decision that the selection of students for college shall not be on the basis of birthplace, economic circumstance, race, sex, or creed. Higher education, in one form or another, the citizens of the United States have decided, should be available to all who want and are able to profit from it. This new experiment in the world reflects our pioneering tradition and our abiding democratic faith in the power and value of education. This decision, however, imposes upon us heavy responsibilities in determining the most perceptive means rather than clinging to the most *traditional* methods of selecting those who are most able to profit from the opportunities of a higher education.

In selecting students for admission to college, multiple, rather than single, criteria are proving to be the more useful. A combination of overall grade average in high school, the results of tested achievement and scholastic aptitude, and the recommendation of school officials who know the pupil well, has yielded the highest results. Rewarding new ventures in predicting college success may be forthcoming by experimenting with tests of performance in simulated life situations, and devising creative methods for assessing the strength and direction of the motivating forces of adolescents.

Unprecedented increases in enrollment during the next decades face both the high schools and the colleges in California. This requires that each critically analyze its problems

and plan constructively for the future. In so doing, the relationship between the systems of secondary and higher education must be considered, for new patterns will certainly be required as the two expand to include new groups and interests. The symposium in the *Journal* this month has been designed to assist in the discussion of the one phase of this problem which is of such vital concern to secondary educators and, we believe, also the higher institutions. Stressed throughout is the necessity for all of the high schools and all of the collegiate institutions to become better acquainted and to work more closely together.

Do the high schools have the freedom they wish in shaping their educational program? Do they use the freedom they now have? Do the colleges allow the high schools as much freedom as is consistent with the highest type of preparation and bases for selection? While the answers to these questions are probably negative, there is evidence of substantial progress toward greater freedom and mutual respect between the colleges and the high schools. They both have important opportunities and responsibilities as they face the future.

The *higher institutions* have two important avenues through which they may work. One is in the direction of encouraging the high school to fashion a program of its own design rather than a replica in content or method of the college. The other is in the participation of all departments in the university in preparing the best possible teachers for the great demand that is imminent. The directing influence of the leadership of the colleges and universities upon the high schools in the next decade cannot be underestimated.

The *high schools* can continue to examine themselves and to build a strong functional program for all of their students, strengthening their guidance programs so that *each* student receives the type of preparation that will best fit him for the road ahead. Rather than ascribe present inadequacies to domination from the outside, they might well take courage from the achievements of the past and become even more constructive in meeting the challenges of the next decades.

In the same issue of the *Journal* quoted above, Cosand [10:12–18] analyzes nine criteria for admission to college, as indicated by the literature on the subject. Five of the most important ones are: average high school grade; rank in high school graduating class; entrance tests; recommendations of principal, counselor, and teacher; and personal interview. The use of multiple criteria, rather than of a single criterion, is gaining acceptance.

In making a study of "College Entrance Requirements Ten Years After the Eight-year Study," on the basis of returns from 138 liberal arts colleges, Emanuel concluded that college entrance requirements have become more liberal and that "secondary schools may no longer hide behind the smoke screen of college-entrance demands but should be encouraged to provide functional education for all youth."[13:526]

Other problems of continuity in public education, which have not been solved, deserve mention. Too often, especially in high school, there is a lack of articulation between subjects or subject-matter departments even at the same grade level. Furthermore, there is a danger at all school levels of a lack of articulation between school experiences and those of the outside community.

Another problem which administrators face in providing continuity in curriculum planning is related to teacher turnover. "Half of the young men and women who began teaching in the United States last year expect to stop teaching within five years, according to an Office of Education survey" (reported in the *Phi Delta Kappan,* December, 1957, page 94). Furthermore, "only 28 per cent of the men and 14 per cent of the women" plan to make classroom teaching their lifework. Without a more or less permanent staff of teachers dedicated to teaching as a career, provision for continuity in curriculum planning becomes a discouraging proposition.

Related to the task of defining the scope and sequence of learning experiences, as well as to the articulation difficulties discussed above, is the matter of curriculum organization or design. Saylor and Alexander define *design* as "the pattern or framework or structural organization used in selecting, planning, and carrying forward educational experiences in the school." [30:245]

In the June, 1957, *Review of Educational Research,* Herrick has identified the following curriculum patterns or designs: "subject, broad fields, problems of living, and emerging needs approaches of the elementary school, and the subject and core curriculum approaches at the secondary-school level." [3:270] Two of these patterns, the subject and the core, have already been discussed in Part Two, pages 239–252. In the June, 1954, *Review of Educational Research,* Saylor indicates that, while there was great activity in the preparation of guides for designing the curriculum in the 1930's, such guides have been prepared by few local or state systems in recent years. He does believe, however, that there is as much experimentation and effort as ever to improve curriculum design with school systems working cooperatively and involving the entire staff. [4:204–213]

In his study of "Patterns of Curriculum Organization in Large Secondary Schools," based on responses from 252 high schools, Brink concluded that, although "all the schools provide either a multiple or constants-and-variable type of organization," programs vary considerably in scope, number of specialized curricula, and number of courses provided, in depth, and in objectives, usually stated in quantitative terms, if at all. [8:377]

CONTRIBUTIONS OF RESEARCH TO CURRICULUM PLANNING

The scientific study of educational problems dates back less than a century, but in that time considerable research has been done, especially in certain areas, such as reading, for example. Every three years the *Review of Educational Research* summarizes the research in curriculum development, supplemented by reviews of research in related areas, such as instructional materials and subject-matter fields.

There is an evident swelling tide of opinion that more application of research findings needs to be made to learning experiences in the classroom. However, numerous obstacles to the implementation of research have been indicated by Cooper [9], Johnson [19], Shane [32], and others.

Three barriers to the use of research findings in the classroom that are often cited are the following: (*a*) the extent and quality of research pertaining to the curriculum; (*b*) failure on the part of teachers, as well as administrators, to make use of known research findings; and (*c*) insufficient evaluation of the effectiveness of research.

The first problem relates to the extent and quality of research. In the *Review of Educational Research* for June, 1957, Fleming concludes that "there is almost a frightening scarcity of research in curriculum." [3:300] Other reports on the present status of curriculum research serve to substantiate the above conclusion.

In the April, 1953, *Review of Educational Research,* Sowards and Stendler state that the research literature lacks "studies of content for the elementary school designed to answer the basic question: What should children study in the elementary school? Research and discussion have instead centered on the *process* of curriculum development rather than on the *content* of the curriculum." [5:158] In this connection the reader may refer to the criticism of content of elementary-school readers made by Thompson and Rafferty, page 199.

At the secondary-school level, Gilchrist and Dutton indicate in the February, 1954, *Review of Educational Research* areas which have been almost entirely neglected by research workers. In their "concluding statement" they make this generalization: "The reviewers found most research studies to be in the area of the communication skills. As has been previously stated, there is need for much more research in terms of other specific objectives of secondary education. Research studies were rather piecemeal and did not give good coverage of all main objectives of secondary education. Some areas were almost entirely neglected." *

In reviewing twenty-five years of educational research, Cook, Hovet,

---

* From American Educational Research Association, "The Educational Program: Adolescence," *Review of Educational Research,* 24:49 (February, 1954). Quoted by special permission of the Association and the authors. Robert S. Gilchrist is Superintendent of Schools, University City, Missouri. Wilbur H. Dutton is Associate Professor of Elementary Education, University of California (Los Angeles).

and Kearney report in the June, 1956, *Review of Educational Research* that curriculum research since 1931 has been "piecemeal, specialized, repetitive, prosaic, or lacking in pertinence or philosophical background." [6:225]

A second problem in educational research relates to application of findings to the classroom. Why do teachers, as well as administrators, not make more use of the results of research in their work? These reasons are often cited: lack of familiarity with research reports; technical vocabulary used in reporting results; difficulty experienced in applying results to practical situations; and lack of time and energy on the part of teachers and administrators, whose efforts are channeled into diverse activities.

In discussing research as a means to curriculum change, Russell and Parker remind the reader that many factors influence curriculum change—tradition, educational philosophies, social aims and patterns, instructional materials, school organization, and teachers. They then proceed to suggest helpful teacher guides to six areas of educational research—the learning process, growth and development, functional curriculum, individual capacity and achievement, group procedures and dynamics, instructional materials—and indicate a number of ways to implement "research knowledge." They conclude that "using research to point the way in curriculum change is a cooperative endeavor involving many talents." [29:276]

Emphasis upon the role of the classroom teacher and the local setting in research is made by Fleming when he makes the point that "research carried on locally should become the key to selection of curriculum content." In the same article Fleming summarizes the research procedures which can be used as a basis for the selection of curriculum content.

Procedures in Research   by ROBERT S. FLEMING

From Robert S. Fleming, "Research Procedures in the Selection of Curriculum Content," *Educational Leadership,* Vol. 13, No. 7 (April, 1956), pages 404–405. Reprinted by special permission of the editor of ASCD publications and of the author. Robert S. Fleming is Professor of Education and Chairman of Early Childhood and Elementary Education, New York University.

Throughout this article an effort has been made to show that many research procedures which aid in identifying student problems and needs are relatively simple and easy to execute. By and large, it becomes a logical and systematic approach to evaluation. Actually, the identification of goals, problems, and curriculum activities is an initial phase of the evaluation process. In sizing up pupils (either as groups or as individuals), the following "research" procedures seem reasonable and can serve as a basis for selecting curriculum content:

1. *Assessment of pupils' academic needs.* This may be done by such activities as:
   a. The use of standardized tests given early in the year (by teachers to their pupils)
   b. Analysis of pupil performance
   c. Analysis of products of students' work
   d. Systematic interviews with other teachers who are currently working with the pupils
   e. Analysis of existing school records and conferences with teachers who prepared such records for clarification and specific information
   f. A series of observations of pupils' performance by principal, supervisors, and parents followed by appropriate summary conferences with the teacher and pupils
2. *Assessment of pupils' interests, attitudes, values*
   a. Observation of students' responses to specific situations
   b. Analysis of a series of writing assignments in which students discuss their feelings, concerns, beliefs
   c. Use of existing tests, such as:
      (1) Interest Index
      (2) Science Research Associates, *What I Like to Do*
3. *Assessment of pupils' emotional needs*
   a. The Wishing Well
   b. Self-portrait
   c. Long, Long Ago
4. *Assessment of youth problems*
   a. Mooney *Problem Check List* (Junior or Senior High form)
   b. Science Research Associates, *Youth Inventory*
5. *Assessment of pupils' skill in critical thinking*
   a. Watson-Glaser, *Critical Thinking Appraisal*
   b. Interpretation of data (various forms)
   c. Logical reasoning
6. *Assessment of pupils' work habits*
   a. Observation in a variety of situations
   b. Science Research Associates, *Can You Find the Answers?*
7. *Assessment of problems of a particular community*
   a. Summary of existing studies
   b. Survey of certain aspects of community life
   c. Pooling of findings from existing resources (agriculture agent, Health Department, occupational studies, etc.)
8. *Analysis of life demands of children and youth in the community*
   a. Analysis of employment opportunities of students
   b. Analysis of home responsibilities
   c. Analysis of community activities
   d. Analysis of school activities
9. *Assessment of past school experience of the group*
   a. Analysis of school records
   b. Analysis of student responses

c. Analysis of conferences with other teachers

d. Analysis of parent interviews

10. *Assessment of available resources for curriculum enrichment*

    a. Identification of competencies available in faculty, parent group, and student body

    b. Inventory of vital centers for industry or for facilitating industry in the area

    c. Inventory of historical spots and people in the community who know them

    d. Survey of library resources, educational situations and agencies

11. *Assessment of major research concerning characteristics of the particular age group with which one works*

12. *Assessment of findings of studies of our society and needs and demands it imposes upon effective participation therein*

The suggested procedures listed above are merely illustrative of approaches to the selection of content. Such procedures are dignified as "research" *to the extent that teachers employ systematic, comprehensive, and objective procedures* in these activities. Results of one test certainly cannot be viewed as a comprehensive accumulation of data. Yet, if such data are carefully collected, with results viewed as an hypothesis, and validated by subsequent findings, one could have more faith in the process.

In spite of all the procedures listed, doubtless teachers must place greatest weight on a careful and systematic assessment of what they *observe* and what they *hear* from their students.

Perhaps one of the most significant aspects of the research potential in identifying content for students is that of recording carefully what was done, bases for such activity, and descriptions of progress made. Without such an activity, the process is often lost and future teachers must begin all over again.

Such an approach to curriculum development is often confusing to teachers since it is developmental and hence one cannot block out an entire year's work in advance. Also it is confusing since many supervisors and principals still adhere to a procedure which is outlined and described as "standard" for a particular grade. This calls for careful involvement of such people in the process. It also calls for continuously interpreting the procedure to all concerned.

Teaching in today's school is an exciting experience. We used to start our automobiles with a crank and primer. Research in technology has brought striking changes in automobiles. Often we fail to recognize that research in the curriculum field has brought about changes which are even more striking. Research activities carried on locally should become the key for the selection of curriculum content.

In an editorial introducing the May, 1955, issue of *Educational Leadership,* Ahrens further emphasizes the fact that changes in the curriculum as a result of research depend upon a cooperative, "grass-roots" approach, involving teacher participation.

Editorial: Leadership for Curriculum Research

by MAURICE R. AHRENS

From *Educational Leadership,* Vol. 12, No. 8 (May, 1955), pages 450–452. Reprinted by special permission of the Association for Supervision and Curriculum Development and the author. Maurice R. Ahrens is Professor of Education and Head of Elementary Education, University of Florida.

Most of the curriculum improvement programs of the past and many which are being carried on today are based upon the assumption that an individual or a few individuals can plan and develop curricula for the use of teachers in the classroom. Our belief in this assumption is reflected in our willingness to accept as valid experiences for children what is written in textbooks and courses of study and by our mute approval of the "gospel" expounded by curriculum specialists, administrators, and other so-called experts. It is not uncommon for schools and school systems to develop courses of study, teaching guides, and other curriculum materials by selecting what appears to be the best from materials produced in other school systems. Neither is it unusual for a school system to permit and encourage the curriculum staff, the administrative staff, small groups of teachers, or an outside curriculum specialist to determine the experiences which its teachers will carry on with children in the classroom.

When this approach to curriculum improvement is used it is evident that the leadership is completely oblivious of the processes involved in helping teachers to improve their practices in the classroom. Changes in the curriculum involve, first and foremost, changes in the thinking and behavior of teachers. This means at least two things—that the problems which are of concern to teachers should be the focus of a curriculum improvement program and, in addition, that the teachers concerned should be provided the opportunity to participate in the solution of these problems.

Since changes in the thinking and practices of teachers are more certain to take place if teachers participate actively in the solution of problems which are of concern to them, it is important and necessary that curriculum planning be a cooperative enterprise. There is, however, one other essential procedure—that of testing the solution of problems and plans of action in real classroom situations. Too often we are guilty of implementing "paper" plans without setting up ways of evaluating the degree to which the plan of action has resulted in the achievement of the objectives.

A Frontier Movement

Cooperative curriculum research which involves application of scientific methods of problem solving, participation in the solution of problems of all who are concerned, and testing of the solutions against the realities of the classroom or school program is still in its infancy. Although there is much experimentation yet to be done, this comparatively new scientific procedure offers much promise for the improvement of school programs. It is worthy of trial by all who are interested in better education for children and youth.

Whether cooperative research becomes the usual and accepted procedure in curriculum development depends, to a great extent, upon the leadership in public schools and in teacher training institutions. Where leadership involves a quest for power, a struggle for self-approval, a drive for security at the expense of others, and a greed for achieving personal motives and goals, there is little possibility for a research approach to curriculum improvement. Moreover, the leader who is skilled in group dynamics and understands his role as a leader but does not have the "know-how" in cooperative research procedures may thwart teachers and others in their efforts to improve in their work with children. The need, then, is for leaders who are sensitive to the needs of teachers, who have relatively stable personalities, who work democratically with teachers in assisting them to solve problems and achieve goals which they feel are important and significant, and who are conversant with the concepts and techniques of cooperative research.

* * *

ACTION RESEARCH

All of the preceding articles stressing a local, "grass-roots" approach to curriculum planning with more participation by classroom teachers point the way to a type of research known as *action research*. A number of definitions of action research have appeared in current literature. One clear, concise definition is the following description of action research by Taba and Noel: "Action research, as the term is used in this booklet, is that research which is carried on by educational practitioners to solve their own problems. Thus defined, it means, first, that such research deals with problems of immediate concern to teachers and curriculum workers. It means, second, that research is a co-operative enterprise in which practitioners and research technicians together decide what to study and how to go about it." *

After analyzing several definitions of action research, some of which seem to be synonymous with such terms as "the evaluative process" or "in-service training," Wiles raises a number of incisive questions about the distinctive characteristics of this type of research. [36:408–410, 432]

In summarizing a more complete treatise on the subject, appearing in book form, Corey further clarifies the meaning of action research and suggests the potential values it has in improving school practices.

Action Research in Education   by STEPHEN M. COREY

From the *Journal of Educational Research,* Volume 47 (January, 1954), pages 375–380. Reprinted by special permission of the editor and the author. Stephen M. Corey is Dean of Teachers College, Columbia University. A more complete coverage of "action research" is contained in Corey's *Action Research to Improve School Practices* (New York: Bureau of Publications, Teachers College, Columbia University, 1953).

Action research in education is research undertaken by practitioners in order that they may improve their practices. The people who actually teach children or supervise teachers or administer school systems attempt to solve their practical problems by using the methods of science. They accumulate evidence to define their problems more sharply. They draw upon all of the experience available to them as a source for action hy-potheses that give promise of enabling them to ameliorate or eliminate the practical difficulties of their day by day work. They test out these promising procedures on the job, and again accumulate the best evidence they can of their effectiveness. They try to generalize as carefully as possible in order that their research will contribute to the solution of future problems or the elimination of future difficulties that they face in

* From Hilda Taba and Elizabeth Noel, *Action Research: A Case Study,* Association for Supervision and Curriculum Development, a Department of the National Education Association, March, 1957, pp. 1–2. Quoted by special permission of the Association and the authors. Hilda Taba is Professor of Education at San Francisco State College. Elizabeth Noel is Curriculum Coordinator of Washington Unified School District, West Sacramento, California.

their teaching or supervision or administration.[1]

The practice of conducting research in order to improve decisions and practices that have to do with practical educational activities is not new. The term "action research," however, is relatively recent,[2] and was first used by Collier,[3] and Lewin and his students.[4] Action research means much the same thing as "operational research," which was the name applied to a type of inquiry undertaken by various planning groups during the Second World War.[5] In education a great deal of the work done by the evaluation staff of the Eight-Year Study is closely anal-

ogous to action research.[6] Herrick[7] was referring to the same kind of inquiry when he cited the advantages of cooperative curriculum studies over curriculum surveys. The recent summary of Taba and associates[8] of the work of the intergroup education project of the American Council on Education describes numerous action research studies of interpersonal relations.

One of the psychological values in action research is that the people who must, by the very nature of their professional responsibilities, learn to improve their practices are the ones who engage in the research to learn what represents improvement. They,

[1] Tress Banks, Edgar S. Farley, Oscar Powers, Floyd Vandermeer, Robert Waldorf, and Stephen M. Corey, "We Tested Some Beliefs about the Biographical Method," *The School Review,* 59:157–163, March, 1951. A. Wellesley Foshay and James A. Hall, "Experimentation Moves into the Classroom," *Teachers College Record,* 51:353–359, March, 1950. Mary Neel Smith, "Action Research to Improve Teacher Planning Meetings," *The School Review,* 60:142–150, March, 1952. Kenneth D. Wann, "Teachers as Researchers," *Educational Leadership,* 9:489–495, May, 1952. Kenneth D. Wann, *Teacher Participation in Action Research Directed Toward Curriculum Change,* Ed.D. Project Report (Typewritten) (New York: Teachers College, Columbia University, 1950), 240 p.

[2] Isidor Chien, Stuart W. Cook, and John Harding, "The Field of Action Research," *The American Psychologist,* 3:43–50, February, 1948.

[3] John Collier, "United States Indian Administration as a Laboratory of Ethnic Relations," *Social Research,* 12:265–313, May, 1945.

[4] Kurt Lewin, *Resolving Social Conflicts* (New York: Harper & Brothers, 1948), 230 p. Ronald Lippitt, *Training in Community Relations* (New York: Harper & Brothers, 1949), ix, x, 21 f.

[5] Committee on Operations Research, *Operations Research with Special Reference to Non-military Operations* (Washington, D. C.: National Research Council, April, 1951), 12 p.

[6] Eugene R. Smith, Ralph W. Tyler, and the evaluation staff, *Appraising and Recording Student Progress* (New York: Harper & Brothers, 1942), 550 p.

[7] Virgil E. Herrick, "The Survey Versus the Cooperative Study," *Educational Administration and Supervision,* 34:449–458, December, 1948.

[8] Hilda Taba, Elizabeth Hall Brady, and John T. Robinson, *Intergroup Education in Public Schools* (Washington, D. C.: American Council on Education, 1952), 337 p.

rather than someone else, try out new and seemingly more promising ways of teaching or supervising or administering, and they study the consequences. There are two alternatives to action research as a method of improving educational practices. One is a procedure that most of us commonly resort to as we try to do our own jobs more adequately. Under the pressures of our work, we are disposed to change, if at all, on the basis of subjective impressions as to what our problems are. And with a minimum of emphasis on reality testing or the accumulation of relatively objective evidence, we form judgments about the consequences of our attempted improvements.[9] As Lundberg has said, ". . . the scientific mode of thought is very recent in human affairs, . . . is practiced by only a small percentage of our own generation, and . . . is uncongenial to a large number of otherwise admirable people."[10]

The second alternative to action research is to ask the professional educational investigator to study our problems and to tell us what to do. There are two basic difficulties with this alternative. In the first place, the professional investigator can never study our problems in any strict sense. They are unique to the situations in which we are working, and we ourselves are part of the problem. A second limitation is that even when the recommendations make sense to us as we read them, we have great difficulty getting these recommendations into our behavior patterns.[11] We find it relatively easy to talk a better type of teaching or supervising or administering as a consequence of reading or hearing what others say that we should do. But there is a vast difference between this modification in our vocabularies and any substantial modification in the way we behave. An integral part of action research is our actual practice of the procedures that give *a priori* promise of enabling us to cope more effectively with our professional problems.

Probably the major difference between action research and the more traditional type of educational research has to do with the motivation of the investigators. In fundamental research, the basic motivation is to conduct an inquiry that will result in generalizations of broad applicability. In a real sense, the traditional educational researcher is motivated by his desire to arrive at the truth. If he is cautious and circumspect this truth is usually reported in relation to certain conceptions about proba-

---

[9] Stephen M. Corey, "Educational Research and the Solution of Practical Problems," *Educational Leadership,* 9:478–484, May, 1952.

[10] George A. Lundberg, *Can Science Save Us?* (New York: Longmans, Green and Company, 1947), p. 13.

[11] Paul R. Mort and Francis G. Cornell, *American Schools in Transition* (New York: Bureau of Publications, Teachers College, Columbia University, 1941), p. 53.

bility. But to the degree that the investigation results in generalizations of the widest applicability, it is considered to be excellent research.

In considerable contrast to this kind of motivation, those who engage in action research, as has been said, are conducting their inquiries primarily because they wish to improve their own practices. Action research is conducted in the heat of combat, so to speak. It is conducted by teachers or supervisors or administrators in order that they may have evidence as to whether or not they are accomplishing the things that they hope to accomplish.

The differences in investigational methodology between traditional research and action research are minor. Each type of investigator attempts to define the problem being studied with precision, to derive his hypotheses from as rich a background of information related to the problem as possible, to design an inquiry in such a way as to result in a genuine test of the hypothesis, to use facts or evidence throughout the research procedure rather than subjective impression, and to generalize cautiously and tentatively from the evidence collected. The situational circumstances under which the traditional investigator or action researcher carries out this process of inquiry, however, may differ appreciably. By various techniques the traditional investigator in education tries to exercise control over a situation so that many of the variables involved in real life teaching or supervising or administrating are ruled out by definition or by laboratory control. This practice results in a more definitive test of the stated hypotheses. But this precision is gained with a comparable loss in applicability of findings. People who conduct action research conduct their inquiries in the complicated psycho-sociological climate of ongoing school activities. Because of the multiplicity of variables involved in these real situations, the action research inquiry is often lacking in precision, but in compensation it is realistic. The results have meaning for practice because they are a consequence of inquiry under lifelike circumstances.

Whether the research be traditional or action oriented, its quality must be viewed in relative terms. It is possible to progress by small increments of improvements in procedure from the casual and impressionistic method that most of us use to cope with our practical difficulties to a methodology which is rather scrupulously scientific.[12] In the degree that we are able to incorporate these increments of improvement in our action-research methodology, we can have increasing confidence in the inference and generalizations that we draw from our research data.

These improvements in method of inquiry can characterize any aspect

[12] Corey, *op. cit.*

of the total process of research. To expect to leap all at once from the method most of us employ as we try to do a better job to a method that incorporates the best scientific procedures is unrealistic. But to improve gradually requires little more than a commitment to the method of science as a way of coping with practical difficulties and a willingness to take the chances that are always involved in experimentation. This commitment to the method of science is more apt to result from the persuasion of events than from the persuasion of other men. In the last analysis, it must be the more dependable consequences of scientific problem solving that argue most strongly for this method of coping with practical problems. These consequences are available for evaluation only when the scientific method is used. The best way to learn how to conduct action research, as well as the values it possesses, is to try it.

Action research in the field of education need not involve the cooperative activities of a number of people, but in most instances that is highly desirable. The reason is that a great many of the improvements that need to be made in teaching or supervising or administration cannot be brought about unless a number of people modify their perceptions and their practices and their points of view.[13] Because this is the case, as many as possible of the people who will be affected by attempts to better a difficult situation should be involved in the action research on which the attempts are based. The cooperative efforts of all of these people will tend to result in better problem definition, a more realistic consideration of the numerous possible action hypotheses, easier translating of these hypotheses into action, and a more adequate understanding of the meaning of the evidence that is procured to test them.[14]

Making action research cooperative in the above sense introduces all of the complications that are involved in group work. In few areas of human activity have precedents become more firmly entrenched. They have even been codified in manuals of rules of order for group meetings. For cooperative action research to be maximally effective, members of the working group must feel free to introduce modifications in their methods of procedure.[15] Their ways of working must be appropriate to the job they are working on, and they must have numerous opportunities to try out and evaluate group procedures that give promise of increasing productivity.

If the quality of the methods now

[13] Alice Miel, *Changing the Curriculum: A Social Process* (New York: D. Appleton-Century Company, Inc., 1946), 242 p.

[14] G. Robert Koopman, Alice Miel, and Paul J. Misner, *Democracy in School Administration* (New York: D. Appleton-Century Company, Inc., 1943), 330 p.

[15] Floyd C. Mann, "Human Relations Skills in Social Research," *Human Relations,* Vol. 4, No. 4 (1951), pp. 341–354.

being employed by teachers and supervisors and administrators to improve their practices is to be bettered, there must be considerable change in the working environment and atmosphere of most school systems. Whether or not these changes will be effected, whether or not conditions will be established that are conducive to action research as a method of improvement, depends largely on things that the status leader is in the best position to accomplish.[16] It is the school superintendents, principals, and supervisors who can do most to make it possible for school people to admit and discuss their own professional limitations, to hypothesize creatively and insightfully, to have the facilities and consultative help that are needed if these seemingly promising innovations are to be identified and put into practice, to get the best possible evidence on the consequences of these changes, and to derive from this evidence generalizations that are sound and provide helpful guides to future behavior.

There is considerable reason for believing that research methodology will not begin to have the influence on American education that it might have until thousands of teachers, administrators, supervisors, and school patrons make more frequent use of the methods of science as they cope with their own practical problems. In the last analysis, action research in education is no more than attempting to solve practical school problems by using research methods.

In further support of action research, Foshay makes the point that curriculum *change* can be brought about in a number of ways—by means of "committee decision," "faculty vote," or "legislation"—but *improvements* are more likely to take place when teachers themselves use research methods. [15:265–266]

In agreement with Corey's comment (page 343) that action research, in practice, is not new, since the background for it appears in the work of Lewin and Collier, Foshay and Green point out, however, that the concept has recently been refined by the Horace Mann–Lincoln Institute of School Experimentation group, notably by Corey. [4:248]

Today, a good many educators are convinced that action research, in spite of present confusion concerning the concept, offers considerable promise as an approach to curriculum improvement. In order to further clarify the process and make it more effective in action, Foshay and Goodson point out the need for curriculum workers to observe certain principles or conditions, such as "testing by reality," making

[16] Stephen M. Corey, "Conditions Conducive to Curricular Experimentation," *Educational Administration and Supervision*, 36:209–216, April, 1950.

personal values explicit, recognizing the role of cultural values, modifying certain cultural stereotypes, and producing principles of action.

Some Reflections on Cooperative Action Research
by ARTHUR W. FOSHAY and MAX R. GOODSON

From *Educational Leadership,* Volume 10, No. 7 (April, 1953), pages 411–418. Reprinted by special permission of the Association for Supervision and Curriculum Development and the authors. Arthur W. Foshay is Professor of Education, Teachers College, Columbia University, and Executive Secretary of the Horace Mann–Lincoln Institute of School Experimentation. Max R. Goodson is Dean of the School of Education, Boston University.

Cooperative action research is the name of a process intended to improve action systematically. In this paper, we wish to state and elaborate certain concepts that must be clarified as this process continues to be studied. We shall place certain terms in relationship: reality, valuing, cultural expectations, and the development of principles.

Testing by Reality

Cooperative action research is an approach to making what we do consistent with what we believe. It is an attempt to deduce what is necessary to improve a real situation through a systematic examination of the situation itself. It cannot, therefore, be planned in the absence of a real situation; it must function in the presence of reality. The research pattern evolves as teacher and consultant test their perceptions of a real situation against data obtained from the situation itself. In this sense, cooperative action research is constantly tested by reality.

One's notion of what is real is compounded from one's values, as they operate, and whatever preconceptions concerning what is real one has accumulated. Thus, one's perception of the school curriculum is heavily influenced by personal values, and also by what one has been led to think a school curriculum is.

The reality that is of most concern to teachers and consultants is, of course, boys and girls learning and growing in school. This reality is children laughing at one another; it is the giving and receiving of report cards; the faculty meeting that no one liked; the unit of work that really succeeded (or didn't). It is the recognizable interaction that makes up a school.

Practical, immediate problems growing out of this reality lead the consultant and the teacher, working together, to the gathering of data that will aid clarification of the problem. The interpretation of these data leads to an expression of some opinion concerning ways the problem may be studied further, or solved. But all of this is undertaken while the action continues, and within the practical, everyday setting in which the action is located. That is, it takes place in a real situation, with all the stresses and contradictions of reality operating. All the unknown factors are in the action research, exerting whatever force they usually have. They are not scrubbed out in the process of "cleaning up" the problem. Such scrubbing strips the situation of its real meaning. Reality is messy. Scrub it up, and you've made it into something else.

To keep our research practical, we have to have a pattern of inquiry that permits these unknown factors to have their effect. Cooperative action research is such a pattern.

Suppose, for example, that a school staff has identified tardiness as a problem around which some cooperative action research is to be undertaken. It is decided to silence the school bell during passing periods. But complications develop. Other school staffs disapprove; some members of this school staff scoff at the idea; an angry letter is written to the superintendent. At this point the activity is no longer strictly experimental; it is something that must be defended. More than tardiness is now at stake. If the relationship among the researchers is really cooperative,

this situation can be used for further research, rather than abandoned. Look at the food for thought in what has happened! Data are now available on such important action problems as relationships with the public, the dynamics of the school staff, how to work successfully with the superintendent, and so on. If the staff will only look at what has happened, the chances are very good that they will come quickly to examine problems of great significance to them.

In this cooperative relationship, the action research consultant faces a special risk—that of distorting his perception of what is real, while thinking about it in isolation. There is a dilemma here. All the participants in the research must both be in the situation and reflect upon it. But for the consultant, the risk is especially severe that in the course of reflecting upon it, he will distort his perception of the situation to fit some preconception.

Thus, one of the present writers decided that the difficulties identified by a group of teachers all arose from an authoritarian school climate. Having so judged the situation, he could not continue to cooperate openly with the staff. He had made a judgment he could not report to them, and his judgment led him to make private interpretations of their subsequent problems. This being so, his relationship with the staff rapidly became less and less important both to him and the staff members and he eventually lost contact with them.

Later events showed him that had he not lost contact with the staff, he and they might have captured an opportunity to study something of great significance—what factors lead many teachers to behave in an authoritarian manner in spite of themselves.

Making Values Explicit

Any action represents an attempt to apply values to reality. We ordinarily are aware of reality through the application of our notions and scientific principles. But we frequently are unaware of the way our own values are operating as we choose among alternative actions. Whenever we choose among alternative ways of acting, we choose on the basis of values, whether they are conscious or not. Teachers choose all the time, and the values on which their choices are made are central to their teaching. We cannot choose whether or not to have values; we can choose only whether or not to attempt making them explicit. In the degree that this attempt is successful, we reduce the number of unknown factors operating in cooperative action research.

Most of us were brought up to believe that research must be objective, and that personal or group bias destroys objectivity. Bias is a hidden preference that grows out of experience and basic personality structure of which we are frequently unconscious. These sources of hidden preferences and their effects upon behavior are inevitable. To reduce bias, the process of valuing itself must be examined by the researcher, who, through this examination, may hope to make values conscious and thus avoid distortion of his perceptions. The importance of conscious valuing arises from two considerations: first, if research is to be significant to the researchers, it must align with their values; second, as has been indicated, unconscious valuing may operate in a capricious, hidden manner. Making values explicit enhances the probability of the first of these, and reduces the danger of the second. At two points in the research process, deliberately making values conscious will have a desirable influence on the significance and utility of research: at the beginning, when hypotheses are formed, and at the end, when implications for action are explored.

At the beginning of an action research process, it is crucially important that careful effort be made to make explicit the values of the participants, because these values determine whether the hypotheses formulated are significant to the participants. For example, if I don't value expressiveness and creativity in children, hypotheses about these things are not significant to me.

When a significant hypothesis has been stated, the researcher adopts techniques for testing it that are as unbiased—as free from unconscious personal or group value—as possible. He submits to the principles of evidence. He attempts to gather data that describe *the whole* of what is relevant to the hypothesis, including possibilities repugnant to him. When these data are examined, again the researcher tries to adopt a mode of examination that allows what is repugnant to him to appear and be studied. Once the data are objectively gathered and analyzed, however, and it is time to state implications, the researcher must make choices, and his values operate.

However, if this inevitable interaction between personal and group values and the research process is to be more than capricious and accidental, values must be stated. It should be observed that ordinarily they are not stated, but rather are left submerged, to operate without much deliberate control.

In a cooperative action research project, failure to make values explicit often leads to an apparently aimless shifting of interest instead of an orderly evolution of activity. In any case, values, rather than surface logic, control what is studied. For this reason, values determine the persistent direction for research.

Role of Cultural Values

Cultural values, as well as personal values, influence curriculum research, especially when teachers and others are cooperating to improve what is done in school. These cultural values may not be violated. They limit what may be undertaken. We shall mention four of them.

First, *usefulness*. The purpose of curriculum experimentation must be to add (or improve) something use-

ful, or to remove something useless. Parents allow experimentation with classroom committees, for example, only as they see group skills and positive social attitudes as useful to children.

Second, *way-of-life*. Experimentation that might make a child too different from others is intolerable. Similarly, we may not (nor would we want to) risk destroying a child's reverence, or the liking of his fellows.

Third, *psychological security of the parent*. We may not experimentally (even by accident) risk having a destructive effect on parent-child relationships. When a parent cannot understand the ideas a child learns at school, he is threatened, and behaves accordingly. When a teacher, for example, tolerates some minor "sassiness" in order to have a permissive climate in class, many a parent is threatened and shouts "poor discipline."

Fourth, *educational welfare*. A proposed experiment, to be allowed, must hold the promise of an improved child. Mere surveying of the achievement of children without using the results for improving teaching may be rejected by parents, who call it a waste of time. The educational welfare of the child must be safeguarded in the experimental process, or this value is violated.

Participants in cooperative action research have the task of locating these boundaries as they really are. In the process, they should seek the help of parents and others who guard the boundaries. Failure to do so sometimes leads to retribution.

Valuing enters into the cooperative action research process at several points. If we are to make such research realistic and practical, it is imperative that the values both of the researchers and of the culture be made concrete and visible, and that continued attention be given them as the research process unfolds.

Breaking Some Cultural Stereotypes

Participants in cooperative action research need to recognize that this kind of activity requires them to change their expectations of one another. A figure in our culture called "the expert" is likely to intervene in the research process in which teachers and consultants are attempting to work on the basis of close cooperation. When teachers make the assumption that the expert can tell them what their problems are and how they can solve them, cooperative action research is blocked.

Blockage likely occurs because the first task of the participants is to reach a mutual understanding of the nature of the situation. This task requires them to postpone organizing the situation for research until they have achieved a functionally similar understanding of the important variables. Such achievement requires of the consultant that he conduct himself with great humility and that at the outset he honestly profess ignorance of the situation. Such a humble approach violates the cultural stereo-

type of the expert. Evidence is provided that the stereotype is undergoing change as teachers in the situation increasingly become involved in describing their situation to the expert.

Other cultural stereotypes need to be modified. One is that teachers cannot do research. This stereotype is based on two assumptions: teachers may assume that they cannot do research; administrators and experts on curriculum may assume that teachers cannot do research. These assumptions are usually modified as teachers become experienced in research.

A second stereotype is that the teacher does not possess sufficient freedom in the situation to make a change in it. Teachers frequently possess in fact greater autonomy than they think they have.

A third notion which has to change is that leadership is a status function. This stereotype has to shift so that leadership is seen as an interpersonal or group function in which the teacher may participate as well as the consultant and administrator.

In the fourth place the teachers' assumptions about the nature of research need to change if cooperative action research is to flourish. The direction of the desirable shift is toward the idea that the teaching situation is a laboratory possessing the necessary resources for doing research. Although additional procedures such as the use of specially designed measuring instruments may have to be added, nevertheless the classroom possesses potentially the essential conditions and tools for the conduct of research.

The success of cooperative action research depends upon a reconstruction of the school's social culture which embodies assumptions and expectations such as those that we have described. The reconstruction of the school's social culture is thus an outcome of cooperative action research. By examining the changes that have taken place over a period of time in the school's culture one may grasp the contribution that research has made to the improvement of the curriculum.

It is urgent that attention be given to the process whereby the social culture of the school is changed. As is true with any subculture in a community, the school subculture possesses a great force for perseverance. The assumptions and expectations among people interlock them with one another in such a fashion that their culture has a tenacious life of its own. A few may honestly desire change but people generally resist change. Resistance and counter-moves for protecting the *status quo* are to be expected. Therefore, when such culture stereotypes as those we have mentioned are in the process of being broken it is important that the people involved comprehend what is happening and prepare themselves for the consequences. For example, the consultant may be accused of insincerity, or teachers may surprise

their superintendent by asking for something they have never requested before—school time for meetings.

Having described what must happen to the school's culture if cooperative action research is to become a normal operation we now turn to suggestions for meeting and managing the problems that are involved. The first consideration is that assumptions and expectations have to be communicated before they can be changed. Such communication requires a permissive atmosphere.

Second, the assumptions and expectations that are presently operating in a situation have to be examined and validated. Likewise, this requires a permissive atmosphere in which people, without hurt, can be objective toward one another.

Third, as cultural stereotypes are being broken the participants involved in cooperative action research need to explore the breaking-up process itself. This exploration needs to be regulated and carried on at the level of conscious attention. For example, as cultural stereotypes are being broken people become insecure and act as insecure people act. Some person involved in the process must understand that people are acting out of their insecurity and comprehend what is causing the particular behaviors of people manifested in the situation. Here the skills and understandings of the consultant very likely become strategic.

At this stage the behavior of the consultant is crucial. As cultural stereotypes shift in a situation where people are undertaking cooperative action research it is usually first the consultant and then a status leader, such as a principal, whose behaviors come under fire. They must be prepared, for example, to accept hostility and even moves by associates to set aside temporarily their influence and potency in the situation.

After assumptions and expectations about the role of the consultant and perhaps the principal are settled, the behavior of any person who shows an unusual amount of anxiety requires the attention of the group.

If the consultant can contain his feelings enough to protect others from the expression of his own anxieties, it is more likely that cultural stereotypes will change, and a new and more functional set of assumptions about people will become established.

Crucial to the favorable outcome of the process of examining cultural stereotypes is human relations skill and understanding exercised by the people who are involved. It is at this point that the importance of group work and the reason for improving group functioning enter the process of cooperative action research. Group work is important because it gives people an opportunity to evaluate their assumptions of one another and to set new and more valid expectations for one another. A recognition of the social psychological forces at work as people try to cooperate is the crux of *cooperative* action research.

Producing "Middle-Ground" Principles

The appropriate outcome of cooperative action research is the development of principles of analysis and method. These principles are related both to statements of fundamental theory and to real situations like those mentioned above. They stand between the two. They are "middle-ground" principles.

Middle-ground principles are action statements. They relate directly to the recognizable problem as it is usually seen. To be helpful, they must be stated in the same terms the teacher uses to describe the learning problems of a real child. The teacher's problem is how to figure out why a child is having trouble (analysis), and what she should do about it (method). Middle-ground principles are principles of analysis and method.

We teachers are now operating on the basis of certain fundamental principles of teaching and learning. The success of their application depends on whether the principles of analysis and method that lie between fundamental principles and action itself have been developed. Some have been developed in detail; others have not.

Take the principle of readiness, for example. The idea that there is such a thing as readiness has great and immediate appeal. It is one of the great principles of learning, so true that it is almost self-evident, yet so sophisticated that it had to be discovered and proclaimed. When this fundamental principle is applied to reading, classroom teachers can deal with it because during the past two generations it has been studied with sufficient attention to reality to provide a set of "middle-ground" principles. Teachers can apply the principle of readiness to many reading problems; they can apply it to writing; many primary grade teachers can apply it to determine rather subtle readinesses for various kinds of communication activity.

But the same is not at all true with respect to readiness for other kinds of subject matter, such as arithmetic. And such middle-ground principles are almost wholly lacking with respect to our understanding of children's readiness for the various kinds of social interaction.

How can we apply such fundamental ideas as "readiness" to problems of social development in ordinary classrooms? Questions like this are answerable only through action research. Through massive action research programs, we can hope for the gradual emergence of statable middle-ground principles that will allow us to make use of this fundamental idea in our day-by-day teaching. As things stand, we simply don't know how to use it.

The same thing might be said about other fundamental principles now available to us. The many studies of human relationships have given us principles of mental health, now useful primarily to psychiatrists. Many of us are trying, with varying degrees of success, to use them in classroom situations. But it is obvious that the same operating principles that can be used by a psychiatrist with a client cannot be used by a teacher with a class. We will have to develop our own principles for classroom application of the principles of mental health.

We have considered some needs. Now let us consider some accomplishments.

Hilda Taba (in *Diagnosing Human Relations Needs*) suggests the means by which teachers may discover the human relations needs in their own classes, and in the process carry on learning experience significant to children. She has in effect offered some middle-ground principles: some operational generalizations.

Ruth Cunningham and Associates (in *Understanding the Group Behavior of Boys and Girls*) re-examine social climates in schools. When they call "authoritarian" by the name "teacher rule–child obedience," they have at once described the phenomenon so that it can be recognized in a classroom, and also contributed significantly to the meaning of the fundamental idea of authoritarian climate as it is expressed in an elementary classroom. They have entered the middle ground that exists between Lewin and Lippitt on the one hand, and the thousands of us who are concerned about the way these ideas work in the classroom, on the other hand. These researchers have put tools in our hands that allow us to achieve purposes only partly indicated by the developers of the fundamental insights.

Cooperative action research, then, can be expected to produce principles of action—middle-ground principles —as its major outcome. And it is precisely these principles that are required by those of us who must deal with the day-to-day reality of children, teachers, schools, and educational goals.

EXPERIMENTAL PROGRAMS

Numerous experimental programs of various types have been initiated in recent years to improve learning experiences of boys and girls. One such experiment is the ungraded plan for the elementary school. In the March, 1955, *NEA Journal,* Goodlad indicates three twentieth-century movements that are contributing toward a break in the traditional graded lock-step type of school organization—"the child-study movement," studies of effects of nonpromotion on pupils, and attempts to relate instruction to what we know about "children, content, and the learning process"—and reports on ten centers which are experimenting with continuous pupil-progress plans in the primary grades. [16:170–171] In the May, 1955, *NEA Journal,* Goodlad briefly describes the "ungraded unit plan" and gives an appraisal of results on the basis of reports from sixteen school systems using it.

More About the Ungraded-Unit Plan   by JOHN I. GOODLAD

From the *NEA Journal,* May, 1955, pages 295–296. Reprinted by special permission of the National Education Association. John I. Goodlad is Professor of Education and Director of the Center for Teacher Education at the University of Chicago.

The ungraded-unit plan of elementary-school organization offers one possible means of encouraging continuous pupil progress and of reducing the incidence of nonpromotion.

Thus far the plan exists primarily as an idea, since only a small fraction of 1 per cent of the elementary schools in the nation have some adaptation of it in operation. But there are enough such programs to provide a basis for a general appraisal of the ungraded-unit idea as it works out in actual practice.

Material for such an appraisal was furnished me by persons connected with sixteen school systems in as many states where some form of continuous-progress plan is in operation. As I analyzed the information about how these plans were organized and how they function, certain patterns became evident. The following generalizations are based on these findings.

As I mentioned in my article on this subject in the March *Journal,* the ungraded-unit plan came into being as a possible answer to some of the current dissatisfactions with existing school practices. In each of the school systems studied, there was some definite reason why it was thought best to do away with the rigid grade-by-grade promotion and start a new system which would encourage continuous pupil progress.

The ungraded-unit plans which have evolved as a result of these dissatisfactions are not all alike, but there are several basic organizational features that are common to all of them. In each case, several years of the conventional graded system are replaced by a single unit.

For instance, the work usually done in grades 1–3 may be included in one unit and that of grades 4–6 in another. Each unit has a number of progress levels, usually eight to ten, and these, in most cases, are geared to reading attainment. There is always variability in the amount of time used for moving through a unit.

Children advance by "work levels" composed of tasks suited to individual readiness, instead of "grade levels" made up of arbitrary subject-matter limits. Emphasis throughout is for creating the best possible placement for the individual child. Pupils may be reclassified at any time and, if it is deemed advisable, shifted to another teacher.

If major shifts in patterns of school organization are to work, they must be accompanied by changed emphasis in curriculum organization. Under the ungraded, continuous-progress plan, the curriculum must be organized along vertical, sequential lines more than along horizontal, graded lines. Concern for long development of basic concepts, skills, and values must replace concern for mastering specific, graded chunks of subject matter.

Appraisal of children's progress at frequent intervals is essential to proper placement on the developmental levels of any continuous-progress system. Hence, there is greater emphasis upon standardized tests in school systems moving into such plans. A new era of test-making lies ahead if truly useful instruments for this purpose are to be devised.

Those who have pioneered with continuous-progress plans have gained experience that will be helpful to others who decide to replace their present system with a program of this type.

First, they emphasize how essential it is that those who are to be involved in or affected by the new curriculum structure be educated to its acceptance. One school suggests that both parents and teachers have a full year of study in child development before attempting any change. If possible, they should visit other centers where this type of organization is being used.

It was pointed out by some of the schools that this educative process has no ending, since new children, new parents, and new teachers are constant and continuous phenomena. As they come, they must be inducted into the operation of the new plan and into the thought behind it.

The importance of getting a right start cannot be overemphasized. An ungraded plan that is not accepted or understood may soon meet a serious pitfall common to all processes of change—that of making the change itself the scapegoat of all ills.

Beginning should be gradual and carefully planned for present and future acceptance. One school suggests that a unit be built a year at a time, beginning with the kindergarten or first grade and extending into the higher levels as the children advance upward. Another school, a large one, suggests that pilot schools be selected and used as experimental centers before the plan is put into effect throughout the entire school system.

Some of the schools that have successfully established this new curriculum structure have made the recommendation that ungraded units and new school buildings be planned together. Admittedly, many existing school structures are not well suited to what is going on or should be going on within them. Since ungraded units promise to be a significant organizational structure of the future, and since so many schools are being built or are about to be built, there should be careful planning to assure compatibility between plant and program.

In this connection one observation deserves special emphasis: *The good teacher finds ways of operating effectively in any setting, but no setting guarantees good teaching.*

The ungraded unit seems to free the good teacher from some frustrating restrictions and to facilitate bringing the total program into a more harmonious relationship with the character of pupil growth and of sound curriculum development. But unfortunately there are some persons, lacking insight into the realities with which they deal, who would set up within the more permissive framework a structure as rigid as that previously abandoned.

Because of this, any effort to move toward ungraded, continuous-progress plans should be accompanied by in-service education designed to acquaint all concerned with what they do and do not facilitate. Above all, there should be clear recognition of the fact that no scheme of school organization by itself sweeps away the basic problems involved in teaching children to live and learn.

Ungraded-unit plans are too new and too few to be measured in conclusions that would satisfy scientific rigor. Nevertheless, there are some results that are already apparent to those who are watching this new curriculum pattern develop.

Most centers report that tensions in children are reduced as the concept of individual adequacy replaces that of personal rivalry. It is also evident that there is a wider leadership opportunity because of the reduced grade-level stratification of pupils.

One of the most significant concomitant outcomes reported by the schools surveyed is that of increased teacher awareness of pupil individuality. In the conventional, graded setup, the spread of difference is readily lost to view. But in the continuous-progress plans, the reality and extent of individual differences are at the very core of the teaching effort. In seeking to identify and provide for individuality, teachers accept this concept as a guiding principle of their daily work.

Another significant outcome is that of increased parental understanding of the school, its organization, its purposes, and its problems. The sympathetic attitude developed by informational efforts goes far beyond a mere acceptance of the new plan and tempers every aspect of home-school relations.

More teamwork on the part of faculty members is another result that was noted. Working together successfully on a major school project brought the teachers a sense of shared accomplishment and united purpose. The teamwork thus generated is now paying rich dividends in the form of other projects successfully accomplished.

NOTE: For illustrations of how the ungraded primary school plan works, the reader is referred to Robert H. Anderson, "The Ungraded Primary School as a Contribution to Improved School Practices." *Frontiers of Elementary Education II,* Vincent J. Glennon, editor. (Proceedings of a Conference on Elementary Education. Syracuse University Press, 1955. Pages 28–39.)

Two administrative procedures designed to promote continuity, flexibility, and better provision for individual needs are the "little school" idea and the "self-contained unit" in the elementary school, briefly described in the January, 1958, *NEA Journal.*

With school enrollments increasing at the rate of 1,000,000 pupils per year, some measures have to be taken to overcome sheer bigness and to help individual pupils and teachers preserve their identity in school units of monstrous size and numbers. The "little school" or "schools within a school" idea is one proposed solution to the problem.

Under this plan, the large school is subdivided into a number of smaller units of 250 to 300 pupils, each with its own coordinator and faculty. Special features include teacher-planning sessions with teachers working together as a team, flexibility in time schedules, and classrooms grouped around a large workroom or general-education laboratory, where pupils spend half of their time on common learnings. For the remainder of the day, the pupils engage in specialized activities elsewhere. [11:26-28]

In the "self-contained unit" of the elementary school, the teacher and a group of pupils (preferably not more than twenty to twenty-five) work together "all day, every day, for a year or more." The self-contained unit is described as a workshop, "a home away from home— a living room for learning." Strong features imply an emphasis on children's needs; a more thorough understanding of individual pupils by the teacher; closer cooperation among parents, children, and teacher in "planning and executing educational experiences"; and better provision for mental health of pupils by means of an environment of security, color, and warmth. [21:18-20]

A program or project launched in 1949 at Teachers College, Columbia University, for the purpose of improving citizenship education of youth is known as the *Citizenship Education Project* (CEP). In order to assist schools in combining knowledge and action through laboratory practices, the following materials have been provided: (a) *Premises of American Liberty,* a booklet listing the basic principles and beliefs of American democracy; (b) a *materials card file,* known as the "Green Box," containing over 1200 annotated cards of references to books, pamphlets, films, and records which may be used in various areas of the curriculum; and (c) a *Laboratory Practices Card File,* referred to as the "Brown Box," containing specific suggestions for more than 300 laboratory practices which have proved useful in teaching.

Although the above materials may be purchased from the CEP, it is recommended that representatives of schools which plan to use the materials should participate in one or more of the CEP workshops. [17:369-375]

In the April, 1956, *Bulletin of the National Association of Secondary-School Principals* Tompkins reports: "Within the last fifteen months, four projects dealing with secondary education have been initiated in the following areas: Outdoor Education, Economic Education, Science and Mathematics Teaching, and a comprehensive Scholarship Program. Although many other projects pertaining to secondary education are now being conducted, these four are significant programs because they are new and are almost certain to have a real impact on secondary-school program and personnel." * The remainder of the article describes the purposes, details, activities, and future plans of the projects.

CURRICULUM AND GUIDANCE

Today there appears to be a growing awareness of the fact that there is a much closer relationship between guidance and curriculum than has been hitherto recognized. That teachers and counselors must work together as a team has become increasingly evident in theory, if not always in practice. The interrelationship of "child study, curriculum, and guidance" is well summarized in the following article by Strang.

How Guidance Relates to the Curriculum   by RUTH STRANG

Reprinted from *The Personnel and Guidance Journal,* January, 1954, pages 262–265, by special permission. Ruth Strang is Professor of Education, Teachers College, Columbia University. This paper was given at a joint meeting of the Los Angeles County Guidance and Research and Curriculum Staffs, February, 1953.

Tony had been referred to the counselor by his English teacher who had written the following note: "Tony does absolutely nothing in my class—except to disturb it. When I asked him if he were going to sit there and do nothing all term he replied, 'That is my intention.' You can see what effect such behavior would have on the morale of my class. I think he should be transferred to another school."

In the course of the interview with Tony the counselor asked, "What's wrong with school, Tony, that makes you dislike it so much?"

Tony: "It don't make sense."

Counselor: "You mean. . . ."

* From Ellsworth Tompkins, "New Projects Affecting Secondary Education," *Bulletin of the National Association of Secondary-School Principals,* April, 1956, p. 448. Quoted by special permission of the Association. Ellsworth Tompkins is Assistant Secretary for Administrative Service, National Association of Secondary-School Principals, a department of the National Education Association.

Tony: "I don't see any use for the subjects I'm taking. I want to quit school and go to work."

Counselor: "What kind of work are you interested in, Tony?"

Tony: "I'd like to work in a print shop."

Counselor: "Perhaps you could while you're still in school."

Tony: "But there's no print shop in this school."

Counselor: "That's true, but there's a print shop in town. Maybe we could arrange to have you work there in the afternoon. One of our graduates owns the shop and I think we could arrange it with him. Let's ask Mr. B (the principal) if he will approve this program for you."

In this case the principal was willing to make any adjustment that would be for the good of the individual student. The counselor arranged for Tony to take English, civics, and physical education in the morning and to work in a print shop in the afternoon. There he was supervised by a former graduate who was willing to cooperate with the school in providing experiences this pupil needed.

But many times the counselor is blocked in his efforts to help a student discover and develop his potentialities by lack of suitable experiences under the control of the school.

At present the relation of guidance to the curriculum is unclear. Some writers treat the two as distinct areas of education: teachers are responsible for the intellectual development of pupils; guidance workers for their social and emotional development. Others would include guidance as part of the curriculum—as merely one of the educational experiences that the child has in school.

Possibly the relation between the two may best be represented by two overlapping circles. There is an area common to both curriculum and guidance; on the other hand, each has distinctive features of its own. The common area is where guidance and curriculum merge and interact; the curriculum affects guidance and guidance influences the curriculum. The special curriculum area includes all the technical aspects of establishing and modifying a curriculum, and the ways and means of providing each child with the experiences which he needs. The guidance area emphasizes the individualized aspect of teaching, plus all the technical aspects of counseling and psychotherapy.

A film illustrated this distinction quite well. In one classroom the teacher was reading aloud an appropriate selection from a great play. The pupils were apparently having a fine experience in the appreciation of literature; they were giving wholehearted attention to the reading. The pupils' response to or interaction with this educational environment was of high quality. In another room the pupils were watching and listening with equal absorption while the teacher demonstrated a principle of physics. In each class the pupils were having a worthwhile educational experience; each pupil was extracting from it whatever was of immediate use and value to him. Both classes were receiving curricular experiences, but not guidance *per se*. In a third classroom, however, the teacher observed that one boy took no part in the class discussion. She had also noticed that he stood apart on the playground. She sat down beside him and talked with him; she began to see how school looked to him. Learning that he had a good singing voice, she asked him to take a solo part in a program which a class committee was giving. This was guidance—establishing a personal relation, gaining understanding of the individual pupil, and making available to him an experience which he needed for his best development.

Some will say, "Every good teacher does that." True, but according to the present terminology this constitutes the guidance aspect of teaching. Providing suitable experiences and materials of instruction comprises the curriculum aspect of education.

Guidance and curriculum are closely related in at least five ways:

1. An unsuitable curriculum will create more problems than a large staff of counselors can correct.
2. An inadequate curriculum will block effective guidance.
3. Insights gained in the guidance of individual pupils should be used in curriculum modification.
4. Many phases of guidance may lead toward curriculum modification.
5. Guidance through groups is an important part of the curriculum.

Effects of Unsuitable Curriculum

Many pupils become behavior problems and delinquents because of dissatisfaction with school. One gifted pupil wrote, "When I was in elementary school I was one of the worst citizens there was. Then a certain teacher I had gave me a chance to use my ideas to advantage, instead of thinking up ways to misbehave." Another said, "Until I reached the fourth grade I was continually bored. I knew the answers, but the teacher got tired of calling on me. So I took to conversing with my neighbors, for lack of anything else to do." Of 187 boys studied at New York State's Randall Island Reformatory, not one could read at his level of mental ability; 90 per cent had failed in school. Among 347 juvenile delinquents at the Delaware County, Pennsylvania, Juvenile Court two-thirds had misbehaved at school, played truant, or disliked school. The sequence leading to juvenile delinquency is well known: unsuitable curriculum and poor methods of instruction→truancy→association with a gang of older delinquents→law violation→a court record, and, as a result, difficulty in getting accepted by the community.

Equally important, though less obvious, are the other kinds of maladjustment which result from an unsuitable curriculum: Pupils have little opportunity for purposeful learning; gifted children lapse into lazy habits; feelings of inferiority and inadequacy of others are intensified; and many experience academic failure with all of its family reverberations.

The counselor is up against a blank wall, if, after he has helped a pupil discover his needs, he finds there is no provision for meeting them. Too often, counselors feel that they have to take sides with the school against the pupil and support outmoded educational philosophy and practices. Under these conditions, their job becomes one of helping pupils succeed in an unsuitable program. Or they go their own way, working aloof from the teacher and the curriculum committee.

The counselor is fortunate who has a guidance-minded principal who will sanction the use of community resources to supplement the experiences offered by the school. For example, in the case of Tony, who was taking an unsuitable academic curriculum—the only one available in his school—the principal arranged for him to work in a print shop in the town as part of his high school program. In New York City, a number of specialized high schools serve pupils who have specific interests. In Pittsburgh, Saturday morning art classes at the art museum enrich the curriculum of talented pupils.

To make counseling fully effective, curriculum makers must, in various

ingenious ways, provide the educational experiences which "developmental counseling" shows are desirable and necessary for each pupil.

Curriculum Modification

From intimate contact with individual pupils, the counselor gains insight into their needs. For example, the counselor finds many reading problems on all grade levels. These discoveries should lead to: (*a*) an examination of the methods of teaching reading in the primary grades; (*b*) more effective developmental reading throughout elementary and high school (learning to read is a lifetime process); (*c*) provision of reading material suitable to the wide range of reading ability and interest represented in every class.

In his interviews with pupils and parents the counselor also detects dissatisfaction with school which stems from a curriculum that seems remote from daily living, and fails to afford many pupils a reasonable amount of success. This discovery raises the questions of how to make schoolwork more meaningful, how to teach so effectively that the pupil will progress step by step without unnecessary failure; and how to adapt instruction to individual needs.

Almost all phases of guidance lead to curriculum modification. For example, Richard March of the Los Angeles County staff described how parent conferences led to a more specific study of the reading curriculum. The teachers were confronted with the question of what to report to parents: What were their reading objectives in a given grade comprising a wide range of reading ability? So the teachers began to think through the progression of reading experiences desirable in their grades. The next question was one that parents might raise: "Why is this particular objective important?" Parents might also ask teachers, "How do you help children to attain this objective and why do you teach it that way?" Thus teachers who were at first interested in improving parent conferences, and not at all in curriculum modification, began to work on curriculum in a most fundamental and specific way.

Guidance techniques also serve as a source of insights into curriculum needs:

1. Through *observation* teachers can see where pupils' interest is high, where apathy prevails; where class work is too hard or too easy for individual children; where a particular learning process has been well or poorly analyzed.

2. Through *testing* teachers see where pupils are under-achieving or over-achieving. This points to the need for further study of these pupils and raises the questions "Why?" "With what consequences?" "In what specific areas?"

3. Through *subjective compositions* by the pupils teachers gain in-sights into the effectiveness of the curriculum and methods of instruction.

4. Through *follow-up studies,* often made by guidance workers, teachers may become aware of poor instruction in English; they may be encouraged by the appreciation of mathematics courses expressed by boys who have gone into the service; they may recognize students' desire for more life-adjustment content in the curriculum.

5. Through *interviews* in which, for example, retarded readers have told how they were allowed to sit in class and do busy work, without receiving any help—at least that's the way it looked to them. Often, of course, pupils fail to recognize the learning that is actually taking place.

Child study, curriculum, and guidance interact with one another. Child study uncovers needs for educational experiences which the curriculum can supply. Through guidance, individual pupils are helped to choose and succeed in experiences that help them to develop their potentialities. Both curriculum and guidance have specialized aspects which are difficult to combine in the training of a single person. Only by working closely together can curriculum and guidance departments most effectively contribute to the development of all the children.

Ellis stresses the need for an "intelligent use of guidance services" in making "an integrated attack upon curriculum problems," especially in meeting individual needs of children. [12:221–226]

NOTE: Further evidence of an increasing emphasis on the close relationship between curriculum and guidance is the fact that the 1955 Yearbook of the Association for Supervision and Curriculum Development is on the subject of *Guidance in the Curriculum.*

SUMMARY

The setting for the process of curriculum development in American public education for the past half century has been a complex society of shifting movements and forces. In order to cope with the situation, those charged with curriculum revision have had to revise their mode of operation. The need for unity, continuity, flexibility, and simplicity in curriculum planning has been recognized and has been reflected in newer procedures of curriculum development.

No longer is curriculum building considered the sole province of professional experts. Today, many groups of people—professional people, parents, pupils, and the public—participate in curriculum planning.

Although educational leadership, both at the state and local levels, continues to grow in importance, more and more the role of the classroom teacher as a curriculum builder has come into the spotlight. As a result, there has developed a new concept of research, known as "action research," by which the classroom teacher uses the techniques of research to study his own teaching problems. Closely allied to the action research approach to curriculum improvement is the so-called "grass roots" movement in which individual schools become the focal point in curriculum activity.

Further evidences of encouragement of more creativity in the classroom are the development of more flexible courses of study or curriculum guides, experiments with new curriculum designs, and attempts to free lower schools from domination by higher schools of learning.

The demand for better articulation or more integration of educational experiences from school to school, grade level to grade level, subject to subject, and school to community (as reflected in the 1958 yearbooks of the National Society for the Study of Education and the Association for Supervision and Curriculum Development) is a recurring theme in present-day publications on education.

10

THE DIRECTION OF
CURRICULUM DEVELOPMENT:
A SUMMATION

Direction is determined by goals. The goals which the American people have set for themselves and their schools are real and compelling, but incapable of complete achievement. Steady progress can be made toward them only to have them continuously recede as does the horizon. In order to measure progress, attempts have been made to assess the present in comparison either with the past or with hopes of the future.

The schools have progressed and developed continuously. For some, the changes have seemed to be too little and too slow; for others, they appear to be too rapid and misguided. It all depends upon one's orientation with regard to the past and future. Nevertheless, any sincere attempt at appraisal will indicate to some extent two things: what has been accomplished and, at the same time, what remains to be done.

HOW WELL HAVE WE DONE?

In Part One of this book, attention was given to the voices raised in criticism and in defense of the schools. What does an investigation of the contemporary pupil achievement in comparison with past results indicate? Elicker has summarized research studies bearing upon this aspect of the question.

How Good Are Our Schools?   by PAUL E. ELICKER

From the *Bulletin of the National Association of Secondary-School Principals,* November, 1954, pages 1–5. Reprinted by special permission. Paul E. Elicker is Executive Secretary of the National Association of Secondary-School Principals, a department of the National Education Association.

Much has been said and written about today's education for our youth. Some of these presentations proffered by self-appointed appraisers of our educational system have been caustically critical of today's education. In many of these published "attacks" on public education, it has been found that these were hasty generalizations based on a personal experience with the school involving one or two children or some unusually unfavorable experience with the school or its personnel. Other appraisals have appeared in our popular magazines that have attempted to tell the unbiased truth about our education and to present the current issues and problems facing educators. This confused and often contradictory "evidence" has created a condition of concern and even suspicion among many parents and other citizens about our schools and our present-day programs of education.

The Facts About Our Education

The average youth today, unless he is the exception, and there are always some of these in every school community, receives a better education than the youth a generation or two ago. Enough tests, based largely on a mastery of the fundamentals, have been given to establish this claim. Here are a few of them.

Study I. In 1848, forty of the brightest youngsters ranging in ages from ten to nineteen—all in the eighth grade—in four Cleveland, Ohio, schools took comprehensive tests in definitions, mental arithmetic, written arithmetic, American history, grammar, and geography. In 1947, forty of the best students in four Cleveland junior high schools, ages twelve to fourteen—all in the eighth grade—took the same tests with an over-all score of 955 correct answers for the 1947 group as compared with 924 for the 1848 group.

Study II. In Dearborn, Michigan, all the youngsters in the fourth, fifth, and sixth grades took a test in 1951 which had been given to children in these same grades in 1926. Result: the 1951 "kids" were a year and a half ahead in reading and a half year ahead in arithmetic. In oral and written English the 1951 group was two years ahead of the group twenty-five years ago. In spelling, however, there was a slightly better total score for the youth of 1926.

Study III. In Lincoln, Nebraska, 5,690 children in the third through the eighth grades were given a reading test in 1921. In 1947, in Lincoln, 5,100 youngsters, comparable to the 1921 group, took the same test. Note the median reading scores, grade by grade:

Grade	1921	1947
3	44.34	57.69
4	65.29	73.28
5	76.47	90.13
6	79.69	91.96
7	89.50	94.01
8	89.19	92.92

It should be noted that the fifth-grade group in 1947 read better than the eighth-grade group in 1921.

Study IV. In Evanston, Illinois, fifty-two children from the fourth grade in 1952, comparable in age, general intelligence, and family background, were given the same tests in reading, vocabulary, spelling, and arithmetic taken by fifty-seven children in 1932. Result: the 1952 group showed an advance of eight months in reading, vocabulary, and arithmetic. In spelling, the 1932 group excelled by a small margin.

The above four studies in four different states are typical of many other group tests in other school communities. It should be remembered that most of these tests were definitely geared to the interests of youth twenty to thirty years ago and that

greater stress was placed on passing examinations then. Today, youth are taught more competences and knowledge usage in contrast to lengthy memory drills of a generation ago. Teaching today includes: (*a*) using libraries, source material, and current magazines; (*b*) speaking before groups and serving as responsible leaders of groups; (*c*) cooperating in community and group study; (*d*) learning more about the human and social aspects of world geography; (*e*) engaging in original and creative thinking in many areas; and (*f*) working in many other learning areas that make youth of today, in general, better informed and better equipped mentally and physically to live and enjoy the complicated world in which they must live.

Study V. Professor John Warren Tilton, Yale University, made a very interesting comparison of the intelligence levels of the members of the Armed Forces in 1917 through the Army Alpha Tests and Army General Classification Test given in 1940–1945 to millions in the Armed Forces in World War II. In general, the amount of schooling as measured by these tests of the millions that were in the Armed Forces in World War I and World War II showed an increase of 3.7 grades—from a 6.8 grade level in World War I to a 10.5 grade level in World War II. The educational gain during this twenty-five year period was substantial, showing a greatly improved status in reading competency and arithmetical reasoning ability. In fact, three-fourths of all persons in the Armed Forces in 1940–1945 were above the middle score of the total group in 1917. We had a better educated Armed Force in 1945 than in 1917 and a better educated citizenry—all achieved during the twenty-five year period.

The Situation in Our Secondary Schools

We hear much about the inadequacy of our American program of secondary education when compared to the English system of secondary education. All such statements cannot be justified by the limited data available. However, through the Kinsmen Trust, the National Association of Secondary-School Principals has selected a number of public secondary-school students to spend a year in some of England's best private schools, such as Rugby, Magdelene, St. George's, and other schools of high academic standing. These American students for the past nine years—the number of years this scholarship project has been in existence—have compared most favorably with English school youth in their own schools. In some learning areas, American youth definitely excelled English youth.

Another source of convincing evidence is the record of the American Rhodes Scholars at Oxford University. Our American youth, the products of our schools and colleges, have creditably "held their own" not only with British scholars but also with scholars from other countries attending Oxford.

Now the Case of the Public School

All of the public criticisms have been directed at the public schools, largely because nearly 90 per cent of all school-going youth attend them, and also because all citizens are obligated by law to support public schools financially. Frequently comparisons are made by persons unacquainted with the facts, or a general criticism is made based on a few cases in public and private schools.

It must be noted that there are good and inferior public schools. A similar condition exists in our private schools, except that the aggregate number of private or independent schools is only one-eighth of the total number of approximately 25,000 public secondary schools. However, when the facts are known, the public-school graduates excel the private-school graduates academically in their college performance.

Study I—The Phi Beta Kappa story. At Harvard, twenty-four persons were elected on March 17, 1954, to Phi Beta Kappa, the national honorary scholastic society. Of this number, seventeen were public school graduates. Approximately 50 per cent of all students at Harvard are public-school graduates.

At Yale there was a total of seventy-nine members of Phi Beta Kappa in

May, 1954. Of this number, forty-five were public school graduates. About 45 per cent of all students at Yale are public-school graduates.

At Colgate, of the twenty-nine persons elected to Phi Beta Kappa, twenty-five were public-school graduates. About 60 per cent of all students at Colgate come from public schools.

The above facts are given to show that, in the aggregate, where both public and private school graduates attend the same colleges, the academic honors, as shown by election to Phi Beta Kappa, go in greater number to public-school graduates.

Study II—The College Entrance story. We often hear that the public schools do not prepare their students adequately to meet college standards. Let's examine the only records available, the scores of students that took the examinations of the College Entrance Examination Board. The examinations are generally recognized as setting the highest academic standards for college admission.[1]

Results on these examinations, given five times during the academic year 1951–1952 and four times in 1952–1953, are available. The reports on the March, 1952 and 1953, examinations are given in the table below. At this time of the year the greatest number of candidates take the examinations and all the different kinds of subject examinations are given. The results of examinations given at other times during the year are similarly comparable to those given on the following page.

An examination of these statistics shows that in March, 1952, the average intelligence was about the same for both groups with a mean score of 483 in the verbal section of the *Scholastic Aptitude Test.* However, in nine of the thirteen subject achievement and aptitude tests, students in the public schools excelled those from independent schools. In 1953 there were better mean scores by public school graduates in ten of the thirteen subject achievement and aptitude tests.

It is generally recognized that conditions for teaching in independent schools are better than in public schools. Favorable teaching conditions in many independent schools include: small classes; better student study arrangements; school control of students for the entire day, especially in boarding schools; more homogeneous classes; and a lighter total teaching load for the teacher.

A Valid Conclusion

All studies show that our schools are providing a better education for more youth today than in the "good old days" a generation ago. This great achievement has been made under increasingly adverse conditions for effective teaching, such as larger classes, inadequate teaching equip-

[1] Henry S. Dyer, *College Board Scores* (Princeton, N. J.: College Entrance Examination Board). Copy 1 gives the 1952 results; the *Supplement* gives the 1953 results.

COLLEGE BOARD EXAMINATIONS

	Mean Scores [1]— March, 1952		Mean Scores [1]— March, 1953	
Kinds of Examinations	Public Schools	Independent Schools	Public Schools	Independent Schools
Scholastic Aptitude				
Verbal Section	483	483	489	486
Mathematical Section	505	494	518	496
Achievement Tests				
English Composition	506	508 *	515 *	514
Social Studies	494 *	484	518 *	505
French Reading	503	534 *	527	548 *
German Reading	507 *	482	516 *	489
Latin Reading	573 *	558	562 *	551
Spanish Reading	477	488 *	494	499 *
Biology	479	483 *	496 *	491
Chemistry	507 *	493	544 *	522
Physics	556 *	522	551 *	526
Intermediate Mathematics	534 *	505	535 *	499
Advanced Mathematics	592 *	586	598	599 *
Aptitude Tests				
Spatial Relations	529 *	520	537 *	514
Pre-Engineering Science Comprehension	524 *	465	547 *	494
Total Number of Examinations Taken	81,632	57,126	90,193	65,153

[1] To aid the reader to interpret the scores, the possible range in scores in these examinations is 200 to 800, with 500 regarded as the arithmetical average or mean score for college entrance examinations.

* Starred numbers indicate highest scores.

ment, many obsolete and crowded buildings, heavier teaching loads and assignments for teachers, more community demands on the teaching staff, and an inadequate number of qualified teachers.

Your community should know the facts.

Your citizens should support their schools so they will continue to grow and improve.

Your parents should ever strive for a better education for their children and cooperate with school officials to make improvements and intelligent changes that will provide a more effective instructional program for all youth.

Additional evidence from a business publication "that public education today is the best it has ever been" is printed in the June, 1954, issue of *Changing Times* in an article entitled "The Truth about Our Public Schools." The same publication, in a later article, gives further reassurance to parents and reminds them of their part in curriculum improvement.

High Schools: Are They Doing Their Job?

from CHANGING TIMES

From *Changing Times, The Kiplinger Magazine,* July, 1956, pages 27–31. Reprinted by special permission.

If you are the parent of a youngster in a public high school, you may have been disconcerted lately by repeated charges that the schools are falling down on their job.

These charges are basically three:

1. Public high schools, which once were citadels of cultural learning, have abandoned even the pretense of teaching the classical subjects. Instead, they offer instruction in beauty culture, dressmaking, industrial sewing, animal husbandry, radio and television repair, gas station management, and a host of other business and industrial subjects.

Therefore, say some critics, college-bound boys and girls who want to study such quaint things as languages, mathematics, history, and the sciences soon will have to enroll in private schools in order to get them. And since private schools are beyond the financial reach of most parents, academic learning will come to be established on a class basis, and will, if the present trend continues, disappear for the great bulk of youngsters.

2. Even in those high schools that still offer the remnants of a college-preparatory course in the so-called liberal arts subjects, the instruction is heavily watered down. The charge here is that the curriculum is diluted with minor elective subjects such as band, glee club, dramatics, and driver training, for which academic credit is frequently given.

Students who go through such a course today more often than not will find that they have spent so much time studying these nonessential "play," or diversionary, subjects that they have neither the credits to get into college nor the skill or knowledge needed to earn a living.

3. As a result of the vocationalization of the curriculum and the dilution of such classical teaching as is left, subjects basic to scientific and

engineering training are hardly being taught.

It is said that whereas Russia is turning out twice the number of engineers and thirty times the number of technicians each year that American schools and colleges are producing, fully half of the American public high schools fail to teach either physics or chemistry. Moreover, in the schools where these two sciences are taught, only 4 per cent of the students take physics, compared with 19 per cent in 1900, and only 7 per cent take chemistry.

What's more, a third of the high schools allegedly do not teach advanced algebra, solid geometry, or trigonometry. Only 27 per cent of today's high school pupils are said to study algebra, and an even slimmer 13 per cent take geometry.

All those are distressing charges. They are not made only by a few crackpots and malcontents bent on stirring up trouble over the schools for obscure or ulterior motives. The figures have been cited by sincere people who are genuinely concerned with educational problems and the nation's welfare.

What are the facts? Are the charges true? Is it possible to get a fair perspective on the whole picture?

1. *Traditional Courses: What Has Happened?*

In 1900 fewer than 10 per cent of the 6,100,000 American youngsters between fourteen and eighteen years of age went to high school. High school was an experience for the intellectually elite, and the total enrollment was only some 519,000 boys and girls, practically all of whom took a classical course. Indeed, that was about the only course offered.

The secondary schools of that period were essentially college-preparatory schools, and youngsters who didn't care for classical subjects or were not on their way to college had the alternative of going to work.

Today approximately 80 per cent of American youths of high school age are enrolled in junior and senior high school classes. As nearly as anybody can estimate it, the total enrollment is a whopping 7,200,000 pupils, give or take a few hundred thousand. Literally, almost everybody goes to high school now—not just the academically inclined. In the 1800's a free elementary-school education became the birthright of every citizen. The first half of the twentieth century was the period in which a free secondary-school education was added to that prerogative.

A number of economic and social factors have brought this result about. Technological progress in industry and on the farm has all but eliminated the need for child labor. Higher family incomes also have lessened the necessity of children's having to work. Untrained youngsters are, in fact, neither needed nor overly welcome in the labor market. The place for them to be is in school, and laws have been passed to enforce their attendance. In many states today the minimum legal age for leaving school is sixteen. Several states won't let students quit till they are eighteen.

All this has posed an enormous problem for educators. Of the vast new hordes of young people descending upon the public high schools, greater and greater majorities come without interest in the traditional classical subjects or the ability to grasp them. They are not planning to go to college. They couldn't care less about Latin or math or science.

What should the schools teach these kids?

Commercial and vocational subjects began to edge into high school curricula about 1910, when it became obvious that many youths who were not going to college could profitably be taught subjects that would help them make a living.

Commercial training for girls was built largely around shorthand, typing, and business English. Vocational training for boys was built around the trades and crafts. Sometimes separate high schools were constructed to house classes in these subjects. More often the high schools were expanded into comprehensive schools that offered all types of courses.

But with the onrush of youngsters that began in the jobless thirties, these courses were not enough. Not all girls who planned to work after graduation wanted typing and short-

hand. Shorthand was beyond the capabilities of some, and others had no real interest in office work. Not all boys wanted to be electricians or machinists. So the variety of business and technical courses was broadened until today every conceivable commercial and vocational subject is taught in some high school somewhere.

Frequently such courses are supplemented by on-the-job training during the students' last two years in high school. For example, boys and girls taking today's course in "distributive education"—school terminology for wholesale or retail selling —will work in local stores part-time during their junior and senior years. A boy learning gas station management will work in a service station under the eyes of both his employer and his high school principal or counselor.

Naturally, such unscholarly goings-on bring gasps from adults who have been accustomed to thinking of high school in terms of the old college-preparatory institutions. But the fact is that these courses usually find their way into the curriculum because the parents and taxpayers of the community want them there. They are valuable to the students who take them, and they have added vastly to the power of the high schools to hold youngsters that are not academic-minded. Even so, far too many children drop out of school as soon as the law permits. Almost half of those who enter high school fail to graduate.

2. How Diluted Is the Curriculum?

Yes, the traditional curriculum, where it still exists, is now supplemented with a wide choice of minor elective subjects. (These electives, like the vocational subjects, wouldn't be there unless there was demand for them.) Yet most high school youngsters who are preparing for college do arrive at the college gates with the required number of admission credits.

The established pattern of entrance requirements tends to insure this. School administrators know what they are and shape their preparatory courses accordingly. Some states set up minimum requirements for college-preparatory programs to make sure that their high schools toe the mark academically. Finally, the high schools are periodically evaluated by the various college and secondary-school accrediting associations that cover the country. Schools that fail to measure up are barred from the associations' accreditation lists.

A typical college-preparatory course includes four years of English, a minimum of two years of foreign-language study, two to three years of social studies (including history), two years of mathematics, and two years of science. This makes a total of twelve or thirteen of the sixteen credits usually required for graduation from high school and admission to college. Three or four other credits should be earned in major subjects for which college entrance credit is given. Credits for minor courses are supposed to be extra.

Successful completion of a course like this will land your youngster in any one of 95 per cent of the colleges in the nation—at least as far as academic requirements are concerned. "Successful completion," however, means that your child should be in the top part of his class. An eastern suburban high school has set this standard as a guide for its students who plan to go on to college: 60 per cent A's and B's in the junior and senior years and no mark below a C.

If your college-bound youngster isn't following a program fairly similar to the one outlined above, you would do well to look into the matter. You might also make inquiry if he seems to be taking too many "fun" courses, such as band or glee club.

Many high schools do a conscientious job of checking on a youngster's progress through school. Many require parents' written approval of the subjects elected by pupils. But some do neither, and it may be largely up to you to make sure that your young man or young lady winds up high school with the right credits.

Now, what about the quality of instruction in the academic subjects? The answer is that schools, like everything else, do vary in quality. In our better secondary schools, instruction is extremely good. For instance, work in English literature in the junior and senior years at the best modern high schools is the equiva-

lent of that offered in college freshman classes a generation ago. Many
schools are instituting programs for
advanced work for superior students
in certain subjects, and some youngsters enter college with advanced
standing in those courses.

Approximately 13,000 high school
students apply each year for the National Honor Society scholarships offered by the National Association of
Secondary-School Principals. They
come from everywhere, and they submit straight-A records. Their records
are replete with such courses as
speech, typing, debate, art, home economics, band, choir, health, social
goals, driver training, and other minor subjects for which they have received credit. But their applications
are based primarily on marks in the
good solid academic subjects—English, mathematics, history, the sciences, and languages. The applications seem to demonstrate both the
general availability of academic instruction and the excellence of at least
one large segment of the high school
population in academic work.

In answer to the argument that it
will soon be necessary for students to
attend private schools in order to prepare for college, it is noteworthy that
public high school students do better
than private-school pupils in most
subjects in College Entrance Board
examinations.

Here, for example, are comparative
mean scores of all public and private
secondary-school pupils who took
College Board achievement tests in
March, 1954, the latest period for
which complete figures are available.
The possible range in these examinations is 200 to 800 points, with 500 regarded as average.

Public high school youngsters out-
scored their private-school contemporaries in these fields:

	Public	Private
Social Studies	525	511
German	509	492
Latin	557	530
Biology	508	491
Chemistry	540	522
Physics	549	518
Intermediate Mathematics	530	495
Advanced Mathematics	582	575

Only in English composition,
French, and Spanish did the private-
school pupils do better than the public-school youngsters, with comparative scores of 523 to 521, 526 to 506,
and 500 to 486 in the respective subjects. In aptitude tests the public-
high kids beat the private-school boys
and girls 484 to 482 in the verbal section, 514 to 492 in the mathematical
section, and 543 to 525 in the examinations having to do with spatial
relations.

3. *Tomorrow's Engineers and Scientists*

The statistics purporting to show
that in today's scientific-minded
world half of America's high schools
are not teaching chemistry or physics
are harrowing indeed. But happily,
the figures are not accurate. The error came about this way.

In a study made by the U. S. Office of Education all public secondary schools, big and little, were surveyed to see how many offer chemistry and physics. The big ones reported that they teach both subjects every year. But many small schools, where the teaching staffs are limited, alternate yearly between physics and chemistry. Schools that were teaching only chemistry when the survey was made neglected to report physics, and vice versa. The fact is that 23 per cent of the public high schools offer neither science, not the alleged 50 per cent.

More significantly, because these schools are small, they account for only 6 per cent of the total U. S. high school enrollment.

The figures showing that a third of the high schools do not teach advanced algebra, solid geometry, and trigonometry are correct. But here again some comfort may be taken from the fact that most of these schools are small institutions, accounting for a small percentage of the high school students in the country.

It is also true that only 4 per cent of all students take physics, but here the statistics, though accurate, are misleading. Youngsters usually are not eligible for physics until the twelfth grade. About 302,800 twelfth-graders do take the subject, some 23.5 per cent of all those who are eligible to do so. Nearly 32 per cent of all eligible students take chemistry, 65 per cent of those eligible take algebra, and 37 per cent take geometry.

How It All Adds Up

The truth about our public high schools seems to be that the great bulk of them are doing a fine job. Vocational and commercial instruction has been broadened because of the great number of pupils who need and want it. But the old college-preparatory instruction is still available. The prerequisites for careers in science and engineering are still being offered.

All this is not to say, of course, that there is nothing wrong with our public high schools. Even though the main charges against them can be answered or explained away, there are still some very serious things wrong.

• Those figures on the smaller high schools indicate one trouble spot. Of the 25,000 junior and senior public high schools in the U. S. today, fully half have no more than two hundred students. A substantial number have fewer than one hundred.

It is in these small schools that the educational short-changing of students generally occurs. The schools are just not big enough to offer a complete educational fare. In some remote areas youngsters must take correspondence courses to get a full program of academic work. One answer to this problem is the modern consolidated high school, to replace small scattered high schools.

• Classroom space is short almost everywhere, and is getting shorter as the throngs of war babies now in grade school push on into high school. Crowding limits a school's capacity to offer much range in its curriculum and to provide such desirable facilities as shops and laboratories. Youngsters may receive little individual attention in the classroom and only cursory guidance in choosing courses. Some high schools can't do their job, no matter what that job is supposed to be, because they just don't have elbowroom.

• The greatest shortage, however, is not of space but of teachers. Teachers of all kinds are scarce, especially science and mathematics instructors. Good teachers of these subjects can command twice the salary in industry that teaching will bring them, and into industry many of them go. The solution to this problem is obvious. Pay higher salaries.

Where You Come In

What can be done if your high school seems to be inadequate? Re-

member that there is no such thing as a national school policy to establish standards and to see that they are maintained. Education in the United States is a local matter. Each state sets a broad pattern to be followed within its borders.

Within that outline, goals and standards vary. They vary with the sense of values of local school boards and of voters in general—and sometimes with their whims and prejudices.

You and your neighbors are called upon to make three judgments:

• What the schools should teach, and why.
• What you can afford to spend on your public school system.
• What you actually are willing to spend.

The job done by your high school —and by all the public schools in your community—will reflect those judgments.

Granted that genuine progress has been made, is it evident in all needed aspects of the program? Has it reached somewhere near its potential? Alberty shatters any tendency toward complacency in the editorial which follows.

Editorial: What Is Progress in Secondary Education?

by HAROLD ALBERTY

From *Educational Leadership,* Vol. 10, No. 8 (May, 1953), pages 466–469. Reprinted by special permission of the Association for Supervision and Curriculum Development and the author. Harold Alberty is Professor of Education, Ohio State University, Columbus.

The overarching theme of this number of *Educational Leadership,* "Secondary Education Reports Progress," makes news at a time when secondary education is under fire for its failure to meet the challenge of the times. This editorial is being written without knowledge of the progress which is being reported in this number. This fact may explain the note of pessimism which is sounded in this brief statement. The writer sincerely hopes that the reports of progress in this issue will change his attitude.

In one sense it is possible to report a great deal of progress in secondary education. Witness the new functionally designed buildings that have sprung up all over the land since World War II; the enormous increase in guidance and "extra"-curricular programs; the proliferation of elective subjects designed to meet the special needs and interests of students; the increases in teachers' salaries; the improvement in textbooks; and the strengthening of libraries. These are significant gains and not to be depreciated.

Has corresponding progress been made in the very heart of the secondary program—general education? In this time of crisis when the very existence of our free society is threatened from within and without, what is the secondary school doing to strengthen that part of the program which is primarily designed to develop the common values, understandings, and skills of living that are essential for *all* American youth?

A half-century of experimentation has shown that it is possible and desirable to break down the compartmentalization among subjects, and to center the curriculum—particularly in the area of general education—upon the needs and problems which grow out of the interaction of the student and his environment. The best elementary schools have long been organized in terms of broad comprehensive units of work. Extensive experience in student-teacher planning and the application of democratic group processes has demonstrated the feasibility of breaking with the tradition of logically organized subject matter doled out in terms of daily assignments from textbooks. The Eight-Year Study demonstrated that students gain more of the cherished values essential to effective citizenship, if the design of the curriculum is changed from the subject-centered to the experience-centered approach. The fear that graduates from such programs would not succeed in college proved to be completely unfounded. In 1944, the National Association of Secondary-School Principals endorsed a "common-learnings" program in *Education For ALL American Youth,* and attempted to popularize it through wide publicity. The "Ten Imperative Needs of Youth" are quoted glibly by school administrators and teachers. We have the "know-how" to introduce this program into the schools and we have the research to prove that to do so would really constitute progress.

In spite of the fact that we know how to transform our static program of general education in the high school into a dynamic one based upon the vital problems which beset youth in a culture that is becoming increasingly confused about its basic values, the program of general education is still defined in terms of Carnegie units, ground to-be-covered and lessons to-be-learned. This situation is well documented in recent studies by Wright.[1]

These studies indicate that only 3.5 per cent of the public secondary schools of the United States have departed from the traditional design of general education. More than four-fifths of the changes are at the junior high school level, and even in this area, the changes are frequently limited to the seventh and eighth grades. To face the problem realistically, it is necessary to look more closely at the actual changes which have been made. *Most of the programs reported merely combine social studies and English in a double period.* Only a handful of schools have actually developed an Adolescent Problems program in general education throughout the junior and senior high schools. Noteworthy among these schools are Garrett County, Maryland; Fairmont Heights High School, Prince Georges County, Maryland; and the Ohio State University School, Columbus, Ohio.

A Realistic Appraisal

Must we continue to describe progress in secondary education in terms of curriculum tinkering, resulting in the addition of a few courses, which however valuable they may be, fail to improve the basic design of the curriculum? Will the new pronouncement published in 1952 by the Educational Policies Commission— *Education for ALL American Youth: A Further Look*—have any more effect on the schools than did the original volume published in 1944?

Will the present emphasis upon Life Adjustment suffer the same fate as did the Eight-Year Study? Perhaps we need to look at the blocks which seem to interfere seriously with curriculum before we can find an answer to these questions.

1. *The climate in which the high school operates today is not conducive to basic curriculum development.*

A fundamental factor in this climate is the fear and anxiety of the public engendered by the struggle between the free world and totalitarianism. This fear and anxiety is manifested in the willingness of many people to accept as true the charges of pressure groups that feed upon unrest. Schools are not likely to trans-

---

[1] Grace S. Wright, *Core Curriculum in Public High Schools: An Inquiry into Practices,* 1949, Bulletin 1950, No. 6 (Washington: Federal Security Agency, U. S. Office of Education, 1950). *Core Curriculum Development Problems and Practices,* Bulletin 1952, No. 5 (Washington: Federal Security Agency, U. S. Office of Education, 1952). "Core Curriculum Why and What," *School Life,* XXXIX, 71 ff. (February, 1952).

form a passive and relatively ineffective curriculum which imparts "tried and true" subject matter into one which centers on the vital problems of living when they witness so many examples of attacks upon such programs. No teacher was ever accused of subversion for teaching Caesar's Gallic Wars, but teachers who deal with controversial social-economic issues are likely to be attacked on the ground that they are undermining the "American System of Free Enterprise." Loyalty oaths and legislative investigations have served to dampen the enthusiasm of schools for curriculum reform. It is easier to retreat to the teaching of the "fundamentals," and the classics.

However potent this climate of fear may be, it is not sufficient to account for the lag between theory and practice in curriculum development. We must search further.

2. *School administrators by and large are not prepared to direct curriculum-development programs.*

Many administrators define their jobs in terms of school buildings, finance, public relations (which means keeping the public happy), and developing a smoothly running machine. Their graduate professional programs have been largely taken up with these matters. They have had no time or opportunity to become students of society or of the curriculum. Thus they tend to feel insecure when faced with the difficult task of curriculum development, and often compensate for their insecurity by keeping themselves so busy with details of administration that they have no time to devote to more important matters.

3. *Teacher-education institutions have not given sufficient emphasis to curriculum development as an important aspect of the work of the teacher.*

Most institutions are hopelessly compartmentalized. On the one hand, prospective teachers build up majors and minors by "taking" a series of specialized courses quite out of relationship to the function of the various fields of knowledge in helping youth to solve basic problems of living. On the other hand, the student acquires professional credits in prescribed courses, each one of which is divorced from the other. The emphasis is upon "school management" and general and special methods rather than upon the organization of classroom activities. Finally the student is thrown into a teaching situation in which the curriculum is ready-made in terms of fixed quotas of subject matter derived from a textbook. And all this is divorced from his academic program. This neat scheme is usually perpetuated by certification requirements. Only a few professional schools have recognized the need for preparing teachers for core programs in the high schools.

4. *College entrance requirements are still defined largely in terms of Carnegie units.*

The Eight-Year Study proved as conclusively as could be expected that there is no *one* curricular pattern that is more satisfactory than another for preparing a student for college. At the conclusion of the study an attempt was made to acquaint college officials with the results. However, traditional practices still persist and school officials and parents fit the student into the pattern. Suggestions for changing the high school curriculum are met with the objection that the new program might not satisfy the demands of the colleges. True, some colleges have changed, but often these changes are not known to school officials—and particularly to parents.

5. *By and large, laymen have not participated effectively in curriculum-development programs.*

It is recognized in public addresses made by educators that "the schools belong to the people." And it is not difficult to find illustrations of laymen working side-by-side with educators in selecting school sites, carrying bond issues for new buildings, improving safety programs, and the like. It is much more difficult to find good illustrations of democratic participation in curriculum development by laymen. The conditions under which laymen may participate successfully have not been clearly determined. The result is that school officials tend to fear that any attempt to bring laymen into the program will result in disaster. Yet it is a well-known fact that public support of education depends upon active, well planned participation by all who have a stake in the enterprise.

How may these blocks be removed? It is not likely that any simple formula can be developed that will result in immediate improvement of the present situation. Yet it is possible to find many instances of school programs which have succeeded in spite of the obstacles which have been enumerated. A study of how such programs were developed should be helpful. Possibly this issue of *Educational Leadership* will provide some good illustrations.

Not all attacks on the schools have succeeded. Battle Creek, Michigan and Arlington, Virginia are illustrations of successful resistance to unfair tactics by pressure groups. There is now a large body of literature in this field which is available to schools. The current yearbook of the Association, *Forces Affecting American Education,* is a good example. The Kellogg Foundation's experiments in leadership which are now under way promise a great deal of help in improving the training of administrators. Such institutions as the University of Minnesota, Temple University, and New York University have developed promising programs for preparing core teachers. The new broad-fields programs which are being developed in the colleges are bound to affect general education procedures in the high school. Successful in-service programs are legion. These tend to make up for the deficiencies of the teacher's formal educational preparation. The National Citizens Commission is pointing the way to successful lay participation in school programs.

The high school has at its disposal all of the resources that are necessary to transform itself into a dynamic institution designed to provide leadership in perpetuating and refining our way of life. To date these resources have not been widely utilized. Perhaps we need to take a "further look" at what really constitutes progress in secondary education.

That a continuous, cooperative evaluation of the curriculum in operation is a necessity no one would deny. But *how* it is to be done poses a real problem and involves considerable organization and effort. Fortunately, a number of instruments and procedures have been developed in recent years to facilitate the study of the curriculum in operation. Evaluation may be made of a great many aspects of the total school program—achievement of students, promotional policy, holding power, follow-up of drop-outs and graduates, hidden costs, participation in extra-class activities, teachers' guides and other instructional materials, and activities of teachers. Some of the procedures now being used to evaluate the school program, with examples of each, are as follows:

(*a*) Opinion polls. See Harold Hand, *What People Think of Their Schools* (Yonkers, N. Y.: World Book Company, 1948); also the Roper poll.

(*b*) Studies. See the Illinois Curriculum Program, Superintendent of Public Instruction, Springfield. (Refer to pages 307–308 of this book.)

(*c*) Self-appraisal. See *Evaluative Criteria* (Washington, D. C.: Cooperative Study of Secondary-School Standards, 1950 edition); "How Good Are Our Schools?" *NEA Journal,* November, 1958, pages 549–555; *The Texas Handbook for Self-Appraisal and Improvement of Elementary Schools,* revised edition (Austin, Texas: State Department of Education, 1948).

(*d*) Experiments. Refer to publications of the Eight-Year Study (New York: Harper & Brothers, 1942–1945).

For illustrations of appraisal devices, see William H. Burton and Leo J. Brueckner, *Supervision: a Social Process* (New York: Appleton-Century-Crofts, Inc., 1955), pages 382–396.

WHAT REMAINS TO BE DONE?

Two orientations are evident in American education: one which stresses development and the psychological factors in learning; another which insists upon the transmission of our heritage. Antithetical as they may appear, they have in common the basic matter of communication. Without effective communication, learning does not take place, nor is the heritage transmitted. The articles which follow deal with this common aspect of the problem from different points of view.

Since both curriculum development and evaluation of it are continuous processes, appraisals from time to time will indicate next steps to be taken—new challenges growing from things learned and progress made. Significant among these is the advance in knowledge of how children develop and learn. Zirbes has outlined some of the things we know and their application to communication in learning.

That All Children May Learn WE Must Learn

by LAURA ZIRBES

Reprinted by permission of the Association for Childhood Education International, 1200 Fifteenth St., N.W., Washington 5, D. C. From *Childhood Education* of September, 1957, Vol. 34, No. 1, pages 3, 50–54. Laura Zirbes is Professor Emeritus of Education at Ohio State University, Columbus.

That all children may learn WE must learn. WE, with a capital W and a capital E, to help us to inflect it properly and to get ourselves into it. Our concern is worldwide. We are herewith challenged to identify ourselves as very special persons concerned with children, persons who must learn and continue to learn, that they all may learn. It is indeed inspiring to be one of the people on whose concern the next generation's potentiality depends.

Do Better What We Can Do

What must we learn? We must learn to do better what we can do and what we DO do as parents, as teachers, as citizens, as members of ACEI. Many of us have things to unlearn; and that is the hardest kind of learning—the unlearning. Our identifications must be expanded because we must expand children's identifications. If we are tight, close little people, we do something to restrict the identifications of children; and in this troubled world, that is a very important matter. Our human relations must be benign and outgoing, so that they can experience those benign, warm, outgoing human relations, as a climate conducive to their own well-being and to the well-being of all others. There are things which children learn growing in that kind of climate, with that kind of human relations. They are not on page 69. They are not in the course of study. They are not required by edict. But they are required for human survival.

We must learn how important environment is as a climate and conditioning factor in the development, growth, and learning of the rising generation—of all children. In a school, the conditions of that climate are largely of the teacher's making, whether he is teaching in one of our beautiful schools or in a hovel. Children are ever learning. All who are concerned with them must learn that all children's learning is conditioned by the climate in which the learning is going on. We must learn what to DO about the environment.

Learn Not to Do Some Things

We must learn also NOT to do some things. I do not believe the old saw that you never learn from the negative. We certainly do learn by considering the distance between the negative and the positive or optimum degree of anything; and only those people who are sensitive to the negative as something to move away from find themselves going as far and as fast as they can in the opposite direction. We must learn what NOT to do and what to DO about the environment. In an environment which is crowded, as it is in many of our schools, some good things do not happen. There is not enough living space. Almost every positive is related to some negative. Too much crowd-

ing is not enough space, is it not? And we need to see that by looking at those two things together we get a hint of what to do. If it is too much crowding, not enough space, we must provide more space and reduce crowds. It is that kind of simple orientation that sometimes gives us a cue to problem solving, and that is better than being told what to do.

Understand Drives of Growing Organism

We need to learn to understand children themselves—their developmental needs. How can we contribute to fulfillment if we do not understand the dynamic drives of the growing organism, the personality, as it seeks satisfaction in whatever way it can, as best it can, and in so doing makes its best better? It is out of the birth cry that language develops. It is out of the random movements and then the creeping that the walking and the coordinated skills develop. We must understand that the drive to reach and the drive to grasp, the drive to communicate, the drive to form, are basic, inherent, organic human drives. The drive to love is another. It is out of those drives that personality is shaped and skills are developed creatively. When we proceed mechanically, out of relation to children's drives and needs, we get "dead-end" learning, not developmental learning. We must learn and understand that. If the learning is motivated by incentives which are out of relation to intrinsic drives, the behavior is "dead end," because the motivation does not carry over. A need is really a deficit of something that the organism is reaching for and searching for. This need, this internal drive of the organism, is the basis for the possibility of satisfaction, the possibility of awareness on the part of those who are concerned with children's development. Consequently we watch the manifestation of drives, needs, and lacks in order to be aware of what we can do for child development.

We must understand the whine, not just stop it. It is a cue to some need. It may be a cue to the need for warm acceptance. It may be a cue to the need of release from discomfort. Whatever it means, it must speak to us. The language of children's needs can be interpreted only by those who understand behavior even before it is articulate, when it is still a whine, a groping, and not a skill. As we respond to these drives and these needs we must channelize, channel or guide, the action or behavior of children in ways which make for forward adjustment.

The word "channelize" is a little bit unusual. I got it from the psychologist, Gardner Murphy. Much that we need to learn about children we can get from psychologists, but not all. Some things we must get from working with children, some from sociologists, and some from anthropologists. They did not give me those in my pre-service training. That is why I went on seeking and learning.

What I had was not enough. We must learn more after we get diplomas, degrees, certificates, and contracts.

I have found Gesell, Piaget, Murphy, Cantril, Allport, and Havighurst very much more helpful than the earlier psychologists who emphasize the fixing of habits. Children's learning is and should be more flexible than conditioning. It should not proceed without cultivating aspirations and creative capacities. It should have forward reference but should also provide immediate satisfaction. These things are clarified by Prescott, Plant, Frank, Hymes, and Lowenfeld.

Developmental Sequence of Learning

All children who have normal musculature learn to walk, but not by walking lessons—not even by following verbal directions or instructions about the elements of walking movements. They try out their limited powers as means to satisfactions. They reach for things, they kick to free themselves of restraints, they attempt to climb, they creep and reach to get objects of their desire; in the course of all this they learn and develop their powers to the point where standing, toddling, and walking become possible. They cast off creeping when it becomes less effective after they have developed the coordinations which creeping launched to the point where rhythmic walking and running are possible. If we understand the developmental sequence we do not press anxiously for skills. It is not a matter of conditioning. We must understand that.

Importance of Expectancy

We must also understand the importance of expectancy in learning. Gesell and Murphy both talk about how, in the warm variable climate of the home, infants and young children learn to expect to be fed, expect to be listened to, expect to be cared for, expect to go to bed. Some children fuss about it, and what they need to learn is the right expectancy. This is very important. A child learns to expect reality and to accept it flexibly. He learns not to fuss about the inevitable, to adjust to the channelized business of going to bed, not necessarily by doing it exactly the same way every night. There can then be an exception when Grandmother comes from far away without upsetting the child. When habits are fixed by conditioning, the child is spoiled by the exception. The difference is important. Regimentation is a conditioning process. Expectancy is what the infant uses in adjusting to the regimen of his life, in knowing when the bottle comes what comes next, in knowing when the bath water begins to gurgle what comes next, in anticipating. And it is by that forward adjustment to coming experience that the child really becomes "at home" in his life, in his world. We must understand that these flexible expectancies have to be set up. That has very practical bearings for schools. For instance, I saw the emotional temper change in a school when, instead of ringing the bell at the hour, they rang it a minute ahead of time and told the children, "The bell says it's almost time." Then they expected and composed themselves. They moved instead of "fussing" or rushing to where they were going.

There are so many phases in school living in which the child must learn to look ahead. He needs to learn to stretch and adjust his expectancy. One minute is not very long, but you have to learn to expect in terms of the realities that have to be met. That is a basic life adjustment that is very fundamental, at least as fundamental as the three R's. It even has to do with the three R's.

Many Related Learnings

One wonders how people ever arrived at the notion that there were only three things fundamental. We must learn that there are many more; that they are not all learned in separate categories, as subjects in books. Most of them are learned functionally in the process of doing something; we must learn that there are very few specific learnings that are learned better one at a time. We confuse children by separating related learnings. That explains why children say, "Are you going to mark for Spelling, or is this just Composition?" "Do we have to write this nicely, or isn't this Handwriting?" Education will be improved when we put things together that should be learned together and let the learnings reinforce each other and function. They do not then become "dead-end" learnings, in compartments unrelated to life, filed for storage but unrelated to life.

We must relate ourselves and the child's behavior to other children. Only thus is the child going to feel safe and secure with other children, outgoing in his human relations. Infantile security in the bosom of the family needs to be expanded to security with peers, security with neighbors, security with community. Acceptance in the family needs to be expanded to acceptance by peers, acceptance in the classroom. The woman who told me she was going to give her child kindergarten at home did not understand. She had one child. She hovered over him. What he needed more than anything was peers to work with and not the ABC's. We must understand that you do not do a developmental job when you start too soon to do such things. His mother could have given premature priority to symbols in isolation from meanings at the very time when priority should have been given to direct experiences in social living. Why? Not because I say so in contradiction to what Flesch recommended, but because such direct experiences are the developmental resource which makes all language learnings meaningful. They are a spur to oral communication which develops concepts that are expressed and recorded and identified. Gross recognition then becomes a dynamic spur to the finer

discriminations on which a meaningful approach to reading depends. We the teachers of young children developed in American schools the first juvenile reading public to stimulate the development of a demand for books, children's libraries, a profession of authors and illustrators of children's literature, a literate rising generation. We did this when we got away from elements first, to meanings first, to ideas and stories and then, of course, to analysis and skills, and to satisfaction in and through more reading and self-selected reading. It is hard for some people to understand that, but there are statistics to prove it, in spite of the fact that some critics would have us go back.

Developmental Learning vs. Logical Learning

We as teachers must learn to understand all this developmentally and to help others understand how, when we begin with experience, experience gets put into words; the words get spoken; they get recorded; and then they get identified as phrases, as sentences, as statements, before they are "learned" as words, sounds, or letters. Of course, it can be done the other way, but we should not upset the order of developmental learning and substitute the order of mechanical, logical learning. We should not expect the child to approach learning from the standpoint of an adult. When we do, we must motivate artificially and use pressure. We need to learn the patience that begins with the developmental way and pace it to individual needs.

Learning from Inference

We also need to understand that children learn a great deal from inference, from insight, not from instruction and direction alone. Much of their early communication is learned by inference from hearing communication in the social medium of the home. Research has told us how many thousand words children use before they get held down to the vocabulary of a pre-primer that leads into a particular primer. Instead of getting prematurely anxious about word recognition, children should see speech set down and interpreted. They should experience language as the means of communication and learn to expect more than lessons in a basic reader while learning to read.

Some stories about children will help us to learn how they feel about this:

I said to one little fellow in Missouri, "So you are in first grade?" He said, "Yes." "And you are learning to read?" He said: "Well, not exactly. We've got a book that you have to do before you read." And then he added, "Do you know my teacher?" When I said, "No," he went on, "All right, then I'll tell you something." I listened, and I understood when he said: "She told me I couldn't read that book through 'til Christmas, and I did already. She said I lied and I didn't. She lied." I said, "Why did you read the book through?" "I

wanted to see if there was anything in it but just pictures and words at the bottom." I brought him a humorous book and said: "Come on, let's have fun. When you know how to read, you'll be doing this by yourself." He cuddled up close to me in one of those lovely big Boston rockers. I put my arm around him and he listened attentively. Every now and then he would say, "Where did it say that?" and I understood. He was trying to read; but I did not say, "Now I'll teach you." No! I just showed him "where it said that" and read on and on. He kept asking, "Where did it say that?" When we came to the end of the book he said: "Oh boy! Some day I'll be reading books like that!"

A little boy in Georgia was asked by his aunt, "How are you getting along at school?" He said: "Well, not so good. We just go over and over things in a lesson book. How many of those do you have to read before you get a book with real stories in it?"

We put too much confidence in our didactic set-down instruction. We push people around with it, and when they are pushed around they do not get a chance to go where they are going. Once when I was on a New York subway, I was fortunately, mysteriously, the first one to enter an empty coach. A man behind me was evidently conditioned to expect crowds. He put his hand on my back and began pushing me through that car. Three seats before the far end I twitched, and something surprising happened to him! I would like to see some children twitch when they are pushed! That might help people who push to understand that pushing around is not the best way to get children into reading. When a child says, "Oh boy! Some day I'll be able to read a book like that," it is not the result of being pushed around. The youngster who is not pushed around is more responsive to guidance. He gets further, he reads more on his own, and learns to select more intelligently and read more purposefully. In other words, his schooling is educating him, not just pushing him around.

We must understand how much of learning is a matter of inference from situational experiences; and we must learn how rich direct experience is in enlarging meanings, in giving people urges to read, because they have had experiences which make the reading meaningful.

Learning Without Lessons

We certainly must learn to keep the native capacity of the child to learn from experience growing, instead of letting it languish by giving him everything in lessons. I saw a seven-year-old child listen to two new records, musical records. The first one she just listened to. Nobody said a word. She was at home with her mother and me and her little brother. She listened in a relaxed way in her chair. When the next record came on, her whole posture changed! She sat up as though something had struck her. She listened, through the whole long-playing record, and then said, "Mom, would you play that one again?" Her mother complied and then, without a lesson, without a direction, without instruction—and she had none previously—she got up and converted that new record into a beautiful dance. I wish you could have seen it. She felt the music and converted it into motion. Oh, what children can do! But I heard someone, in attempting to teach a group of four-year-olds a dance, start by saying, "Rotate your left hip." She could have said, "Make a circle on the floor," and the hip would have rotated. She could have let them interpret freely. She did not understand. We must learn to understand how children can rise to a situation. We may say not all children can do that. Those who start to move awkwardly can be helped and guided, but let us not think we must tell them all, show them all, beginning with elements and resorting to repetitious formal instruction. We can facilitate learning by letting children respond to the stimulus of music, of color, not by showing them exactly what to do.

Oh, there is no time for me to tell you the stories of what happens to children's creative spontaneity when they draw around patterns of "color in"! According to Lowenfeld's research, that is the way to kill creativity, not develop it. All this has a very practical bearing for us. It has to do with those stencils we use and those Hallow'en ghosts that children are told to trace around and with the "coloring in" of workbooks. I won't belabor the point, for adults can learn from inference too.

Help Children Learn by Experience

We must learn to help children learn by experience even when experience is not planned. I have seen it done beautifully. I have even seen a mess used as an experience in cleaning up. I have seen an accident used as an experience in learning how to play safely. I have seen a bare room used as an experience in making a bare room beautiful. I could go on, but there is no time. Experience can stimulate curiosity, thinking, questioning, asking, expression. As teachers we can guide experience developmentally—not rely on stereotyped methods, orders, and regimentation.

We must learn to understand and recognize developmental sequences so that we do not expect too much, give instruction in the ABC's or formal phonetics prematurely. Let us not go back fifty years because some people adhere to the memories and traditions of their childhood. New insights based on studies of learning and development are better guides. From them we can learn to pace learning, to evaluate children's responses, to evaluate curricular expectations, to evaluate criticism of what we do, instead of getting scared out by people who do not really understand.

Apply Science of Child Development

There is so much to understanding children as children. We must learn more and more to encompass our needs to meet their needs, because there comes our satisfaction. But all that must be channeled and applied to the particular children, to all the individuals who come within our responsibility. All the book knowledge and learning about child development that stays stored in your memory of a course or workshop can come alive if you begin to channelize it, to test it in action and let it grow as you see children. The actual contacts with children are the places in which our science of child development can be transmitted into an art of application. Some people just know their science. The professional people who are creative apply science artistically. We need to learn that, and we do not learn it by blindly following some ready-made method.

Open Way for All Children

We must aspire to understand individuals, their differences, not just to section them. That is not providing for individual differences. It is an attempt to deny the need for such provision. As I remember it, when I was a classroom teacher—and I was an elementary teacher for seventeen years—I found it necessary to work with children as individuals. Some were gifted, some were slow learners, or problems. I had to encourage Bernice who lacked self-confidence. I had to give Donnie those extra books he wanted to read, because he loved reading. I had to let Abner begin with easier books and to help him more. I had to give Arthur a chance to experiment. I had to take Jimmie to the art museum with the whole class but pay particular attention to Jimmie on that occasion because he was wild about knights and knighthood. I had to read parts of "When Knighthood Was in Flower" to the class and encourage Jimmie to go on with it on his own. That was in 1916. And then, two years ago, when I was directing a workshop on the gifted child, I picked up the current issue of *Time* and saw Jimmie's picture and read that Jimmie—now known as James Rohrheimer—had been named director of the Metropolitan Museum. When interviewed for the *Time* article, Jimmie said, "When I was nine a teacher interested me in knighthood." Now, Jimmie did not have a tag on him saying, "I'm the future director of the Metropolitan Museum." We must open the way for all children to develop their special as well as their general potentialities; but to do that we must learn what makes them click, what makes them flower, so that their uniqueness and promise can be realized, instead of just being potential. We must realize how mass handling and regimentation miss and mangle individual aptitudes and needs. Even if you do have to handle some learning in groups—and I know you do—that does not say that there is nothing in the individual touch and the personalized guidance of groups. There is a kind of impersonal management that violates and deadens individual initiative, as well as dynamic group involvement. When children find what they are to do from orders, they do not listen to the still small voice inside, they do not learn by discovery, they do not find themselves.

Now where can we learn all the things which were not part of our pre-service training? It is never too late to learn. The frontiers of child development are not old frontiers. Some things must be learned in action. We must discover them in our classrooms, and then when we run across them in books or in magazines they mean much more because they were also in our experience.

Go Beyond the Best

But listen, folks! We need to be lifted to the level of aspiration which enables us to learn creatively beyond books, beyond facing our problems, beyond our learned habits and skills. We must go beyond the best we have ever done, and that is why we go to conferences and work together in study groups. That is why we realize what a wonderful thing it is to have access to the fellowship of all those who come together with the aspirations and concerns that find expression in our array of study groups, as well as in other phases of our conference activities. We have the need to learn, the urge to learn, the resources for learning. WE must learn, that all children may learn.

As times change they bring about changes in what is considered the vogue. Although the term "progressive" in education has fallen into disrepute, many of the concepts fostered by the movement are with us to stay. Olgin has undertaken an examination of the advent of progressive education, its waning, and its subsequent synthesis into current practices.

Let's Re-examine Progressive Education   by PHILIP OLGIN

From the *Phi Delta Kappan,* May, 1957, pages 309–313. Reprinted by special permission. Philip Olgin is an Associate Professor of Education in the Graduate School, Long Island University, Brooklyn, N. Y.

1. *What conditions prevailed in "traditional" schools that pointed to the need for progressive education?*

Arbitrarily using the 1920's as the time during which "traditional" education was at its peak, and necessarily referring to the extreme of the "average" program, we may create the truest picture of the education of that period by characterizing it as a "listening" school with the primary emphasis on verbal and intellectual learnings. Personality, character, and social traits were considered important "concomitant" goals and were designated as "secondary" outcomes of the educational program. Often these traits were not consciously sought, a practice justified by the doctrine which held that a scholar would normally develop desirable disciplinary, behavioral, and social traits during the intellectual development process. Serious objections were voiced by the educational psychologists of that pre-Gestalt period; not only did they advocate considering the growth and development of the "total" profile of the student, but they considered personality, character, and social traits as primary goals which could only be achieved through a conscious and directed training program.

A "part-learning" curriculum was developed to a high degree by the traditionalists. Logically-organized materials were arbitrarily assigned to the various grade levels with a sequence of simple to complex. This was an additive curriculum which faced difficult instructional and administrative obstacles before it could be realized. It did not meet the objections of the advocates of the science of education who insisted that only instructional planning which considered individual differences, level of maturity and growth, and context of comprehension could accomplish the individualization of mass instruction and behavioral learning. It was a perfectionist curriculum which had difficulty in justifying its existence in the light of psychological findings relating to the curve of forgetting, transfer of training, and nature of the "whole" learning process, with its emphasis on a flexibility which takes growth and maturation into account.

The traditional educators held for an intellectual hierarchy, a classicism in democratic education which spelled out failure for those who could not achieve an arbitrary numerical or grade level. Under usual circumstances, a student had one-half year—at most one year—in which to prove his competence, regardless of his background, purposes, readiness, or maturity. In full bloom, the "failure" philosophy functioned to eliminate from the school's responsibility those who were intellectually below par. Children were often classified for instruction according to their "IQ," which was considered a measure of "native" ability. Yet this valuable information was handled in practice as a constant measure of achievement rather than as a variable measure of capacity. The severe administrative bottleneck which developed at all levels was considered a necessary evil; there was little to be done except wait for the minimum age of release designated by the state to relieve the school of its responsibility.

The classroom was usually administered in an autocratic fashion with little or no provision for democratic pupil-planning or training in democratic experiences. The instructional materials were considered the ends of instruction; it was the function of the teacher to set up provisions for mem-

orization of compartmentalized materials most often found in textbooks and designated as "subjects." Consequently, the teacher taught subjects to a child rather than the actual child in terms of his needs and abilities. Individual differences were recognized, as previously indicated, only to the extent of eliminating the intellectually unfit. Little concern was shown for future citizenship responsibilities of those who could not meet the standards of mastery of the subjects; these children would have to accept their burden and bear it.

Part-learning instructional methods were utilized by the traditional educators to aid in conquering the instructional materials. The teacher would lecture (tell and explain), and all practice materials used in the classroom as well as the assigned homework had the primary purpose of drilling on that portion of the total materials being considered. The children would then return to the classroom to demonstrate their competence in a "recitation" period. Mastery of each portion of the subject would be evaluated by an achievement test and these tests would be averaged, usually numerically, to determine the total achievement or passing grade. The purpose in measurement, therefore, was to determine the degree to which the instructional materials had been mastered rather than the degree to which the aims and objectives of the total instructional program were achieved in a behavorial context. Curriculum specialists were critical of this inconsistent relationship between the practices and procedures of the instructional program and the guiding purposes which were supposed to give direction to the total instructional program.

2. *What were the basic ideals, purposes, principles, practices, and procedures of the early progressive educators?*

The early progressive educators were concerned with individualizing mass instruction; they reinterpreted the findings of the science of education within the philosophical framework of training our young for the responsibilities of citizenship in a democracy. They were concerned with all aspects of the child's growth and development and consciously sought to improve the dynamics of the learning process so that it would result in mastery of skills and knowledges in a desirable behavioral context. These early pioneers rejected the perfectionism of total memorization of compartmentalized materials and directed their efforts toward insuring that each child would be educated in accord with his needs, background, interests, level of maturity, talents, and aptitudes.

The early progressives recognized that social skills and desirable behavior would have to be taught directly and consciously. Knowledge was no virtue unless it could be applied and only if it would result in desirable behavior in a meaningful democratic context. The autocratic teacher-domi-

nated classroom gave way to a teacher-pupil planning ideal. The minimum outcomes of any instructional program so conceived would at least be basic democratic experiences for all children, emphasizing regard for the general welfare.

Toward these purposes, the instructional program became the vehicle for the application of consistent practices and procedures in accord with the science of education. The part-learning curriculum was replaced in theory by unit concepts of learning; instead of subjects being considered the ends of instruction, behavioral outcomes were stressed. Such terms as "controls of conduct," "units of activity," and "centers of interest" came into use. *The basic concern of the progressive educators was to integrate all of the areas of learning in seeking broad, socially significant purposes despite the fact that subjects were then considered the best organized sources as a means toward these purposes.*

The classroom was organized as a "miniature democracy"; discipline was interpreted as the development of individual democratic responsibility. The "failure" philosophy was replaced with a policy of "continuous progress." This policy was justified as a further attempt to individualize mass instruction. Reason and experience indicated that children of the same age at least have compatible social interests. Group work in accord with readiness in each skill or content area was designed to offer differentiated instruction. Progressives reasoned that with proper administrative adjustments it would be possible to have children of similar age groups working at different remedial tasks designed to bring them up to "grade" level at the earliest possible time. The curricular experience of the traditional educators was not rejected in entirety during this period; actually, an attempt was made to fuse their more recent ideas into the established school organization. Progressives considered the intelligence quotient as extremely valuable information to round out their knowledge concerning the child's background and capacities rather than as a base for classification for instructional purposes.

The early progressive educators broadened the scope of instructional materials to include community resources as well as abstract, compartmentalized materials. In order to synthesize theory and practice, more weight was given to excursion experiences. In the new regime, the "whole" method of learning was accepted as a vital replacement for the part-learning method. In seeking the broad, socially-significant goals of unit activity, a teacher-pupil planning and a motivating phase preceded the activity proper. During this phase an attempt was made to encourage some contributions from all of the children —the ugly duckling could be part of the plan and of service too. Instead of the lecture, assignment, recitation,

testing sequence, the group worked as a reasonable whole; committees, individual assignments, and similar individualized projects became vehicles for exploring the instructional materials in the light of the purposes of the unit. Drill periods were scheduled as necessary and advisable. Evaluative techniques were broadened too, to measure progress in the light of the purposes of the unit; subjective techniques were used if more refined techniques were not available. The perfectionism of memorization was rejected. Measurement became a flexible instrument and functioned as a realistic aid to further individual guidance; the optimum goal was to give the child many well-rounded cultural and broadening experiences as well as vital skills and knowledges.

3. *What occurred during the period of synthesis of traditional and progressive education which led to misconceptions and, consequently, a rejection of the label "progressive"?*

Criticisms of the early progressive programs were in some instances justified. It is difficult to develop practical and consistent procedures in the early stages of any revised educational program.[1] Major policies needed revision and in many instances critics of progressive education were not informed about the true merits of this new concept of education. Unfortunately, too, district political considerations and emotional conflicts combined to favor the

---

[1] Stephen Corey, Dean, Teachers College, Columbia, says, "It takes eighteen years for 3 per cent of the public schools to accept an educational innovation."

rise of many misconceptions concerning the new program. These misconceptions usually revolved about the following indictments:

(*a*) Progressive education is a radical movement connected with communism and atheism.

(*b*) Progressive education is too permissive; it results in poor discipline and delinquency.

(*c*) Progressive education is concerned only with catering to the child's interests; children do not learn skills and knowledges as well as they did in the "good old days."

(*d*) Progressive education expounds the theory that all children should be "promoted"; consequently, in accord with human nature, children will not work hard at school studies.

In scrutinizing these charges for substance, one who has a working knowledge of our schools and of progressive education must find it difficult to see an actual controversy between progressive and traditional education. Some explanation other than a professional diagnosis must account for the heated attacks made upon our schools. In reality, a synthesis has taken place between these two schools of thought in education. The result has been that more of the characteristics of traditional education have been retained than the controversial features of progressive education. This merger will be considered more fully in the next section of this paper.

An objective appraisal will reveal that progressive education is not a radical movement; rather, it is designed to perpetuate the democratic ideals and practices of a patriotic, nationalistic, individualistic America as defined by our Constitution and other great public documents. The type of internal individual responsibility it fosters in each child of our classroom miniature society is certainly more in accord with American democracy than is an autocratic approach employing fear as a motive for learning. Self-discipline and reason have not yet been replaced in our scheme. There is no substitute for knowledge and cooperative performance in the maintenance of our leadership among the nations of the world.

There are, of course, complex causes for loose discipline and delinquency among school-age children. Those who would make a scapegoat of progressive education are guilty of the worst kind of *post hoc, ergo propter hoc* fallacy. They overlook the fact that the worst delinquency areas in many of our cities are the very areas where the schools are least affected by progressive methods. All educators, conservative and progressive alike, expect and demand socially-approved and proper behavior in the classroom. License in the name of liberty is to be condemned under any system.

One of the favorite themes of the "anti-progressive" is the cry that children do not actually learn anything in progressive schools. The "language of love" has not only been misinterpreted as appeasement of improper conduct, it has been further misrepresented as a functioning "guide, friend, and advisor" who miraculously removes any and all obstacles in the learning process. In practice and in reality, drill is the order of the day when the need arises and the time is psychologically right. We might lecture until we were blue in the face and the children would not necessarily learn anything if the instructional materials were beyond their level of readiness and comprehension; similarly, we could drill and repeat—and repeat—exercises in the skill areas without success if the children did not understand the concepts involved. *The gross misrepresentation is that performance in terms of knowledge and skill is not sought in progressive education; actually, superior standards of performance must be maintained. Without them it would not be possible to attain the socially significant ends progressive educators are concerned with.* Modern studies of the relative effectiveness of traditional and progressive methods of learning do not substantiate the charge that children learn more from the unmotivated mass drill methods of the "good old days." The facts support whole-learning methods.

Finally, the argument against "easy promotion" loses validity when we consider that "continuous progress" need not be 100 per cent promotion. This administrative plan attempts to remove the emphasis from grades as ends in themselves; rather, evaluation is stressed as progress in terms of growth. It is difficult to see that educators have any choice in resolving this problem; it would seem ludicrous to justify over-age children struggling with materials not attuned to their stage of development in the company of children several years younger, merely awaiting the minimum age of departure, completely defeated, frustrated, and maladjusted in the grade level. The logical (and progressive) solution lies in special classes, remedial teaching on each grade level, and a motivated approach designed to get the best from the children we are working with. Children will work and learn if they are interested and properly motivated; they will not all learn the same things in the same way at the same rate and we will inevitably lose many of them. The "continuous progress" concept in practice will keep a child from advancing to the next grade level only if his total profile reveals that he cannot profit from instruction in the next grade.

4. *What gains were made and held; which portion of the early progressive education program have we lost in the process of merger with "modern" education?*

During the stage of initial impact with traditional educational programs, even in those systems and schools where progressive education was accepted as worthy of experiment, the concept of education of the "total" child influenced actual practice to a slight degree. Despite the fact that the philosophy of progressive education, as found in the professional literature, was accepted as the end of instruction by more and more influential educators as time progressed (in the 1930's), the program of "modern" education which resulted was not similar in all respects to the educational program envisaged and conceived by the early progressive educators. Portions of the early program were accepted and adopted over a period of years: the continuous progress policy, classification by chronological age, socialized and permissive methods, excursions and a broadened scope of instructional materials, and in fewer instances broader bases of evaluation of purposes. *What has been lacking, however, in almost all of the modern programs, has been the faith early progressive educators had in broad, socially significant experiences and purposes as the ends of instruction and a program of measurement geared to evaluate achievement in terms of these purposes.*

We're Still Teaching Subjects

In the "modern" period we have been reluctant, and justifiably so in many instances, to trust vague normative aims and objectives which do not yield easily to attainment. We have been content to keep subjects as the end of instruction, under many labels and disguises. These practices have resulted in much confusion in our modern programs. There is no guarantee that mastery of a rehashed "content" unit (from a subject area) will lead us into the promised land of desirable behavioral, conceptual knowledge more rapidly than the subject activities of our traditional brothers. The early "developmental" unit of the progressives which was designed to be "integrated" and to cut across subject lines has not often been utilized in our modern systems; WE ARE MORE OFTEN INTEGRATING CONTENT UNITS, and the end result has been, ironically but truly, that we are still concerned with the teaching of subjects as the end of instruction. We may, indeed, be content with this turn of events as a preliminary forward step at this time. *But we shall not attain the social or intellectual goals that the early progressive educators held as ideals merely by achieving superficial socialization of classroom organization and instructional methodology. Until we construct a curriculum which cuts across subject lines and which is designed to attain socially significant behavioral goals, and until we develop a supporting measurement program which consciously seeks to measure achievement of these goals, we will fall short of the dreams of our early progressive leaders.*

The pendulum may swing in the direction of more or less drill, more or less democracy in classroom organization and methodology, and more or less pupil failure—but this is not the real issue; until we break the shackles of the subjects as ends of instruction, children will not share the fruits of the promised land of the early progressives who really wanted to meet their needs and give more than a superficial substance to the scope of instruction. *Unless we have enough faith in our classroom experiences to utilize subjects as sources toward more meaningful social goals, i.e., "controls of conduct," "centers of interest," "persistent life situations," we have missed the fundamental purposes of progressive education.* We have never quite achieved in public education a curriculum flexible enough, measurement programs broad enough, and individual guidance in the classroom competent enough to meet the needs early progressives felt we must meet and conquer if we were to prepare our children for life's problems.

5. *What of the future? Have we some unfinished business with progressive education?*

The term "progressive" is now in much disrepute in education. Many educators feel that modern education is such an improvement over the traditional type of education that a battle of terminology will serve no useful purpose. Hence the following professional blueprint for the future seems reasonable:

(*a*) Teachers and college professors should take to the rostrum to dispel the charge that there is a current "traditional versus progressive" contro-

versy. Modern education is very much with us; the science of education is young and there is room for improvement. The job of educating the public in this professional area rests with the school personnel themselves.

(*b*) Curriculum committees should evaluate programs in individual schools and systems to insure that the practices of the educational program are consistent with the stated goals of the program. This procedure should lead to a re-evaluation of educational purposes as well as a critical examination of instructional principles, practices, and procedures.

(*c*) Curriculum committees may lead their school systems to experiment with broader, more socially-significant educational purposes in terms of life adjustment in our democracy. Pioneers have already worked in this area. For example, Stratemeyer, Forkner, McKim, and associates[2] have formulated a group of socially-conceived behavioral aims and objectives from early childhood through adulthood; these educators have also developed a supporting program designed to achieve these goals. More research should be pursued in this vital area and interest revived in these tasks if we are to improve modern education. A prudent program may encourage educators to examine critically the perfectionism inherent in the desire to master sub-

[2] F. B. Stratemeyer, H. L. Forkner, M. G. McKim, and cooperating members of the Childhood-Youth Education Committee, *Developing a Curriculum for Modern Living* (New York: Bureau of Publications, Teachers College, Columbia University, 1947).

jects; we shall perhaps come forth with a program which better meets the needs of our children and results in better-functioning, more emotionally stable citizens. The times are hard and time is valuable; we cannot afford to waste it in a dismal cycle of memorizing and forgetting. Our goals must be woven of worthy substance rather than of platitudes too vague or too difficult to attain. We must recognize that transfer will not take place in a mystical fashion; identical components must be present in instruction in a series of life situations.

(*d*) Plans should be inaugurated at all levels of instruction to make admission and content requirements of the curriculum more flexible in terms of the purposes of the instructional program. Guidance techniques must be improved if they are actually to function in meeting individual needs. Verbal aims which exist only on paper must be eliminated from our curricula.

What of the future of progressive education? Our problems are not common to any level in particular; they are present whether we are trying to master logically-organized materials in preparation for a local achievement test, a Board of Regents examination, or College Entrance Board examination—if these materials are considered to be the ends of instruction in themselves! More problems present themselves in the high school and college, where some solution must be found to the organization of the curriculum around subjects. The fact remains that we must bolster our classroom efforts toward behavioral goals with a more favorable type of curriculum organization. Perhaps the activity program in the form of an enlarged core period will be the answer. We might even compromise temporarily with an activity room in the morning engaged with problems of social living and a drill period in the afternoon designed to prepare students for college entrance examinations in specific subjects.

This phase is part of the future, part of our unfinished business with progressive education.

Certain traditional practices have resisted the developmental point of view described in the two preceding articles. None is more resistant than the subservience of teacher and pupil to the dullness and dogma of textbooks. The result is poor communication and inadequate learning. Handlin decries this situation and places a large share of the responsibility for it with teachers themselves.

More culpable than the publishers and the authors are the teachers who are the instruments of a crime against their students.

Some teachers acquiesce because they know no better. Reared themselves on the textbook, they would be lost without it, and they see no reason why their charges should not suffer as they themselves once did.

Most teachers, however, do know better. Everything their course in educational psychology taught them about the learning process contradicts the assumptions under which the textbooks they use are written. The more conscientious ones recognize the discrepancy and devote their lectures and discussion to remedying the deficiencies of the text. Let the book supply the facts, they seem to argue, while the interpretation emerges in the classroom. While this procedure has merit, the textbook remains a tiresome repository of data to be remembered in the hope that significance may later be attached to it. The exceptional, inspiring teacher can rise above these limitations. But all too often, when the ability or will is lacking to go beyond what the text offers, the teacher forgets theory altogether and accepts practice as the book defines it.

The great majority of teachers, whether they know better or not, are content to go along. To depart from the organization of the text or to dispense with it entirely calls for original thought, consistent effort, and the willingness to buck the inertia of accepted method.

And then, the text has one inestimable virtue—the aid it offers in grading. Assign a chapter, and each paragraph has built into it a specific question with a right or wrong answer. Some texts, or the teachers' manuals that accompany them, even simplify the process by supplying the questions readyframed. To the compilers of objective tests these books are mines from which hundreds of facts can be drawn to be marked plus or minus.*

An even greater problem is the fact that a generation brought up on textbooks and TV has not itself learned to read with intelligence.

The use of textbooks is not to be confused with the development of reading skills and enjoyment. Riesman reminds us that "books bring with them detachment and a critical attitude that is not possible in a society dependent on the spoken word." He also points out that much of the critical emphasis upon reading fails to stress the mentally liberating quality of books, and falls back instead upon fears that heritage will be lost.

It may be that some residual feeling of this sort—some fear that children may be growing up as barbarians and away from us of the older generations—may be one element behind the ominous success of Rudolf Flesch's demagogic best seller, *Why Johnny Can't Read,* a book that would lose the exaggerated edge of its power if *its* readers could read, or were not too frightened to keep their wits about them. Flesch and his followers never ask the crucial question I am asking here: namely, what distribution of not only reading skills but reading enthusiasms, for what systems of notation (includ-

* Oscar Handlin, "Textbooks That Don't Teach," *The Atlantic,* December, 1957, p. 113. Quoted by special permission. Oscar Handlin is Professor of History at Harvard University and was awarded the Pulitzer Prize for History in 1952.

ing music, languages, and mathematics), is desirable if we are not only to pass on the heritage—the world's library of art and imagination—but also to contribute to it? They take it for granted that Johnny should read just because John Alden or John Adams did read; in the case of most of the reactionary critics of our public schools who are riding so high today, such terms as "heritage" are merely snob tags, status labels, which they can use to pull rank on schoolteachers, educationists, psychological counselors, and other relatively defenseless people. I suspect that many such critics would like to restore drill and to make reading more of a chore than it needs to be as a sublimated form of hazing the young, though some chore and bore elements will certainly be part of any educational program which aims to reach all who can possibly be reached by books or by any other media which connect people with a non-contiguous world, the world of yesterday and tomorrow as well as of the here and now.*

WHAT ARE IMMEDIATE AND PRESSING CONCERNS?

The launching of the first satellite into a space orbit, a satellite not of U. S. origin, has confounded the American people. Again the voices have been raised—in fear, in bewilderment, in censure, in demand, and even sometimes in sober reflection. A weighty proportion of the clamor is directed toward the public schools.

The demands now tend to cluster around a general toughening-up of the curriculum, special education of the gifted, emphasis on science and mathematics, and the preservation of a well rounded education in the humanities and liberal arts.

Are our educational needs now of a different order? President Eisenhower, when he was president of Columbia University, declared that the greatest need of American soldiers was for "better understanding of, and increased devotion to, the American way of life and its values." [34:3] On November 14, 1957, at Oklahoma City, he said: "I wish that every school board and every PTA would this week and this year make one single project their special order of business: to scrutinize your schools' curriculum and standards to see whether they meet the stern demands of the era we are entering.

"As you do, remember that when a Russian graduates from high school, he has had five years of physics, four years of chemistry, one

---

*From David Riesman, "Books, Gunpowder of the Mind," *The Atlantic*, December, 1957, pp. 124–125. Quoted by special permission. David Riesman is Professor of Social Sciences at the University of Chicago.

year of astronomy, five years of biology, ten years of mathematics through trigonometry, and five years of a foreign language." [26:183]

Roy E. Larsen, president of Time, Inc., and chairman of the board of directors of the Fund for the Advancement of Education, announced at a conference in Chicago: "The education program of the American high school must be toughened up to meet a level of unprecedented challenge or, like generals who fight the wrong war, the nation will be producing schools which can only serve yesterday's needs." [25:94]

The same theme is developed by Walter Leibrecht who finds the sickness essentially in our society. "In no other country do parents have so much to say in matters of schooling and curriculum, but parents do not really insist that their children be put to work. . . . We have provided our children with a soft bed, but have robbed them of responsibility and the need to work hard." [22:164]

In January, 1958, President Eisenhower approved a plan proposed by Marion B. Folsom, then Secretary of Health, Education, and Welfare. The plan calls for a four-year program at a cost of one billion dollars to promote science and mathematics in the public schools and to attract more graduate students into college teaching.

A recent report indicates the reactions of some highly articulate citizens and educators. [24:18–19] Their reactions are scattered, conflicting, and confusing. Schools could not possibly follow them without riding in all directions. Conant, former president of Harvard, thinks that the gifted can best be served in strong, special programs within regular high schools. On the other hand, Rickover, who fathered the atomic submarine, proposes the establishment of twenty-five elite high schools where gifted children will be educated separately. Wells, president of Indiana University, cautions specifically against raising salaries of science and mathematics teachers above the average level as ruinous to the morale of other teachers. DuBridge, president of California Institute of Technology, states that many science and mathematics teachers are incompetent because of inadequate preparation and wants to raise the requirements for them. Carr, president of the National Education Association, advocates a plan costing five billion dollars to be given to the states on the basis of $100 per school child, which the states would use for educational purposes. Faust, president of the Fund for Advancement of Education, would make teaching more attractive by eliminating clerical and janitorial duties.

Schoolmen have heeded these voices but have shown unwillingness to be stampeded or to become unnecessarily defensive. Jack Rees, president of the California Teachers Association, addressed the State Council thus: "We of the public schools accept the challenge and will do our utmost to cope with it. We do so, however, without apologies for the past in which public education has contributed so much to the welfare, progress, culture, and defense of our country." [28:11]

John Fischer, superintendent of public instruction, Baltimore, sees the schools of the future growing as an expansion from the tasks of the past. "The difficult task of the high school is, in the light of the goals, now to extend the opportunity for sound education to more young people, of more diversified backgrounds, with a greater range of occupational objectives, in a world of incredible complexity and amid an unprecedented expansion of knowledge." [14:24]

Hollis Caswell states that "if we permit fear of Russia's material strength to determine the emphasis in our curriculum, we most certainly shall not have an education which meets the broader range of educational needs in our country." [34:3]

A scientist, Ruben G. Gustafson, president of Resources for the Future, Inc., raises the question of where we shall find help in making value judgments which are the basis of action. His answer is: "Not in science because science is not concerned with value judgments. There is a better chance in the humanities, because here, over the centuries, have been recorded man's experiences in making these judgments." [25:94]

Finally Carl Jung, a psychiatrist who has devoted a long life to the study of individuals and their psychic disorders, says this about the questions raised by the world situation today: "I am neither spurred on by excessive optimism nor in love with high ideals, but am merely concerned with the fate of the individual human being—that infinitesimal unit on whom a world depends, and in whom, if we read the meaning of the Christian message aright, even God seeks his goal." [20:63]

Bibliography

1. AIKIN, WILFORD M. "The Eight-Year Study: If We Were to Do It Again." *Progressive Education,* 31:11–14, October, 1953.
2. ALTER, HARRY M. " 'Ask the Graduates'—a Method of Curriculum Improvement." *California Journal of Secondary Education,* 32:473–478, December, 1957.
3. AMERICAN EDUCATIONAL RESEARCH ASSOCIATION. "Curriculum Planning and Development." *Review of Educational Research,* 27:237–304, June, 1957.
4. ———. "The Curriculum: Organization and Development." *Review of Educational Research,* 24:191–261, June, 1954.
5. ———. "The Educational Program: Early and Middle Childhood." *Review of Educational Research,* 23:111–189, April, 1953.
6. ———. "Twenty-five Years of Educational Research." *Review of Educational Research,* 26:199–344, June, 1956.
7. BARNES, FRED P. (ed). *School Begins with Kindergarten.* The Subject Field Series, Bulletin No. C-One. Illinois Curriculum Program. Springfield, Illinois: State Superintendent of Public Instruction, September, 1957. 97 pages.
8. BRINK, WILLIAM G. "Patterns of Curriculum Organization in Large Secondary Schools." *School Review,* 63:372–377, October, 1955.
9. COOPER, DAN H. "The Impact of Research on Education." *Phi Delta Kappan,* 35:16–20, 44, October, 1953.
10. COSAND, JOSEPH P. "Admission Criteria: a Review of the Literature." *California Journal of Secondary Education,* 28:12–18, January, 1953.
11. CROSS, EVA A., and RUTH S. FORD. "Program Can Have Priority in Building Secondary Schools." *NEA Journal,* 47:26–28, January, 1958.
12. ELLIS, G. GORDON. "Guidance Services—Red Tape or Red Blood." *The High School Journal,* 36:221–226, May, 1953.
13. EMANUEL, WILLIAM H. "College-Entrance Requirements Ten Years after the Eight-Year Study." *School Review,* 61:521–526, December, 1953.
14. FISCHER, JOHN H. "High Schools for the Fabulous Future." *NEA Journal,* 47:23–25, January, 1958.

15. Foshay, Arthur W. "Curriculum Improvement Through Action Research." *NEA Journal*, 46:265–266, April, 1957.
16. Goodlad, John I. "Ungrading the Elementary Grades." *NEA Journal*, 44:170–171, March, 1955.
17. Johnson, B. Lamar, and William R. Harless. "Implications of the CEP for the Junior College." *Junior College Journal*, 25:369–375, March, 1955.
18. Johnson, Eric H. "Purposes and Activities of the Illinois Curriculum Program—a Report to the Steering Committee." Presented on April 28, 1956. (Johnson is Director of ICP.)
19. Johnson, Loaz W. "Educational Research and Its Dissemination." *Educational Leadership*, 10:423–427, April, 1953.
20. Jung, Carl G. "God, the Devil, and the Human Soul." *The Atlantic*, 200:57–63, November, 1957.
21. Koopman, G. Robert, and Edith Roach Snyder. "Living Room for Learning—a Self-Contained Unit." *NEA Journal*, 47:18–20, January, 1958.
22. Leibrecht, Walter. "A Sickness in Society." *Phi Delta Kappan*, 39:162–167, January, 1958.
23. Lieberman, Myron. *Education as a Profession.* Englewood Cliffs, N. J.: Prentice-Hall, Inc., 1956.
24. *Life*, 44:18–19, January 13, 1958.
25. *Phi Delta Kappan*, 39:94, December, 1957.
26. ——. 39:183, January, 1958.
27. ——. 39:185, January, 1958.
28. Rees, Jack D. "Sputnik and the Schools." *CTA Journal*, 54:11, 30–33, January, 1958.
29. Russell, David H., and J. Cecil Parker. "Using Research to Point the Way to Curriculum Change." *Educational Leadership*, 12:269–276, February, 1955.
30. Saylor, J. Galen, and William M. Alexander. *Curriculum Planning for Better Teaching and Learning.* New York: Rinehart and Company, Inc., 1954.
31. Schutter, Charles H. "Should We Abolish the 7th and 8th Grades?" *School Executive*, 74:51–54, May, 1955.
32. Shane, Harold G. "Responsibility for More Functional Use." *Phi Delta Kappan*, 35:45–48, October, 1953.
33. Swenson, Esther J. "Issues Concerning Articulation Between Elementary and Secondary Schools." *High School Journal*, 38:281–288, May, 1955.
34. *T. C. Topics*, 6:3, Winter, 1957–1958.
35. Toy, Henry, Jr. "Planning Curriculum with Citizens." *The School Executive*, 74:19–21, November, 1954.
36. Wiles, Kimball. "Can We Sharpen the Concept of Action Research?" *Educational Leadership*, 10:408–410, 432, April, 1953.

Name Index

This book contains numerous references—[5:392], for example—to specific pages of works listed in the bibliographies at the end of Parts One, Two, and Three. This Index includes all pages on which a writer or his work is referred to, whether or not the writer's name is mentioned. When a page number is italicized, reference is made to a page number in one of the bibliographies.

Name Index

Subject Index